ROLE TRANSITIONS
IN ORGANIZATIONAL LIFE
An Identity-Based Perspective

LEA's Organization and Management Series

Arthur Brief and James Walsh, Series Editors

ROLE TRANSITIONS
IN ORGANIZATIONAL LIFE
An Identity-Based Perspective

Blake E. Ashforth
Arizona State University

LEA LAWRENCE ERLBAUM ASSOCIATES, PUBLISHERS

2001   Mahwah, New Jersey   London

Lawrence Erlbaum Associates, Inc., Publishers
10 Industrial Avenue
Mahwah, New Jersey 07430-2262

Cover design by Kathryn Houghtaling Lacey

Library of Congress Cataloging-in-Publication Data
Ashforth, Blake E.
    Role transitions in organizational life : an identity-based perspective /
    Blake E. Ashforth.
       p.   cm. -- (LEA's organization and management series)
    Includes bibliographical references and index.
    ISBN 0-8058-2892-3 (cloth : alk. paper) -- ISBN 0-8058-2893-1
    (pbk. : alk. paper)
    1. Organizational change. 2. Social role. I. Title. II. Series.

  HM796 .A74   2001
  302.3'5--dc21
                                                    00-026457

Printed in the United States of America
10 9 8 7 6 5 4 3 2 1

*To my parents, Phyllis and Ross,
and my wife, Deb, with love*

Contents

Series Editors' Foreword

Identity-based approaches to understanding thoughts, feelings, and actions in organizations have produced, particularly in recent years, an array of rich insights that truly have broadened the domain of organizational behavior. Blake Ashforth's book perhaps is the first attempt to bring these insights together in one source and use them collectively to stretch further the boundaries of the discipline. He does this by creating new ways of viewing the many forms of role transitions evident in organizational life. Thus, Ashforth's unique book creatively accomplishes two scholarly objectives. It provides a needed review, critique, and integration of what is known about being socially defined in an organizational context, and it provides fresh and intriguing perspectives on the dynamics of role engagement and disengagement both within and between organizations.

Given the aforementioned, we obviously are delighted to have Blake's book join LEA's Organization and Management Series. We are confident his book will help the series achieve its goal as a collection of scholarly works that open promising new avenues of investigation or meaningfully alter the course of existing ones in organization studies.

Arthur P. Brief
Tulane University

James P. Walsh
Michigan University

Preface

Years ago, when I was a newly minted assistant professor, I taught an off-campus MBA course to would-be managers. My wife, Deb, would often pick me up when class ended. One time she arrived early and stood outside the classroom door, out of sight, listening to me do my thing. Afterward she said, "Where did you get that professor voice?"—which I took to mean "authoritative and compelling," whereas she meant "dry and preachy."

It got me thinking: Where *did* I get that professor voice and *why* did I get a different voice at all? Wasn't I the same person no matter where I was or what I was doing?

In the course of a day, we may wear many different hats: Spouse, parent, colleague, friend, subordinate, manager, customer, worshipper, sports fan, and so on. And over the course of years, we outgrow some hats and try on new ones: For example, the student becomes an assistant manager, then a manager, and then establishes her own business. What's more, the number and variety of hats we wear over time may well be increasing.

This book attempts to answer what happens to the *I*—to the person—as he or she dons and doffs these many hats over the course of a day and over the course of a life. In short, it focuses on *role transitions,* on the process of exiting one role and entering another.

And so, in my best professor voice . . .

Acknowledgments

I never quite knew what the phrase *a labor of love* meant until writing this book. Fortunately, on the labor side of the equation, I was blessed with steadfast support from some wonderful people.

I thank Art Brief and Jim Walsh for inviting me to write a book for the Lawrence Erlbaum series on organization and management and not blinking when I proposed a different topic than they had in mind. They gave me enough rope to either lasso something worthwhile or hang myself and conveyed their confidence that I'd do the former. Art and Jim also provided very helpful feedback on the entire book: No good cop–bad cop here, they were both tremendously supportive throughout the project. I'm also deeply grateful to Anne Duffy, senior editor, for her firm stewardship through the difficult shoals of the publication process.

I'm greatly indebted to Vikas Anand, Peter Hom, Angelo Kinicki, Carol Kulik, Mike Pratt, and Cheri Ostroff for their very insightful comments on individual chapters. Angelo served double duty as an ongoing sounding board, allowing me to pour him frequent glasses of whine. Mel Fugate, Scott Johnson, and Glen Kreiner were not only terrific coauthors on chapters 8 and 9, they have been staunch colleagues throughout the entire project. Karen Little did a superb job preparing the figures and putting up with my nickel-and-dime changes with a wry smile. I'd also like to thank Bill Glick, chair of the Department of Management at Arizona State University, for fostering a truly supportive and collegial atmosphere where faculty are encouraged to follow their muse.

Portions of the early chapters and much of chapter 9 are adapted from Ashforth, Kreiner, and Fugate (2000). I very much appreciate the helpful comments on that article offered by Chris Early and three anonymous reviewers at the *Academy of Management Review.*

Stretching back a lot further, I've also been blessed with a set of wonderful mentors that I've never properly thanked: Hugh Arnold, V. V. Baba, Martin Evans, Bob House, Gary Johns, and Dick Osborn. I very much appreciate the attention that each of you lavished on a green kid. I've also benefited enormously, both personally and professionally, from long-time research collaborations and friendships with Ron Humphrey, Ray Lee, Fred Mael, and Alan Saks.

Finally, I'd like to thank my wife, Deb Salac-Ashforth, for her unflagging love and support through the ups and downs of not only the writing process but also of the last 20 years and counting. Speaking of role transitions, she dated a teenager, married a banker, supported a doctoral student, and stuck by a prof—all within the same marriage to me. She is my touchstone.

—*Blake Ashforth*

1

Roles and Role Transitions

I feel like I'm pretending at work that I don't have a family and pretending at home that I don't have a job. This week we lost a director, had production problems, I took my daughter to the doctor yesterday and was up all night with her. . . . I have her in a school co-op. . . . Wednesday afternoon I actually had to leave her home sick to do my shift at the school and then got a call from my office that I had to come back and go to this meeting. So I rushed back here and then had a meeting for the school that night at seven-thirty to talk about kindergartens. My kids don't go to bed 'til late—ten or ten-thirty—because that's my time with them—and then I start reading scripts. I can't remember the last time that I did something luxurious—got my nails done or had a religious experience. And I have good day care, a cook, and a house-keeper. I'm lucky.

—executive, Walt Disney Productions (Friedman, 1996, p. 129)

There are two great trends affecting how we, as individuals, interact with and within organizations. The first is that organization-based roles are steadily proliferating and becoming institutionalized in industrialized societies (D. Katz & Kahn, 1978; Ritzer, 1996). For example, in the 20th century, health clubs, nursing homes, summer camps, day-care centers, dating services, and so on formalized tasks that were once performed informally in the home or neighborhood, thereby creating roles such as health club member and nursing home patient.

As the once-private realms of life are colonized by organizations, everyday life becomes increasingly mediated through roles vested in organizational settings. To satisfy personal needs and desires, individuals must often enter organizations and adopt more or less formal roles. For example, to maintain good physical health, one may enroll in a health club and abide by the rules and procedures in effect for its members. Experiences are constrained and filtered through institutionalized structures such that the very sense of self in many situations is derived largely from the role one is enacting.

Furthermore, because roles are institutionalized, they can be learned and enacted by a range of individuals. The role occupants are to some extent substitutable and perhaps even interchangeable. The role perseveres, but the occupants do not. This strengthens the resilience of the organization and its structure but potentially constrains the expression of individuality—the very stuff that fosters interpersonal liking and relationships.

As the opening quote from the Walt Disney executive attests, the colonization of personal life by organizations has created an awareness among laypeople and scholars alike of the many roles that one may play in the course of a typical week (or even day). Because these roles are typically associated with differentiated social domains, they are typically enacted for differentiated audiences, creating concerns with interrole conflict and the fragmentation of self (Gergen, 1991; Zurcher, 1977). It is no accident that it was only in the 20th century that the social-scientific concept of *role* became firmly established in its own right as something consequential and different from the concept of *person* or *self* (Oatley, 1990).

In short, the colonization of the private means that people increasingly interact as role occupants rather than as individuals per se, as organizational members and clients rather than as Jim and Susan, devoid of institutional ties. As we will see, however, entering a role for the first time involves more than learning the role; it involves colonizing the role in the service of the person—negotiating a personal space in how one understands and enacts the role.

The second great trend affecting how we relate to organizations is the escalation of the *rate* of change: The treadmill is moving ever faster. The globalization of the economy and the escalation of competitive pressures have fostered a relentless urgency to develop new products and services, to make fewer mistakes, to make more with less, and to do it all as rapidly as possible. Discoveries and innovations have led to the creation and reinvention of entire industries; technological developments and organizational restructurings have created tremendous turbulence; and emerging organizational forms have rewritten the very way many firms and industries do business and view their employees. Moreover, the explosion in information technologies and the growing interdependence of nations and regions have effectively hardwired the world such that emerging issues and developments are rapidly disseminated throughout the industrialized world.

As the rate of change escalates, traditional assumptions about stable jobs and careers, punctuated with periodic changes, are becoming increasingly antiquated (e.g., Arthur & Rousseau, 1996b; Cappelli et al., 1997; D. T. Hall & Associates, 1996). The stereotypical notion of a career as a patterned series of upward moves, often within a single organization, is becoming increasingly rare. The emergent reality is unstable jobs and careers punctuated with periods of stability. As Nicholson (1987) put it, "change, through the core mechanism of transition, is the norm and stable equilibrium the exception" (p. 168). Individuals are constantly in a state of *becoming*, of moving between and through various roles and their attached identities and relationships. And yet, as Stephens (1994) noted, "until recently, research . . . has emphasized continuity over discontinuity" (p. 480).

In particular, little attention has been paid to the nature of individuals' *role transitions*, that is, the psychological and physical (if relevant) movement between roles, including disengagement from one role (*role exit*) and engagement in another (*role entry*; Burr, 1972; Richter, 1984). Given the increasing proliferation of organization-based roles (Trend 1) and the increasing rate of change affecting those roles (Trend 2), this book focuses on the dynamics of role transitions, of *transitioning*. How does one simultaneously enact the role of subordinate, peer, and manager in a meeting? How does a newly hired person navigate through her work role? How does a newly retired chief executive officer (CEO) cope with the loss of identity and status? The book charts the processes by which individuals move between roles during the workday (e.g., from spouse to employee as one commutes to work) and over the worklife (e.g., through promotions, retirement).

We begin this journey with two related questions: What are roles? And what are role transitions? This material provides a foundation for the chapters to follow. I then provide an overview of the central arguments and the format of the book. The chapter closes by introducing two additional themes that pervade the book, normalization and interactionism.

WHAT ARE ROLES?

The term *role* derives from the theater and refers to the part played by an actor (E. J. Thomas & Biddle, 1966). The term began appearing in the social science literature in the 1920s and 1930s, and its usage has escalated to the point where Biddle (1979) suggested that "role theory is a vehicle, or perhaps the major or only vehicle, presently available for integrating the three core social sciences of anthropology, sociology, and psychology into a single discipline whose concern is the study of human behavior" (p. 11).

There are two basic sociological perspectives on roles, the structural-functionalist and the symbolic interactionist. Structuralists define roles "as sets of behavioral expectations associated with given positions in the social structure" (Ebaugh, 1988, p. 18), and view roles as functional for the social system within which they are embedded (e.g., Merton, 1957b; T. Parsons, 1951). In this book, a role is defined simply as a position in a social structure, and the "behavioral expectations" component is reserved for the later discussion of role identity. *Position* means a more or less institutionalized or commonly expected and understood designation in a given social structure such as accountant (work organization), mother (family), and church member (religious organization). Role transitions in organizations, then, means psychological and, if relevant, physical movement between jobs, occupations, committee appointments, and other positions.

That said, my perspective draws heavily on the symbolic interactionist perspective on roles. Symbolic interactionists view roles as emergent and negotiated understandings between individuals (e.g., Blumer, 1969; Mead, 1934). Based on subjective perceptions and preferences, individuals attempt to coordinate their behaviors and come to jointly define what constitutes a given role. Whereas structuralists tend to view roles as fixed and largely taken-for-granted positions, symbolic interactionists tend to view roles as fluid and always negotiable shared understandings.

I stake a middle range position in this paradigm divide: In the context of organizations, positions do indeed tend to become more or less institutionalized (as per the structuralists), but the *meaning* imputed to a given position and the way in which an individual *enacts* a position are negotiated within structural constraints (as per the symbolic interactionists). Creating a position in an organization is a starting point for negotiation, not an ending point (Ilgen & Hollenbeck, 1990). This tension between institutionalization and negotiation constitutes a strong subtext of the book.

Three attributes of roles are particularly relevant to role transitions: Role boundaries, role identities, and role sets.

Role Boundaries

The word *define* is derived from the Latin term for *boundary* (*finis*). To define something is to mark its boundaries, "to surround it with a mental fence that separates it from everything else" (Zerubavel, 1991, p. 2). According to what may be loosely described as *boundary theory*

(Michaelsen & Johnson, 1997; Nippert-Eng, 1996a, 1996b; Zerubavel, 1991), individuals erect mental fences as a means of simplifying and ordering the environment. Fences are erected around geographical areas, historical events, people, ideas, and so on that appear to be contiguous, similar, functionally related, or otherwise associated. The process results in the creation of slices of reality that have particular meaning for the individual(s) creating and maintaining the boundaries. Home, work, and church are examples of the social domains created by boundaries (Nippert-Eng, 1996a).

The boundaries are real in the sense that the individual perceives them as such and acts as if they were real (cf. Weick, 1979). Although a given social domain may be more or less institutionalized, Nippert-Eng (1996a, 1996b) showed that the boundaries around domains are somewhat idiosyncratically constructed (e.g., one person allows home to cross over into work, whereas another keeps them separated). Furthermore, by circumscribing domains, boundaries enable one to concentrate more exclusively on whatever domain is currently salient and less on other domains.

Within and across social domains, boundaries tend to be further drawn around roles. Thus, a *role boundary* refers to whatever delimits the perimeter—and thereby, the scope—of a role. Given the institutionalized nature of organizations, roles tend to be bounded in both space and time; that is, they are more relevant in certain physical locations and at certain times of the day and week. Consequently, a role transition typically involves movement between settings and circumstances, that is, through *space* (commuting from home to the office), *time* (ascending a career ladder), or both. Crossing a role boundary tends to cue the associated role.

Because boundaries must be imposed or socially constructed, there is an element of choice and arbitrariness in how individuals define roles and thus, transitions. For most employees, there is a clear distinction between family roles and work roles, but for the owners of a small family business, there may be little distinction between the two such that the notion of a role transition is not very meaningful. Moreover, once constructed, role boundaries tend to become taken for granted and seen as natural and perhaps immutable. Indeed, "people become invested in boundaries because their sense of self, their security and their dignity, all are tied to particular boundary distinctions" (C. F. Epstein, 1989, p. 576).

The importance of role boundaries will become most apparent when frequent and recurring role transitions (e.g., a daily commute between home and work) are discussed in chapter 9.

Role Identity

Given the importance of role identities to the book, chapter 2 explores the concept in detail. For now, let me simply define a role identity as the goals, values, beliefs, norms, interaction styles, and time horizons that are typically associated with a role. A role identity provides a definition of self-in-role, a persona that one may enact. A role's boundaries facilitate the articulation of a role identity by circumscribing the domain of the role—by demarking what activities belong to the role and what belongs to other roles.

Role Set

Roles are embedded in social systems comprised of interdependent or complementary roles (Biddle, 1979). For example, organizations are comprised of senior executives, middle managers, supervisors, front-line employees, staff analysts, and so on, and these roles are in turn interdependent with suppliers, distributors, customers, government regulators, and so on. The various roles that are more or less directly linked to a focal role are referred to as the *role set* (D. Katz & Kahn, 1978; Merton, 1957a). Thus, a production supervisor's role set includes his or her subordinates, manager, fellow supervisors, and various members of staff groups (e.g., production schedulers, human resource management employees).

Because the roles in a social system tend to be differentiated by function and power, the nature of the interdependency—and thus the nature of the interaction—between any two roles in a role set tends to be more or less unique. Thus, our production supervisor likely interacts with her manager about different issues and in different ways than she would with a subordinate. This notion of differentiation has several implications for the enactment of a role. First, it suggests that a role identity is largely defined by its role set. The role identity of supervisor is defined largely by the complementary role of subordinate. As such, complementary roles serve as *foils* for one another. Second, the notion of differentiation suggests that a given role is multifaceted in the sense that a role occupant will display a certain characterization of the role toward each member of the role set. The production supervisor may be relatively directive toward a subordinate but relatively deferential toward her manager. Third, differentiation suggests that role conflict is inherent in any given role because the role occupant must respond to the ongoing and varying demands of multiple role set members. A peer requesting immediate assistance may have little knowledge of or sympathy for the competing demands on the supervisor's time.

WHAT ARE ROLE TRANSITIONS?

In Louis' (1980a) formulation of career transitions, a transition occurs when an individual either moves from one role to another (interrole transition) or changes his or her orientation toward a role already held (intrarole transition). I focus primarily on transitions *between* roles rather than *within* roles, although theories of socialization, work adjustment, personal and role change, turnover, and so forth are relevant to the exiting and entering phases of between-role transitions.

There are many types of interrole transitions—or simply, role transitions. Research has focused overwhelmingly on *macro role transitions*, defined as the psychological and (if relevant) physical movement between sequentially held roles. The most common macro transitions are entry or reentry into an organization, intraorganizational transitions (e.g., promotion, transfer, demotion, short-term assignment), interorganizational transitions, interoccupation transitions, and exit from an organization (e.g., quit, dismissal, retirement, layoff, leave of absence; Bruce & Scott, 1994; Louis, 1980a). Often, a single change can involve multiple transitions, as when a manager quits a firm to start his own small business. As these examples suggest, macro role transitions usually involve infrequent and more or less permanent changes within the social domain of work organizations.

Micro role transitions are defined as the psychological and (if relevant) physical movement between *simultaneously* held roles—what V. L. Allen and van de Vliert (1984) referred to as "role alternations" (p. 9). Examples include shifts between one's home and work roles, one's at-work roles of supervisor and subordinate, one's at-home roles of parent and spouse, and between work or home roles and roles lodged in other social domains (e.g., church, school, health club). As these examples suggest, micro role transitions usually involve frequent and recurring movement both within and between social domains.

Because the book focuses mainly on macro role transitions, I will drop the term *macro* and refer simply to *role transitions* (unless otherwise indicated). As noted later, the topic of micro role transitions is deferred until chapter 9.

Why Study Role Transitions Now?

Organizations In Flux.   The escalation of change was mentioned earlier. One emerging development is Arthur's (1994; Arthur & Rousseau, 1996b) notion of the "boundaryless career." As noted, several forces have converged to drastically undermine the stereotypical notion of a career as a sequence of vertical moves within a single paternalistic organization. Furthermore, the current shift from an industrial society to a knowledge society is creating an ongoing emphasis on individual-based learning— and hence diverse experiences and adaptability—rather than on position-based power (Arthur & Rousseau, 1996a). In addition, the flattening of conventional hierarchies, the emergence of new organizational forms such as the network and cellular organization, the job creation success of small firms, and the inability and unwillingness of organizations to sponsor individuals for an entire career are creating a sea change in how individuals view organizations and vice versa (Cappelli et al., 1997; Miles & Snow, 1996). Increasingly, individuals are expected to manage their own careers by actively seeking developmental opportunities, regardless of functional, organizational, and even national boundaries. Careers are beginning to resemble a series of short-term appointments or projects with multiple employers or in multiple networks. Consequently, the locus of work identification is likely shifting from organizations to professions and roles— to more localized and portable sites for vesting the self. A boundaryless career thus places a huge premium on individual initiative, networking, and learning (Arthur & Rousseau, 1996a).

Bridges (1995) further argued that a "job shift" is underway such that even within a given organization the notion of a role is unclear. According to Bridges, discrete jobs are dissolving into a "field of work"—a fluid sphere of activity accomplished by temporary coalitions of people. In such a work world, fixed positions give way to emergent tasks, stability gives way to improvisation, and individual accomplishment gives way to teamwork. Thus, the boundaries that define and separate organizational members tend to blur. As a result, organizational members must actively work at creating and maintaining a sense of workplace identity as well as of meaning, control, and belonging—four key psychological motives that are argued in chapter 3 to be activated by role transitions. Individuals must articulate a narrative thread that connects possibly disparate experiences into a coherent story about themselves (Weick, 1996).

What concepts such as the boundaryless career and job shift suggest is that individuals are losing their secure and predictable moorings in the workplace. They must cast about for roles that appear to resonate with their needs and desires. The premium placed on initiative, networking, and learning in turn suggests that a knowledge of how individuals accomplish role transitions is vitally important to the health of individuals and organizations alike.

Individuals in Flux. Greek mythology tells us that Proteus was able to change his shape at will, from lion to fire to flood. As the world becomes more dynamic and cacophonous, lifestyles and choices proliferate, tradition fades, geographic mobility increases, and values and truths become relativized. Lifton (1993) argued that the resulting fragmentation of contemporary life has given rise to a "protean self," one who actively experiments with diverse roles, identities, and behaviors. The protean person, in short, is highly adaptable. Indeed, protean people may eschew commitments and stability to retain flexibility; their identity may be based more on seeking change than on finding stability. The protean world is one of flux and perpetual change, where roles are easily adopted and discarded as circumstances warrant. Social commentators have argued the merits and demerits of this emphasis on flexibility, suggesting that although it promotes adaptability, it also impairs the ability to form deep and lasting attachments to others and to values and norms.

Given the flux of organizational life, the notion of the protean person is readily applicable to organizations. As Zaleznik (1989) argued, "organizations need people who are flexible, can take on many roles, and can abandon roles without becoming disabled by a sense of loss" (p. 192). D. T. Hall (1976; Hall & Mirvis, 1996) described the "protean career" as one that is driven more by the individual than by the organization. In the absence of formerly reliable benchmarks of progress and success (e.g., education credentials, long-term organizational memberships, symbols of authority) and of organizations that are willing and able to shepherd their members, individuals must—by design or default—take more responsibility for managing their work lives (Cappelli et al., 1997). In the protean career, success is defined by the individual rather than by the organization or social expectations; by subjective rather than objective or consensual standards. Success is thus more idiosyncratic; it depends on the individual's values and goals. As D. T. Hall and Associates (1996) put it, "the driving questions are now more about meaning than money, purpose than power, identity than ego, and learning than attainment" (pp. xi–xii).

The dilemma is that the very flexibility that enables one to pursue one's dreams may undermine the capacity to *know* one's dreams. If the flux of organizational and individual life indeed impairs one's ability to attach oneself to others and to ideas, then there may be no bedrock meaning, purpose, and identity to direct and ground experience; no subjective standards—only a kaleidoscopic succession of events (Gergen, 1991). In Lifton's (1993) words, "proteanism . . . is a balancing act between responsive shapeshifting, on the one hand, and efforts to consolidate and cohere, on the other" (p. 9).

By exploring the social psychology of role transitions, we will better understand how roles, identities, and careers are socially constructed in an inherently dynamic environment; how individuals struggle to create coherent and more or less stable definitions of themselves in part through the roles they play in organizational life—and in so doing, find meaning and purpose.

OVERVIEW OF THE ROLE TRANSITION PROCESS

The concepts of role boundaries, role identities, and role sets provide the basic building blocks for the analysis of macro and micro role transitions. This section provides an overview of the basic transition process that will be elaborated on throughout the book.

Unfreezing–Movement–Refreezing

Lewin's (1951) field theory maintains that various social states are neither fixed nor permanent; rather, they are "quasi-stationary equilibria" (p. 199) held more or less in place by a set of counterbalancing forces within a given domain. For example, a person may continue in a job because the benefits appear to outweigh the costs. However, if the forces were to shift, the relative balance could be upset, resulting in an "unfreezing" (p. 228) of the equilibrium and movement toward a new equilibrium. Thus, an unwanted change in job duties may upset the positive ratio of benefits to costs and prompt the person to search for a better job. A "freezing" (p. 228) of a new equilibrium occurs if the opposing forces again become counterbalanced. The person may find and accept a new job that indeed appears to offer a more desirable ratio of benefits to costs. Although the terms *unfreezing* and *freezing* imply a movement from one fixed state to another, like water turning into ice, Lewin noted that there is often considerable fluctuation within a given state as the opposing forces wax and wane.

Field theory is readily applicable to role transitions because the transitions, by definition, involve movement across boundaries—across the spatial and temporal markers that circumscribe positions and their context (e.g., department, hierarchical level, organization, industry, nation). As the earlier example of the job leaver suggests, unfreezing corresponds to role exit, and freezing corresponds to role entry.

Furthermore, as Trice and Morand (1989) pointed out, Lewin's theory provides a framework for van Gennep's (1960) seminal work on *rites of passage,* defined as rituals or ceremonies that facilitate movement of one or more individuals from one role to another. Rites may include the presence and involvement of significant others, the manipulation of emotionally charged symbols (e.g., settings, props, clothing), and the use of well-defined dramaturgical parts and more or less scripted behavior. These attributes underscore the importance of the event and evoke strong emotion, affirm group values and ideologies, renew group cohesion, and encourage the internalization of the role identity as a definition of self (i.e., *role identification*; see chaps. 2 and 3). However, the manifest purpose of the rites is to signal, both to the individual and to members of the role set(s), the change in roles and associated role identities and status, allowing all concerned to acknowledge the change. This acknowledgment serves to either deinstitutionalize (in cases of role exit) or institutionalize (in cases of role entry) the individual(s) in the role and to affirm the network of roles in the face of a change of role occupants. The rites of passage are necessary for an effective—or smooth—transition; that is, one that either minimizes the social-psychological and organizational disruptions of a role exit or that facilitates the fulfillment of the entering individual's psychological motives for identity, meaning, control, and belonging (see chap. 3) and the organization's role performance requirements.[1]

As discussed in chapters 5 and 6, the rites of passage include three forms: (a) rites of separation (unfreezing), which facilitate role exit, (b) rites of transition (movement), which facilitate the journey between roles, and (c) rites of incorporation (refreezing), which facilitate role entry (van Gennep, 1960). Figure 1.1 integrates the role transition process with the models of Lewin and van Gennep.

Although Fig. 1.1 shows the old and new roles as highly segmented for ease of illustration, in reality: There is typically some overlap in the

---

[1]It should be noted that the individual's interests may not always mesh with the interests of the organization or of members of the role set (see chaps. 5 and 6). In such cases, the effectiveness of a transition must be judged relative to each participant's interests.

features that define the two roles and their associated identities, role entry usually begins *before* role exit as the individual mentally prepares for the actual or physical transition, and role exit usually continues for some time *after* role entry as the individual continues to mentally disengage from the prior role.

Transition Bridges.   Rites of passage heighten the salience of role boundaries and of differences between the identities of the exited and entered roles by calling attention to the act of role exit and entry. In short, rites of passage underscore the discontinuity experienced by the individual even as they help preserve the continuity of the roles.

Thus, unless one is seeking a complete break from the past, one may need a mechanism—a *transition bridge*—to preserve a sense of personal continuity as one moves between roles. In particular, the concepts of identity narratives, transitional roles, anticipatory identification, sentimentality, nostalgia, grieving, mementos, comforting rituals, mediatory myths, and exroles are discussed throughout the book as mechanisms by which individuals can develop and perform in new roles while retaining a sense of attachment to the past. These transition bridges are helpful even if the transition is welcomed as a means of furthering personal development. However, a particularly disruptive transition (in the terminology of chap. 4, typically a high magnitude, socially undesirable, and involuntary transition) may simply overwhelm the efficacy of bridging mechanisms precisely when they are most needed.

Boundary Crossings

There are numerous models of what Van Maanen (1982) referred to as "boundary crossings." My perspective on role exit and entry draws on an eclectic array of models including models of organizational role transitions (Ashford & Taylor, 1990; Brett, 1984; Nicholson, 1984; Stephens, 1994), organizational socialization (Feldman, 1976; Fisher, 1986; Van Maanen & Schein, 1979; Wanous, 1992), and work adjustment (Dawis & Lofquist, 1984; R. Katz, 1980; Louis, 1980b). However, three major provisos are warranted. First, these models focus on role entry and do not discuss the complementary issue of role exit. Accordingly, I draw heavily on Ebaugh's (1988) work on role exit, which encompasses roles in a variety of social domains (e.g., home, work). Second, the models focus on short-term processes and outcomes. In chapter 8, the discussion is broadened to include transitions associated with an individual's career and applies Nicholson's (1987) "transition cycle" to transitions within roles, between roles, and over the course of one's career. Third, these models do not discuss micro role transitions. As noted, the topic of micro transitions will be deferred until chapter 9 and draws on the work of D. T. Hall and Richter (1988) and Nippert-Eng (1996a), among others.

Two important boundary conditions of the book need to be mentioned. First, I assume that the individual views work as a relatively central life interest (Dubin, 1992). As will be discussed, the more the individual is involved in and identifies with work, the more consequential and potentially taxing the transition process tends to be for the individual. Thus, in cases where the individual does *not* view work as a central life interest, the social-psychological dynamics of role exit and role entry are likely to play out in more muted form. Second, role transitions necessarily unfold within a particular cultural (or cross-cultural), historical, and economic context. There is tremendous variance in the nature of roles, role boundaries, role identities, role sets, and role transitions across nations, industries, organizations, and subunits—and over historical periods. The arguments in the book are intended to generalize to Western industrialized nations, although much of the evidence on which the arguments are based is derived from work organizations in the United States, Britain, and Canada. My intent is to abstract commonalities or generic principles from a variety of settings and nations rather than to explore specific differences between settings and nations.

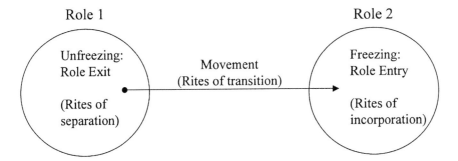

FIG. 1.1. The role transition process. (Note. The roles are depicted as highly segmented for ease of illustration. The model applies to any two roles that are not completely integrated.) (Reprinted from B. E. Ashforth, G. E. Kreiner, & M. Fugate, 2000, "All in a day's work: Boundaries and micro role transitions," *Academy of Management Review*, in press. Copyright © 2000 by the Academy of Management. Reprinted by permission of the Academy of Management via the Copyright Clearance Center, Inc.)

Role Exit. The process of role exit is discussed in chapter 5. Following Ebaugh (1988), most of the discussion focuses on voluntary exit. It is argued that certain events—disappointments, external changes, milestones, impending events, and internal changes—may trigger first doubts about the long-term viability of role occupancy. If the doubts persevere, the individual may search for information to confirm or disconfirm the doubts. However, the stronger the doubts, the more likely the individual will seek—and find—confirmation rather than disconfirmation. To the extent that confirmatory information is perceived, the doubts escalate—particularly if validated by valued members of the role set.

As doubts crystallize, the individual may seek and weigh alternatives and may begin to identify with favored prospects. The individual's psychological fulcrum may shift from the present to the future, and his or her reference group may shift from the current role to the anticipated one. If a turning point is experienced (typically a further external event or an internal resolution of doubts), the individual physically exits the role and, with the assistance of rites of separation, constructs an exrole identity. Individuals generally desire to retain socially desirable, functional, and fondly recalled features of their former role identities. Role exit may trigger *liminality* (van Gennep, 1960), a social-psychological state where the individual lacks a self-defining connection—an identity moor—at least to that social domain. If one anticipates the assumption of a new role or substitute activities within a reasonable time frame, the experience of this limbo state may actually be positive.

Although the exit process has been couched in largely rational terms, the process is fraught with bias, emotion, and contradiction. For example, doubters may profess to be open-minded about their role but seek confirmation of their doubts; they may display their doubts as a way of precipitating a crisis; they may examine alternatives in a very cursory manner; they may become entrapped by *side-bets* (e.g., personal ties, sunk costs; Becker, 1960); and they may retrospectively construct reality to justify their desire to leave.

Role Entry. The psychological motives cued by role entry are discussed in chapter 3, and the process of role entry is discussed in chapters 6 and 7. As noted, role entry activates motives for identity (self-definition in the organization), meaning (sense-making and purpose), control (mastery and influence), and belonging (attachment). The more a role fulfills these motives, the more subjectively important the role becomes, the greater the identification with the role, and the more faithfully one enacts the role identity and meets objective and subjective criteria for success.

Role entry involves a negotiation between individual and organization. On the one hand, entry tends to foster surprise and uncertainty, galvanizing newcomers to learn about and adapt to the situation. Thus, newcomers tend to be most receptive to personal change during the initial period of role entry. Organizational socialization practices are intended to help resolve the uncertainty in a manner that addresses organizational goals.[2] The more rigorously socialization practices constrain the experiences of newcomers and the lessons they derive from those experiences, the stronger the situational control is said to be. Indeed, organizations may create a "social cocoon" (Greil & Rudy, 1984) where individuals are subjected to intense and relentless pressure to adopt the role and organizational identities espoused by management. Facilitated by rites of transition and incorporation, newcomers may experience an identity transformation and adopt the prefabricated self offered by the organization. On the other hand, newcomers are not passive recipients of the organizational word. Newcomers often engage in proactive behaviors to learn more about the role context and to shape it to their wishes. Preliminary empirical work suggests that personal and role change are largely independent and that each is associated with certain individual differences.

Behavior can foster congruent affect and cognition as the newcomer enacts the role and endeavors to make sense of his or her behavior; alternatively, affect and cognition can foster congruent behavior as the newcomer endeavors to display his or her actual or hoped-for self. Either way, a role identity is unlikely to take root if the newcomer's enactment of the identity is not affirmed by valued members of the role set. Role entry is also facilitated by selectively forgetting aspects of former identities that conflict with the current role identity and by transition bridges that quell the sense of discontinuity.

Purpose and Overview of the Book

The purpose of the book is to provide a provocative examination of certain facets of the *multi*faceted dynamics of role transitions in organizational settings rather than to build a single unified model of the transition process.

---

[2]The term *intended* is used because organizations often institutionalize practices that are actually antithetical to long-term goals. For example, Ashforth and Saks (1996) argued that organizations generally promote role conformity even when role innovation may be preferable.

My intent is not to simply summarize the literature in selected areas but to use it as a springboard for speculating about the nuances of the social-psychology of transitioning.

A friendly warning is in order: Readers looking for detailed discussions of such conventional organizational behavior or human resource management topics as selection, training, role stress, gender differences, and turnover, or of specific role transitions such as promotion, transfer, and retirement are apt to be disappointed. Rather than review the voluminous literatures in these domains, I focus—as noted—on the intersection of role and identity. Thus, the book explores such relatively uncharted territory as normalization, dis- and deidentification, transitional and temporary identities, role exit, liminality, selective forgetting, role reversals, transition bridges, turning points, time compression, identity narratives, micro role transitions, and transition scripts.

The arguments throughout the book are illustrated with an eclectic assortment of studies—from the education of medical students to the socialization of torturers and from the adjustment of camp counselors to the retirement of CEOs. Although the diversity of settings is inherently interesting, it is the *commonalities* in role and identity dynamics across these settings that is truly remarkable. As Hughes (1970) concluded in a retrospective commentary on occupational research, "if a certain problem turned up in one occupation, it was nearly certain to turn up in all" (p. 149). As will be seen, the same can be said for identity dynamics.

The game plan is as follows. Chapter 2, "Role Identities," explores the nature and development of role identities, the interaction between one's global identity and one's role identities, and the nature of temporary role identities. Chapter 3, "Psychological Motives Aroused by Role Transitions," examines the four motives noted earlier (identity, meaning, control, and belonging) and how they affect one's propensity for role identification, disidentification, and ambivalence. Chapter 4, "Attributes of Role Transitions," discusses seven key characteristics of transitions (high vs. low magnitude, high vs. low desirability, voluntary vs. involuntary, high vs. low predictability, collective vs. individual, long vs. short duration, and reversible vs. irreversible) and how they affect the difficulty and valence of role transitions. As noted, chapter 5, "Role Exit," explores the phenomenology of disengagement (first doubts→seeking and weighing alternatives→the turning point→creating the exrole); chapter 6, "Role Entry: Situational Context," examines how normative controls, entry shock, and socialization processes may induce a transformation of identity; and chapter 7, "Role Entry: Individual Dynamics," looks at the other side of the coin: How individuals address the four psychological motives and attempt to personalize their roles and secure social validation for their role enactments. Chapter 8, "Role Transitions and the Life Span," examines the cycles of preparation→encounter→adjustment→stabilization that play out not only within a role but over the succession of roles that constitute a career, and discusses how individuals construct identity narratives to make sense of their transitions over time. Chapter 9, "Micro Role Transitions," argues that everyday transitions between social domains can be regarded as a boundary-making and -crossing activity where individuals construct or confront temporal and spatial boundaries around their roles and develop scripts for regularly surmounting those boundaries. Finally, chapter 10, "Epilogue: Summary and Major Themes," briefly recaps the major arguments of the book and distills eight central themes (role and self, dynamic interactionism, transitioning, events, normalizing, role exit↔role entry, role identification, and social influence).

Intended Audience for the Book. The discussions should provide a solid introduction for advanced students of role transitions as well as a stimulus for theorizing and empirical work for scholars who are well versed in the topic. The major social science disciplines that I draw upon and that the book will likely appeal to are organizational behavior, human resource management, and various branches of psychology (particularly social, cognitive, developmental, and industrial and organizational). The book also includes occasional doses of sociology and anthropology for good measure.

ADDITIONAL THEMES

Two motifs pervade the discussion of role transitions and identity throughout the book: Normalization and the interaction between the person and the situation. These motifs are briefly foreshadowed here.

Normalization

D. Rosenthal (1990) conducted an ethnographic study of Los Alamos, New Mexico, the birthplace of the atom bomb and at the time of her study still a major home for nuclear weapons design. Indeed, Los Alamos was a company town, where the company was the U.S. government.

Rosenthal was curious about the effects that weapons design might have on the attitudes and behaviors of the townspeople. Surely, living "at the heart of the bomb," as her book is titled, would leave some obvious traces if not psychic scars. However, what is most striking about her findings is the very *lack* of the extraordinary. Aside from the high proportion of scientists, engineers, and technicians, Los Alamos at the time appeared to be a rather ordinary small town. The daily transitions from bomb designer to parent and from weapons technician to neighbor appeared relatively seamless. This is not to say that such roles are antithetical, only that an outsider might expect to find some evidence of awkward or unresolved integration.

A recurring theme of the present book is that role transitions are partly about *normalization* or *normalizing* (Ashforth & Kreiner, 2000); about rendering the new, the unexpected, the strange, and the frightening more or less ordinary. The potential leveling power of normalization is demonstrated by the fact that it is usually only outsiders who are surprised by the very ordinariness—the taken-for-granted routinization—of the seemingly extraordinary.

Interaction Between Person and Situation

A longstanding debate in psychology concerns the relative impact of the person and the situation on behavior. Those favoring the former argue that the individual has an array of attributes and dispositions that lead him or her to behave in more or less predictable and reliable ways in a given situation over time and possibly across situations. Those favoring the latter counter that external pressures and constraints curtail the individual's latitude, thereby negating individual differences and leading to marked inconsistencies across situations. Not surprisingly, the person versus situation issue constitutes a subtext in many theories of organizational behavior and occasionally flairs into an explicit debate (e.g., Davis-Blake & Pfeffer, 1989, vs. House, Shane, & Herold, 1996).

As Bell and Staw (1989) noted, a critical concept that emerged from the person versus situation debate is that of *strong versus weak situations.* According to Mischel (1977), a strong situation exists where: (a) everyone construes the situation in much the same way, (b) everyone has the same understanding of what behaviors are appropriate, (c) everyone is capable of performing those behaviors, and (d) those behaviors are reinforced. In short, there is strong consensus on the "right way" and the "wrong way" to behave. Conversely, a weak situation is less structured and more ambiguous such that it is unclear or may be construed in multiple ways. Under such conditions, there may be no consensus on what constitutes appropriate behavior. The concept of strong versus weak situations thus suggests that the stronger the situation, the less variance in behavior across individuals and the less the impact of individual attributes and dispositions on behavior.

Extensions to the Debate. There are four critical provisos to the person–situation debate and strong–weak situation issue that are relevant to role transitions. First, by definition, strong situations constrain only behavior—potentially observable actions—*not* goals, values, beliefs, needs, wants, or other psychological and (directly) unobservable phenomena (House et al., 1996). Thus, a newcomer may display the expected behaviors and yet retain highly dissonant readings of the situation. The importance of this proviso will become evident in chapter 7 when we discuss the ABCs (affect/behavior/cognition) of role entry and how any of the ABCs may lead and cue the others, leading ultimately to role identification or role *dis*identification. It is argued that dissonance among the ABCs is difficult to maintain over the long run, such that convergence tends to occur.

Second, most scholars have gravitated away from a strict person versus situation conception of the debate and have assumed an *interactionist* position. This position holds that behavior within a given setting is determined by the interaction of individual differences *and* situational characteristics (Chatman, 1989; Hattrup & Jackson, 1996; House et al., 1996). For example, job characteristics theory maintains that enriched jobs (situation) foster high motivation and effort (behavior) among individuals with high growth needs (individual; Hackman & Oldham, 1980). Interactionism suggests that a person's behavior is not necessarily consistent across situations (as the person argument would suggest); rather, it is *coherent* (Magnusson & Endler, 1977; Schneider, 1983). A given setting is likely to present a unique combination of situational characteristics, thus rendering certain individual differences more relevant and salient and others less so. For example, Sheldon, Ryan, Rawsthorne, and Ilardi (1997) found that university students "reported being relatively most extroverted in the friend role, most neurotic in the student role, [and] most conscientious in the employee role" (p. 1390). The interaction of these idiosyncratic couplings of situation- and person-based attributes will likely lead to different patterns of behavior across situations (moderate consistency), and yet the behavior will continue to reflect the nature of the person (high coherence).

I argued earlier that an individual develops local or situation-specific self-conceptions that often differ markedly across situational contexts. In enacting these local identities, the individual remains true to his or her self-conception *within each situation*, and the more valued the identity, the stronger the desire to remain true. Furthermore, these localized enactments tend to interact with the individual's more abstract global identity such that there is a continuous and reciprocal relation between site-specific identities and a generalized and more or less coherent sense of self. Thus, interactionism helps explain how individuals can experience themselves as both one self and many selves.

Third, as Hattrup and Jackson (1996) discussed, person- and situation-based approaches offer fairly static views of the individual and situation. There is little sense of *process*, of how the individual learns about, adapts to, and affects a given situation over time. Indeed, many interactionist accounts are equally static, examining how one variable moderates the impact of another on some outcome of interest. What is needed is a more *dynamic interactionism* (Hattrup & Jackson, 1996; cf. reciprocal determinism, Bandura, 1986) where it is recognized that persons affect situations and situations affect persons such that the unfolding of time produces continuous changes in both the person and the situation. Thus, dynamic interactionism focuses on the ongoing processes through which individuals and contexts mutually affect one another. For example, once evoked, a high need for achievement may lead one to actively seek role clarity and feedback and to set challenging goals. In turn, these behaviors may influence the situation and reinforce the need for achievement, setting off further cycles of person–situation interactions. In this book, I am less concerned with long-term person–situation interactions than with the short-term interactions surrounding exit from one organizational role and entry into another.

Finally, person-based approaches offer a fragmented view of the individual. Demographic attributes, traits, needs, attitudes, values, and so on are often studied in isolation or in limited combinations. The typical study participant is described as having so many units of, say, self-esteem or need for power. What is missing is a *holistic sense of the person*, of how the various attributes cluster together into a profile that represents a flesh-and-blood individual.[3] The constructs of role identity and global identity

---

[3]The fragmented approach also ignores interactions between the personal attributes themselves (Chatman, 1989). For example, individuals with high self-esteem may enact the need for affiliation differently than individuals with low self-esteem.

potentially offer a more holistic as well as dynamic approach to under-standing the individual. Identities, whether role specific or global, offer more or less articulated personas that enable individuals to navigate across contexts and over time. Moreover, as a more holistic and dynamic con-ception of the individual's sense of self, identity has the elasticity to accommodate a host of phenomenological and affective variables that are often neglected by fragmented person-based models, including excite-ment, ambivalence, intuition, disappointment, and hopes and dreams.

CONCLUSION

In emphasizing continuity over discontinuity (Stephens, 1994), research-ers have often viewed role transitions as discrete steps between fixed states, much like climbing stairs. What is missing is a clear sense of tran-sition*ing*, of the social-psychological dynamics of disengagement from one role (role exit) and engagement in another (role entry). Role transi-tions are fundamentally about crossing role boundaries and in so doing, doffing one persona and donning another. Thus, many of the social-psy-chological dynamics of role transitions lie at the intersection of roles and identities, and it is there that much of our attention will be focused in the chapters to follow.

2

Role Identities

I'm also getting a little worried about July. In July I'm going to be magically trans-
formed into a junior resident. I like the idea of not being an intern anymore, but I'm
not sure I like the idea of being a resident. I mean, residents are people the interns
turn to when they have questions and concerns. Residents are figures of authority.
For some reason, I can't seem to imagine myself as an authority figure. I can't imag-
ine giving interns advice. I wouldn't trust advice I gave to myself. Of course, that
sounds kind of ridiculous.

—a medical intern (Marion, 1990, p. 299)

Our quest to understand the intersection of roles, role transitions, and the self must begin with the seminal construct of identity. The construct has been used in many ways in many contexts such that it is in danger of encompassing everything—and therefore nothing. The perspective adopted here focuses primarily on models of identity that examine how the self is constructed in social contexts and how it mediates the impact of the social context on individual cognition, affect, and behavior.

Specifically, the perspective represents a meld of two major theories, social identity theory (SIT) and identity theory (IT; see Hogg, Terry, & White, 1995; Thoits & Virshup, 1997), as well as allied work under the general rubric of identity (e.g., Brewer, 1991; Burke, 1991; Cheney, 1991; Schlenker, 1986; Thoits, 1991; R. H. Turner, 1978). I draw liberally from this material to define role identity and articulate its basic dynamics. I then discuss the development of role identities vis-à-vis one's global or general identity and close with a discussion of identities adopted for relatively short periods of time—temporary role identities.

SOCIAL IDENTITY THEORY
AND IDENTITY THEORY

Social Identity Theory

According to SIT (W. P. Robinson, 1996; Tajfel & Turner, 1986) and its extension, self-categorization theory (J. C. Turner, Hogg, Oakes, Reicher, & Wetherell, 1987), the individual's sense of self is comprised of a *personal identity* that includes idiosyncratic attributes (e.g, dispositions, abilities) and a *social identity* that includes salient categories of people (e.g., nationality, production team; although SIT does not focus on roles per se, roles can be viewed as a specific type of social category[1]). As such, SIT helps reconcile the two poles of identity flagged in Graafsma, Bosma, Grotevant, and de Levita's (1994) interdisciplinary review of identity: Being a unique individual (personal identity) and being one with others (social identity).

Individuals categorize themselves and others as a means of ordering the social environment and locating themselves and others within it. Thus, categories are selected to provide meaningful distinctions between people or subgroups of people. Individuals define a category according to the most widely shared attributes of category members (prototypes) or specific persons that exemplify the category (exemplars), or both (Ashforth & Humphrey, 1995). These social identities are "relational and comparative" (Tajfel & Turner, 1986, p. 16): They define members of a category relative to the members of other categories. For example, the category of *doctor* becomes meaningful in relation to the category of *patient*. As the comparison categories change, so might the salience of certain aspects of the focal social identity. Huntington (1957) found that virtually all of the first-year medical students she surveyed thought of themselves as students when dealing with medical faculty and classmates, whereas 12% and 31%

---

[1]The term *social category* is more inclusive than organizational group or organizational role. Social categories such as nationality or gender can be quite abstract with relatively unclear goals and norms and perhaps minimal interaction between members qua members (e.g., two Americans may interact not *because* they are American but because they share a mutual interest). Groups such as a production team or committee tend to be more exclusive, concrete, and context specific, with much clearer goals, norms, and member interdependencies, and therefore, more interaction as members (Deaux, 1996; Rabbie & Horwitz, 1988). Roles, in turn, tend to be even more exclusive and concrete, with particularly clear goals and norms, although interdependencies and interactions are often stronger *between* roles than *within* them (e.g., a personal secretary is more interdependent with his boss than with other personal secretaries; cf. Brewer & Gardner, 1996; Thoits & Virshup, 1997). I thank Mike Pratt for suggesting this argument.

[handwritten top margin: SI identify with the SC/role - on two levels ① cognitive (you have a sense of membership) ② evaluative (this awareness is related to some value) + this awareness is related to some value]

thought of themselves as doctors when dealing with nurses and patients, respectively. Moreover, because individuals are motivated to hold positive identities, they tend to accentuate differences between their category/role and other categories/roles that favor their own (Haslam, Oakes, Turner, & McGarty, 1996).

Social identification is the perception of oneness with or belongingness to the social category or role. Tajfel (1982) added that: "In order to achieve the stage of 'identification,' two components are necessary . . . a cognitive one, in the sense of awareness of membership; and an evaluative one, in the sense that this awareness is related to some value connotations" (p. 2). The cognitive component reflects the perception of various social categories and the location of oneself in one or more of them. The affective component of identification serves a signaling function (Harquail, 1998; Thoits, 1989), drawing one's attention to the identity. The potency or strength of the emotions aroused conveys the importance of the identity to oneself, whereas the positiveness or negativeness of the emotions conveys the evaluation of the identity.

[handwritten: → is a process you are evaluating the how strength of it & emotions that draws you to the role & if that; Identity carries a +/- emotion.]

By identifying, individuals perceive themselves as psychologically intertwined with the fate of the social category or role, sharing its common destiny, and experiencing its successes and failures (cf. Deaux, 1996). As individuals begin to identify, they usually assume the perceived prototypical or exemplary characteristics of the category or role as their own.[2] This *self-stereotyping* amounts to the depersonalization of the self: When the category or role is salient, unique attributes are downplayed as individuals come to see themselves as more or less exemplifying the category or role (J. C. Turner, 1985; J. C. Turner & Oakes, 1989). Once internalized, these attributes may outlive the individual's active involvement in the category or role (e.g., Banks et al., 1992). Thus, individuals develop a

[handwritten: Individuals begin to assume/explain characteristics of the category, once those attributes are internalized they may outlive the individual's membership in that category → this is internalization results in individuals norms, etc being influenced by their social category.]

---

[2]Of course, the individual may have these characteristics (or at least an affinity for them) prior to entering the category or role. Indeed, the literatures on vocational identity, job search, and person–job/organization fit usually assume that individuals have a more or less clear and stable sense of who they are and simply search for positions and organizations that match or reflect these attributes. However, it may be more accurate to say that individuals—particularly the young and inexperienced—have a somewhat equivocal and malleable sense of who they are that is shaped and only becomes truly known through concrete action and reflection in specific settings. In short, the self is most knowable when grounded and enacted in specific settings. Individuals search for roles and organizations that *appear* to resonate with who they are and what they want, but it is in the course of learning and enacting the new role that individuals crystallize and enact these actual and desired self-conceptions. As discussed in chapters 6 and 7, role entry is therefore a complex process of role learning, personal change, and role innovation. In short, the process of identification is often less about discovering fit than *creating* it.

sense of who and what they are—their goals, values, beliefs, and normative ways of thinking, acting, and even feeling—at least partly from their social memberships. When the social identity is salient, the individual thinks and acts as an exemplar of the category or role.

Although not specified by SIT, internalization is likely related to identification in a reciprocal manner as internalization of the social category's or role's perceived attributes ("I believe") may induce one to identify with the category or role ("I am"; Mael & Ashforth, 1995). The significance of this statement will become apparent in chapter 7 when it is argued that affect, behavior, *or* cognition—the ABCs of role entry—can instigate role identification. Furthermore, although individuals tend to seek and value social identities that enhance their self-esteem and status (cf. Hogg & Abrams, 1990), they may also identify with categories and roles that are not joined by choice (e.g., family, task force) and may tenaciously maintain identification in situations involving failure, loss, and unpopularity (Ashforth & Mael, 1989). As Abrams (1992) put it, "the question 'Who am I?' takes precedence over the question 'How good am I?'" (p. 66).

Identity Theory

IT (McCall & Simmons, 1978; Stryker, 1980, 1987) emerged from symbolic interactionism, which contends that one's sense of self is largely grounded in the perceptions of others (Mead, 1934). Through social interaction and the internalization of collective values, meanings, and standards, one comes to see oneself through the eyes of others and constructs a more or less stable sense of self (Burke, 1991; Stryker, 1980).

IT adds the contention that this socially constructed sense of self is firmly anchored to the discrete roles that one plays in society (although IT acknowledges the impact of other social categories and of personalities). When interacting with another person, one necessarily occupies a particular role such as friend, spouse, or coworker. The associated role prescriptions and how one enacts them strongly affect how one is perceived. Moreover, because values, meanings, and standards—and reference groups—tend to vary across the many roles one may occupy, one's sense of self also tends to vary across roles. A particular role calls forth a particular self such that the individual is actually a portfolio of selves.

IT further argues that one's role identities are arrayed in a hierarchy of salience (Stryker, 1980), defined as "a readiness to act out an identity" (Stryker & Serpe, 1994, p. 17) or the probability of an identity being activated in a given situation. According to Stryker, this readiness inheres in

(handwritten margin note:) Example of how a tough manager, however, need to be an empathetic mother. (1) Example of how a tough manager, however (2) home you need to be an empathetic mother.

the person, not the situation.[3] The greater the number of valued relationships that are predicated on the role, the greater the role's salience. For example, Callero (1985) surveyed blood donors and found that the greater the number of important relationships associated with the act of donating blood, the more salient was the donor identity to the individual. Thus, two people in the same context may behave quite differently because of the salience they accord certain role identities. Individuals enact their salient role identities as a means of expressing themselves and gaining support and acceptance from members of their role set (McCall & Simmons, 1978).

INTEGRATING THE TWO THEORIES

Thus, both SIT and IT view the self as *socially defined*, where the definitions are derived largely from the individual's membership in or occupancy of certain social categories (SIT), including roles (IT). As Ebaugh (1988) noted, when individuals are asked "Who are you?", they typically respond in terms of social categories (e.g., female, wife, French, lawyer). Following IT, to the extent that a role cues or connotes a certain persona—replete with goals, values, beliefs, norms, interaction styles, and time horizons—we can speak of a role-based identity or simply, role identity. Role identities are socially constructed definitions of self-in-role (this is who a role occupant is). Role identities anchor or ground self-conceptions in social domains. To switch roles is to switch social identities.

I would elaborate this perspective in three ways. First, role identities consist of core or central features and peripheral features. Core features tend to be important, necessary, or typical characteristics of the identity and more defining of the identity (Perry, 1997). For example, Greenhaus and Beutell (1985) suggested that the stereotypical managerial role identity emphasizes the core features of "self-reliance, emotional stability, aggressiveness, and objectivity" (pp. 81–82), whereas more peripheral features may include intelligence and charisma. Core and peripheral features also may include aspects of the context(s) that help situate the role identities such as geographical location, role set members, and a role's relative status.

Second, role identities can vary from strong to weak. A strong role identity is widely shared (i.e., role occupants and role set members have a

---

[3]However, in McCall and Simmons' (1978) version of IT, salience is a function of personal and situational factors.

similar understanding of the identity) and densely articulated (i.e., the identity has a set of tightly integrated core and peripheral features that leave little ambiguity or equivocality regarding what the role entails). Note that each role set member may have a clear perception of the identity of a focal role but may nonetheless perceive the identity very differently than some other members or the role occupants themselves (e.g., a subordinate expects her manager to support her even if it means bucking the rest of the organization, whereas the manager's boss expects the manager to put the organization first). Such cases of interrole conflict undermine the strength of an identity.[4] Note also that a densely articulated identity does not necessarily imply low autonomy. A role identity may have well-articulated goals and values but accommodate a variety of means of realizing them; and even where means are clearly specified, there is typically room for idiosyncratic enactment (see chap. 7). Finally, roles that are new, in flux, and that are associated with underdeveloped selection and socialization mechanisms are likely to have weak identities.

Third, a given role occupant may or may not actually accept a role identity—whether socially or idiosyncratically constructed—as defining himself or herself ("This is who *I* am"). That is, individuals may occupy and enact a role without actually regarding it as self-defining. Following SIT, *role identification*—a specific form of social identification—is said to occur if the individual indeed comes to define himself or herself in terms of the role identity.[5]

Role Contrast

A key concept affecting role transitions is the *contrast* between the identities of the exited role and the entered role. The magnitude of the contrast is determined by the *number* of core and peripheral features that differ between the role identities and the *extent* of the differences, where core features are weighted more heavily (cf. Louis, 1980b). For example, just as Greenhaus and Beutell (1985) noted that the stereotypical managerial role identity emphasizes self-reliance, stability, and so on, they also noted

---

[4]However, just as role identities have core and peripheral features, so some role set members are more core or peripheral than others. Interrole conflict between core role set members undermines role identity strength more so than conflict involving peripheral members.

[5]IT theorists refer to role identities as "self-definitions that people apply to themselves as a consequence of the structural role positions they occupy" (Hogg et al., 1995, p. 256). In contrast, I refer to role identities as socially constructed definitions rather than self-definitions and reserve the term *identification* for the process by which one actually accepts a role identity as self-defining.

that a manager's family members may expect him or her "to be warm, nurturant, emotional, and vulnerable in his or her interactions with them" (p. 82). The greater the magnitude of this contrast between the role identities of manager and family member, the greater the magnitude of the transition from one role to the other and thus the potential difficulty of the transition (where *difficulty* is defined as the effort required to become psychologically and, if relevant, physically, disengaged from one role and psychologically and physically engaged in a second role). The difficulty lies in "switching cognitive gears" (Louis & Sutton, 1991, p. 55); disengaging from the identity implied by one role and reengaging in the dissimilar identity of a second role. In the words of one manager:

> When I come home and try to get involved with my family I have a difficult time switching from my cognitive, directive management style to a more emotional, cooperative one. The very things I'm paid to do well at work create disaster for me at home. . . . I guess I just don't know how to turn off directing everything and everyone. (DeLong & DeLong, 1992, p. 171)

A high-magnitude transition may involve large changes in many core and peripheral features (relative discontinuity), whereas a low-magnitude transition may involve small changes in a few core features or large changes in a few peripheral features (relative continuity). In between these two poles, various mixes of the two criteria are possible. A moderate change may be the product of a few core features that change greatly (e.g., geographical location) or many core and peripheral features that change in small ways.

Multiple Identities

Furthermore, because an individual tends to be a member or occupant of multiple categories/roles, he or she is likely to have *multiple* social identities (SIT) or role identities (IT). The notion of multiplicity is particularly relevant to role transitions because it raises the question of how a particular role is activated and reconciled with other roles one may retain. Both SIT and IT address the issue of which identities will assume salience or psychological prominence in a given situation. SIT emphasizes situational factors, whereas IT, as noted, emphasizes personal factors. Combining these perspectives, I argue that the salience of a role identity to an individual in an organizational context is determined by both sets of factors; specifically, subjective importance and situational relevance (cf. accessibility and fit,

Oakes, 1987; J. C. Turner, Oakes, Haslam, & McGarty, 1994). These factors can be regarded as dimensions or continua that range from low to high and that are conceptually independent but tend to be correlated in practice.

Subjective Importance. The first dimension can be termed the *hierarchy of subjective importance*, analogous to IT's hierarchy of salience. I prefer the former term to the latter because IT's notion that salience inheres in the person rather than the situation can be easily confused with the notion of identities being rendered more or less "salient" by situational cues (e.g., a uniform) or by the interaction of personal attributes and situational cues. In contrast, the notion of a hierarchy of subjective importance places the locus of the hierarchy squarely within the individual.

A subjectively important role or other social identity is one that is highly central to an individual's global or core sense of self (as described more fully shortly) or is otherwise highly relevant to his or her goals, values, or other key attributes (cf. N. Miller, Urban, & Vanman, 1998). The greater the importance one attaches to a given identity, the more weight it carries in determining one's global sense of self. Individuals generally gravitate toward and place more value on positively regarded social categories/roles. However, an important identity is not necessarily regarded positively, whether by the individual or his or her referents. For example, a member of a stigmatized occupation such as funeral director may view his or her occupational identity with ambivalence or even embarrassment and yet continue to regard that identity as a central component of self (Ashforth & Kreiner, 1999). That said, individuals are adept at reframing the meaning of stigmatized categories/roles they occupy so that they can feel more positively about them. Thus, funeral directors state they are helping relatives and friends of the deceased deal with grief rather than processing dead bodies and profiting from their work (W. E. Thompson, 1991).

Individuals vary widely in the degree of importance they typically ascribe to a given role identity, and given role identities vary widely in the degree of importance that individuals typically ascribe to them. Generally, subjective importance is higher if the role identity is strong (recall, widely shared and densely articulated) and the role itself is permanent, visible, socially desirable, and instrumental to valued goals. In turn, the more subjectively important the role identity, the more densely articulated (although not necessarily widely shared) the identity tends to become, the more permanent and visible the enactment of the identity tends to become, and the more instrumental the identity tends to become in realizing goals.

Thus, one is likely to view one's role identity as a coworker as far more important than one's role identity as a customer at a local store.

It is important to differentiate subjective importance based on affective commitment ("I like") from that based on behavioral commitment ("I do") or normative commitment ("I should") (Meyer & Allen, 1997). As one develops *side-bets* (Becker, 1960; Meyer & Allen, 1984) over time—role-specific relationships, capabilities, and rewards; and a role-specific reputation—one may come to feel dependent on or obligated to the role and members of the role set. Overall subjective importance may remain high but may be based on extrinsic rewards and normative expectations as much as (or instead of) intrinsic satisfaction. Indeed, the longer one stays in a role, the more difficult it may become to initiate a role transition, even if role identification is low. One may become entrapped by one's history, particularly if one's role entry and continued role enactment are perceived by oneself and others "as involving free choice, when [they] cannot be reversed or denied, and/or when one confirms [them] in front of other people" (Pratt, 1998, p. 199; Salancik, 1977; Staw & Ross, 1987). In short, behavioral and normative commitment tend to increase over time such that subjective importance may ultimately be based on all three forms of commitment or only on behavioral and normative commitment.

The more subjectively important the identity, the more likely one is to define a given situation as identity consistent, to be receptive to identity-related cues, to actively seek opportunities to enact the identity, and to retain and recall identity-related information (particularly identity-consistent information; e.g., Stryker & Serpe, 1994; Swann, 1990). Like the parable of the boy with a hammer who found that everything needed hammering, individuals are predisposed to perceive situations through the lens of subjectively important identities and to act accordingly. For example, Hunt and Benford (1994) described how members of peace movement organizations routinely interpret mundane personal activities, such as putting a child to bed, as reflections of the conflict between peace and war.

The book focuses on role identities and transitions that are typically viewed as important to the role incumbents or to members of their role set or both.

Situational Relevance. To act in any given context, individuals need a definition of the situation including their role(s) and their relationships with others who may be present. Role and other social identities tend to be highly salient when one is in an organizational context. The presence of institutional symbols (e.g., a doctor's office, a bank) or people, or both, triggers the need for social categorization, including of oneself, thereby cuing relevant identities. Whether a roomful of people are categorized as friends, clients, or rivals has enormous consequences for the role identity one invokes in that situation and consequently, for one's thoughts, feelings, and behavior.[6]

Thus, I call the second dimension along which role or other social identities can be arrayed the *hierarchy of situational relevance*, where situational relevance is defined as the degree to which a given identity is socially appropriate to a given situation (i.e., a specific context, setting, or encounter). By *socially appropriate*, I mean that the identity would be considered by others to be legitimately applicable to the situation. Whereas subjective importance is defined by internal preferences, situational relevance is defined by external norms. However, as illustrated by the Hunt and Benford (1994) study discussed earlier, the greater the subjective importance of an identity to an individual, the more likely that *he or she* will believe the identity is relevant—and, likely, vice versa. For example, a dedicated insurance agent may regard a New Year's Eve party as an occasion to recruit insurance prospects, whereas most others would regard the invocation of the occupational identity as totally inappropriate. In this case, the situational relevance of the occupational identity would be considered low.

The categories into which an individual groups himself or herself and others depends largely on the context and its mix of people and roles. Once an individual adopts a given role or other social identity, aspects of his or her *personal* identity will be more or less applicable to the matter at hand. Thus, the definition of the situation and the most relevant role identity(ies) provide a psychological framework within which more individuated attributes are manifested (Abrams, 1990). For example, a work context that cues the identity of supervisor thereby also cues and legitimates certain behaviors (e.g., directive, supportive), but different supervisors will likely have different preferences for displaying those behaviors.

---

[6]In the absence of an organizational context and clear cues for roles, self-categorization theory (J. C. Turner, Hogg et al., 1987) argues that a person categorizes individuals into collectivities on the basis of the perceived similarities and differences among them and accentuates intragroup similarities and intergroup differences. These twin processes distill the mass of individuals into relatively clear and separate categories. I would add, however, that personal identities may instead be invoked if individuals appear quite dissimilar such that grouping is difficult or the individuals are already grouped under a common social identity (e.g., young adult) that is meaningful to the context.

As Fig. 2.1 illustrates, the dimensions of subjective importance and situational relevance interact to determine the *salience* of a given identity to an individual, where salience is defined (following IT) as the readiness to act out the identity. An identity will be most salient when the two dimensions are both high, moderately salient when only one dimension is high, and least salient when both dimensions are low. A particularly intriguing area for research is those occasions where salience is only moderate because it is not clear under what circumstances a moderately salient identity will actually be invoked, how sincere the role enactment will be in cases where the role identity is situationally relevant but not subjectively important, and how members of the role set will respond to the enactment of a subjectively important identity that is deemed low in situational relevance.

It is important to note that salience is not the same as conscious awareness. For example, as a newcomer becomes increasingly familiar with her organization and job, her work role identity may come to be activated automatically by routinized cues (e.g., entering the workplace at 9 a.m.), thus precipitating role-consistent behavior, thought, and feeling with minimal reflection (see chap. 9, "Role Transitions Over Time"). Indeed, it is often when smooth role performances are disrupted that people become most aware of the role-based nature of their actions.

Finally, the situational relevance of a given identity tends to vary widely across contexts. The more contexts in which an identity is applicable, the greater the *breadth* of its relevance; and the more strongly an identity applies to a given context, the greater the *depth* of its relevance. For example, consistent with footnote 1, the social identity of female may be

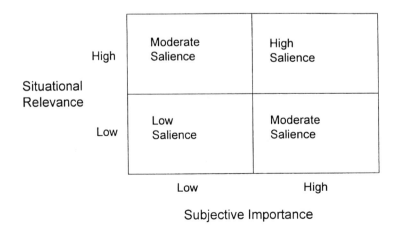

FIG. 2.1. Salience of a role identity to an individual in a given context.

relevant to many contexts (high breadth) but it may be far less relevant than other social identities within some contexts and far more relevant in others (varying depth). Generally, the more abstract an identity, the higher its breadth and the lower its depth; and the more specific an identity, the lower its breadth and the higher its depth. For example, the rather abstract identity of middle manager may be applicable to a wide variety of situations in an organization (high breadth) but may have less relevance in most of those situations (low depth) than more specific identities such as marketing manager or turnaround specialist.

The book also focuses on role identities and transitions that are likely to be viewed as situationally relevant.

Conclusion

What makes the concept of social/role identification compelling is that it provides a fundamental psychological connection between the individual and valued social categories, such as department member and secretary, situating the individual within the organizational context. Identity cuts to the core of what a social entity is thought to be, and by identifying with an entity, the individual effectively becomes a *microcosm* of it, reflecting prototypical or exemplary attributes. Analogous to R. H. Turner's (1978) notion of *role–person merger*, to then faithfully enact the identity is to be true to oneself. By extending the self to include the entity, the individual's self-interests also come to include the entity's interests.

However, it should be emphasized that identification does not mean that one becomes a mindless automaton. First, as noted, SIT contends that individuals also have a personal identity, a sense of their own uniqueness. The personal identity often emerges in juxtaposition to valued social/role identities as the individual seeks some distinctiveness within the homogenizing context of the collectivity (Brewer, 1991). Indeed, the perception of a common bond may enhance the appreciation of differences, at least on peripheral features of the identity. Second, although a social/role identity establishes goals, values, and so on, there is usually considerable latitude in the specific manner in which these qualities are enacted. Third, identification speaks to the *process* by which a role or other social identity becomes the individual's; it does not specify the *content* of that identity. Thus, if a role encourages initiative, creativity, innovation, and constructive conflict, identification will be positively rather than negatively related to an inclination to challenge the status quo (Ashforth & Mael, 1996).

Finally, of particular relevance to role transitions is the notion from SIT that social/role identities are relational and comparative and that individuals are motivated to hold positive identities. As I will argue, macro role transitions involve withdrawing psychological and often social investments from one role and placing them in another. This process of separation and reincorporation is abetted when one is able to draw clear and self-enhancing distinctions between the two roles, although such distinctions may appear arbitrary and trivial to an outsider. Thus, L. A. Hill (1992) found that newly promoted managers were initially excited about the perceived prospects of increased power, but these perceptions ultimately proved illusory. Nonetheless, the anticipated role contrast facilitated their movement from the role of subordinate to that of manager.

DEVELOPMENT
OF ROLE IDENTITIES

The Global Identity

The *global identity* is those portions of the individual's personal and social identities (including role identities) that are integrated into a roughly coherent self-system or self-theory (S. Epstein, 1980). As such, the global identity may consist of goals, values, beliefs, traits, competencies, time horizons, and ways of acting, thinking, and feeling. The global identity forms early in life but continues to develop throughout the life course (e.g., Kroger & Haslett, 1991; Waterman & Archer, 1990). Features of the global identity tend to be abstracted from myriad concrete experiences, with one's family acting as the initial primary reference group and mediating the impact of the wider culture (Mortimer, Lorence, & Kumka, 1986). Through the social learning processes (Bandura, 1977) of observation, imitation, and instruction, coupled with direct experiences such as trial and error and self-reflection, one learns and internalizes the qualities that define a family member (social identity) and oneself in particular (personal identity; see chaps. 6 and 7 for more detailed discussions of role learning, personal change, role innovation, and social validation).

The concrete experiences and learning are arranged in a hierarchy of progressively broader, more inclusive, and more abstract concepts. For example, successful performance at table tennis, swimming, and baseball may contribute to the integrated midlevel conception of good athlete, which may in turn contribute to the higher level conception of good performer

(S. Epstein, 1980). Moreover, similar concepts may link horizontally into a network—good performer may be linked with intelligent and attractive.

A global identity tends to function as a *positively regarded, self-fulfilling template* (S. Epstein, 1980). First, following hedonistic or reinforcement principles, individuals tend to gravitate toward and value activities at which they are adept, that are extrinsically rewarded, and that are experienced as intrinsically satisfying (e.g., Kohn & Schooler, 1983; Mortimer, Lorence et al., 1986). The more positive the valence of the activity, the more likely that it will be incorporated into the global identity as self-defining. Adler and Adler (1991) described how college basketball players typically come to view their athletic role as more subjectively important than their academic role: The former role encounters far more social affirmation and personal success than the latter. Furthermore, because the higher order features of the global identity are abstract, they may be generalized or applied to a variety of new situations such that one effectively projects oneself into a new context. The good performer may embrace her first job with high confidence and positive expectations.

Second, by shaping choices and expectations, the global identity shapes its own destiny. The good performer may be attracted to challenging goals that further build skills, confidence, and credibility. In addition, individuals give concrete form to their ideals, aspirations, hopes, and fears via what Markus and Nurius (1986) termed *possible selves* (e.g., to be a high performer, a valued student). Possible selves provide a future orientation for identity. For example, current personal and social identities that are undesired or equivocal can be recast as short term and instrumental to longer term identity goals.

Third, because the global identity is couched in abstract terms, is predicated on myriad experiences, and tends to be self-fulfilling, it is resistant to disconfirmation. By providing a more or less coherent sense of self and one's place in the world, the global identity shapes not only choices but sense-making such that the range of new experiences is constrained by the old and the meaning derived from the new must be reconciled with the old. As a result, the global identity typically becomes more densely articulated over time as new encounters tend to reinforce and extend current self-schemas. Also, individuals tend to be versatile at invoking various ego-defensive biases, such as the occupational reframing mentioned earlier, to ward off threats to social and self-esteem (Breakwell, 1986; Sedikides & Strube, 1997; C. M. Steele, 1988; S. E. Taylor, 1989). Thus, although the global identity is a distillate of experiences, those experiences tend to be selectively perceived and retained.[7] In short, the global identity does not include every self-relevant experience (Berzonsky, 1990). Experiences and abstractions that are not perceived to fit the emerging global identity may be explained away (e.g., external forces were responsible), effectively forgotten, or compartmentalized outside the global identity ("This does not reflect the 'real' me"—the generalized sense of self). However, if a higher order conception *is* invalidated (e.g., through repeated or particularly dramatic disconfirmation), then the impact on the global identity can be great because the conception subsumes a hierarchy of more concrete conceptions and is networked to similar conceptions. Invalidation may thus provoke what is popularly known as an *identity crisis* (cf. Baumeister, 1986).[8]

Continuity Versus Discontinuity.   The notion of resistance to change raises the intriguing issue of continuity versus discontinuity (Demo, 1992; Mortimer, Finch, & Kumka, 1982; L. E. Wells & Stryker, 1988). On the one hand, stability and self-continuity are major themes in life (see chap. 3). It was argued earlier that the global identity provides a basic platform for subsequent experience such that it functions as a self-fulfilling prophecy. On the other hand, diversity, change, and self-exploration are also major themes in life. First, normal maturation processes and changes in life circumstances (see chap. 8)—including role transitions—often provoke at least some personal change. Second, as discussed in chapter 6, role entry may entail a divestiture process whereby the newcomer's incoming identities are deliberately stripped away so that the organization can rebuild the newcomer in the image of the desired member. Third, an exited role may serve as a foil for a new role whereby one adopts the latter's identity precisely because it differs from undesired aspects of the former's identity. For example, a person's dissatisfaction

---

[7]However, individuals who regard themselves negatively (through genetic predisposition, an abusive parent, lack of growth opportunities, traumatic events, etc.) may form robust global identities around this negative core and may actually labor to preserve the core such that it too becomes self-fulfilling (see chap. 3).

[8]It seems likely that an identity crisis will be more devastating for individuals who have engaged in minimal identity exploration and have instead unreflectively internalized an identity (or identities) espoused or modeled by their parents or other social referents (what Marcia, 1966, drawing on E. H. Erikson, 1963, termed *identity foreclosure*). Given the relative lack of exploration, such individuals have few identity alternatives—and perhaps few skills for exploration—to fall back on if their identity is invalidated.

with the lack of autonomy in his corporate job may prompt him to rethink his deeply held values about security and loyalty and to become self-employed (Ebaugh, 1988). Fourth, a person may seek at least a temporary break from her past to encounter new and stimulating experiences: Indeed, diverse experiences may extend the breadth and depth of the global identity. Finally, rather than reconcile disparate experiences and roles within a given level of one's global identity, one may differentiate experiences and roles such that one becomes more cognitively complex and retains multiple and perhaps antagonistic potentialities. As S. Epstein (1980) put it, "To assert that there is unity in the self-system is not to deny that there is also differentiation, and even inconsistency, within the system" (p. 119).

In short, continuity and discontinuity are two sides of the same coin. The global identity acts as a ballast or keel for role transitions, providing stability and control but not necessarily determining the specific social domains or the breadth of experiences that one may venture into.

The Global Identity and Role Identities

Thus, the global identity provides the initial basis for role identities. As one matures, one engages in the developmental task of *identity exploration* (E. H. Erikson, 1968), defined by Grotevant (1987) as "problem-solving behavior aimed at eliciting information about oneself or one's environment in order to make a decision about an important life choice" (p. 204). One actively adopts various informal and formal roles outside the home such as friend, student, Girl Scout, and athlete. Each role, particularly the formal ones, may be embedded in and cued by specific contexts (e.g., school, church) with local reference groups and more or less idiosyncratic subcultures. Exploration unfolds within a certain historical and cultural context that renders some processes and roles more or less socially desirable (E. H. Erikson, 1968; Waterman, 1988). For example, U.S. society tends to encourage active exploration and individuality.

When one first adopts a role, one relies on social learning to simulate role performance (see chap. 7). Initially, the global identity and preliminary expectations help inform the role identity, creating a certain conception of self within the role (self-in-role schema) comprised of goals, values, beliefs, traits, competencies, time horizons, and expected ways of acting, thinking, and even feeling. As one is progressively socialized into the role, one learns and may internalize the local schemas such that the global identity gives way to a more narrowly bounded role identity. The local reference group becomes a primary group for *that* setting, providing information about the content of the role identity and shaping and reinforcing its adoption and display.

The more one comes to value the role identity, the more its content is likely in turn to inform the global identity. Indeed, the more valued the role identity, the more likely that the role identity per se (e.g., athlete) rather than just its inferred features (e.g., tough, persevering) will be incorporated into the core conception of self, the global identity. Furthermore, a valued role identity may have a greater impact on the global identity when one is young and the latter is yet inchoate. Conversely, as the global identity becomes more clearly articulated with age and experience, it may exert a stronger impact on the selection and enactment of role identities.

By adulthood, one has typically adopted many roles of varying formality and specificity. Some adoptions are only tentative and for short periods of time, some are playful, and others are strong and for extended periods. The outcome for many individuals (but by no means all) is a more or less clear sense of self-definition, what the developmental theorists refer to as *commitment* (E. H. Erikson, 1968; Marcia, 1966) to a given global identity and perhaps specific role identities.[9] For example, Schmitt-Rodermund and Vondracek (1999) found that identity exploration among German teenagers was associated with identity formation and occupational preferences.

For committed individuals, the identity structure has been depicted in various ways. These include concentric circles, where the global identity forms the center and role identities the outer layers; partially intersecting circles, where role identities comprise the circles and the global identity is found where they intersect; and a tree, where the global identity forms the trunk and role identities form the branches (e.g., D. T. Hall, 1968; Leonard, Beauvais, & Scholl, 1995; Rossan, 1987). What is common to these and other images is that the core conception of self is thought to be a combination of attributes that have been abstracted from diverse experiences.

Figure 2.2 provides one representation of the intersection of the global identity and a subset of role identities. The size of a circle (identity) denotes its *scope* or the number of core features that define the identity. Thus, the role identity of spouse has a greater scope than the more limiting identity of health club member. The greater the scope, the greater the number of potential identification hooks for the individual.

---

[9]If contemporary society is indeed giving rise to proportionately more protean people, then identity exploration will become a *permanent* rather than temporary life theme for many people. As discussed in chapter 3, it seems likely that both themes—commitment and exploration (or continuity and discontinuity)—coexist within most people.

In addition, the greater the overlap between a role identity and the global identity, the more relevant the role identity is to the individual's core conception of self. Thus, consistent with the developmental model described earlier, the core conception includes the more highly valued role identities. As noted, identities can be arrayed on a hierarchy of subjective importance where important identities are more likely to be internalized as central and enduring aspects of self. Thus, valued identities are more likely to be activated and inform a given situation.

One Self or Many?

A burning issue that has intrigued psychologists as far back as William James (1890/1950) and social observers long before that is whether there is one integrated self or only many fragmented selves. Is there an essential I or only a series of context-dependent personas? The integrated-self perspective has led to a search for consistencies in behavior and self-concept across situations and over time, informing much research on personality and adult development (e.g., Lecky, 1945; Mortimer, Finch et al., 1982). The working assumption is that behavior and the sense of self tend to be determined by more or less stable individual differences.

Conversely, the fragmented-self perspective has led to a search for the situational forces that shape behavior and the sense of self, informing

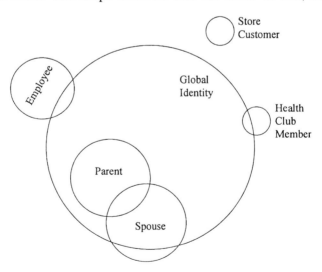

FIG. 2.2. Hypothetical mapping of an individual's global identity and a subset of role identities. (The size of the circle denotes the scope (number of core features) of the identity.)

much of the work under the rubric of symbolic interactionism, drama-turgy, and IT (e.g., Goffman, 1959; Stryker, 1980). The assumption here is that behavior tends to be cued by the situation.

The notion that a person has both a global identity and myriad role identities suggests that one reason the question of one self or many has persisted is because neither alternative provides a complete answer. Each person is *both* one self and many selves. The world is necessarily experienced in localized contexts—home, work, school, and so on—where role identities tend to be highly salient. Most individuals are able to recognize and distinguish between contexts, are acutely aware of at least some of the situational pressures operating within each context, and are able to describe their in-role behavior and attitudes with some accuracy. At the same time, most individuals are able to step back from their specific role identities and describe themselves in more abstract and generalized terms. In short, their phenomenological experience is usually one of coherence across situations: They believe that they *recognize* themselves (their global identity) within given roles (e.g., Ashforth & Tomiuk, 2000).[10]

Thus, depending on whether the global identity or specific role identities are cued, a person may view himself or herself as consistent over time and across situations or as different. For example, Roberts and Donahue (1994) found that women were able to describe themselves in general in coherent terms and yet describe themselves somewhat differentially across four roles (partner, friend, worker, and daughter). Furthermore, Roberts and Donahue found that the more satisfied the women were with a given role, the stronger the association between the role and their general self-descriptions. However, there are limits to the elasticity of self: Donahue, Robins, Roberts, and John (1993) cautioned that high levels of self-concept differentiation across roles is associated with emotional distress, interpersonal difficulties, and lower self-esteem and well-being. As they put it, "specialization of behavior across roles is adaptive and contributes to adjustment, whereas the subjective experience of a divided self . . . reflects poor adjustment" (p. 845). Sheldon et al. (1997) added that a sense of consistency and a sense of authenticity across roles contribute to well-being.

---

[10]It is important to note that this felt resonance of specific role identities and an overarching global identity is strongly abetted by various ego-defensive biases. For example, individuals are motivated to seek and find cross-role consistencies, to impute more control over local contexts than may be warranted (particularly when enacting valued role identities), and to selectively perceive identity-consistent behavior and to rationalize away identity-inconsistent behavior (see chap. 3; Banaji & Prentice, 1994; S. E. Taylor, 1989).

In summary, although role identities are enacted locally and therefore tend to vary across contexts, individuals generally remain able to abstract perceived similarities from the morass of idiosyncratic experiences and construct a more or less internally consistent and stable self-conception, a global identity. As the global identity is articulated and reinforced over time, it shapes the choice of contexts and the meaning of and weight placed on the experiences that are abstracted. Thus, there is an ongoing reciprocal influence between the global identity and specific role identities.

TEMPORARY ROLE IDENTITIES

The remainder of the chapter switches gears and focuses on a peculiar kind of role identity, the temporary identity. A *temporary role identity* is an identity that one knowingly adopts for a relatively short period of time. As such, temporary identities are usually associated with short-term reversible role transitions. The concept of temporary identity should not be confused with a weak identity (i.e., one that is not widely shared and densely articulated); for example, where the role is novel or there is a lack of consensus on the implied identity. Temporary identities have at least three distinct origins: Short-term role enactments, games and play, and long-term role enactments where identification is low.

Short-Term Role Enactments

In a short-term role enactment, one is temporarily immersed in the experience of the role. In an employment context, short-term assignments include contract work, training assignments, temp work, task forces and committees, projects, summer jobs, interim or acting positions, and relief assignments. In other contexts, short-term enactments include customer in a store or restaurant, patient in a hospital, student in a night course, and so on.[11]

It is important to note that short-term role enactments are psychologically and socially quite different from being roleless in a given social domain (i.e., experiencing liminality, in the terminology of chap. 5). In short-term enactments, the role is nonetheless viable—that is, a recognized and institutionalized portion of the network of roles in the domain—although an individual's occupancy is circumscribed in time. The role provides a basis

---

[11]A role enactment that is brief but recurring, such as a weekly visit to one's bank, is considered long-term because the individual experiences the role as intermittent rather than temporally bounded.

for both self-categorization and the categorization of self by others and thus, a basis for interpersonal relationships. In short, unlike liminality, the individual is psychologically and socially *grounded* in the context.

It could be argued that role identification is likely to be minimal in short-term enactments. First, because identification is partly a function of role tenure, individuals may simply lack sufficient time to internalize the role identity. Second, because individuals know that the assignment is bounded in time, they may be more inclined to go through the motions, that is, refrain from investing themselves emotionally, cognitively, and behaviorally in the role identity. Thus, although research on transitions into short-term enactments is scarce, there is some evidence that individuals may essentially suspend their normal sense of self and develop site-specific temporary identities. For example, Henson's (1996) research on temps revealed that many create a client-specific persona to function in a specific role and workplace without placing their core sense of self at risk, and Wertsch (1992) found that children raised on military bases coped with their parents' frequent transfers by developing chameleon-like skills for quickly adapting to a particular locale without really vesting their emotions in that locale.[12]

However, I argue that the operative factors in identification with short-term roles is not time per se but the role's valence, current salience, and opportunities for social validation.

Valence.   *Valence* is defined as the attractiveness of a role transition to the transitioner where positive valence means attractive and negative valence means unattractive. Valence depends largely on whether the attendant role identity is consistent with a desired actual or possible self (or inconsistent with an undesired or feared self; see chap. 4). In general, the greater the social desirability of the role and the perception of gain rather than loss, the more positively valent the change. However, because short-term roles are temporary and often reversible, the issue of gain versus loss is less important than the social desirability of the role and its potential for helping one affirm or realize a desired self.

The more positive the valence, the greater the willingness to identify, even if the enactment is known to be short. For instance, an individual

---

[12]With the growth of contract work and the frequency of role transitions, many careers are essentially a series of short-term assignments. In such cases, individuals may come to resemble Henson's temps and Wertsch's military children, developing certain *meta-competencies* (D. T. Hall, 1986; D. T. Hall & Mirvis, 1996) for survival: The ability to quickly read and learn from situations and adopt locally desired personas while perhaps leaving the global identity largely unaffected.

might willingly embrace a training assignment regarded as instrumental to long-term goals or an interim or acting position that will help a valued sub-unit weather a difficult period. Waskul (1998) described how some camp counselors came to identify very strongly with their work and camp despite knowing that the camp would close after 9 weeks. Indeed, short-term enactments can induce a major identity shift, although such dramatic change is probably rare.

Conversely, negatively valent transitions may induce strong resistance to identity change and a strong desire to cling to and reaffirm a prior iden-tity(ies). Schmid and Jones (1991) studied new prison inmates incarcerated for a short term. The researchers found that inmates feared that prison might change them for the worse either through the deliberate efforts of rehabilitation staff or the hardening effects of the prison environment. Accordingly, the inmates resolved not to change and to avoid all nonessen-tial contact with inmates and staff. They distinguished between their "true" outside preprison identity and a "false" prison identity created to cope with the prison environment. By suspending their preprison self and playing the part of the tough but cautious inmate, they hoped to finish their sentence in peace and leave relatively unscathed. Schmid and Jones reported, however, that the inmates were only partly successful. The radical discontinuity of the prison environment—the magnitude of the transition—indelibly marked them in various ways such that their postprison identity was a meld of their revived preprison self and their prison experience. Reversible tran-sitions, in short, are seldom *psychologically* reversible (see chap. 4).

Current Salience.   Schmid and Jones' (1991) findings illustrated that some identification is possible even in negatively valent short-term roles. A current role—even a short-term one—may have an immediacy or temporal salience that overwhelms active consideration of the future. Demanding roles can foster a strong press on the here and now, preoccu-pying one's thoughts and time and creating a self-sustaining momentum where the future is essentially relegated to the role of a continually unfold-ing present. D. T. Hall (1995) described his experience as acting dean of Boston University's business school. He found that "the interim period does not *feel* interim or temporary. It feels (and is) very real" (p. 85), as if the period had "virtual permanence" (p. 71). Thus, whether a demanding short-term role is regarded as positively valent, as in D. T. Hall's study, or negatively valent, as in Schmid and Jones' study, individuals frequently report being swept along by situational events and pressures such that they are captured by the present. They become caught in the moment and find it difficult to step back and fully recognize that their time is bounded. Intellectually, they understand that their incumbency is short term, but phenomenologically, they may not.

Opportunities for Social Validation. The importance of social validation to role identification is discussed in chapter 7. For our purposes here, occupants of short-term assignments are more likely to internalize the role identity (even if it is perceived to be negatively valent) if members of the role set treat them as exemplars of the role or as if they were permanent role occupants. Although the abbreviated nature of the assignment may impair true social acceptance, social cues that one is a bona fide exemplar remain powerful. Thus, D. T. Hall (1995) found that because members of the dean's role set were compelled to interact with him to accomplish their own work, an air of normalcy developed around his social interactions, creating the appearance of acceptance such that he came to feel he belonged in the role. Conversely, Katovich and Hardesty (1986) interviewed academics in temporary positions, such as adjunct professor, and found that permanent faculty were generally unwilling to invest much effort or personal concern in the temporaries. In the absence of social validation and a "future anchor" (p. 337), it became difficult for the temporaries to regard themselves as authentic academics. As one said:

> I think the real issue of being temporary is an emotional one in the sense that you feel at odds with the place you're employed. You feel as if you're just a hanger-on, an onlooker at a banquet. That's the real disadvantage, the sense of being unimportant, transient, [and just] passing through. (p. 342)

As will be seen in the discussion of role exit (chap. 5), a major impetus to psychological and social role disengagement is the sure knowledge that one is leaving. Temporaries, socially defined as such, have no "temporal capital" (p. 336) to offer members of their role set and so tend to remain at least somewhat marginalized.

In summary, the desirability of a short-term role, coupled with the every-day pressures of role performance and with being treated by others as an "authentic" role occupant or as if one's incumbency were permanent, may induce the incumbent to identify with the role despite its impermanence.

Can the Short Term Affect the Long Term? Identification with a short-term role may be of little consequence if it quickly dies upon role exit. It seems likely that the long-term impact of identification with a short-term role will depend on the extent to which: (a) the short-term role is similar to later roles, such that the role identity may generalize and be further reinforced, and (b) identification infuses the global identity, such that the identification comes to transcend any particular role. For example, Ricks (1997) interviewed U.S. Marines who had left the Marine Corps shortly after boot camp but who nonetheless appeared to retain a strong attachment to the Corps. The exMarines seemed to have deeply internalized Marine Corps values (e.g., honor, peer support) that transcended any one role, and some may have migrated to occupations that drew on Marine Corps training (e.g., policework).

In the absence of either role identity continuity or a modification of the global identity, identification with a short-term role may gradually dissipate once the assignment ends. The greater the magnitude of the transition both into and out of the short-term role, the less likely that the identity of the short-term role will generalize to other roles. The same discontinuity that renders one receptive to change (that unfreezes identity, in Lewin's, 1951, terms) makes it difficult to integrate (freeze) that change with one's subsequent roles. Waskul (1998) found that when camp counselors returned home, the unique experiences and perspectives they had gained were often gradually submerged and possibly forgotten over a period of months amidst the mundane realities of the real world. Similarly, the lasting impact of off-site training, company retreats, overseas assignments, and so on is often muted by the discontinuity between contexts, leaving only traces on the global identity. As Waskul stated, such "removal-reflection experiences are exceptionally easy to compartmentalize precisely due to the same qualities that give these experiences their transforming potential—they are apart from the realities of everyday life" (p. 51).[13]

Games and Play

In games and play, one's normal social identities and the rules of everyday life are temporarily suspended—or perhaps are preserved in stylized form through the structure and rules of the game or playful activity. The role identities associated with games and play are said to be temporary because one is cognizant that the role entails a strong element of playacting for a limited period of time.

---

[13]An important exception to this muting of memory may occur if the short-term enactment was associated with acute emotions. For example, a traumatic hospital stay or a very enjoyable summer job may produce vivid images such that one can recall the experience "as if it were yesterday." Barring an impact on identity, however, these memories are likely to remain bottled (sealed and self-contained) unless consciously or unconsciously cued.

This notion of temporary identities in games and play is analogous to Zurcher's (1970) concept of *ephemeral role*: "a temporary or ancillary position-related behavior pattern *chosen* by the enactor to satisfy social-psychological needs incompletely satisfied by the more dominant and lasting roles he or she regularly must enact in everyday life positions" (p. 174). Thus, in Zurcher's formulation, ephemeral roles serve to complement—or compensate for deficiencies in—one's more permanent roles. For example, in a study of bowlers, P. D. Steele and Zurcher (1973) found that participation in an ephemeral role provided a means for self-expression, belonging, relaxation, catharsis (a satisfaction of desires, such as for competition, in a socially approved manner), and separation (a temporary disassociation from other roles). Zurcher (1978) also suggested that ephemeral roles may serve as an *extension* of other roles, such as when a competitive executive becomes a competitive golfer. Games and play may also serve an educational and socialization function, imparting skills in teamwork, competition, sportsmanship, rule compliance, and so forth that may generalize to other roles.

Games and play can also be viewed as a metaphor in the sense that one "plays at" a new or potential role identity. For example, life crises such as a layoff or divorce often stimulate experimentation with identities as people strive to reattach themselves to society by rediscovering who and what they are or might be and who and what they are not (e.g., Schouten, 1991). Similarly, Markus and Nurius' (1986) possible selves can exist in fantasy form as one plays at alternative futures. Such imaginative ruminations may provide a temporary respite from an oppressive status quo and may serve as *role rehearsals* (Ebaugh, 1988) for later *real* role transitions. Collinson (1992), for instance, described how shop floor workers often spoke about starting new endeavors such as their own small business.

Games and play offer at least three qualities that make them attractive platforms for temporary identities: Safety, role contrast, and immersion.

Safety. Games and play allow one to adopt identities in a relatively safe and structured environment, sampling experiences and venturing behaviors. For instance, J. W. Gibson (1994) described how the game of paintball enables individuals to play at the identity of warrior:

> At one moment the game can be seen as a test of true grit. Minutes later a player can simply see himself as having become a kid again for an afternoon, with presumably no implications for his adult life. . . . This is, after all, only a game. (pp. 140–141)

It is partly the temporal, physical, and normative boundedness that makes games and play appealing. Emotions such as fear and sadness are usually defined as negative. Yet, people buy tickets on roller coasters and to theaters in part to experience such emotions within the safe (i.e., bounded) confines of the activity. Scheff (1979) attributed the pleasurability of otherwise negative experiences to the controllability of emotional distance. Temporary and playful engagement in emotionally stimulating roles enables one to regulate the experience of strong emotions, thereby creating a catharsis.

Role Contrast. As highlighted by P. D. Steele and Zurcher's (1973) study of bowlers, much of the appeal of many forms of game and play is that they represent a sharp contrast from people's more "serious" everyday roles. It is partly because the games and play constitute a distinct break from these other roles—a "time-out" (Van Maanen & Kunda, 1989)—that they are experienced as stimulating. Ethnographies of work, particularly routinized work, are replete with examples of how people actively seek opportunities to engage in playful activities during the workday (e.g., Balzer, 1976; Roy, 1959–60). Even where games and play represent an extension of other roles, a sense of contrast may still be derived from the change of settings, players, and rules.

Note that the sense of role contrast is pleasurable largely because of the temporary nature of the identity. Play derives its meaning and enjoyment partly in comparison to the more serious business of work. Play and work serve as a recurring foil for each other, enhancing the salience of the unique qualities of each. Remove the work, and play may lose much of its appeal; remove the play, and work may lose much of *its* appeal.

Immersion. It is important to emphasize that a temporary role is not necessarily one that a person regards as unimportant or enacts lightly. Individuals often take their games and play very seriously, perhaps more so than their so-called serious roles. Indeed, Goffman (1961b) argued that being fully immersed in the role is what makes games fun. Similarly, Csikszentmihalyi (1990) argued that losing oneself in an activity contributes to a state of *flow,* where mind and body merge in an enjoyable experience of the moment. Csikszentmihalyi argued that eight elements contribute to flow:

> First, the experience usually occurs when we confront tasks we have a chance of completing. Second, we must be able to concentrate on what we

are doing. Third and fourth, the concentration is usually possible because the task undertaken has clear goals and provides immediate feedback. Fifth, one acts with a deep but effortless involvement that removes from awareness the worries and frustrations of everyday life. Sixth, enjoyable experiences allow people to exercise a sense of control over their actions. Seventh, concern for the self disappears, yet paradoxically the sense of self emerges stronger after the flow experience is over. Finally, the sense of the duration of time is altered; hours pass by in minutes, and minutes can stretch out to seem like hours. (p. 49)

Allison's (1994) description of the Tokyo hostess club circuit provides a good illustration of the transformative potential of immersion. Many male executives are expected by their employers to meet after work—frequently and often for long hours despite having families at home. The hostesses are paid to sit demurely with the men, agreeing with what they say (regardless of content), flattering them as virile and clever, and generally affirming their masculinity and importance. The more gracious and graceful a hostess' conduct, the greater her pay. However, it is generally understood by all that there are real boundaries to the hostesses' duties: They are not allowed to date clients or perform sexual favors. The men recognize the playful and ritualistic quality of the hostesses' performances and reciprocate by teasing and flirting with the hostesses. Allison concluded that the reason that Japanese firms pay for club memberships is that the hostesses and alcohol cue the managers to enact a communal male identity in a more informal setting than found in the office, thus fostering cohesion among the managers. By playing at flirting, they bond as male comrades.

More to the point, the temporary identity of highly desirable male is experienced as very engaging, attesting to the seductiveness of social validation. Although the men are keenly aware that the attention and approval of the hostesses are bought, they come to expect and then rely on these formulaic affirmations of their masculinity and power. As Allison (1994) put it, the "men come to recognize themselves in the images created for them by paid hostesses" (p. 25). At first, the men allow themselves to forget temporarily that it is just a game; ultimately, they forget entirely.

Thus, part of the attraction of games and play is that they frequently offer a safe but highly seductive persona—one that may even induce identity change that goes beyond the bounds of the game. Like any role identity, a temporary identity adopted during a game or play may shape and reinforce the global identity, just as the global identity may have shaped the choice of games and play in the first place.

Long-Term Role Enactments
Where Identification Is Low

A normative requirement in many organizations is that members act as if they are committed to the organization and their role(s). Overt acts of low commitment may only be tolerated in "backstage" regions (Goffman, 1959) among trusted colleagues. Thus, individuals who do not identify with their work roles nonetheless often need to *act* as if they do—particularly if they occupy professional, managerial, or salaried positions where they represent the organization or a subunit, obligations are diffuse, hours are open-ended, and a strong work ethic is part of the role identity (e.g., Jackall, 1988).

As a result, individuals who lack role or organizational identification but are expected to display identification may adopt a temporary identity for impression management purposes (Schlenker, Britt, & Pennington, 1996). As in the games and play discussed earlier, individuals may "play at" being an exemplar of the role or organizational identity. Kunda (1992) discussed how members of a high-tech firm actively participated in top management presentations as signaled by laughing, applauding, nodding, and note-taking. However, before and after the presentations, members struck a more cynical stance as signaled by criticizing management and parodying conventions. In short, they played the role of loyal subordinate during the presentation. Indeed, it may have been precisely because they had dramatized their lack of identification with the subordinate role prior to the presentation that they felt sufficiently comfortable to temporarily don that role (Ashforth & Mael, 1998).

In sum, low role identification coupled with normative pressure to display identification may lead to the adoption of a temporary identity for impression management purposes. However, recurrent short-term playacting may *become* long-term identification if one's recurring actions gradually persuade one that the attachment to the role must be real (see chap. 7). Ashforth and Tomiuk (2000) quoted an interview with a security consultant with 25 years of experience:

> Q: Now, if a friend were to watch you talking to a client, would that friend say this is the man that I know or . . . ?
>
> A: Definitely not the person I know. . . . [But] it becomes you at some point in time. You put on a mask and you wear it long enough, it becomes you. (p. 190)

In closing, a temporary role identity is not necessarily either a weak identity or weakly identified with identity. If the role identity is positively valent or currently salient, offers social validation or safety, or a welcome role contrast or immersion, then it may affect one's global identity and other role identities long after one's official involvement has ended.

CONCLUSION

Role identities are role-based personas complete with goals, values, beliefs, norms, interaction styles, and time horizons. The more these features are tightly coupled and widely understood, the stronger the identity is said to be. In addition, the more subjectively important and situationally relevant the role identity, the greater its salience. However, individuals can occupy a role and enact its identity without accepting the identity as self-defining. Role identities interact in an ongoing reciprocal manner with the global identity (a generalized knowledge structure abstracted from myriad specific experiences) such that each informs the other.

The key implication for role transitions is that to exit one role and enter another is to switch personas—and if one identifies with the roles, to switch the very conception of self. This in turn suggests that role exit may at times be quite traumatic (as will be seen in chap. 5) and that it may be very difficult to learn a new role and be accepted by one's role set as a bona fide role occupant (as will be seen in chaps. 6 and 7).

3

Psychological
Motives Aroused
by Role Transitions

You become your job. I became what I did. I did become a hustler. I became cold, I became hard, I became turned off, I became numb. Even when I wasn't hustling, I was a hustler. . . . People aren't built to switch on and off like water faucets.

—a prostitute (Terkel, 1975, p. 102)

Walking down the street in that uniform and seeing blue-haired old matrons turn to look at you like, "Thank God, you're here," it really is a wonderful thing. It's like Dodge City and you're the sheriff. . . . You've done something, you're important. Up until then in your life you may have done absolutely nothing. Now all of a sudden, at the ripe old age of twenty-one, there's a whole lot of people looking to you to protect them from the madhouse around them.

—a police officer (M. Baker, 1986, p. 18)

The role I'm required to perform, sitting up here in front and smiling and typing and being friendly . . . it's all bullshit, it's just a role, and there isn't any satisfaction in it for me. I'm more than that, and I want to be seen as a person apart from the work I do. This eight or nine hours is a waste, damaging, I think, to my own growth and what I think about myself.

—a receptionist (W. A. Kahn, 1990, p. 706)

Three competing reactions to work: The first person reluctantly became her role; the second did so proudly; whereas the third defiantly did not. This chapter focuses on the relationship between role and self—on the psychological motives aroused by role entry and how they play out in terms of role identification, role disidentification, and ambivalence. (The relevance of the motives to role *exit* is touched on in chap. 5.)

Figure 3.1 provides an overview of the model. Role entry, whether anticipated or actual, arouses psychological motives for identity, meaning, control, and belonging. The more subjectively important the role identity,

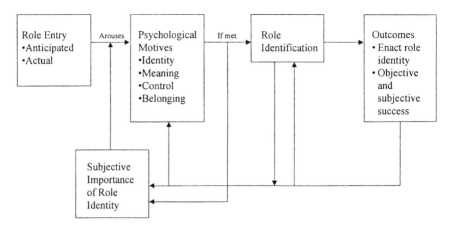

FIG. 3.1.   Role transitions and the self.

the greater the arousal of the motives such that a newcomer is more likely to seek to fulfill them within the context of the role. And the more that the motives are actually met or are expected to be met the greater the identification with the role. A newcomer is more likely to internalize roles that seem to provide salutary answers to his or her pressing needs. In turn, identification leads the newcomer to faithfully enact the role identity: To be true to the role is to be true to oneself. Faithful performance results in both objective (e.g., productivity) and subjective (e.g., well-being) indicators of effectiveness. Finally, role identification and the experience of success in turn reinforce the subjective importance of the role identity and the fulfillment of the motives.

The discussion is divided into three sections. First, the bulk of the chapter focuses on the four motives aroused by role entry. Second, the impact of the motives on role identification—and also role disidentification and ambivalence—is considered. Third, I close by discussing why role identification and disidentification matter to the individual and organization.

PSYCHOLOGICAL MOTIVES

Transitions within and between organizations are necessarily embedded in specific contexts. In the absence of a firm sense of the context, it is difficult for one to settle into the role and focus on content. Thus, adjustment is largely about becoming *situated* in a local context. The four psychological motives aroused by the process of becoming situated include identity, meaning, control, and belonging.

Figure 3.2 summarizes the motives. The motive for identity is a quest for self-definition ("who am I") in the organization and will be the primary focus of our discussion. The motive for meaning is a blend of sense-making (what) and searching for purpose (why). The motive for control is a drive to master and to exercise influence (how). And the motive for belonging is a desire for attachment with others (who). The motives are experienced simultaneously, not sequentially, and tend to interact (as briefly described later).

This model of psychological motives is adapted from a variety of perspectives on work adjustment and the person–role interface, including the work of Ashford and Taylor (1990), R. Katz (1980), and W. A. Kahn (1990). I recognize that scholars have proposed a vast number of motives. The four-motive scheme attempts to balance parsimony with adequate

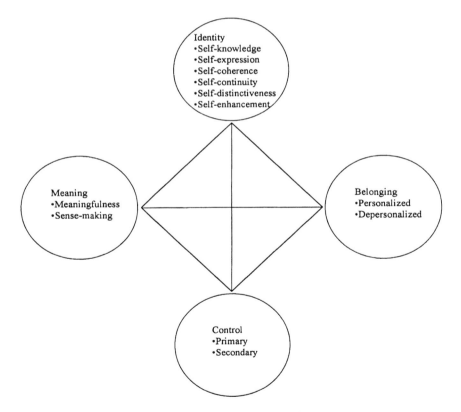

FIG. 3.2. Psychological motives cued by role transitions. (Note. The more the motives for primary control and personalized belonging are satisfied, the less relevant are the motives for secondary control and depersonalized belonging, respectively.)

coverage of the motive domain. Furthermore, some motives proposed by others are essentially synonyms for certain aspects of the motives discussed next such as power and achievement (control), self-actualization and status (identity and meaning), and affiliation (belonging). Other motives are specific examples of the four such as creativity and altruism (identity).

Identity

SIT and IT maintain that desires for self-esteem motivate identification (with positively valued social categories/roles) and identity-consistent behavior (to affirm valued identities). However, identity theorists working in allied domains have attributed a wider variety of self-oriented motives to the individual (Banaji & Prentice, 1994; Dutton, Dukerich, & Harquail, 1994; S. Epstein, 1980; Erez & Earley, 1993; Gecas, 1986; Markus & Nurius, 1986; Pratt, 1998; Sedikides & Strube, 1997; Shamir, 1991; C. M. Steele, 1988; Swann, 1990; Waterman & Archer, 1990). These motives span both personal and social identities, although the focus here is primarily on the latter. I discuss motives for *locating* and learning about the self (self-knowledge), for maintaining *integrity* between self and behavior (self-expression) both within and between situations (self-coherence) and over time (self-continuity), and for attaining a *positive* sense of self through differentiation (self-distinctiveness) and betterment (self-enhancement).

Self-Knowledge. As noted, to act in a given organizational context, one must understand the situation, one's place within it, and one's capabilities for enacting the necessary behaviors. In short, one must locate or situate oneself in the context and learn about oneself (R. Katz, 1980). An understanding of the situation and one's place and capabilities are closely intertwined: A sense of *where* one is complements a sense of *who* one is and what is expected (Ashforth & Mael, 1989). For example, Mansfield (1972) reported that new hires assigned to a series of short-term posts found it difficult to develop a coherent work-related identity. Presumably, they were only able to do so when they were permanently assigned to a specific department.

Once situated in a role, newcomers elaborate their knowledge of self-in-role—or, simply, self-knowledge—by learning more about the role identity and their personal articulation of it. Chapter 6 focuses largely on how role identities are imparted, whereas chapter 7 focuses on how individuals personalize those identities. For now, it should be noted that the articulation of self-knowledge is constrained by: (a) the extant knowledge about self in this and other roles and (b) the other self-motives. Regarding the first, as discussed later, research indicates that individuals tend to seek clear and accurate evidence of their attributes provided that the evidence does not moderately or strongly contradict what they already believe about themselves (Banaji & Prentice, 1994; Swann, 1990). Regarding the second, self-knowledge operationalizes desires for coherence, continuity, and so on such that the search for self-knowledge is not random or impartial: It is motivated and biased. For instance, a desire for self-distinctiveness can lead one to perceive and internalize attributes that appear to distinguish one's role (or execution of one's role) from that of one's coworker. Thus, a different coworker may have prompted a different conception of self-in-role.

It is important to underscore that self-knowledge is not the same thing as identification. Self-knowledge refers to information about the self within the context of the role and organization. This implies a blend of knowledge about: (a) prototypical or exemplary role occupants—people who embody the role identity ("This is who I should be") and (b) one's *own* skills, abilities, preferences, and so forth within the context of the role and organization ("This is who I appear to be"). Identification refers to one's embracement of this knowledge as a legitimate reflection of self ("This is who I am")—as self-*defining*. A salesperson may be aware that prototypical salespeople act in an extroverted manner and that she does so as well when enacting the role but that it does not feel authentic or genuine—it does not reflect her own self-conception. Thus, her self-knowledge is clear (salespeople act as extroverts, and I am capable of doing so as well), but her role identification is low. However, I will argue in chapter 7 that it is difficult to remain distanced from one's own role behavior over the long run.

Self-Expression. Individuals seek opportunities to enact identities they value (identify with). This is the motive for self-expression (D. Katz & Kahn, 1978; Shamir, 1991). Gecas (1986) posited that individuals have a need for authenticity, to display their "real self." Self-expression enables individuals to immerse themselves in their valued identities largely for the intrinsic pleasure of simply being true to their self-conceptions—"being themselves"—thereby affirming the worth of the identities, at least to themselves (Ashforth & Tomiuk, 2000).

Moreover, identities tend to assume a moral cast as they are internalized. The goals, beliefs, norms, and so on come to be seen not merely as convenient self-descriptions but as the right way for one (but not necessarily others) to be. The goals, beliefs, and other aspects become moral benchmarks or imperatives such that to live up to the implicit standards is experienced as being good, whereas failing to do so is experienced as being bad (cf. Higgins, 1987). Indeed, acting directly contrary to salient and valued identities arouses feelings of guilt, hypocrisy, and shame—even if such actions meet with social approval and are instrumental to other goals. For example, whistle-blowers may sacrifice their careers to uphold morals derived from their other social identities (e.g., family, church; Near & Miceli, 1987).

Self-Coherence.   This refers to a desire for a more or less internally integrated and consistent sense of self (S. Epstein, 1980; Shamir, 1991). Research on various consistency theories, such as cognitive dissonance theory (Festinger, 1957) and balance theory (Heider, 1958), indicates that individuals value and seek a sense of coherence among their goals, values, beliefs, emotions, and actions. C. M. Steele's (1988) research on self-affirmation indicated that inconsistencies between cognitions or between cognition and behavior are anxiety provoking not because of the inconsistency per se but because of the implied threat to the integrity or coherence of the self—the global identity.[1] Individuals appear to value the sense that there is an underlying *I*, a fundamental self that informs action, thought, and feeling. Thus, the desire for coherence is apt to be particularly strong for core rather than peripheral features of the global identity.

As discussed in chapter 2, the global identity is manifested in part through the specific roles that one adopts, and the implicated role identities may in turn inform the global identity. However, because roles in contemporary society are highly differentiated, the role identities that one assumes in the course of a day are not necessarily consistent and may even be contradictory (see chap. 9). Thus, self-coherence across situations is often problematic. Nonetheless, as also noted last chapter, individuals tend to *experience* a sense of more or less coherence. This is probably

---

[1]This research indicates that individuals can cope with specific inconsistencies as long as the integrity of the global identity is preserved. Thus, individuals may address inconsistencies by affirming the global identity, perhaps in ways that seem quite irrelevant or specious to an impartial observer. For example, an employee who commits a costly error at the office may restore his sense of competence by helping his son with his homework that evening. In short, an identity threat in one domain may be countered by an identity affirmation in another domain. However, it seems likely that compensatory acts will have more impact if they occur in the same domain and directly confront the threat (e.g., making amends for the error)—particularly if the role is strongly valued (cf. C. M. Steele, 1988).

because: (a) individuals actively work to inform their role enactments with valued aspects of their global identity or desired selves, (b) they are adept at affirming their global identity in the face of identity threats or attributing those threats to external forces (strong situations), and (c) they are adept at selectively perceiving and recalling instances of consistency (as Fiske & Taylor, 1991, put it, "Actual inconsistency that is not perceived as such does not yield psychological inconsistency," p. 11; Breakwell, 1986; S. Epstein, 1980; Fiske & Taylor, 1991).[2]

Self-Continuity.   Closely related to the desire for self-coherence is the desire for a sense of stability in the self over time (Dutton et al., 1994; Ruble, 1994; Swann, 1990). And just as individuals tend to experience a sense of coherence across situations, they also tend to experience a sense of continuity over time.

There are several reasons why this is so. First, the psychological forces discussed earlier that foster an experience of self-coherence similarly foster an experience of self-continuity. Thus, abundant research indicates that individuals tend to seek identity-confirming information and perceive more than exists, avoid or discredit identity-disconfirming information, and manage their environments to acquire confirming evidence (e.g., by displaying *identity markers* such as role-related attire, selecting interaction partners who are more likely to echo what they want to hear, and soliciting affirmation; see chap. 7; McCall & Simmons, 1978; Sedikides & Strube, 1997; C. M. Steele, 1988; Swann, 1990). For example, research on self-verification indicates that if the self-concept is strong, individuals tend to react against self-discrepant feedback (Swann, 1990). In one laboratory study, dominant people mislabeled as submissive tended to become more assertive, whereas submissive people mislabeled as dominant tended to become more submissive (Swann & Hill, 1982). The tendency to self-verify is abetted by the equivocality of much role-based experience, the reluctance of others to offer negative feedback, and by individual differences in openness to disconfirming experience (see chap. 7; Ashford & Taylor, 1990; Berzonsky, 1990).

Second, various theorists argue that identities are essentially *narratives* that are crafted to provide meaning and closure to phases of one's life

---

[2]Fiske and Taylor (1991) subdivide selective perception into several forms: "selective exposure (seeking consistent information not already present), selective attention (looking at consistent information once it is there), and selective interpretation (translating ambiguous information to be consistent)" (p. 469).

(Gergen & Gergen, 1988; McAdams, 1992). In McAdams' (1992) words, "the person is both historian and history—a story-teller who creates the self in the telling" (p. 325). As one matures and moves through various roles and contexts, the evolving narratives provide a sense of continuity for oneself and members of one's role set. As a story, a narrative retrospectively highlights and may even invent important themes while downplaying missteps and inconsistencies that would disturb the orderly plot line. As Weick (1996) observed, "tales of continuity and discontinuity can be constructed from the same facts" (p. 52). Thus, a sense of continuity may be conferred after the fact. Moreover, a narrative encourages one to act prospectively to maintain and embellish the plot line. In short, one continuously writes and acts out one's biographical self (see chap. 8; Ludwig, 1997).

Third, if one identifies with the role, one gains an ongoing psychological connection between the self and the social system. By investing one's self-definition in a valued role, one becomes a microcosm of the system and thereby imports the stability of the system into the self. Indeed, psychodynamic perspectives suggest that a major allure of identification is the sense of immortality it confers (Denhardt, 1987).

This is not to say that the global identity or a given role identity is either fixed or monolithic, as self-continuity and self-coherence may imply. As suggested last chapter, there is often differentiation and some loose coupling within and between identity schemas, allowing for flexibility over time. Moreover, normal maturation processes and new experiences tend to invite growth and development. Indeed, as hinted in chapter 2, change itself may constitute a thread in the life narrative: In a life buffeted by change, one may find continuity in the very fact of discontinuity. Thus, how one adapts to (and possibly seeks) change may become a recurring subtext of identity. Finally, identities do tend to change if repeatedly or dramatically disconfirmed (Burke, 1991). The weight of disconfirming experiences may simply overwhelm one's defense mechanisms.

Self-Distinctiveness. Social identities were said last chapter to be relational and comparative. Individuals are motivated to seek and find differences (whether real or imagined) between the identities held by themselves and those held by others as a means of affirming their own uniqueness and therefore specialness. In short, individuals value a sense of distinctiveness (Ashforth & Mael, 1989; Brewer, 1991, 1993; Dutton et al., 1994; Oakes & Turner, 1986; C. R. Snyder & Fromkin, 1980). In the context of groups, the motive for distinctiveness gives rise to what Smith and Berg (1987) termed the *paradox of identity*: The desire to be unique and yet meld with the group.

The motive of self-distinctiveness is particularly relevant to organizations because of their differentiated systems of interlocked units. Brewer (1991) argued that members of large and heterogeneous groups gravitate toward subgroups that offer a sharper and more homogeneous identity—that provide *optimal distinctiveness*, that is, membership that simultaneously balances the desire for inclusion (one is a member of the local subgroup) with the desire for exclusion (one's social identity is differentiated from that of the broader overarching collective). Thus, members of large and complex organizations may identify primarily with their role, workgroup, or department (R. M. Kramer, 1991), although the strength of identification across *nested* units tends to remain moderate to high (Ashforth & Mael, 1996; C. R. Scott, 1997).[3] Furthermore, because the local unit is associated with more concrete and perhaps coherent activities than the overarching unit, it provides a potentially rich identity; and because the local unit is smaller and has fewer members, it is easier for the individual to perceive his or her impact on the unit and to directly know the other members.

However, the search for optimal distinctiveness can become quite complex in large organizations because there are many potential foci for identification of varying exclusivity and inclusivity and because many of these foci are cross-cutting (Urban & Miller, 1998). A marketing manager can identify with her role, department, hierarchical level, division, cross-functional committees, and organization—in addition to a variety of demographically based social categories such as gender and age cohort. Moreover, as the context changes, so too does the optimal distinctiveness of a given social identity (Brewer, 1993). In a cross-functional committee of managers, the marketing manager's departmental allegiance may become an optimally distinctive basis for identification, whereas back in the manager's department, her hierarchical level may become optimal.

Finally, if the desire for self-distinctiveness is indeed addressed by differentiating one's role from other roles, then the maintenance of salient role boundaries becomes very important. Without boundaries, there can be no differentiation; and without salience, there is no awareness of different others. For example, the role identity of a mailroom clerk who interacts

---

[3]However, if aspects of the focal unit's identity are perceived to conflict with those of other units, identification with the focal unit may be *negatively* related to identification with those other units (e.g., M. E. Brown, 1969).

only with other mailroom clerks may not be particularly salient to the clerk. The shared identity is simply the water they all swim in (Ashforth & Mael, 1996). Thus, the clerk may resort to his *personal* identities and his idiosyncratic enactment of the role identity to attain distinctiveness. Thus, he may take pride in his unusually strong work ethic and low absenteeism rate and in being an avid reader.[4]

Self-Enhancement. As noted in chapter 2, SIT and IT hold that individuals tend to value identities that are socially desirable and enhance their self-esteem. The self-enhancement motive is the desire to perceive oneself favorably (Banaji & Prentice, 1994; Pratt, 1998; Sedikides & Strube, 1997). The motive appears to have two related aspects. The first is experiencing one's currently held role identities in a positive manner. This can be accomplished through a variety of mechanisms including immersing oneself in the enactment of the role (see "Immersion," chap. 2), accomplishing identity-related goals, engaging in role-consistent impression management, securing positive feedback from members of one's role set, claiming credit for successes and deflecting blame for failures, overrating one's performance, selectively recalling and reminiscing about events, and being symbolically associated with a socially desirable or prestigious role. A classic example of the latter is Cialdini et al.'s (1976) study of "basking in reflected glory." They found that after university football victories, students were more likely to wear school-identifying apparel and to use the pronoun *we* in describing the outcome than after nonvictories. In addition, the tendency to bask was greater when individuals were induced to think they had done poorly on a test: Basking was apparently used as a salve for their wounded esteem. As Cialdini et al. noted, what makes this tendency intriguing is that the one who basks has done nothing to bring about the other's success: Nonetheless, through identification (even if superficial), one partakes of the pride of the victor.

The second aspect of the self-enhancement motive is experiencing a sense of growth or progress, that one is becoming a truer exemplar of a valued identity. Chapter 2 mentioned Markus and Nurius' (1986) concept of the possible self—a vivid projection of what one might become, what one wants to become, or what one is afraid of becoming. A possible self

---

[4]Of course, the salience of a given role boundary and identity remains highly dependent on situational cues. For example, an external threat to the mailroom (e.g., rumored layoffs) may at least temporarily cue the role identity and induce individuals to forget their individual differences and band together.

gives concrete form to expectations, ideals, goals, hopes, and fears and thus may function as a beacon or "vision of the self" (p. 961) to motivate one's development (either toward an ideal self or away from a feared self) and as a standard against which to evaluate one's current self and relative progress. Beyer and Hannah (1996) interviewed engineers and other professionals in the semiconductor industry who were assigned to a consortium. Beyer and Hannah concluded that adjustment to the consortium was associated with one's ability to connect the consortium experience with either valued prior selves (thus addressing the self-continuity motive) or valued possible selves (thus addressing the self-enhancement motive). Individuals who failed to connect with either experienced a disconnection between themselves and the consortium.

The motive for self-enhancement may at times conflict with the motives for self-coherence and self-continuity. When this occurs, the latter motives usually prevail (Swann, 1990). As Burke (1991) observed, most research supporting self-enhancement has focused on persons with relatively high self-esteem. It is only when self-esteem is low that the motives for self-enhancement and self-verification diverge. In such cases, self-enhancement may still occur if it does not involve an identity claim that cannot be sustained (C. M. Steele, Spencer, & Lynch, 1993; Swann, 1990). For example, laboratory research by J. D. Brown, Collins, and Schmidt (1988) found that high self-esteem subjects self-enhanced by rating their own group most favorably, whereas low self-esteem subjects self-enhanced by disparaging a comparison group; that is, they self-enhanced in a manner that essentially preserved self-continuity.

Conclusion. The identity motives create a tall order for newly entered roles. The desires for self-knowledge, -expression, -coherence, -continuity, -distinctiveness, and -enhancement operate more or less simultaneously and for each subjectively important and situationally relevant (i.e., salient) role identity. Indeed, the less a person is able to address an identity motive within a given role, the less subjectively important the role identity will tend to become. However, because the identity motives are largely complementary, enacting the role identity may address multiple motives simultaneously. For example, Rachlin (1995) chronicled how a neophyte police detective came to feel more like a bona fide exemplar of the role (self-knowledge and self-enhancement) by handling a succession of challenging cases (self-coherence and self-continuity) and developing his own style in doing so (self-distinctiveness and self-expression).

Meaning

If identity addresses the existential concern of "Who am I?", meaning addresses the existential concern of "*Why* am I?" Individuals need to make sense of their world, to find purpose, and to connect themselves to that purpose so that they believe they matter. Accordingly, individuals are predisposed to seek and infuse meaning in themselves and their relation to the world (Frankl, 1962; Gecas, 1986; K. O'Connor & Chamberlain, 1996).

The discussion focuses on two forms of meaning: (a) the purpose and significance of a role (*meaningfulness*) and (b) an understanding of the nature of the role (*sense-making*; Brief & Nord, 1990; Morin, 1995). Although the discussion centers on the *individual's* quest for meaning in organizational roles, I recognize that individuals are necessarily embedded in rich cultural contexts, from the local subunit to society as a whole. And the stronger a given culture, the more densely articulated and integrated is the set(s) of meanings available to the individual. Indeed, the leadership of complex social systems is largely about the management of meaning (Ashforth & Mael, 1996; Pfeffer, 1981). Thus, the individual's quest for meaning is necessarily both culturally and historically bounded.

Meaningfulness. Meaningfulness refers to a sense of purpose and significance associated with a role beyond the role's obvious formal duties and requirements (cf. Hackman & Oldham, 1980). Individuals seek meaningfulness because they are defined by others and themselves partly in terms of their roles: If the roles are meaningless, then so are they. Even if a role is not regarded as self-defining, the sheer expenditure of time and energy on role performance necessitates some kind of justification. Finally, given the various trends noted in chapter 1—the loss of tradition, the relativizing of values, the escalation of occupational and geographic mobility, and so on—it can be argued that many members of contemporary Western organizations are "in search of meaning," as Pauchant and Associates (1995) titled their book (also see Briskin, 1996; Pratt, 1998).

Unfortunately, the notion of purpose has not received much attention in theories of motivation in organizations. Shamir (1991) argued persuasively that motivation theories typically assume that individuals are rational maximizers of personal utility. Individuals are thought to exchange their time and effort for valued rewards, particularly when supported by specific and challenging goals and clear effort–performance and performance–outcome expectations. Even theories that incorporate intrinsic motivation tend to reflect an "individualistic hedonistic bias" (p. 409) centered on the immediate task. Although motivation theories are able to predict specific task-related behaviors, they do not adequately explain motivation at the more molar level, particularly in weak (vs. strong) situations. For example, motivation theories have a difficult time accounting for: (a) long-term perseverance entailing self-sacrifice, frustration, and obstacles and where there are no obvious rewards or goals or both are distant and possibly unattainable; (b) organizational citizenship behaviors and moral obligations; and (c) diffuse and open-ended commitments where personal utility appears to be traded for some greater good.

What is missing, Shamir (1991) contended, is a focus on meaning, on the power of ideas, values, ideals, and hopes to confer purpose and significance and thereby enable individuals to transcend their narrow self-interests and immediate situation. Individuals seek meaning and are adept at making meaning in even the most objectively sterile and hopeless situations. Ashforth and Kreiner's (1999) analysis of so-called "dirty work" (i.e., occupations that are morally, socially, or physically stigmatized such as exotic dancer, prison guard, and sewer worker) indicated that meaning is in the eye of the beholder and that occupational members often perceive purpose and weight that outsiders do not. Meaning is subjectively (and often socially) constructed and thus may bear little relation to "objective" reality.

Role identities help provide meaning in at least two ways. First, by embedding one in the larger social system, role identities encourage one to embrace goals and values beyond idiosyncratic self-interests. The more subjectively important and situationally relevant the role identity, the more likely is the role occupant to view himself or herself in terms of the identity. This self-stereotyping induces the occupant to think, act, and even feel as he or she imagines a prototypical or exemplary member would (see chap. 2). To the extent the individual identifies with the self-definition afforded by the role, he or she comes to embody and exemplify the role: The meaningfulness of the role to the organization and its constituents becomes the meaningfulness of the individual. He or she becomes part of something much bigger and consequential than himself or herself.

Second, the self-enhancement motive—specifically, through possible selves—gives concrete form to aspirations, hopes, and fears and provides a meld of proximal and distal goals that give purpose and direction to everyday action beyond that provided by context-specific role identities. Possible selves, as "representations of the self in future states . . . often have not been verified or confirmed by social experience" and may not exert their influence "in direct proportion to the ease with which [they] can be formulated or . . . realized" (Shamir, 1991, p. 414). Although some possible selves may be readily attainable, others may be quite fanciful or quixotic and yet strongly affect behavior. Such is the power of meaning.

Sense-Making. Van Maanen (1977) described organizational entry as a transition that "thrust(s) one from a state of certainty to uncertainty; from knowing to not knowing; from the familiar to the unfamiliar" (p. 16). Thus, role entry activates a motive to make sense of the role and the surrounding organizational context.

Sense-making is an interpretive process where one organizes stimuli into some kind of intelligible framework (Weick, 1995). The need for sense-making is prompted by ambiguity and surprise. Ambiguity arises in novel and unfamiliar situations where past learning and expectations provide limited guidance. The individual needs to resolve the ambiguity to act with purpose and confidence. Surprise arises in situations where one's expectations are not realized (Louis, 1980a, 1980b). Unpleasant surprises trigger particularly earnest sense-making as the newcomer must determine why his or her expectations were in error (e.g., "Was I misinformed? Naive?"), whether and how the surprises should be addressed, and what the implications are for longer term role enactment (e.g., "Will there be other surprises? Can I trust the organization?"; Weiss, Ilgen, & Sharbaugh, 1982; Wong & Weiner, 1981). Indeed, the literatures on attribution and accounts are largely predicated on the need to explain (and justify) surprise to oneself and perhaps to members of one's role set.

It is important to note that situations are inherently equivocal, that is, open to multiple interpretations. Thus, sense-making is not about discovering an existing truth, like a prospector panning for gold; it is about imposing or inventing one's own "truth." In Weick's (1995) words, "sensemaking is about authoring as well as reading" (p. 7). Sense-making is inherently intertwined with action and observation as one tentatively enacts the role and then formulates theories to explain what has occurred and will occur. Sense-making is thus retrospective (Weick, 1995) in that one crafts a history or a narrative.

Furthermore, sense-making is not an impartial exercise: It is strongly *motivated* by the desires for identity, meaningfulness, control, and belonging. That is, individuals resolve ambiguity and surprise in ways that address these needs. For example, Schmid and Jones (1993) reported that individuals about to begin prison terms tended to be concerned about potential violence and uncertainty in prison. On entry, these concerns gradually gave way to a sense of boredom despite the regular occurrence of prison assaults, rapes, and homicides. Schmid and Jones explained this apparent anomaly as an outcome of sense-making: Inmates learned to explain violent episodes as a consequence of prison norm violations, thereby providing a sense that violence was controllable and avoidable. Sense-making is thus largely about normalization: Rendering the chaotic and extraordinary seemingly ordinary (Ashforth & Kreiner, 2000).

Role identities greatly facilitate sense-making by providing localized and more or less developed frameworks for resolving ambiguity and surprise. For example, Belknap (1969) found that because doctors in a state mental hospital were concerned with treatment, they organized patients by malady, whereas the ward attendants, concerned with order, organized the patients by their degree of cooperativeness. However, the link between identity and sense-making is reciprocal in that role identities are themselves constructed (psychologically and socially) through sense-making processes (Weick, 1995). Throughout the book, terms such as *role-playing*, *role learning*, and *role innovation* are used to refer to the mechanisms through which identities are actively constructed to address the motives for identity, meaning, control, and belonging. In short, sense-making focuses not only on the context but also on one's relationship to that context.

In summary, the motive for meaning is essentially a search for a role-based ideology. An ideology is a system of more or less internally consistent beliefs and values that define what is good and bad, true and false, and the means for navigating between these polarities and realizing "goodness" and "truth." Well-developed role identities articulate why the role matters and how to understand role-related phenomena.

Control

A motive for control is a motive to master and to exercise influence over subjectively important domains. The term *control* is a loose federation of many concepts, spanning ability (e.g., competence, expertise), discretion (e.g., autonomy, self-determination), and power (e.g., impact, influence).[5]

Control is often regarded as a basic psychological need (Alloy, Clements, & Koenig, 1993). In Gecas' (1986) words, "the *experience* of agency ... seems to lie at the very heart of the experience of self" (p. 140).

---

[5]The ability portion of the control motive shades into the self-knowledge and self-enhancement aspects of the identity motive. Research on feedback seeking and identity suggests that individuals attempt to evaluate their role-related capabilities as a means of improving their competence and more accurately understanding themselves as role occupants (Ashford, 1986; Sedikides & Strube, 1997).

The need or motive for control underlies many perspectives on organizational behavior, from motivation to newcomer adjustment and from power and politics to stress and burnout (Ashford & Black, 1996; Ganster & Fusilier, 1989). A central premise of such perspectives is that having discretion over the parameters of work enables one to adapt those parameters to one's desires and creates a sense of involvement and responsibility. Similarly, a sense of control over the enactment of a role identity enables one to personalize and "own" the identity, to more fully internalize it as an authentic expression of self.

The motive for control is apt to be particularly strong during role transitions because of their upending nature. The new role tends to be at least somewhat unfamiliar to the newcomer, and he or she may be unsure of what is appropriate and whether he or she is capable of responding (Ashford & Black, 1996). In addition, as the newcomer becomes acclimated, the desire to personalize the role becomes more salient (R. Katz, 1980). In chapter 7, I discuss how newcomers often express the motive for control through behaviors variously described as *information seeking*, *feedback seeking*, *proactive behavior*, *self-management*, and more generally, *newcomer proactivity*.

Following Rothbaum, Weisz, and Snyder (1982) and Heckhausen and Schulz (1995), the discussion focuses on two forms of control: Primary and secondary.

Primary Control. Primary control refers to attempts to influence the environment and has been the overwhelming focus of organizational research on individual-level or personal control. Studies of autonomy, participation, empowerment, power and politics, leadership, decision making, and conflict often revolve around participants' implicit desire to exercise influence over organizational events.

Role identities strongly affect perceived opportunities to exercise influence. Role identities delimit domains of authority and expertise, thereby legitimating control by the role occupants over certain spheres of activity. Moreover, role identities articulate the make-up of the role set and perhaps the nature of relationships among its members, thus fostering networks and interactional patterns—and thereby, pathways of influence. And role identities may specify norms for how influence is to be exercised and for which issues.

There are limits, however, to the motive for control. For example, control may not be desired by role occupants if they lack the ability or resources to wield it, if they do not perceive their tasks or decisions to be inherently meaningful, if the control conveys undesired performance expectations, or if they lack identification with the role (Ashforth & Saks, 2000). Furthermore, the desire for control has been characterized as an individual difference variable where some people experience chronically lower levels of the desire than others (Burger & Cooper, 1979; McClelland, 1985; Nicholson, 1984; see chap. 7).

Secondary Control. In roles where there are few opportunities to exercise primary control, or one is unable or unwilling to exploit such opportunities, or one's attempts have failed, the motive for control may still be at least partly addressed through *secondary* control. Whereas primary control involves "bringing the environment into line with [one's] wishes," secondary control involves "bringing [oneself] into line with the environmental forces" (Rothbaum et al., 1982, p. 5). If primary control can be generally characterized as direct, behavioral, proactive, and externally oriented, secondary control is more indirect, cognitive, reactive, and internally oriented (Heckhausen & Schulz, 1995). Secondary control is essentially compensatory.

According to Rothbaum et al. (1982), there are four kinds of secondary control: (a) *vicarious control*, where one identifies with powerful others and indirectly partakes of their power, (b) *illusory control*, where one associates oneself with chance (e.g., "born lucky"), perhaps through superstitious rituals, (c) *predictive control*, where one avoids disappointment by drastically lowering one's expectations and efforts, thereby ensuring a predictable—albeit aversive—outcome, and (d) *interpretive control*, where one attempts to make sense of an uncontrollable situation so as to at least salvage some salutary meaning (e.g., seeking "a silver lining").

Role identities are potentially potent sources of secondary control, particularly in the absence of primary control. To the extent that an identity conveys an ideology geared to the identity motives of role occupants (i.e., that provides a sense of self-knowledge, -coherence, -continuity, -distinctiveness, and -enhancement),[6] it will tend to provide accounts that flatter the occupants. Accounts that link the role to powerful others (e.g., the organization) and provide salutary interpretations of otherwise negative events (e.g., "Our misfortune is attributable to jealous rivals") appear to be particularly common. A classic example is Festinger, Riecken, and Schachter's (1964) study of a religious sect that claimed a cataclysmic

---

[6]The remaining identity motive—self-expression—is realized through enacting the identity, not through the articulation of the identity itself.

flood would occur on a certain day. When that day came and went, the sect faced a severe challenge not only to its sense of control but to its very identity. The sect responded by concluding that their strong beliefs—"a force of Good and light" (p. 169)—had in fact caused God to abort doomsday. In one swoop, the account carried them from farce to glory.

It is important to reiterate, however, that not all roles are regarded positively by their occupants and that occupants may seek to preserve the coherence and continuity of even stigmatized roles. In such cases, the search for secondary control may only perpetuate the negativity. For example, Shield (1988) found that nursing home residents were often treated as if they were dependent children. Rather than actively resist the stigma, many residents passively conformed as a means of at least securing predictive control.

Belonging

Baumeister and Leary (1995) posited a need to belong, which they described as a "pervasive drive to form and maintain at least a minimum quantity of lasting, positive, and significant interpersonal interactions" (p. 497). More broadly, the motive to belong reflects a desire for attachment with others (Bowlby, 1969), to be part of a community where there is at least some underlying commonality of interest (Pratt, 1998). The discussion focuses on two forms of belonging: Personalized and depersonalized.

Personalized Belonging.   This form of belonging refers to the sense of attachment that an individual derives from knowing that one or more others are familiar with and like him or her *as an individual.* In other words, personalized belonging derives from interpersonal attraction (Hogg & Abrams, 1988). Role identities help foster this form of belonging. First, just as an individual needs to situate himself or herself and others in a given context to engage in meaningful interaction, others need to situate the individual. Roles serve as prominent *identity badges* facilitating this mutual placement. In addition, the greater the number of subjectively important and situationally relevant social identities that two individuals perceive they have in common, the greater their perceived interpersonal similarities and, thus, their predisposition to like and interact with one another (Byrne, 1971).

Second, social networks in organizations tend to form around salient social identities, particularly those attached to occupations, hierarchical ranks, and departments. Physical proximity, task interdependence, and actual similarities grounded in selection, socialization, and attrition processes (R. M. Kramer, 1991; Schneider, 1987) predispose individuals to interact and develop interpersonal attachments. As a result, the satisfaction of the motive to belong is often yoked largely to one's roles. Also, role transitions usually necessitate that an individual exit one social network and join another that may have minimal overlap, thus reactivating the motive.

Depersonalized Belonging. In the discussion of meaning, I noted that role identities embed one in the larger social system, enabling one to become part of something more consequential than oneself. Similarly, identification with a role or other social category enables one to become part of a community. The sense of belonging is said to be *depersonalized* when it is not predicated on the interpersonal bonds that tend to form between individuals who come to know one another as individuals but on the social identity that a group of people share (Brewer, 1981). In short, depersonalized belonging is based on *social attraction* (Hogg & Abrams, 1988). The group members tend to assume, by virtue of their common identity, that they share certain goals, values, beliefs, and a commitment to the collective. They gain a sense of fellowship from the knowledge that others share their valued identity(ies)—*even if they remain interpersonal strangers.* For example, one can be a dedicated hockey fan without ever leaving one's living room, gaining a sense of belonging simply from watching one's favorite team on television and sharing the emotions expressed by the spectators.

In an organizational context, depersonalized belonging often complements personalized belonging. Only in small organizations is it feasible for one to develop interpersonal bonds with most members of the organization. The larger and more structurally differentiated and geographically dispersed the organization, the more likely that the personalized belonging derived from interpersonal bonds at the local level will be complemented with depersonalized belonging derived from identification with more abstract social categories (e.g., the organization, the division). However, even in a small organization where one knows everyone at a personal level, there is apt to be some depersonalized belonging derived from the common membership: The organization, as a collective, usually retains an identity that is more than the sum of the individuals (Albert & Whetten, 1985).

Like the motive for control, the motive for belonging has been characterized as an individual difference variable ("need for affiliation,"

McClelland, 1985) where some people experience chronically higher levels of the motive than others.

Conclusion

Just as the identity motives were said to be complementary and experienced simultaneously, so too are the motives for identity, meaning, control, and belonging. Indeed, as signified by the arrows in Fig. 3.2, the motives are highly interactive: Identity facilitates meaning, meaning facilitates control, control facilitates belonging, belonging validates identity, and so on. The organizational behavior literature has focused particularly on the link between meaning and control. For example, K. W. Thomas and Velthouse (1990) conceptualized empowerment as an amalgam of meaningfulness and control; Hackman and Oldham's (1980) notion of motivating potential includes experienced responsibility for outcomes (autonomy) and experienced meaningfulness of work; and Ashford and Black (1996) proposed that newcomers who construe events as challenges and opportunities rather than as problems or threats are likely to experience those events as more controllable and to be better able to cope with stressors that arise. It is likely that our understanding of the individual–organization interface can be enriched significantly by also including identity and belonging among the psychological motives that fuel action, thought, and emotion.

A good illustration of the synergies between the four motives is provided by W. A. Kahn's (1990) interviews with counselors at a summer camp and members of an architecture firm. W. A. Kahn found that personal engagement was greater when individuals had a sense of psychological safety—"feeling able to show and employ one's self without fear of negative consequences to self-image, status, or career" (p. 708). This sense of safety or trust was dependent on a supportive climate where expectations were clear and consistent and individuality in the form of initiative and risk taking was encouraged. In particular, a sense of meaningfulness was predicated on: (a) roles that connoted valued identities as well as status and influence, (b) tasks that provided opportunities for self-expression—entailing challenge, variety, creativity, goal clarity, and some autonomy, and (c) interpersonal interactions that involved respect and positive feedback, perhaps blending a personal rapport with a professional one. Conversely, individuals who felt insecure were distracted by anxieties and experienced heightened self-consciousness. "They would focus on external rather than internal cues [and] perceived themselves, consciously or not, as actors on stages, surrounded by audiences and critics, rather than people simply doing their jobs" (p. 716).

I recognize that individuals differ widely in their desire for work roles that offer opportunities for challenge, variety, and so forth (Hackman & Oldham, 1980). The key point is that even in work roles of objectively low motivating potential, individuals still generally attempt to satisfy their motives—within that specific context—for identity, meaning, control, and belonging. And because the satisfaction of these motives exists in the eye of the beholder, identity, meaning, control, and belonging exist wherever individuals are convinced they have found them. A job that seems boring to one person may seem a boon to another.

ROLE IDENTIFICATION, ROLE DISIDENTIFICATION, AND AMBIVALENCE

Role Identification

Last chapter, identification was said to occur when a role occupant comes to define himself or herself at least partly in terms of the perceived role identity. To then enact the role identity is to express a valued conception of self. Role identification has also been referred to as *role embracement, role fusion*, and—as noted in chapter 2—*role–person merger* (Goffman, 1961b; R. H. Turner, 1978).

As depicted in Fig. 3.1, the more that the four psychological motives are met (or one anticipates they will be met), the greater the role identification and the subjective importance of the role identity: A role that addresses the motives provides a very attractive basis for self-definition. However, one does not have to identify with a role to regard it as important. For example, one may regard a role as important if it confers a sense of control or belonging, even if one does not resonate with the role's identity. (That said, it is difficult for a role to fulfill the motives for identity or meaning without also inducing some identification.)

Moreover, role identification also reinforces the fulfillment of the psychological motives, thus producing a virtuous circle. Regarding the motive for identity, role identification provides at least partial knowledge of self within the organizational context ("This is who I am here"), a vehicle for self-expression, a platform for self-coherence and -continuity, and a means of perceiving self-distinctiveness and -enhancement. Indeed, the identity motives tend to presuppose an essential role-related self that one wishes to express, maintain, and enhance. Regarding the motive for meaning, the system of goals, values, and beliefs associated with the role facilitates sense-making and the social construction of meaningfulness: Identification thus predisposes one to accept the proffered identity as meaningful. Regarding control, identification enables one to claim the power and efficacy of the role as one's own (primary control)—even if that power is vicarious, illusory, or allows only predictive or interpretive control (secondary control). Finally, regarding belonging, identification provides a sense that there are others who share the identity (depersonalized belonging) and through that identity may come to know and like the individual as a person (personalized belonging). Thus, as shown in Fig. 3.1, there is a strong reciprocal relation between the four motives and identification: The motives help stimulate identification, and identification helps fulfill the motives.

Transitional Identities and Identification. The process of role learning is discussed in chapter 6. For now, it is important to note that it takes time to learn the expected behaviors, attitudes, and even feelings that typify the role identity. Thus, role entry involves adopting a *transitional identity*, a partially formed understanding and enactment of the role. A transitional identity is a partially realized identity, a way station on the road toward being accepted by oneself and one's role set as a bona fide exemplar of the role identity.[7]

Similarly, the process of identity transformation and identification is discussed in chapters 6 and 7. For now, it should be noted that identification is not all or none; it is a continuous variable ranging from zero to very high. As one begins to identify, one internalizes aspects of the role identity as a reflection of self. In short, one's identification is transitional, a way station on the road toward stronger identification. What distinguishes *transitional identification* from weak or moderate identification is the sense of movement or progress. In contrast, weak or moderate identification represents a quasi-equilibrium point where the strength of identification fluctuates around a more or less stable mean.

---

[7]Transitional identities should be distinguished from what Schwitzgebel and Kolb (1974) termed *transitional roles*. A transitional role is a position that facilitates movement into another role. Transitional roles include: (a) relatively short-term positions that are designed to provide developmental or transformational experiences (e.g., apprentice, patient, intern, parolee) and (b) relatively permanent positions that are regarded by an occupant as a stepping stone to other permanent positions (e.g., supervisor→manager, manager→entrepreneur).

Indeed, what makes the concepts of transitional identity and identification noteworthy is the experience or phenomenology of progress. A newcomer learning her new role derives satisfaction from the emerging sense of mastery and fitting in, reinforcing her desire to learn more. Although her knowledge, skills, and abilities are incomplete, the sense of progress fosters encouragement—not discouragement. Moreover, her role set may also reward her incremental progress such that she is reinforced despite her incompleteness. Conversely, a veteran who has plateaued at the same level as the neophyte will lack this sense of *ongoing* progress and may feel discouraged.

Put differently, transitional identification is somewhat akin to falling in love (Ashforth, 1998) where the growing sense of affinity is inherently rewarding and "the sky is the limit." A veteran who has plateaued at a moderate degree of identification may lack this electric sense of possibility.

Role Deidentification.   If the process of becoming one with a role is termed *role identification*, then the process of again becoming two (person and role) can be termed *role deidentification*. Deidentification is thus the reverse of identification. It occurs when one no longer perceives an affinity with the role, typically because of personal change (e.g., maturation, other changes in one's portfolio of personal and social identities), role or context change (e.g., the role is redefined to include or exclude certain aspects, managerial support is reduced), or an inability to enact the role (e.g., extended sick leave). The importance of role deidentification will become apparent when role exit is discussed in chapter 5.[8]

Role Disidentification

Individuals define themselves not only by what they *are*, but by what they are *not* (J. Aronson, Blanton, & Cooper, 1995; Dukerich, Kramer, & McLean Parks, 1998; Elsbach, 1999; Elsbach & Bhattacharya, 1996). *Disidentification* refers to an "active differentiation and distancing of oneself from the entity . . . this is different from *not identifying*—it is identifying *as not*. . . . Identification focuses on similarities, whereas disidentification focuses on differences" (Dukerich, Kramer et al., 1998, p. 245). One's self-definition is honed by disidentifying with referents that appear to embody goals, values, beliefs, and so on that are inconsistent with what

---

[8]Ebaugh (1988), who figures prominently in chapter 5, used the term *role disidentification* rather than *role deidentification*.

one prizes. As Elsbach (1999) argued, "individuals sometimes find it easier to define themselves by the social groups they do *not* belong to, than
those to which they do belong (e.g., I'm not sure I'm a 'feminist,' but I
know I'm not a 'conservative')" (p. 173). Role disidentification has also
been referred to as *role distance* and *role separation* (Goffman, 1961b).

Although the four psychological motives are positively related to identification, they are not necessarily related negatively to disidentification.
To be sure, if the motives are not met, one is less likely to identify with
the role. However, to *dis*identify, one must perceive that the role somehow
challenges or contradicts valued aspects of the self—that there is an active
antipathy to aspects of one's global identity or other valued role identities.
For example, a new manager who prides himself on not playing politics
may discover that the role involves a great deal of political behavior. As a
person begins to disidentify with the role, his or her psychological motives
for identity and meaning may be met through *opposition* to the role and
organization; for control, through agitating for change or engaging in
resistance and sabotage; and for belonging, through banding together with
other dissidents.

However, strong disidentification is unlikely to occur in role transitions
that are voluntary and of small magnitude (see chaps. 4 and 6) because the
individual will have chosen a role with which he or she is already somewhat familiar. Furthermore, strong disidentification is an untenable long-
term state for either the individual or the organization: Active antagonism
to a role is likely to provoke either voluntary or involuntary turnover.

Transitional Disidentities and Disidentification.   Just as
there are transitional identities and identification, there are *transitional
disidentities* and *transitional disidentification*. The former refers to a partially formed understanding of the antithetical identity, and the latter to a
partially internalized disidentity as a reflection of self. These concepts are
not the same as a weak identity or identification: What makes them transitional is the sense of movement toward fully understanding and internalizing the disidentity.

Role Dedisidentification.   And, just as the process of losing
one's sense of identification is termed *deidentification*, the process of losing one's disidentification is termed (somewhat awkwardly) *role
dedisidentification*. For example, over time, the process of normalization
may render a repugnant role seemingly ordinary and routine. Reed (1989),
a hospital orderly, discussed the initial disgust he felt at handling corpses:

"But after a while, I got used to it. Each time it got a little easier. It's just not that big a deal anymore" (p. 48). Thus, one's repugnance may be blunted into indifference—or even, through the process of identification, transformed into attraction. One may discover a silver lining to the role and come to actually internalize the role as a partial definition of self.

Simultaneous Identification and Disidentification

Following Dukerich, Kramer et al. (1998) and Elsbach (1999), identification and disidentification can be thought of as orthogonal dimensions although they are likely to be negatively correlated in practice (e.g., Elsbach & Bhattacharya, 1996, reported a correlation of $r = -.69$ in a study of outsiders' perceptions of the National Rifle Association, NRA). Crossing high and low levels of identification with disidentification yields the model depicted in Fig. 3.3. As the figure indicates, the opposite of high identification is not high disidentification but low identification, and the opposite of high disidentification is low disidentification.

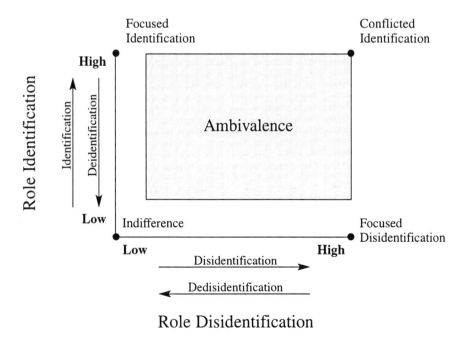

FIG. 3.3.   Role identification and role disidentification.

In cases where identification is high and disidentification is low (termed *focused identification*, after Dukerich, Kramer et al., 1998) or identification is low and disidentification is high (*focused disidentification*), we have the pure cases discussed earlier. When both identification and disidentification are low, the role identity does not resonate either positively or negatively with the individual such that he or she feels no psychological connection or disconnection with the identity. The individual remains *indifferent* to the role identity (what Dukerich, Kramer et al., 1998, termed *apathetic identification*, and Elsbach, 1999, termed *neutral identification*) and lacks a psychic anchor to the role—although he or she may retain strong identifications and disidentifications with other social categories associated with the context (e.g., gender, subunit). An indifferent waiter, for example, may simply go through the motions, performing the role in a mechanical matter, devoid of psychological involvement. Note that the waiter would be said to disidentify with the role only if he harbored an active antipathy or disaffection. Nonetheless, the literature on anomie and alienation suggests that even indifference can have corrosive effects on psychological health over time (Blauner, 1964; Kanungo, 1979).

Ambivalence.   Figure 3.3 further indicates that a role occupant is said to be *ambivalent* about the role identity if he or she at least partly identifies *and* disidentifies with that identity. It seems likely that *most people are at least somewhat ambivalent about each of their roles.* There are at least five paths to ambivalence: (a) conflicts within a role identity, (b) conflicts between multiple identities, (c) fear of loss of self, (d) protection of dualistic values, and (e) social stigma (Ashforth & Mael, 1998). First, because roles are often complex, the individual may be attracted to some features of the role while being repulsed by others. For example, Adler and Adler (1991) described how college basketball players were attracted to the athleticism of the game but often felt very uncomfortable with the public relations aspect associated with their visibility. Moreover, complexity may also give rise to internal contradictions and dilemmas, particularly if a role is emergent or in a state of flux, such that a given action or decision invites ambivalence. A manager may be compelled to lay off subordinates whom she has come to regard as friends.

A second path to ambivalence is interrole conflict. Not only are roles complex and possibly dynamic, they are embedded in role networks where occupants must answer to diverse and often conflicting demands

(Merton, 1976). Thus, it is unlikely that all the facets of a given role identity will mesh perfectly with one's global identity and other role identities. For example, the long hours and frequent travel required of a neophyte management consultant may conflict with his conception of a good parent and spouse. In such situations, one may identify with those aspects of the role that are most consistent with the global identity and highly valued role identities and disidentify with those aspects that are least consistent.

A third path is fear of loss of self. Earlier, Brewer's (1991) notion of optimal distinctiveness and Smith and Berg's (1987) paradox of identity were noted, where individuals struggle with the desires to meld with a group and to preserve a unique sense of self. Given the centrality of the global identity and the sense of individuality it provides and given the multiplicity of potentially attractive role identities, individuals tend to be leery about investing themselves fully in any single role. Indeed, "as a kind of social corollary to Newton's third law, the stronger the attraction . . . the stronger the potential *reaction*" (Ashforth & Mael, 1998, p. 96). For example, Bullis and Bach (1989) described how graduate students wrestled with competing desires for identification with other students and with separation from them.

A fourth path to ambivalence is the protection of dualisms. K. T. Erikson (1976) argued that cultures consist not simply of core values but of *axes* of values where the endpoints are anchored by dualities. A culture tends to award primacy to one endpoint of a given axis but nonetheless retains the capacity for the opposite. These dualities are experienced as ambivalence—the temptation to address *both* endpoints. Thus, a bank manager's role may extol the value of honesty precisely because dishonesty is inherently tempting. In awarding primacy to one side of a series of dualities, a role identity may spawn counterdesires to express that which is denied.[9]

A fifth path is social stigma. Because roles serve as prominent identity badges and because self-perceptions often require a certain degree of social validation (see chap. 7), individuals tend to be concerned about how others evaluate their roles. Roles that suffer from social stigma

---

[9]A poignant and perhaps archetypal example is the fall of evangelist Jimmy Swaggart. As documented by L. Wright (1993), Swaggart was caught frequenting prostitutes. L. Wright suggested that the constant need to publicly enact the role of the anointed one proved exhausting to Swaggart as it denied his human and darker side and fostered a doubt in him about his worthiness. The perpetual suppression of his baser impulses may have ultimately fostered an exaggerated expression of that which was denied. L. Wright suggested that Swaggart acted as if he *wanted* to be caught: He was tired of always being good.

invite ambivalence because the occupants are denied validation, at least from nonrole occupants. For example, Ashforth and Kreiner (1999) noted that individuals performing dirty work tend to be acutely aware of their occupation's stigma and may feel embarrassed when reminded of that stigma through subtle and not so subtle social cues (e.g., intrusive questions at a party).

The degree of felt ambivalence likely fluctuates widely over time depending on what identities and aspects of those identities are most salient. As suggested by the five paths, ambivalence may be aroused by various intrarole and interrole conflicts, by strong demands for role conformity if the demands are perceived to threaten one's individuality or to deny dualistic values, and by social cues that remind role occupants of the low status of the role or features of the role identity.

However, identification may be buoyed and disidentification held at bay if one can separate the conflicts, threats, and demands from the role identity itself. Crocker and Major (1989) discussed several mechanisms by which countercultural groups ward off threats to how members define themselves: (a) they may attribute the threat to the prejudice of outsiders, (b) they may look to each other for social comparison and validation, thus decreasing the likelihood of disadvantageous comparisons to nonstigmatized outsiders, and (c) they may focus on identity features that reflect well on themselves rather than focus on the threatened attributes made salient by outsiders. For example, Ebaugh (1988) described how restrictive edicts from the Catholic church provoked an exodus of nuns. Rather than leave the church, the nuns might have concluded that their role identity was threatened by parties who did not understand or were biased against the role and might have drawn support from one another. In short, rather than regard the role itself ambivalently, the nuns might have rallied around *their* definition of the role identity and confronted the source of the threat. This externalization rather than internalization of threat is apparent in accounts of the mobilization of animal experimenters (Arluke, 1991) and Paris sewer workers (Reid, 1991).

Ambivalence may be manifested in acts that imply strong attachment to the role and in other acts that imply precisely the opposite. P. A. Wells (1988) described how the staff at a Girl Scout camp distanced themselves from the cloying wholesomeness of the Girl Scout identity by ridiculing the identity, defacing the camp uniform, parodying camp songs, and playing pranks that mocked authority. Yet, the staff regarded the "initiation of campers into the traditions and values of Scouting as a sacred trust"

(p. 114) and were careful to support the image of the organization in any dealings with the public.

Thus, ambivalence toward a given role identity is not only common but to some extent healthy (Ashforth & Mael, 1998). A sense of ambivalence enables one to attain a certain ironic distance from an otherwise over-whelming identity and express one's personal identities and other social identities in the space afforded. Ambivalence may also function as a sig-nal that devalued features of an identity warrant attention or that valued features are potentially threatened, cuing one to consciously attend to the identity and possibly renegotiate role demands.[10]

However, ambivalence becomes more problematic as one gravitates toward the upper right corner of Fig. 3.3, simultaneously identifying and disidentifying strongly with the same role identity. Dukerich, Kramer et al. (1998) offered the example of a person who strongly identifies with a prolife organization and its antiabortion stance while strongly disidentify-ing with its sometimes violent methods, "finding a conflict between the protection of life on the one hand, and its destruction on the other" (p. 246). As cognitive dissonance theory (Festinger, 1957) would suggest, such strongly *conflicted identification* (or, what Dukerich, Kramer et al., 1998, referred to as *schizo-identification*) is difficult to sustain and indi-viduals may respond with a mix of dissonance-reducing behaviors and cognitions (e.g., agitating for a change in methods, bolstering one side of the conflict while downplaying the other). However, it seems less likely that identification would vanquish disidentification, or vice versa, than that one would gain somewhat greater prominence while the other recedes in strength and salience to a more tolerable level. Under these circum-stances, the lesser one—whether identification or disidentification—would remain as a latent capacity, occasionally flaring to life as situational cues provoke it. For example, I recall reading about a person who expressed a strong antipathy toward his organization but nonetheless vol-untarily remained with the organization during its slow demise, helping it to liquidate. Indeed, Dukerich, Kramer et al. (1998) speculated that con-flicted identification may be "a precursor to such frequently functional behaviors as whistle-blowing and creative change" (p. 250).

---

[10]Unfortunately, survey measures of identification and other forms of attachment mask ambiva-lence by soliciting only generalized perceptions (Ashforth & Mael, 1998). For example, Cheney (1983) found that an individual who had a moderate organizational identification score described his or her relationship with the company as "just a job" and yet expressed a yearning to identify with the company.

In sum, given the complexity of most role identities, one's momentary prevailing sentiment toward the identity may easily tip from positive to negative or vice versa as circumstances change (Ashforth & Mael, 1996). As the saying goes, a thin line separates love and hate.

WHY DO ROLE IDENTIFICATION AND DISIDENTIFICATION MATTER?

From the perspective of the individual, role identification matters in the humanistic sense that it reflects and helps fulfill the four seminal psychological motives of identity, meaning, control, and belonging. As the perception of oneness with or belongingness to a collectivity, identification bonds the individual with others, placing him or her in a specific context that confers definition, meaning, control, and attachment. Identification, then, is essentially an end in itself (Glynn, 1998).

From the perspective of the organization, identification matters because the individual can then be trusted to faithfully enact the role identity (as shown in Fig. 3.1). Research on role identification in various social domains (e.g., religion, family, college) indicates that individuals tend to choose activities congruent with salient aspects of their identities and support the social institutions embodying those identities (Burke & Reitzes, 1981; Santee & Jackson, 1979; Stryker & Serpe, 1982). For example, Stryker and Serpe (1982) found that individuals for whom a religious role was salient reported spending more time in that role. Also, research on occupational, professional, and organizational identification suggests that identification is associated with compliance with role requirements, good performance, organizational citizenship or prosocial behaviors, job satisfaction and organizational commitment, sense-making and decision making that is consistent with organizational values and beliefs, group advocacy, and lower intentions to quit (Ashforth & Saks, 1996; Bullis & Tompkins, 1989; Cheney, 1983; Dukerich, Golden, & Jacobson, 1996; Elsbach, 1999; Harquail, 1996; Horvath & Glynn, 1993; Mael & Ashforth, 1992, 1995; Pratt, 1998). For example, Horvath and Glynn (1993) found that members' identification with home health care cooperatives was associated with a sense of ownership, the fulfillment of expected duties, and extrarole participation. As Pratt (1998) put it, "the message given by Cheney (1983a) and others is clear: Organizational identification helps organizations retain control over members" (p. 184).

Can these outcomes occur independently of identification? Certainly. However, as discussed in chapter 6, the perception of oneness with a role or organization helps ensure that one thinks, feels, and acts like an exemplary member of the role or organization. Thus, identification obviates much of the need for conventional control systems such as tight surveillance and rigorous specification of procedures. When one identifies with the role or organization, doing well for the role or organization is tantamount to doing well for oneself.

Conversely, disidentification may fulfill the four psychological motives but in a backhanded way. Rather than embrace the identity and gain sustenance from the bond, one flees the identity and gains definition through opposition—whether loudly through voice or quietly through neglect or role exit (Hirschman, 1970; Withey & Cooper, 1989). However, disidentification is inherently harder to sustain than identification because: (a) it is associated with negative rather than positive emotions, and people tend to avoid stimuli that provoke the former, and (b) it only defines what one is *not*; there is no central core to exert a gravitational tug and define what one *is*. As Dukerich, Kramer et al. (1998) noted, "it is much more difficult to perceive the *absence* of something" (p. 251). However, if disidentification prompts the formation of an identifiable outgroup (e.g., a union, a counterculture), then the antipathy may coalesce into a distinctive and situated identity.

Role disidentification may be manifested in many dysfunctional forms including absenteeism, tardiness, alcohol or drug use, daydreaming, inattentiveness, poor motivation, destructive criticism, lack of enthusiasm, sabotage, and so on. Because these behaviors are interchangeable insofar as they express psychological distance (Gupta & Jenkins, 1991), the particular form is less relevant to the present discussion than the magnitude of distance achieved. Unfortunately, organizational scholars tend to focus on idiosyncratic behaviors such as absenteeism or sabotage rather than on the common purpose achieved such that the quality of interchangeability is often overlooked.

However, disidentification may also be manifested in more functional forms, particularly if it leads to the formation of an outgroup with sufficient power and visibility to agitate for change. Concepts such as voice, political behavior, young Turks, dissent, reactance, resistance, whistleblowing, and so on get at this notion of more proactive and potentially constructive change efforts (Ashforth & Mael, 1998; Mintzberg, 1983).

Dukerich, Kramer et al. (1998) and Elsbach and Bhattacharya (1996) argued that disidentification may also trigger a vicious circle. Dukerich,

Kramer et al. noted that strong emotions may become all consuming, lead to biased and pejorative interpretations of equivocal events, foster a sense of persecution, trigger rebellious or resistant behavior, and lead to one being labeled a troublemaker. The upshot may be a "disidentification spiral" (p. 251). Similarly, Elsbach and Bhattacharya's analysis of outsiders' disidentification with the NRA suggests that the counternormative emotions fostered by disidentification—contempt, hostility, and distrust—provoked criticism of the NRA and in a few cases, active opposition (e.g., a boycott). Enacting a disidentity serves to further polarize the individual and the role or organization.

Finally, when an individual exits a role or is considering exit, disidentification may be used as a means of resolving dissonance about foregoing the benefits of the role (J. Aronson et al., 1995). Finding fault with a role may help motivate one to look for a new role, to feel less conflicted about leaving, and to embrace the new role more fully (see chap. 5). Also, displays of disidentification (e.g., criticizing the job and organization) may also be used for impression management purposes to persuade members of the old and new role sets (and oneself) that the decision to exit was indeed rational and that one has truly changed one's allegiance.

In Praise of Balanced Identification

It would seem that role identification is generally preferable to disidentification for both the individual and the organization. However, there is a potential dark side to strong identification as well (Ashforth & Mael, 1996; Dukerich, Kramer et al., 1998; Pratt, 1998), whether with a role or an organization. Roles and organizations are inherently two-dimensional. To become three-dimensional, they must be infused by people who bring with them human experience, emotion, and perspective—people with strong personal identities (e.g., convictions, dispositions) and strong social identities lodged in additional social domains (e.g., family, community, church). Individuals who identify very strongly and more or less exclusively with a given collective risk losing an independent sense of self—along with the independent intuition and moral bearing that act as counterweights to the unavoidably egocentric and myopic cultural control systems that sustain every collective (W. A. Kahn & Kram, 1994).

The key phrase is *identify very strongly and more or less exclusively*. Strong and more or less exclusive identification may be associated with unreflective conformity to organizational demands, resistance to change, ethnocentrism and bigotry, and unethical behavior on behalf of the organization (Dukerich, Kramer et al., 1998; Kets de Vries & Miller, 1984; Schwartz, 1987; J. C. Turner, 1985). Thus, as argued earlier, a certain ambivalence or psychological distance is often healthy for the individual—and ultimately for the organization—because it signals one to be more circumspect than simple role specifications might suggest is necessary. Ambivalence, distance, and circumspection occur when one actively retains personal and social identities anchored in multiple social domains. However, given the often strong pressures that exist in organizations to identify with one's role and organization and to render other identities far less salient, the pursuit of active balance is very difficult (see chap. 6).

Objective and Subjective Indicators of Role Effectiveness

M. E. Poole, Langan-Fox, and Omodei (1993) distinguished between *objective* and *subjective* career success. Objective success refers to observable accomplishments such as pay raises, promotions, and job status, whereas subjective success refers to the focal individual's sense of accomplishment and well-being. Objective and subjective success tend to be correlated in that the former provides social cues that clearly mark and reward achievement and the latter helps foster commitment and motivation that contribute to attaining organizational performance goals.

Given that role identification induces one to carefully enact the role identity, identification is likely associated with both objective and subjective success (see Fig. 3.1). And the experience of objective and subjective success likely reinforces the subjective importance of the role identity, the fulfillment of the psychological motives, and role identification itself. Again, the result is a virtuous circle in that the individual places more weight on roles that are experienced as fulfilling and less weight on roles that are not.

Objective Versus Subjective Success. Although objective and subjective indicators of effectiveness are reciprocally related—whether in a career or within a single role—it is important to differentiate between the two. Success, like the fulfillment of the psychological motives, exists in the eye of the beholder. Korman, Wittig-Berman, and Lang (1981) described managers who were a "career success and personal failure" (p. 342). Similarly, an engineer who declines a promotion because she treasures the autonomy of her role is answering to a subjective criterion of success, not an objective one.

With the growth of boundaryless careers where role options proliferate and individuals manage their own patterning of roles and development (Arthur & Rousseau, 1996b), conventional objective standards may become harder to gauge and less important to the individual. Furthermore, Weick (1996) predicted that tomorrow's employee will look increasingly like today's professional—that is, identified with a complex occupation rather than with an organization, where a premium is placed on learning rather than on upward mobility. If so, then organizationally defined standards of success will pale in importance relative to professional and self-set standards.

To come full circle, organizational research should expand the breadth of subjective criteria considered as legitimate indicators of role success. In particular, measures that capture the relative fulfillment—or better yet, progress toward the fulfillment—of the four psychological motives may capture some of this subjective sense or phenomenology of what makes work matter. Examples include measures of self-awareness, authenticity, dissonance, pride, meaningfulness, learning and growth, mastery, identification, psychological safety or security, interpersonal attachment, cohesion, excitement, frustration, and hope and hopelessness. A significant number of individuals may be objective failures but subjective successes.

CONCLUSION

Because role transitions arouse psychological motives for identity, meaning, control, and belonging, they implicate the self. Role entry is not just about settling into the role and context, it is also about situating and learning about the self and using the role as a platform for expressing that self. The more fulfilling the role, the more likely that one will internalize the role identity as a partial definition of self, leading one to faithfully enact that identity. Identification essentially yokes the individual to the role, for better and for worse. However, given the complexity of roles, individuals may disidentify with certain features that they find repugnant, leading to an overall sense of ambivalence.

4

Attributes
of Role Transitions

*You come right out of a position of advocacy [as a lawyer] into one where you have
to be totally impersonal. It's tough to train yourself not to want to take part in a pro-
ceeding . . . and the longer you stay on the bench, the less of a lawyer you become,
the more you appreciate the constitutional provisions, the rights of people.*
— a judge (Alpert, Atkins, & Ziller, 1979, p. 330)

*I think it'd be totally wrong to go from working in the government on Friday to
commenting on the government on Monday. If you say something critical, you're an
ingrate. If you say something positive, you're in the tank. The audience is confused
about what your role is. I didn't want to look like I was cashing in on the situation.*
— David Gergen on buffering his transition from presidential counselor
to journalist with a brief stint at Duke University
and the Aspen Institute (Kurtz, 1996, p. 320)

Part of what makes role transitions fascinating is the challenge they create
for the individual. As argued in chapter 2, an individual's global identity is
essentially a narrative that he or she crafts to provide meaning and closure
to aspects of his or her life. The individual attempts to weave the multiple
roles that he or she experiences in everyday life (and that precipitate micro
transitions) and the multiple roles that he or she adopts and discards over
time (precipitating macro transitions) into a more or less coherent story.
The story simultaneously provides a sense of continuity and development
and addresses the motives for identity, meaning, control, and belonging.

To understand how role transitions affect the individual, we need to first
understand the nature of the transitions. Previous chapters alluded to role
transitions that involved large changes in role identity, that are socially
desirable, and that are reversible. This chapter combines these threads and
discusses seven key attributes of macro transitions, derived in part from
Ashford and Taylor (1990), Ebaugh (1988), Glaser and Strauss (1971),
Nicholson (1987), and Schlossberg (1981). Each attribute is cast as a

continuum: (a) low magnitude versus high magnitude, (b) socially desirable versus socially undesirable, (c) voluntary versus involuntary, (d) predictable versus unpredictable, (e) collective versus individual, (f) long duration (of the transition period, not the role occupancy) versus short duration, and (g) reversible versus irreversible. To facilitate exposition, I will contrast the transition dynamics at the opposite poles of the continua. Also, I will discuss one attribute that applies to *micro* role transitions: Regular versus irregular.

Each attribute is discussed in terms of its impact on the *difficulty* the transition presents for the individual and of its *valence* for the individual. *Difficulty* was defined in chapter 2 as the effort required to become psychologically and physically (if relevant) disengaged from one role and reengaged in a second role. *Valence* was defined in chapter 2 as the attractiveness of the role transition to the transitioner (i.e., whether it is regarded, on balance, as positive or negative). Transitions usually have both positive and negative qualities, and thus one could create a diagram analogous to Fig. 3.3 with positive valence on one axis and negative valence on the other—and illustrate that most transitions actually foster some ambivalence. However, to ease the exposition of the transition attributes, I will simply focus on net or overall valence (i.e., the difference between the sum of the positive valences and the sum of the negative valences). Overall valence—or henceforth, simply "valence"—is a summary or molar evaluation of the transition, and it exists on a continuum ranging from highly positive, to neutral (no affective import), to highly negative.

Valence is determined by the *process* of transition and by the *content* of the role identities. Regarding process, individuals generally seek to minimize the effort required to change roles. Thus, the more difficult the transition, the more negative the valence is likely to be. (Similarly, the more negative the valence, the more difficult the transition is likely to be as one must summon the psychological energy to exit one role and enter the other.) However, as discussed later, sometimes the very difficulty of a transition makes it positively valent, whether the transition is approached as a challenge to be mastered (prospective sense-making) or is experienced as an ordeal that must be rationalized (retrospective sense-making).

Regarding content, a transition is likely to be regarded as positively valent if: (a) it provides a salutary answer to the motives for identity, meaning, control, and belonging, discussed last chapter, or (b) it is consistent with or activates a desired possible self (or conversely, it moves one away from a feared self; Markus & Nurius, 1986). The motives pertain to one's current adjustment to a role, whereas desired possible selves pertain to one's hoped-for future. Because the motives were discussed in detail last chapter, I will focus on desired selves here.

Whether a transition is consistent with a desired self depends on both the qualities of the role one is adopting and whether the role represents a gain or loss relative to the role one is exiting. For example, a promotion (gain) into top management (desired self) is likely to be regarded as a positively valent transition, whereas a demotion (loss) into a stigmatized position (feared self) is likely to be seen as negatively valent. It seems likely that where the criteria conflict—a transition into a better but still undesirable role versus a transition into a worse but still desirable role—the relative gain or loss would tend to override the role itself. For example, a company president who is demoted to vice president will likely experience the transition as negatively valent, whereas a sweatshop worker promoted to shift supervisor will likely experience the transition as positively valent.

There are two important caveats to this argument. First, because of its evaluative flavor, valence exists in the eye of the beholder. The evaluation of a given feature necessarily depends on the values and preferences of the perceiver. An increase in responsibility may be regarded negatively by one person and positively by another. However, there is strong consensus on the evaluation of some features (e.g., more pay is good, more noxious working conditions are bad). Second, the valence of a transition may be ambiguous because the social cues are equivocal (e.g., is a transfer overseas a reward or a punishment?), the transitioner is unfamiliar with the role or is uncertain how he or she will react, or the features of the role identity provoke such high ambivalence that he or she cannot reliably assess overall valence (e.g., a job change means a big gain in autonomy but a big loss in pay).

Figure 4.1 links the seven attributes of macro role transitions to the perceived difficulty and valence of a transition and thus provides an overview of the chapter.

LOW-MAGNITUDE VERSUS HIGH-MAGNITUDE TRANSITIONS

As noted in chapter 1, the magnitude of a transition is defined by the degree of role contrast; again, the number of core and peripheral features of the role identity that changes and the extent of the changes, where core features are weighted more heavily. In Latack's (1984) operationalization

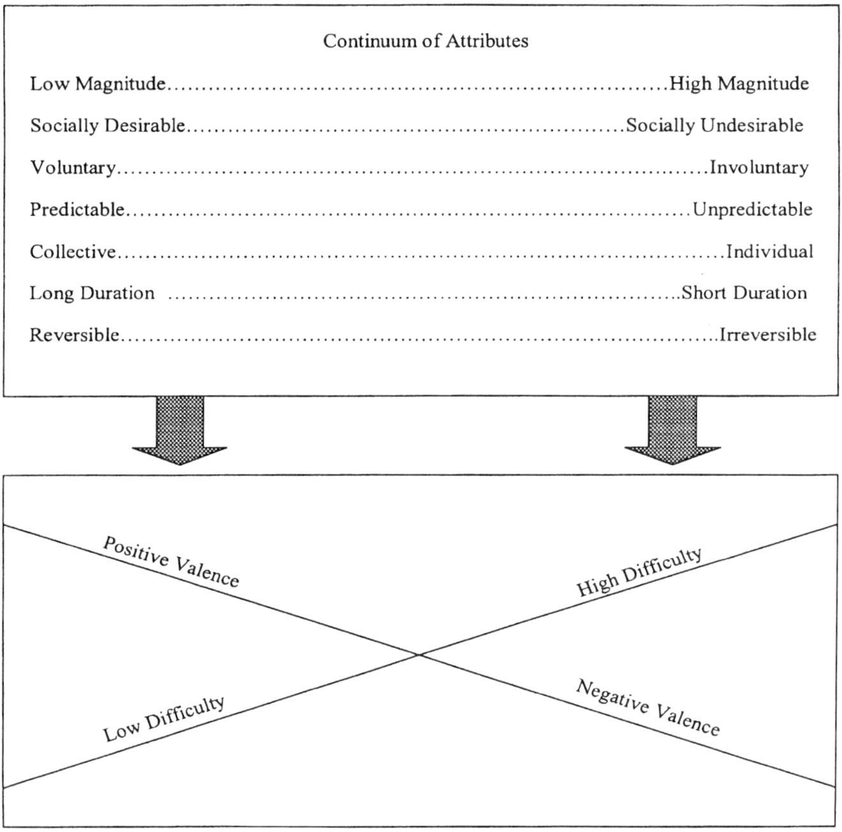

Continuum of Attributes

Low Magnitude...High Magnitude

Socially Desirable...Socially Undesirable

Voluntary...Involuntary

Predictable...Unpredictable

Collective...Individual

Long Duration ....Short Duration

Reversible...Irreversible

Positive Valence

High Difficulty

Low Difficulty

Negative Valence

FIG. 4.1. The difficulty and valence associated with the attributes of role transitions. (Note. "Long Duration" refers to the duration of the transition period, not to the duration of role occupancy.)

of the magnitude of intraorganizational transitions, the smallest change is that of a job, followed by a change in job plus hierarchical level, job plus function, job plus occupation, and various combinations of these changes.[1] This operationalization correlated at $r = .66$ with a subjective measure of magnitude (e.g., "When I moved to this job, it felt like a big change"). If *inter*organizational transitions are also considered, the magnitude would increase further with changes in organization, industry, region, country, and continent. Furnham and Bochner (1986), for example, discussed the culture shock of transitions between countries with large differences in value systems and beliefs.

Latack (1984) also found a positive correlation between the magnitude of intraorganizational transitions and the occurrence of personal life tran-

---

[1]Latack (1984) also included the category of *occupational field*, but this term was not defined.

sitions (e.g., marriage). It seems likely that the correlation was based more on a given organizational transition prompting a personal adjustment (e.g., a transfer necessitating a geographic relocation) than on the reverse (e.g., a divorce prompting one to immerse oneself in work, leading to a promotion). Such domino effects or *role reverberations* can rapidly escalate the magnitude of a given role transition. However, the personal transition→organizational transition relation would likely become far stronger when interorganizational transitions are also considered (e.g., a spouse's transfer necessitating a search for a new job). Thus, the relationship between personal and organization-based transitions is probably reciprocal such that the magnitude of a transition can increase rapidly.

L. A. Hill (1992) provided an example of a common high-magnitude transition. She noted that first-line management is the hierarchical level that generates the most frequent reports of incompetence, burnout, and attrition. In her qualitative study of 19 new managers, she found that the promotion to manager entailed a transformation in role identity from a specialist to a generalist and from an individual actor to a network builder. The abrupt change in identity presented a considerable challenge to the new managers. Indeed, promotions are often thought to involve changes of *degree* (the amount or importance of a given task); however, most promotions—like any role transition—also involve at least some changes in *kind* (the nature of the work).

Less common high-magnitude transitions include the assumption of roles that are highly unique, public, coveted, reviled, or otherwise involve a highly visible discontinuity with previous roles. Induction into the army, election to high public office, joining a major league baseball team, and conviction on a murder charge are examples of dramatic changes in role identity.

Difficulty and Valence

A high-magnitude transition may have mixed effects on the ease of role exit. On one hand, the possibility of a high-magnitude transition may foster anxiety prior to committing to the exit. A fear of the unknown (e.g., "What will it be like? Can I succeed?") and the size of the anticipated challenges may give one pause. On the other hand, if one does commit to leaving the role, the very magnitude of the transition may make it easier to psychologically distance oneself from the exited role (see chap. 5). The lack of role blurring may facilitate a relatively clean break such that one can begin anew in the next role.

A high-magnitude transition is likely to have a far less ambiguous impact on role *entry*; that is, it will tend to impair entry (Burr, 1972). Pinder and Schroeder (1987) studied employees who had undergone *transfers*, defined as a "relatively permanent job reassignment that entails the movement of an employee within an organization from one of its operating sites to another" (Pinder & Walter, 1984, p. 188). Pinder and Schroeder found that the less similar and more difficult the new job was perceived to be compared to the old, the longer it took for an employee to feel proficient in the new job. The authors emphasized that subjective perceptions of contrast, rather than objective changes in function and hierarchical level, affected the time to proficiency.

According to Chao, O'Leary-Kelly, Wolf, Klein, and Gardner (1994), high-magnitude changes increase the amount of role- and context-specific information that one must learn. Similarly, according to Nicholson's (1984) work-role transitions theory, the more novel the job demands are to the individual—that is, the higher the magnitude of the transition—the greater the personal change. The novelty of the role means that prior knowledge, skills, and abilities may be less relevant, prompting the person to adapt to the demands of the role. Indeed, in a survey of U.S. Navy officers, Bruce and Scott (1994) operationalized the magnitude of a role transition as the perceived "degree of personal change required by the average officer" (p. 23). They found that the magnitude of a variety of role transitions was positively correlated with adjustment difficulty and negatively correlated with eagerness toward the event and its perceived desirability. A high-magnitude transition may challenge the continuity and orderliness of one's identity narrative; it may disturb the system of meaning one has constructed; it may introduce role ambiguity, conflict, and overload (Latack, 1984), upsetting one's sense of control; and it may disrupt one's social network, undermining one's sense of belonging. (However, research under the rubric of work-role transitions theory has yielded mix findings regarding the novelty–personal change relation; Ashforth & Saks, 1995; Black & Ashford, 1995; V. D. Miller, Johnson, Hart, & Peterson, 1999; Munton & West, 1995; M. A. West, Nicholson, & Rees, 1987; see chap. 6).

On balance, then, high-magnitude transitions tend to be quite difficult and therefore negatively valent (see Fig. 4.1). However, beyond the mixed effects of magnitude on role exit, there are several major exceptions to the association between magnitude and negative valence. First, because work dissatisfaction and poor performance predict voluntary and involuntary turnover (Hom & Griffeth, 1995), an individual may seek a high-magnitude transition to escape an aversive situation. For example, T. A. Wright and

Bonett (1992) found that employees who changed jobs and occupations displayed greater increases in work satisfaction and mental health than employees who only changed jobs or who remained in their initial job.[2]

Second, regardless of one's level of satisfaction with a prior role, a high-magnitude transition may provide a welcome contrast between roles. As noted, role contrasts are associated with marked differences in role identities, enabling one to explore and experience other facets of oneself. Role contrasts may also provide perspective and balance by enabling one to place each role in a larger and richer context. Waskul (1998) found that the unique world of summer camp enabled some counselors to attain psychological distance from their other roles, permitting them to "step out of themselves" (p. 41) and reflect on their lives and priorities.

Third, there are many instances where a transition is welcomed and relished precisely because of the challenge it presents. Like a mountaineer climbing Everest, the difficulty may represent an opportunity to build and test one's ability, to affirm one's distinctiveness, and to express one's identity as a courageous risk taker. As the literature on so-called stretch goals suggests, difficult challenges are more likely to be accepted if one has control over the goal and the process by which it is realized as well as adequate support and resources to attempt to attain the goal (K. R. Thompson, Hochwarter, & Mathys, 1997). Of course, not everyone has an Everest or the same Everest: For one person, perhaps it is to be the first family member to attend university, for another, to be a partner in a consulting firm.

Fourth, role contrasts enable individuals to temporarily distance themselves from role identities that have been "overworked." Sabbaticals, vacations, hobbies, temporary assignments, and so forth may provide a needed diversion from an otherwise consuming role identity (see chap. 9 regarding ephemeral roles). For example, the literature on stress and burnout advocates frequent respites from roles that are emotionally taxing (Westman & Eden, 1997): As the saying goes, a change is as good as a rest. However, by the same token, role contrasts may also impair transitions back to former roles. Waskul (1998) also found that when the camp counselors returned home at the end of the summer, the cessation of their unique experiences and highly regimented camp life left some feeling disconnected and directionless.

---

[2]However, the differences between employees who changed jobs and occupations versus those who changed only jobs is attributable to the lower preexit work satisfaction and mental health of the former group: No significant differences were found in postexit satisfaction and mental health between the two groups.

Finally, many difficult transitions that are *prospectively* feared become *retrospectively* prized. Bruce and Scott (1994) found that U.S. Navy officers approaching a career event (e.g., promotion, resignation) perceived it as being of greater magnitude and less desirable than did individuals who had already experienced the event. This finding suggests that prior to a transition, individuals may become apprehensive and view the event as more intimidating than it is or that after the transition, individuals are able to retrospectively find meaning and perspective. Regarding the latter, it was noted last chapter that the motive for meaning (both sense-making and meaningfulness) may impel one to seek and find meaning where outsiders see little or none. And as discussed in chapter 6, this resolution of cognitive dissonance ("Why did I put myself through that?") is one of the reasons that initiation activities—deliberately contrived obstacles to role entry—often *enhance* role identification.

In summary, barring these five exceptions, a low-magnitude transition tends to be less difficult and more positively valent than a high-magnitude transition.

SOCIALLY DESIRABLE VERSUS SOCIALLY UNDESIRABLE TRANSITIONS

A socially desirable transition is one that is generally regarded by others in positive terms, where *others* refers to society in general and members of one's role set in particular (e.g., colleagues viewing one's promotion). Social desirability is thus the social or collective analog of an individual's assessment of valence.[3] Social comparison theory (Festinger, 1957) and social information processing theory (Salancik & Pfeffer, 1978) contend that individuals rely heavily on others to understand ambiguous situations ("What is it?") and to evaluate them ("How good is it?"). In short, individuals take their informational and evaluative cues largely from social referents. With regard to role transitions, society provides the social values and standards on which members of the role set at least partly base their assessment of the transition. Thus, the more socially desirable the

---

[3]A key difference, in addition to the level of analysis (group vs. individual), is that valence is assessed by the individual with regard to his or her wants and needs, whereas social desirability is not assessed with a specific individual in mind. Valence is thus particularistic or idiosyncratic. For example, an individual may agree with others that a promotion to management is highly socially desirable but nonetheless regard it as negatively valent for her.

transition (where the role set has a more immediate or proximal impact than the more distal society), the more likely that the individual will view the transition in positive terms.

And just as valence depends on the quality of the entered role and whether it represents a gain or loss relative to the exited role, so too does social desirability. Regarding quality, research on occupational prestige indicates that roles associated with complex tasks, status, power, education, and income are more likely to be regarded as socially desirable (Treiman, 1977). Generally, roles lacking complexity, status, and so on are less likely to address an incumbent's psychological motives—particularly for a salutary identity, a sense of meaningfulness, and primary control (conversely, sense-making, secondary control, and belonging are less likely to be affected by the quality of a role). Regarding gain versus loss, a loss is seen to be counternormative, deviating from what is socially expected (Morris, 1997). A role transition "should" represent progress, not regression or the maintenance of a steady state. The social desirability of continual progress is signaled by derogatory phrases such as "he's just treading water," "she's plateaued," "his career has stalled," and "she's stagnated."

The impact of social desirability on the individual is moderated by the visibility of the transition. For example, M. West, Nicholson, and Rees (1990) found that the negative impact on managers of a downward move in status was greater than that of unemployment. At first blush, this might seem surprising because unemployment represents a termination of one's managerial role (total loss), whereas a downward move preserves the role (partial loss). However, although a downward move in an organization clearly symbolizes failure to members of one's role set, unemployment releases one from the role set and its status system. Anonymity can thus buffer one from the pain of social stigma.[4] Anonymity, however, is unlikely to completely eradicate the pain because the individual, as a member of society, has probably internalized society's standards for assessing role transitions. Mead (1934) termed this inner voice the *generalized other*.

Provisos

The impact of social desirability on the individual needs to be qualified in three ways. First, given the distinction between distal and proximal influence, the impact of society on the individual is largely mediated by the

---

[4]However, if the unemployment were to persevere, the negative impact would likely become far worse (see chap. 5).

more proximal role set. Societal and role set assessments of social desirability may at times be only loosely coupled, particularly if the role set is embedded in a strong subculture. The general standards of society may provide slim guidance for the specific nuances of a particular social domain; a transition may be novel or highly idiosyncratic and therefore defy easy stereotyping as good or bad; and a group may deliberately reject conventional standards. Thus, a transition that appears highly desirable to people outside the role set may be turned down if members of the role set think otherwise (e.g., a professor becoming dean), and a transition that appears undesirable to others may nonetheless be pursued if it is prized by the role set (e.g., a manager applying for a position overseas).[5]

Second, as discussed last chapter, individuals and groups are adept at constructing value where outsiders see little or none (Crocker & Major, 1989). The psychological motives are sufficiently powerful that individuals and role set members may construe a salutary identity and meaningfulness and may impute control (cf. positive illusions, S. E. Taylor, 1989).[6] Indeed, Ashforth and Kreiner (1999) concluded that incumbents of stigmatized roles are highly motivated to socially construct edifying rationales for their work. For example, Bourassa and Ashforth (1998) found that workers on an Alaskan trawler maintained that their onerous work conditions proved their physical and mental toughness: Lesser work would have required lesser people. However, Ashforth and Kreiner (1999) cautioned that role incumbents are nonetheless likely to remain somewhat ambivalent toward their role because outsiders provide ongoing reminders of the role's low social desirability.

Similarly, research on demotions and terminations indicates that whereas most people view them negatively, a sizable minority view them positively (e.g., a release from high stress, an opportunity to start something better; Fineman, 1983; More, 1968). Moreover, if others participate

[5]It is important to note that even the literature on deviant subcultures suggests that groups typically do not wholly reject conventional standards. Instead, they *reframe* them in a manner that is more consistent with the group's goals and beliefs (e.g., Sykes & Matza, 1957). For example, although street gangs may appear to have opted out of conventional society, they nonetheless recognize the importance of role entry (as signaled by recruitment and socialization efforts), role specialization, and "promotion"; and value effective role enactment and social solidarity (e.g., Jankowski, 1991).

[6]However, because primary control reflects influence over the work environment, it is typically less amenable to social construction. Furthermore, belongingness tends to be less of a concern because the external threat of stigma encourages peers to unify under the role banner (Ashforth & Kreiner, 1999).

in the transition (e.g., a plant layoff), or a collective response coalesces (e.g., a lawsuit), or one joins a self-help group, then it becomes more likely that the individual will eke out a salutary sense of identity, meaning, and control—as well as belonging. Collectivities can often foster and sustain salutary beliefs that individuals alone cannot (Hardin & Higgins, 1996).

The third proviso involves the concept of boundaryless careers, discussed in chapter 1. Conventional standards and norms are becoming diluted such that individuals have greater freedom to invent their own career paths (Arthur & Rousseau, 1996b)—a freedom that newcomers to the job market are increasingly exercising (Munk, 1998). Thus, the notion of what is and what is not socially desirable may become increasingly opaque.

In sum, the social desirability of a transition, as mediated by the role set, affects the valence of the transition and thereby its difficulty.

VOLUNTARY VERSUS INVOLUNTARY TRANSITIONS

A voluntary transition occurs when an individual is able to exercise real choice in whether and when he or she exits a role and in selecting or agreeing to accept a new role. Examples of involuntary transitions include demotions, terminations, mandatory transfers and retirements, sick leaves, imprisonment, hospitalization, and new jobs where no real alternatives exist. Although *voluntariness* may appear to be a categorical attribute— one either has choice or not—it is actually continuous (Ebaugh, 1988). Whereas a layoff may represent low voluntariness and a decision to leave one promising career for another may represent high voluntariness, there are many choices that are ostensibly voluntary but are severely constrained. For instance, declining a promotion may reflect badly on one's reputation and foreclose future opportunities, and a decision to attend night school may reflect a fear of obsolescence rather than intrinsic interest.

The importance of voluntariness to the experience of a transition is readily apparent in the lengths that organizations often go to persuade one to "choose" an otherwise unwanted role (e.g., a transfer to a different locale, an unpopular committee assignment). For example, rather than invoke his or her authority or coercive power and force a transition, a manager may attempt to persuade and offer inducements. The reason for this attempt to make the involuntary seem voluntary is rooted in cognitive dissonance theory (Festinger, 1957). Many dissonance experiments are contrived to induce individuals to make choices they would ordinarily not, from eating worms to publicly advocating positions they abhor. The experiments are carefully designed to minimize the possibility of refusal, thereby creating the illusion of choice. The individuals' desire to then make sense of their ostensibly voluntary behavior induces them to change how they feel about the behavior. In short, the perception of voluntariness changes the perceived valence of the activity.

The more involuntary one perceives a role transition to be, the greater is the threat to one's sense of control (even if the role transition is otherwise desirable) and, indeed, perhaps one's ability to maintain a valued identity(ies) and sense of meaningfulness and belonging. Following reactance theory (Brehm, 1993), individuals react against a threat to their perceived control such that they come to desire the foregone alternatives even more. Thus, an involuntary transition may enhance the perceived desirability of the former role and other now-precluded possibilities. Also, highly involuntary transitions often involve a sudden and strong role contrast and throw plans and hopes in disarray. In short, they are destabilizing. Moreover, involuntary transitions are often unexpected, further threatening the control motive. Finally, involuntary transitions also tend to be socially undesirable transitions; hence the need for coercion.

As a result, highly involuntary transitions may induce individuals to at least temporarily lower their expectations and, possibly, their aspirations. By truncating their expectations, they reduce the chances of disappointment and thereby gain some secondary control (Brandtstädter & Rothermund, 1994). Furthermore, highly involuntary transitions tend to induce individuals to focus on their immediate needs for security and stability. They may engage in "firefighting," addressing their current and most pressing concerns. For example, Zamble and Porporino (1988) surveyed and interviewed male prison inmates and found that 79% lived day by day and eschewed planning. As one inmate put it, "No, I don't plan my time. Do I live day by day? No, a day's a long time in here, too much to think about. I just let things happen. I guess you'd say I live minute by minute" (p. 88).[7]

When coupled with high magnitude, a highly involuntary transition may prompt a dramatic reevaluation and change in the life course. The unwanted disruption of one's identity narrative may induce one to cast about for new plotlines. For example, Rosenbaum (1988), a physician,

---

[7]In this example, the tendency to firefight is exacerbated by new inmates' perceptions that prison life is often unpredictable.

described how his experience as a cancer patient at the same hospital where he worked caused him to provide medical care in a far more sensitive and empathic manner than he had prior to the onset of cancer.

In summary, a voluntary transition tends to be far less difficult and more positively valent than an involuntary transition.

PREDICTABLE VERSUS UNPREDICTABLE TRANSITIONS

A transition is predictable when one is able to anticipate the date of role exit, the onset and duration of the role entry period, and the nature of the events surrounding the exit and entry. The more predictable the transition, the better able is one to engage in anticipatory preparation (Ashford & Taylor, 1990), thereby facilitating sense-making and secondary (if not primary) control.

People generally prefer controllability to predictability. Although the former is a realistic objective for most voluntary role exits, the latter is more realistic for most role entries. To be sure, the greater the relative status and power of the individual (e.g., through work experience, unique capabilities, abundant job opportunities), the more control he or she can exercise over the date of exit, the onset of the entry, and the degree and nature of socialization required. However, even a powerful individual must learn about and adapt himself or herself at least somewhat to the idiosyncrasies of the particular organization, subunit, role, and role set members. For most individuals, role entry allows limited amounts of primary control, and therefore, secondary control via predictability becomes attractive.

The importance of predictability to personal well-being is illustrated by the lengths individuals often go to in order to secure it. For example, Westby (1960) described the career trajectories of symphony musicians. The occupational structure is a status pyramid where valued opportunities quickly narrow as one ascends the hierarchy. Openings occur infrequently and suddenly, and musicians have to be ready to pounce. As a result, aspiring musicians keep active tabs on the ages, professional history, ability, and perhaps even the inclination to quit and relationships with the conductor of individuals holding desirable posts in the pyramid. Under such circumstances, it seems likely that a great deal of occupational gossip and politicking would revolve around potential employment opportunities and the abilities and aspirations of peers. In short, much energy is spent trying to render the unpredictable more predictable.

Many organizations recognize that predictable role entry both eases the anxiety of newcomers and provides more organizational control over the nature of early role experiences and the lessons that are drawn. Chapter 6 discusses how organizations often use institutionalized socialization to structure newcomers' experiences. Institutionalized socialization leaves little to chance and has generally been associated with lower role ambiguity and conflict and higher job satisfaction and organizational identification (Bauer, Morrison, & Callister, 1998; Saks & Ashforth, 1997).

In sum, a predictable transition tends to be far less difficult and more positively valent than an unpredictable one.

COLLECTIVE VERSUS INDIVIDUAL TRANSITIONS

A collective transition occurs when either two or more role occupants exit together or two or more newcomers are grouped together and put through a common set of role entry experiences (Van Maanen & Schein, 1979). Regarding role exit, interaction and social comparison with other potential leavers facilitates exit by providing critical information (e.g., evaluation of pros and cons, knowledge of role alternatives), by legitimating thoughts and ultimately the act of leaving, and by providing social support. Thus, Ebaugh (1988) found that it took nuns who left their convent alone much longer to work through the exit process than nuns who left in cohorts. Certain collective role exits are institutionalized, such as graduation from educational institutions and even periodic layoffs from corporations, and thus tend to have more or less structured exit rituals.

Regarding role entry, collective transitions are most prevalent in the movement from outsider to insider, where a basic orientation to the organization and role is needed. Collective transitions are generally associated with organizations that recruit and socialize newcomers in batches to efficiently impart the organization's culture, to shape a common identity, and to prepare the recruits for substantially similar entry-level roles. Thus, collective transitions are more common in large organizations with relatively strong and unique cultures where the basic role identities can be clearly specified (Van Maanen & Schein, 1979). Examples include management training programs, military boot camps, sales training programs, fish processing boats, and police academies.

Conversely, more individualized socialization is associated with smaller organizations that lack the economies of scale for batch processing and with complex role identities that require more intensive one-to-one socialization, as through mentorship and apprenticeship programs. Individualized socialization is also more prevalent for within-organization transitions, such as a promotion or transfer, because individuals are less likely to move in batches and have already learned about the organization.

As with role exit, collective transitions tend to facilitate role entry. Newcomers see their peers as fellow travelers with the same status and developmental needs, creating an in-the-same boat consciousness (Becker, 1964; Van Maanen & Schein, 1979). Peers attempt to resolve the ambiguity and anxiety of the initial transition by socially constructing a definition of the situation and their role within it, sharing emergent answers to developmental issues, and seeking and offering emotional support borne of common experiences and concerns.[8] Thus, collective transitions tend to address each of the four psychological motives, particularly for belonging.

Moreover, the involvement of peers in socialization may reinforce the efforts of organizational socialization agents. Peers may exert pressure on one another to conform with emergent values and norms, particularly if they are grouped into teams and induced to compete with other teams or generalized standards, as in boot camp (Ricks, 1997). Thus, as Van Maanen and Schein (1979) noted, "army recruits socialize each other in ways the army could never do" (p. 233).

However, the segue from a collective transition to regular role performance is often problematic. First, the newcomer cohort may construct answers that deviate from what is espoused by the organization's socialization agents. Consequently, collective transitions are double-edged: The power conferred on newcomers to construct their own meaning may be used to either reinforce or subvert the organization's espoused views (Van Maanen & Schein, 1979). Second, collective socialization is usually not a sufficient basis for job performance because individuals must translate their generalized learning into specific roles in specific parts of the organization. Thus, collective practices are usually augmented with more idiosyncratic practices such as the on-the-job training that a police academy graduate may receive from a veteran squad car partner (Rachlin, 1991).

---

[8]It is important to note that both receiving *and giving* instrumental and expressive social support facilitates one's own adjustment (Schlossberg, 1981). In giving support, one comes to feel valued by and connected to others and engaged in the situation at hand.

In summary, both a collective role exit and collective role entry tend to be easier and more positively valent than an individual exit and entry.

LONG VERSUS
SHORT DURATION
OF TRANSITION PERIOD

The duration of the transition period refers to the length of time between when a person seriously entertains thoughts about exiting a role (or in the case of an involuntary exit, when he or she learns of the exit) and when he or she is expected to be "up to speed" in the subsequent role (that is, expected to perform more or less like a regular role occupant). Typically, individuals have more control over the duration of the role exit period than of the role entry period.

All else equal, the longer the duration, the easier the transition. A long period enables one to prepare for an upcoming role (e.g., through training, role rehearsals; see chap. 5) and fosters a sense of security by providing a grace period in which performance requirements are relaxed and by signaling that the organization regards one's development as a relatively long-term investment. Conversely, a short period may make one feel rushed and unvalued.

However, seldom is all else equal: Typically, organizations allow a grace period for newcomers precisely because the transition is likely to be difficult. Thus, the duration permitted tends to be longer for newcomers who are inexperienced or are entering entry-level roles, complex roles, established work groups, or unique and strong organizational cultures.

Furthermore, the utility of a lengthy exit and entry period depends on how the time is invested. Regarding exit, Ebaugh (1988) cautioned that past a certain point, a long period may provide no marginal benefit (and indeed may lead to a dissolution of momentum): "There seems to be a 'ripe' time for exiting after all known alternatives and pros and cons are carefully weighed" (p. 189). Regarding entry, research on newcomer training suggests that a series of moderately challenging assignments, supported by resources and constructive feedback, gradually shape the individual's capabilities, confidence, and credibility and thereby the individual's capacity to attract resources and further developmental assignments (D. T. Hall, 1976). The result is often a *success spiral*, where success breeds success. Alternatively, newcomers who languish in unchallenging training assignments, perhaps "paying their dues," may begin to question their capabilities and role choice.[9] As development stagnates, enthusiasm wanes. Moreover, even in a well-designed training program, newcomers are usually eager to shed their *trainee* label and be seen by all as a bona fide organizational member. I argue in chapter 7 that it is very difficult for a newcomer to fully settle into a role without social validation by valued members of his or her role set. And validation tends to be meted out only as one actually enacts the role.

Finally, it should be noted that organizations may deliberately truncate the transition period. An organization may get wind of a role occupant's desire to exit and hasten the exit (see chap. 5). Also, an organization may shorten a newcomer's entry period to foment maximum personal change. In terms of Lewin's (1951) field theory, the *reality shock* (M. Kramer, 1974) of an abrupt role entry may unfreeze the newcomer, rendering him or her more receptive to personal change as a means of acclimating to the new situation. Thus, newcomers prematurely thrust into the breech are compelled to learn the role even as they enact it. As chapter 7 shows, in attempting to convince others of their credibility as a role occupant, they may ultimately convince themselves (e.g., Haas & Shaffir, 1982; Ibarra, 1996). However, this kind of induced reality shock is seldom experienced by the newcomer as pleasant.

On balance, a long transition period tends to ease the transition and be perceived as more positively valent than a short period—provided that the individual experiences development and can anticipate the end of the trainee status (see chap. 7).

REVERSIBLE VERSUS IRREVERSIBLE TRANSITIONS

A reversible role transition exists when individuals can exit a role and resume their career almost as if they had never entered the role in the first place. The transition can be said to have been reversed if the role and the transition had little or no effect on the individual and how he or she is perceived by himself or herself and by role set members. In short, a reversible transition is one that can be effectively forgotten by everyone. A transition is more likely to be reversible if: (a) the role is occupied for a

---

[9]However, in the discussion of divestiture in chapter 6, I note that socialization practices are sometimes *designed* to induce this self-questioning as a means of fostering receptiveness to authority and personal change.

relatively short period of time, thus minimizing the impact (e.g., quitting shortly after entry), (b) the occupancy is for a fixed period, possibly enabling the individual to adopt a temporary identity (see chap. 2) and ride out the period with little personal adjustment and then exit with little or no stigma (e.g., a summer job), (c) the role is similar to previous roles held by the individual, thus requiring less adjustment, and (d) relatively few people know the individual occupied the role (e.g., moonlighting as a taxi driver).

In contrast, an irreversible role transition exists when a person is somehow marked by the experience of the role or the transition, if only by how others perceive him or her. A role transition is more likely to be irreversible if the role is long term, open-ended, dissimilar to previous roles, and highly visible or public. Because the individual or members of his or her role set cannot simply forget the role or the transition, the individual has little recourse but to come to terms with the role. This may involve a range of responses from substantive personal change to more superficial accounts offered as an impression management device (e.g., "It was a learning opportunity"). Thus, irreversible transitions are more likely than reversible transitions to arouse the psychological motives—particularly for identity and meaning—as the individual endeavors to reconcile himself or herself with the role (Ashford & Taylor, 1990).

In a sense, however, a role transition is *always* irreversible. Immersion in a socially structured situation, with its own local and pressing reality, leaves a residue of experience—what Ebaugh (1988) termed the *role residual* or *hangover identity*—with all its potential to subtly and not so subtly affect the global identity. In short, biography indelibly marks identity (Ludwig, 1997). For example, all else equal, a person who was a union steward is likely to be a somewhat different manager than one who was never a steward. Moreover, as described in chapter 5, the more public and affectively charged the role, the more the individual will be perceived by others in terms of the imputed qualities of the role, thus making it more difficult for the person to deidentify with that role. Labeling theory, for example, contends that people marked by stigmatized roles—such as convict, school dropout, and prostitute—have a very difficult time escaping the taint (Ashforth & Humphrey, 1995). Similarly, people marked by prestigious roles—such as actor, athlete, and politician—often find it difficult to be regarded as an individual apart from their former role.[10]

---

[10]This argument assumes that one first knew the focal person via their public role. In cases where one knew a person prior to the public role, the earlier knowledge holds a strong first-mover advantage and shapes subsequent role-based perceptions of the person. The president of the United States is known to the world as *Mr. President,* but to his parents, he is still known first and foremost as *son.*

Difficulty and Valence

Irreversible transitions tend to be more difficult because "there is no going back"; the individual must at least attempt to adapt. However, as with high-magnitude transitions, an irreversible transition—particularly if entered voluntarily—may be valued precisely because it entails risk, the anticipation of personal change, or indelible labeling. For example, an employee may resign to start a company in the same industry, thereby earning the enmity of her former employer. Nonetheless, she may relish the opportunity to compete head-to-head.

Furthermore, a reversible transition may ultimately prove very difficult if an individual avoids adapting to the role in anticipation of leaving—but then, for whatever reason, does not. For many people, the long term is essentially a series of short terms, of just-for-now roles that stretch into a career. Tomorrow never comes. For example, research on shop floor workers suggests that many retain wistful aspirations, such as to own a small business, that provide hope for the future but dull the willingness to adapt to the present (Collinson, 1992). As a result, many of these workers become trapped in roles they do not value, and the reversible transition becomes irreversible.

In summary, a reversible role transition tends to be easier and more positively valent than an irreversible one. However, irreversibility may arouse the psychological motives and galvanize change precisely because the transition cannot be undone. Irreversibility commits one to adapt.

REGULAR VERSUS
IRREGULAR TRANSITIONS

As noted, this final attribute pertains only to micro role transitions. A regular transition is one that occurs at more or less the same time (whether measured by the hour or day) and in more or less the same manner. For example, a suburban resident may commute to work at 8 a.m. each weekday, stop at the gym for a workout at 5:30 p.m., and arrive home at 7 p.m. He may visit his parents on Friday evening, attend synagogue on Saturday, and do his grocery shopping on Sunday. The patterning of the transitions' time and manner provides some predictability, which was argued earlier to ease the transitions. Regularity may reduce the conscious effort required to undertake the transition such that it proceeds almost mindlessly. Indeed, as discussed in chapter 9, individuals may develop *transition scripts* or routines to help regularize micro transitions. Moreover, the regular immersion in highly differentiated roles—work, play, family, consumer, worshipper, and so on—enables the individual to concentrate on exercising and exploring highly specific facets of self (without necessarily worrying about potential contradictions *between* the facets) and experience *recurring* role contrasts. For example, the role of worshipper may address personal needs left unattended by the role of employee such that—over the course of a week—the individual experiences a more holistic sense of self. The regularity of the transitions helps ground the individual in specific contexts and provides a rounded sense of identity, meaning, control, and belonging.

In sum, a regular micro transition tends to be less difficult and more positively valent than an irregular transition.

CONCLUSION

The attributes of a role transition affect the difficulty of making the transition and the valence of the transition. Difficulty tends to be reciprocally related to negative valence—although sometimes effort is enjoyed for its own sake and for what it represents (e.g., dedication, development). A role transition will generally be easier and thus more positively valent if it is of low magnitude and long duration and is socially desirable, voluntary, predictable, collective, and reversible (and regarding micro transitions, is experienced regularly).

Although the transition attributes have been discussed one at a time, they are of course experienced jointly. Thus, we need to briefly consider some potential interactions among them. Social desirability, magnitude, and voluntariness may be the three most critical attributes. It seems likely that the evaluative tone of the transition—social desirability—will most strongly influence the experience of the other attributes. A transition that is widely regarded as a net gain is more likely to address the motives for identity and meaning, providing a dominant frame such that the other attributes are in turn more likely to be interpreted as a stimulating opportunity rather than as an overwhelming problem (cf. Jackson & Dutton, 1988). Even then, however, an otherwise socially desirable transition may still threaten the motives for control and belonging.

It also seems likely that the magnitude of the transition will strongly influence the experience of the remaining attributes. Under a low-magnitude transition, where continuity is by definition high, the other attributes become far less consequential. For an experienced bank manager transferred from one retail branch to another, it may not matter much if the transition is unpredictable, individual, irreversible, and allows limited adjustment time. Conversely, a high-magnitude transition exacerbates the difficulties caused by these attributes.

As noted, the voluntariness of role entry is likely associated with its social desirability: Individuals may have to be coerced to accept an undesirable move (e.g., demotion, incarceration in prison). However, the correlation is imperfect: For personal reasons (e.g., family commitments, idiosyncratic values and beliefs), an individual may prefer to decline a socially desirable transition and thus may need to be induced to move. Given the threat that an involuntary transition presents to the individual's motive for control, involuntariness may strongly bias how the individual interprets and experiences the subsequent transition process. The negative expectations provoked by involuntariness may prove self-fulfilling. The importance of voluntariness will become particularly apparent when we discuss role exit next chapter.

Finally, it is important to again emphasize that each of the transition attributes ultimately exists in the eye of the beholder. This underscores the malleability of meaning in the transition process—and thus, the malleability of difficulty and valence. As noted in chapter 3, individuals are often capable of finding meaning in even the most dire transitions. For example, Leach (1994) argued that doctors and nurses had a better chance of surviving prisoner of war camps than other prisoners partly because their medical expertise gave them a purpose that the others lacked. Finding meaning enables one to recast an otherwise difficult and negatively valent transition as serving a larger purpose—as a necessary ordeal.

Also, as argued next chapter under "Liminality," it is much easier to tolerate a negatively valent transition if one can anticipate an eventual end to the role occupancy: Anticipating an end effectively brackets the occupancy period, allowing one to hope and plan for a better day. A recurring theme in concentration camp diaries is that the loss of hope often meant the loss of life (e.g., Bettelheim, 1960).

5

Role Exit

The process of adapting to higher officer . . . hadn't been easy for Batogowski, and in some ways it made him feel lonely. He still lived in a suburban community west of the city, along with some twenty-five other middle and upper-middle managers at Sears, several of whom were the guys he drove to work with and played golf with on the weekends. But now he sensed he was supposed to isolate himself in the name of good management practice, and it made him sad. He knew it was hard for some of his pals who were still buyers or even the heads of departments to talk shop informally in front of him lately, so he figured that once the new house he was building in a different town was done, things would be easier for everyone. . . . [He] figured that [his boss] was pleased he was moving: it indicated his willingness to grow.
—D. R. Katz (1988, p. 454)

Role exits are prompted by a variety of reasons, the most common of which include resignation, termination, promotion, transfer, demotion, retirement, and fulfillment of terms (e.g., contract employment, university graduation). What makes the concept of role exit intriguing is the necessity for *disengagement* (Ebaugh, 1988), for psychological and usually physical withdrawal from the role and the cultural context and web of relationships within which the role is embedded. The stronger the identification with the role, the more difficult the role exit (Latack, Kinicki, & Prussia, 1995; Taylor Carter & Cook, 1995). The departing individual must cease to conceive of himself or herself as a role occupant, perhaps abandoning social identities and relationships that are highly valued. Moreover, disengagement is usually a mutual process in that members of the departing individual's role set must similarly withdraw their role-based attachments to the individual. Thus, just as role entry may involve a long and arduous process of adjustment, so too may role exit.

Although there has been abundant research on the predictors of certain forms of role exit, particularly resignation, dismissal, and retirement (G. A. Adams & Beehr, 1998; Atchley, 1976; Beehr, 1986; Hom & Griffeth, 1995; Jackofsky, 1984), much of that research has focused on somewhat static factors such as job satisfaction and person–organization fit.

109

Comparatively little research has focused on the emergent phenomenology or *experience* of role withdrawal (Nicholson, 1987).

Furthermore, research on role exit (other than turnover) has been far less common than research on role entry (Ebaugh, 1988; Louis, 1980b). There seem to be at least two reasons. First, organizations appear to be more concerned with role entry than exit. Role entry represents the *promise of the future*: Individuals are hired, promoted, transferred, or even demoted to help the organization, and selection, training, and socialization may greatly facilitate their adjustment. In contrast, role exit represents the *termination or even failure of the past*: Individuals are fired or decide to quit or retire, or are promoted, transferred, or demoted to a new slot. It is often not appreciated that the nature and management of role exit tends to influence the nature of subsequent role entry and the morale of those who remain. Second, researchers usually find it easier to study incoming newcomers than outgoing veterans. Newcomers are often hired and begin en masse, providing a convenient sample, whereas veterans tend to depart singly (prominent exceptions include mass layoffs and fulfillment of terms) and often without much forewarning. Also, entry-level newcomers are often recent graduates of university, high school, or training programs, again providing a convenient source.

Because of this lopsidedness in research emphasis, there are far fewer models of role exit than role entry. Perhaps the most developed and best known model of the experience of (voluntary) role exit was articulated by Helen Rose Fuchs Ebaugh (1988). Accordingly, the following discussion of the social-psychological dynamics of disengagement from an organizational role is loosely organized around Ebaugh's model. First, I briefly discuss the origins of role exit to provide a conceptual framework for Ebaugh's model. Second, I discuss in detail each of the four stages of Ebaugh's model (first doubts→seeking and weighing alternatives→the turning point→creating an exrole). Third, I close by expanding her model to include involuntary role exit, "pull forces," and the effects of exit on those who remain.

ORIGINS OF ROLE EXIT

Figure 5.1 shows that role exit originates from two sources: The locus of change (intrarole vs. extrarole) and voluntariness (voluntary vs. involuntary). Regarding the locus of change, a role exit is the product of factors inherent in the role and its enactment (*push forces,* such as job dissatis-

Locus of Change

		Intrarole (push forces)	Extrarole (pull forces)
Voluntariness of Change	Voluntary	Resignation, Retirement (as escape from work role)	Resignation, Retirement (as attraction to other roles and activities)
	Involuntary	Individual termination, Mass layoff	Role progression, Failing health

FIG. 5.1.   Origins of role exit. (Note. All entries are illustrative, not exhaustive; the shaded cell is the primary focus of the Ebaugh, 1988, model.)

faction) or factors external to the role (*pull forces,* such as an inquiry from a headhunter), or both (March & Simon, 1958; Withey & Cooper, 1989). For example, Grove (1992) interviewed nurse practitioners about their occupational choice. Individuals who had been dissatisfied with their previous occupation as a nurse were likely to articulate their role transition as an active and rational attempt to upgrade their professional credibility and status: Dissatisfaction had mobilized them to seek change (push). Conversely, individuals who had been satisfied with being a nurse were more likely to describe their transition in passive terms, as an unexpected opportunity to make a job change (pull).

Regarding voluntariness, as discussed last chapter, a role exit may occur because a role occupant chooses to leave (voluntary) or because other influential individuals or uncontrollable forces necessitate that the occupant leave (involuntary).[1] The phenomenology of role exit is much different when one perceives that the change was voluntary. The illustrative cell entries in Fig. 5.1 show that resignation and retirement are examples of voluntary role exits that can originate from push or pull forces or both. Individual terminations and mass layoffs are examples of involuntary push forces. Finally, *role progression* (e.g., a medical intern becomes a resident, a university freshmen becomes a sophomore) and failing health are examples of involuntary pull forces. These examples represent

---

[1]Although voluntariness is a continuous rather than a dichotomous variable, Fig. 5.1 depicts it as the latter for ease of exposition.

tendencies in that they are often but not always true; for example, one may be coerced into accepting early retirement (involuntary) or one may deliberately make mistakes to induce termination (voluntary).

The Ebaugh (1988) model focuses primarily on intrarole and voluntary transitions, where doubts materialize in the role occupant and ultimately prompt a role exit. In terms of the phenomenology of role exit, this represents the most complex intersection of locus of change and voluntariness because much of the process is intrapsychic. Thus, the Ebaugh model provides the framework for the discussion to follow. Following this discussion, I briefly consider the phenomenology of role exit in the other three cells of Fig. 5.1.

Ebaugh's (1988) model is based on 185 interviews with a variety of "exs," including occupational roles (e.g., exnuns, exdoctors, retirees), family roles (e.g., divorced people, mothers without custody of their children), and stigmatized roles (e.g., exconvicts, transsexuals). For our purposes, a major strength of the Ebaugh model is her focus on the interaction of role and identity; indeed, consistent with the focus of this book, Ebaugh concentrated on exroles that had been central to the identity of her interviewees. The model is divided into four stages: First doubts, seeking and weighing alternatives, the turning point, and creating an exrole. I regard these stages as tendencies rather than as fixed and necessary steps that must occur. An overview of the model, adapted from Ebaugh, is presented in Fig. 5.2.

STAGE 1: FIRST DOUBTS

Precipitating Events

Individuals are often swept along by the demands and routines of everyday life and may not actively reflect on their valued identities, goals, and life trajectories (Langer, 1989). Thus, reflection is often prodded by events— from the momentous to the seemingly innocuous, from the expected to the unexpected, and from the highly negative to the highly positive—that interrupt the flow of life and prompt one to take stock (D. T. Hall, 1986; T. W. Lee & Mitchell, 1994). First doubts occur when one begins to question and possibly redefine previously taken-for-granted meanings.

What makes a given event a *precipitating event* is the meaning the individual derives from it. An event may produce a flash of insight or realization, what Denzin (1989) referred to as an *epiphany*. Denzin identified

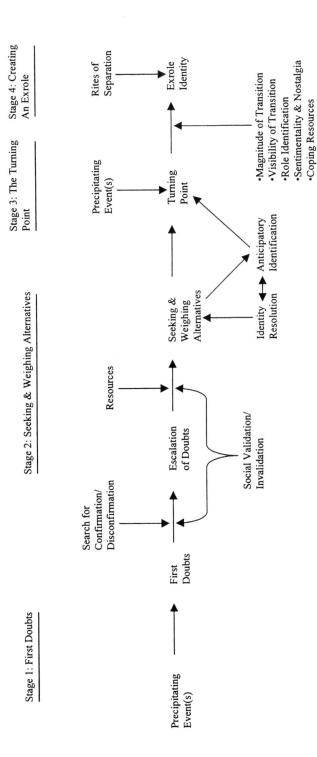

FIG. 5.2. The phenomenology of voluntary role exit. (Note. It is assumed that role exit results largely from push forces.) (Source: Adapted from Ebaugh, 1988.)

four types of epiphanies: (a) minor or illustrative, which reveal underlying tensions, (b) major, which provide moments of truth where the essence of something is revealed, (c) cumulative, where a series of events is revealing, and (d) relived, where one reexperiences an earlier epiphany. Whatever their form, epiphanies may plant seeds of doubt.

Epiphanies and thus first doubts may be triggered by a variety of events.

Disappointments. Because of the high importance accorded to securing a sense of salutary identity, meaning, control, and belonging in a role, doubts are most likely to arise when one has experienced a major disappointment, such as a poor performance appraisal, or a series of disappointments, such as snubs from peers and difficulties in mastering tasks.

Disappointment triggers attributional processes as one searches for an answer to the question, "Why did this occur?" (Wong & Weiner, 1981). According to attribution theory, the more that individuals attribute causality for the disappointment(s) to factors that are perceived to be global, stable, external, and uncontrollable (rather than specific, unstable, internal, and controllable), the more likely that they will conclude that they cannot solve the problem and the more likely they are to decide to exit the role (Martinko, 1995; C. K. Parsons, Herold, & Leatherwood, 1985). For example, Withey and Cooper (1989) found that low job satisfaction and the perception that the situation would not improve each predicted preparation for organizational exit. Thus, role exits are often prompted by a desire to address accumulated disappointments that appear likely to persist.

External Changes. Asking why a role or procedure exists may prompt the response, "Because it's always been done that way." In other words, the more institutionalized a role and its context appear to be, the more *legitimate* they appear to be (Ashforth & Gibbs, 1990). Institutionalization and legitimacy discourage public and collective dissent, thereby reinforcing institutionalization and legitimacy. Ironically, then, *it is precisely during times of change—whether positive or negative—that individuals and groups are most likely to question the status quo.* For example, Goffee and Scase (1992) found that organizational changes and uncertainty induced many managers to rethink their orientation to work and the organization, with some becoming self-employed. External change may help crystallize vague feelings of dissatisfaction, making them focused and salient, thereby galvanizing action. Thus, changes that are intended to better the lot of employees may make the context and nature of work more salient and cause them to question their commitment to it. The act of changing the status quo sensitizes individuals to other possibilities, to the limitless *potential* of change, such that the act may be seen as insufficient (hence the adage, let sleeping dogs lie).

Of course, external changes need not be planned or on a grand scale. Events such as the resignation of a valued peer, the death of a loved one, a sudden opportunity, the onset of a major illness, and so on may similarly provoke reflection and doubt.

Milestones. Milestones are significant signposts that punctuate or conclude a journey. Fulfilling a contract, accomplishing a goal, or simple anniversaries such as New Year's Day or one's date of hire, last raise, or birthday may trigger reappraisals. Milestones are often used as periodic respites, where the temporary cessation of normal activity allows one to reflect on the past, present, and future.

Complex and lengthy role transitions are often subdivided into a series of discrete and tightly structured steps, such as the progression from medical school to internship, to residency, to licensed practitioner. Structuring the process helps define short-term tasks and goals and instills a sense of predictability and progress, which in turn helps motivate the individual to undertake the arduous journey and persevere. However, the act of structuring socialization also creates natural breakpoints when one's goals and resources may be reassessed.

Similarly, symbolic occasions designed to dramatize and thereby heighten commitment may also unwittingly provoke a reassessment. Ebaugh (1988) interviewed exnuns who left the convent shortly before they were to pronounce their final vows. Rather than strengthening commitment, the act of publicly declaring commitment raised doubts in their minds. Such is the power of milestones.

Impending Events. Whether an event is an external change, milestone, or other type, the mere *anticipation* of it may precipitate doubts. Ekerdt and DeViney (1993) argued provocatively that as individuals approach retirement, they increasingly express discontent with the work role as a means of justifying their withdrawal. The justification enables individuals to resolve their inner conflict about leaving an otherwise desired role, allowing them to more easily accept and perhaps even embrace their impending retirement. Ekerdt and DeViney sampled men who were 50 to 69 years old and whose planned age for retirement did not change over the 9 years of the study. Controlling for various factors that could impair job involvement, they found that reported job tension and fatigue indeed became worse with increased proximity to retirement. Thus, as the time remaining dwindled, they appeared to reinterpret their work situations. Similarly, Karp (1985–86) reported evidence of an emergent "exiting consciousness" (p. 98) among academics in their 50s where "retirement has an unreality about it; it is paradoxically near and distant at the same time" (p. 100).

Internal Changes.   Finally, psychological changes may occur in the absence of a discrete and identifiable external event. Two common sources of internally generated doubts are *burnout* and what might be termed the *pendulum effect*. Burnout refers to the process by which demanding roles gradually drain emotional energy such that one becomes unable to perform effectively or derive satisfaction from the role (Maslach, 1982). As T. W. Lee, Mitchell, Wise, and Fireman (1996) noted, traditional models of turnover begin with some level of dissatisfaction. Ironically, it appears to be precisely those individuals who are most strongly—and exclusively—identified with their work role and committed to performing it well that are most susceptible to burnout (Ashforth & Humphrey, 1993; Hallsten, 1993).

The argument for the pendulum effect is that individuals tend to become more habituated to the positive qualities of the status quo than to the negative qualities. Through repeated exposure, the positive qualities come to seem normal and expected; less a privilege and more a right. The "honeymoon period" comes to a close (M. Kramer, 1974; see chap. 6). Thus, unless a role's attractive qualities are at least periodically reaffirmed (e.g., via social comparison, periodic celebrations), they tend to become somewhat taken for granted and fade in salience. A certain complacency and even boredom may set in. Conversely, research on information processing indicates that people attend and react more strongly to negative rather than positive information (e.g., León, 1981). Although a role's unattractive qualities may also come to seem normal and expected (Ashforth & Kreiner, 2000), they may remain somewhat salient if they are viewed as an ongoing problem. Indeed, issues that were once ignored or tolerated may begin to grate if the status quo persists. This potential shift in relative salience is often exacerbated by social information processes (Salancik & Pfeffer, 1978) as group norms frequently favor the expression of the negative in "gripe sessions" over more Pollyannaish sentiments ("Isn't this job wonderful?"; e.g., Collinson, 1992). The upshot may be a pendulum-like shift over time from a predominantly positive attitude toward the role and organization to a more negative attitude (hence the aphorism, the grass is always greener on the other side of the fence).

As either burnout mounts or the pendulum begins to swing, one becomes more inclined to interpret ambiguous events in a critical light and less forgiving of perceived slights. Goodwill accumulated earlier may be gradually exhausted such that one is less willing to concede the benefit of the doubt and ignore seemingly negative incidents. One may even become predisposed to a tipping effect where a seemingly small or innocuous event is perceived as "the last straw"—that is, the most recent negative event in a long series of events—and incites a reaction that is disproportionate to the event itself (Ashforth & Mael, 1998).

Again, what makes burnout and the pendulum effect insidious is that *the status quo may not have changed*: Instead, what may have once been regarded as generally positive now seems more negative.

Improving the Situation

The constructs of proactive behavior and role innovation are discussed in chapter 7. These constructs refer to the tendency of newcomers to attempt to actively manage their roles and the context within which they are embedded to better suit the newcomers' needs and preferences. Similarly, role occupants experiencing first doubts are inclined to attempt to manage the situation to address their concerns (Hirschman, 1970). However, such attempts are less likely to be successful if: (a) the individual has little power or the willingness or ability to wield power, (b) the individual is unsure of how to improve the situation, (c) the situation is institutionalized such that role set members are not sympathetic to the desire for change— or the situation, once changed, simply regresses to the prior state, and (d) the doubts are so many that idiosyncratic changes seem pointless. Given our current focus on role exit, I will assume that role changes are either not attempted or prove ineffective.

Escalation of Doubts

Figure 5.2 shows that the link between first doubts and the escalation of doubts is moderated by the search for confirming versus disconfirming information such that first doubts may escalate if confirmed and may deescalate if disconfirmed.

As first doubts arise, the individual may revisit his or her role history, looking for signs of corroboration. If found, the doubts may solidify such that the individual is apt to become less receptive to signs of disconfirmation and actively *seek* confirmation (Ruble, 1994). Indeed, critical events are often retrospectively inferred, assuming greater significance in hindsight than when they occurred. Once an individual is psychologically committed to exiting, he or she becomes adept at interpreting and reinterpreting circumstances in a way that supports the decision. Incidents that may have aroused little notice earlier are suddenly imbued with meaning. Ebaugh (1988) described how physicians who had earlier seen challenging cases as inherently stimulating came to see such cases as examples of the annoyance and stress of medicine once they began to entertain thoughts about leaving the field. Moreover, the escalation of doubts may spread from a specific focus—such as one's supervisor or tasks—to a more generalized sense that the role and organization are suspect.

What makes this escalation process perilous is that much of it transpires in the mind of the individual: As the process progresses, the subjective doubts may become less and less tightly coupled to current objective conditions. The process of convincing oneself that it is in fact desirable to leave a role makes one susceptible to strong perceptual and sense-making biases. The stronger the doubts become, the more *motivated* one is to validate the doubts by finding reasons to leave. For example, Farkas and Tetrick (1989) concluded from their study of U.S. Navy enlisted personnel that once the intention to quit or to stay crystallizes, job satisfaction and organizational commitment may be adjusted to bolster the intention. Indeed, objective conditions may be *improving* even as doubts are becoming stronger. This suggests that an individual is most likely to be receptive to reality testing and information about the environment early in the escalation process when emergent doubts are ill-formed and the individual is still reasonably impartial.

However, managers often fail to notice or deal with an employee's escalating doubts until they appear to be threatening the health of the employment relationship. Because of the incessant and often unpredictable demands of management, many managers come to operate reactively rather than proactively (Mintzberg, 1973). Moreover, it may be difficult for a manager to justify devoting resources to an issue until it has become defined as an organizational problem (e.g., a threat to quit). This same critical threshold, however, may signify that the individual has already withdrawn psychologically from the job. As a result, organizational attention and resources are often brought to bear *after* the point where they could have reversed the process. In fact, far from reinvigorating the employee, the belated attention often only arouses resentment and confirms the soundness of the doubts.

Ebaugh (1988) suggested that first doubts are associated with various *cues*, intended or unintended behavioral signals that commitment is perhaps flagging and that a change may be desirable. For example, exnuns that Ebaugh interviewed remarked that they wore their hair long and stylishly, contrary to traditional convent rules. Individuals may engage in such behaviors, perhaps unconsciously, for at least two reasons. First, overt acts of defiance may precipitate a response from the organization, thus bringing the issue to a head. By forcing a confrontation, individuals force a potential resolution of their ambivalence. If they are dismissed for their actions, the matter is resolved without actually having to make the difficult decision to leave. If they are not dismissed, they are forced to at least ponder their misgivings. Second, following self-perception theory (Bem, 1972), overt acts provide behavioral indicators that can be retrospectively cited by the doubters as evidence for both themselves and their social referents of their flagging commitment. In essence, the doubters are building a case against their own current social identity.[2]

Indeed, Ebaugh (1988) found that once the decision to exit a role was made, interviewees were adept at retrospectively finding cues in their previous behavior to justify the need for a change: "It was common for interviewees to point out early cues as a way of demonstrating that they were unhappy in their roles long before they made a conscious choice to leave" (p. 70). For example, a former police officer who was relieved to receive a medical discharge from police work (with a lifetime medical pension) remarked that he seemed more accident prone at times when he was frustrated with his work and wondered if he was really looking for a way out without losing his benefits. Similarly, an exprostitute interpreted her carelessness at becoming pregnant as a sign that she was becoming dissatisfied and wanted an excuse to get out. Such cues may or may not have actually been prompted by unconscious doubts: The point is that whatever their cause, the cues were retrospectively *interpreted* to have been prompted by such doubts.

Social Validation and Invalidation

As shown in Fig. 5.2, the escalation of doubt also tends to be moderated by social processes in that validation strengthens doubt and invalidation weakens it.

---

[2]A meta-analysis by Mitra, Jenkins, and Gupta (1992) yielded a corrected average correlation of .33 between absence and turnover, suggesting the possibility of a progression in withdrawal—or in the *inference* of withdrawal ("I've missed three days this month; I guess I don't like the job that much").

Because doubt and uncertainty are inherently anxiety provoking, individuals are motivated to resolve their doubts. The stress literature indicates that anxiety predisposes individuals to seek both instrumental and expressive social support (e.g., Beehr, 1995). Furthermore, because roles are embedded in often dense role networks and role occupants often form strong personal bonds through those networks, the opinions of certain role set members may matter a great deal. Thus, individuals experiencing doubt may actively seek and be particularly receptive to the opinions of their valued social referents—both inside and outside the role network.

Ebaugh (1988) found that sharing doubts served several purposes. First, it enabled reality testing. By its very nature, doubt renders an issue suspect, and doubters often feared they had a biased viewpoint. Doubters felt they could better assess the veracity of their emerging beliefs by comparing them to the perspectives of trusted others who were somewhat more distanced from the issue. Second, others could provide concrete advice, such as about alternative jobs. The more anxiety provoking the doubts, the more difficult it is for individuals to think clearly and realistically about a world beyond the immediate context. Indeed, high anxiety can incapacitate thought and action such that one simply avoids actively considering a dysfunctional situation (Fein, 1990). Ebaugh found that social referents were sometimes able to convince doubters that there were in fact viable options.

Third, expressing doubts serves a signaling function (Breese & O'Toole, 1995). The very act of going public confers weight and clarity on the doubts. As self-perception theory would suggest, the act of articulating doubts informs the doubter and audience alike that the doubts must have reached some threshold of severity to have warranted articulation. Moreover, in responding to the doubter, the audience confirms the reality of the issue and becomes implicated in its resolution. If the grounds for the doubts appear strong, it may prove embarrassing to do nothing or to later recant the doubts.

Depending on the response of the social referents, the initial doubts may be weakened or strengthened or sent into remission pending future events. Ebaugh (1988) provided exemplars of all three from her interviews with ex-police officers, exphysicians, and exnuns. The variance across cases attests to the power of significant others to shape one's very construction of reality (Hardin & Higgins, 1996). However, if doubts escalate, one is apt to seek out others who will *reinforce* the doubts, essentially echoing what one wants to hear, and to phrase doubts in a leading manner, inviting validation.

In sum, the doubting process looks much like a snowball gaining momentum as it runs downhill. After a certain point, the momentum is such that individuals are predisposed to seek and find confirmation for their incipient doubts, creating a self-fulfilling prophecy. However, it should be noted that Ebaugh (1988) found wide variance in the duration of the doubting process. Ebaugh argued that the duration is negatively related to the degree of one's awareness of doubts and one's control over the exit process and the degree to which doubting is externally cued, shared by one's peers, and validated by one's social referents.

STAGE 2: SEEKING AND WEIGHING ALTERNATIVES

As doubts crystallize, individuals may seek and weigh alternatives. The alternatives considered are strongly shaped by what is desired (that is, by what possible selves one wishes to realize; Markus & Nurius, 1986; cf. T. W. Lee & Mitchell, 1994) and strongly constrained by what is feasible (realistically available). Typically, individuals have only a vague awareness of alternatives (Ebaugh, 1988). In some cases, however, knowledge of specific alternatives may galvanize doubt by creating a salient contrast with the status quo. For example, knowledge of a friend's job may cause one to reappraise one's own job.

Ebaugh (1988) found that the degree of rationality involved in Stage 2 varied widely. Rational models of decision making describe a relatively complex process. For example, Janis and Mann (1977) proposed that decisions involve examining a wide range of alternatives, articulating objectives, weighing the pros and cons of each alternative, searching for and utilizing a wide array of information, reexamining alternatives, and developing implementation and contingency plans. Although this process may be followed for some highly consequential decisions where the individual has the required motivation and resources (particularly time and information), the model appears to be more normative or idealized than descriptive (Grotevant, 1987). Thus, Ebaugh (1988) found that:

> In most cases, the process of comparing a current role with role options took place in a vague and off-and-on way over a period of years until the pressures mounted or events occurred which significantly altered the perceived advantages or disadvantages of either the current or the alternative role. (pp. 95–96)

Ebaugh (1988) also found that only 12 of 185 (6%) interviewees left a role without considering alternatives. Given the gravity of most of the role transitions she studied (e.g., leaving a convent, getting divorced, having a sex change), this percentage may approximate the degree of preplanning in most organizationally based role transitions where one more or less identifies with the implicated roles. It seems probable that individuals will be *less* likely to actively consider work alternatives if: (a) they are reacting to an intolerable status quo where an uncertain future is preferable to an odious present, (b) the transition is thought to be reversible or of low magnitude, (c) they are highly confident they can secure a satisfactory alternative (e.g., high demand for employees, reliable job contacts, high self-efficacy; T. W. Lee et al., 1996), (d) they do not regard work as a central life interest (Hulin, Roznowski, & Hachiya, 1985), and (e) they are buffered during the transition by financial resources and social support.[3] It also seems probable that the greater and more generalized the dissatisfaction (i.e., attributed to the role identity or organization as a whole rather than to specific facets), the more likely the transition will be of a high magnitude (e.g., switching careers).

As noted, the alternatives considered are strongly influenced not only by one's possible selves but by pragmatic issues. A prime issue is the side-bets accumulated over time (Becker, 1960; Meyer & Allen, 1984), including personal obligations and ties, financial and job security, retirement benefits, perquisites, and sunk costs such as education and on-the-job learning that is specific to an occupation, organization, or industry. In addition, there are various psychological benefits of longevity and inertia, including predictability and stability and avoiding the unknown and the fear of failure. The longer an individual spends in a role, the more side-bets accumulate, and the more aspects of his or her life become intertwined with the role. This *role entrapment* creates strong inertia such that it often takes a powerful stimulus to provoke role exit (Ebaugh, 1988). Thus, in appraising alternatives, it is not simply a matter of which alternative offers the highest benefits for a given cost; the highest alternative must also offer a significant premium over the status quo to compensate for the foregone side-bets—unless the status quo has become so odious that the side-bets no longer matter.

---

[3]Although these predictors are additive, there are likely to be associations among them (e.g., individuals who do not regard work as a central life interest are less likely to have financial resources).

Resources and Social Validation and Invalidation

Figure 5.2 shows that the link between escalation of doubt and seeking and weighing alternatives is moderated by resources and social validation/invalidation. *Resources* refers to a variety of factors that affect information seeking and the desirability and feasibility of alternatives including personal networks, financial resources, geographic mobility, instrumental and expressive social support, and role-relevant knowledge, skills, and abilities. For example, consistent with the argument last chapter that low-magnitude transitions are less difficult, Ebaugh (1988) found that the transferability of skills and interests predicted the alternatives considered.

Expressive social support is an especially important resource. In particular, social validation/invalidation continue to moderate the causal links in Stage 2. As in Stage 1, individuals may display behavioral cues—perhaps more deliberately and provocatively than earlier—that both reinforce their doubts and induce responses from social referents. If the responses from valued referents are positive (validation), the individuals are more likely to continue to seek and winnow alternatives; conversely, negative responses may retard or derail the exit process (invalidation). For example, Ebaugh (1988) and San Giovanni (1978) found that familial disapproval and the likelihood of social stigma caused nuns to reconsider their desire to exit their convent, and Van Maanen (1983) found that police officers ridiculed peers who evinced a desire for upward mobility. Where a role transition is particularly unusual (e.g., a doctor becoming a realtor), interaction with—or at least knowledge of—others who have traveled the same road may help normalize the transition, making it seem more socially permissible and personally feasible.

Anticipatory Identification

As seeking and weighing alternatives becomes more concrete and thus more vivid and real, exiters report various emotional states from euphoria to tension (Ebaugh, 1988). For some, the anticipation of change fosters relief and calm, for others, confusion and anxiety. The more psychologically engaged the exiter becomes in future possibilities beyond the current role, the less engaged he or she remains in the current role. The psychological fulcrum shifts from the present to the future.

If the alternatives are winnowed to one or a few, the individual may begin to engage in *anticipatory identification* (Ashforth, 1998)—a specific aspect of anticipatory socialization (Merton, 1957b)—whereby one begins to internalize the attributes that are thought to define occupants of the envisaged role. Anticipatory identification may be facilitated by role rehearsal (Ebaugh, 1988) whether by imaginary or actual role playing (e.g., an employee considering returning to school full time may take night courses on a trial basis), by interaction with new role models, and by more indirect sources of knowledge about the role (e.g., prior experience in related roles). If the individual indeed subsequently enters the role, anticipatory identification can greatly facilitate adjustment *if* the identification is predicated on realistic information.[4] Conversely, identification predicated on misinformation, such as occupational stereotypes derived from popular culture, can seriously impair adjustment.

A major transition function served by anticipatory identification is a shift in reference groups from the current role to the anticipated one (Ebaugh, 1988; Levine, Bogart, & Zdaniuk, 1996). As the exiter becomes more concerned with the normative standards of the anticipated group, the current group loses its psychological and behavioral grip on the individual. Furthermore, the current group may sense the growing estrangement and reciprocate. Both processes enable the exiter to more easily cope with any resistance the current group may have to the transition and at the same time gain social validation from the anticipated welcome of the new group (or *actual* welcome if explicit overtures have been made). In Ebaugh's (1988) words, "the person, in a sense, psychologically becomes part of the group before he or she actually becomes a member" (p. 109). As such, anticipatory identification serves as a transition bridge.

I speculate that the greater the contrast between current and anticipated role identities (i.e., the greater the magnitude of the anticipated role transition), the more likely that anticipatory identification will be associated with *de*identification from the current role. Deidentification enables the exiter to gain some psychological distance from the current role. Perhaps surprisingly, I also speculate that the smaller the contrast in role identities, the more likely that anticipatory identification will be associated with *dis*identification on those attributes that most clearly differentiate between the role identities. As argued last chapter, although a small con-

---

[4]This analysis suggests that a major benefit of realistic job previews is that they provide informational hooks for anticipatory identification (e.g., Hom, Griffeth, Palich, & Bracker, 1998; Meglino, DeNisi, & Ravlin, 1993).

trast tends to ease the transition, the overlap somewhat blurs the role identities such that it becomes difficult to attain psychological distance. Thus, distance may be attained by disidentifying with whatever areas offer the highest contrast. As Elsbach (1999) argued, *"it is not organizations* [roles] *that are obviously in conflict with one's identity that are most likely to produce disidentification, but those that are distinct in important ways and confusingly similar in other ways"* (p. 172). For example, a brand manager switching employers may disidentify with attributes that are specific to her old organization and identify with attributes specific to her new organization.

Individual Differences

Identity Resolution.   Figure 5.2 includes a direct link between identity resolution and the seeking and weighing of alternatives. As discussed in more detail in chapter 7, *identity resolution* refers to awareness of one's own abilities, values, and interests (S. Gould, 1979; D. T. Hall, 1976). The greater one's awareness of what role identities best resonate with one's hoped-for self, the more focused the search will likely be for viable alternatives to the current role (Semmer & Schallberger, 1996). Identity resolution is also depicted as having a reciprocal influence on anticipatory identification. The greater the resolution, the more readily one may begin to identify with a hoped-for role: This anticipatory identification may in turn crystallize one's self-definition.

Role Identification.   Role identification *may* act as a significant brake on the process of role exit throughout the four stages. As noted, the stronger the identification, the greater the reluctance to exit the role. Thus, a role occupant may give the benefit of the doubt to the organization such that he or she ultimately becomes *immunized* to doubt, making excuses where others see none. In short, identification may render one unwilling or unable to raise doubts (Schwartz, 1987).

That said, it may also be in *precisely* those cases where identification is high that doubts are most quickly raised because one has a clear idea of what the role represents and thus how it "should" be enacted. Whistleblowers, for instance, may identify strongly with certain values undergirding their role identity (Near & Miceli, 1987). Moreover, role identification is often transferable to other organizations if the role is not unique to a particular organization (e.g., a pipe-fitter who is disenchanted with Exxon may move to Shell). Given the mixed impact played by role identification, it is not included in the model in Fig. 5.2—at least until Stage 4 (discussed later).

In sum, the process of seeking and weighing options generates concrete role alternatives to consider such that the exiter may begin to identify with a hoped-for role and de- or disidentify with the current role prior to actually departing. As the psychological fulcrum shifts from the present to the future, it can be said that role entry has already begun.

Finally, the more difficult the transition is expected to be, the more circumspect the search for alternatives and thus the longer the duration of this stage. Returning to Fig. 4.1, difficulty is associated with high-magnitude, socially undesirable, individual, and irreversible transitions and with short but unpredictable transition processes (one other condition, involuntary, does not apply to the adapted Ebaugh model). Ebaugh (1988) also found that social support facilitates and thus hastens the search process.

STAGE 3: THE TURNING POINT

Even with concrete alternatives in hand, Ebaugh (1988) found that "the vast majority [of role exiters] experienced a more abrupt and dramatic turning point in their decision-making process" (p. 125). Poised at the edge of a break, a final push was often needed to actually trigger the explicit act of leaving. A *turning point* is defined by Ebaugh as "an event that mobilizes and focuses awareness that old lines of action are complete, have failed, have been disrupted, or are no longer personally satisfying" (p. 123). A turning point usually culminates in an external expression of an intent to exit such as a letter of resignation.

As with the first doubts of Stage 1, a turning point is usually triggered by a precipitating event(s) (see Fig. 5.2), whether a disappointment, external change, milestone, impending event, or internal change. Whether large or small, multiple or single, or simultaneous or sequential, precipitating events symbolize and crystallize one's ambivalence and may signal the means for resolving it (Ebaugh, 1988). As noted earlier, an otherwise insignificant event may be perceived as "the last straw," occurring at a point when one is ripe to make a decision.

The event(s) may also provide a convenient excuse for leaving a role. Because roles are embedded in role networks, exiters are often very concerned about how valued members of their role set may construe the exit. Thus, Ebaugh (1988) recounted how physicians seized on health problems and police officers seized on injuries as justifications for exiting their professions because these issues were viewed by their respective role sets as socially acceptable reasons to quit.

To be sure, a role exit may *begin* with a turning point and thereby bypass the first doubt and seeking alternative stages. However, in the absence of first doubts, the event(s) must be construed as highly momentous to trigger a spontaneous exit (i.e., Denzin's, 1989, major epiphany). For example, T. W. Lee et al. (1996) described how a change in hospital policy prompted a nurse to quit immediately. Also, Fig. 5.2 shows that a turning point may occur independent of a specific triggering event(s), perhaps as a logical outcome of seeking and weighing alternatives or of the growth of anticipatory identification.

Regardless of the genesis, turning points often foster a veritable soup of emotions, most notably relief at having resolved the issue and at being released from the costs of the current role and excitement and apprehension at the prospect of beginning anew elsewhere (Ebaugh, 1988). Other common emotions include guilt over leaving the role obligations and ongoing ties with members of the role set, grief over the loss of insider status and all that it implies, and numbness if the precipitating event(s) and act of declaring one's decision are emotionally overwhelming.

Functions of Turning Points

Ebaugh (1988) argued that turning points serve three functions. First, they become the focal point for announcing one's decision to exit. Ebaugh found that many of her interviewees made their announcement within days of the event that finalized their decision and that the majority did so within a month. The act of publicly announcing one's decision further commits one to the exit (Salancik, 1977). Moreover, supporters offer assurances that the decision is correct, and detractors require the articulation of justifications—both of which further reinforce the decision.

Second, turning points help reduce cognitive dissonance (e.g., Vroom & Deci, 1971). Given the escalation of doubts and the knowledge of viable options, the individual tends to be in an anxiety-provoking state of ambivalence prior to the turning point. Turning points resolve doubts to the point where the individual feels able to make and declare a decision. However, the ambivalence is seldom resolved completely because most roles represent a complex package of costs and benefits. Indeed, the decision-making process may cause one to recognize the potential benefits that are now foreclosed (cf. regret theory, Loomes & Sugden, 1987).

Third, turning points help mobilize the necessary energy and resources to carry one through the exit: "The period of deliberation . . . is over and action is now required" (Ebaugh, 1988, p. 136). The act of declaring one's decision to exit commits one to act on the decision, thereby galvanizing effort toward actual exit.

Rites of Passage: Separation

As noted in chapter 1, rites of passage facilitate role transitions (van Gennep, 1960). In particular, rites of separation facilitate disengagement from a role (see Fig. 5.2). Disengagement is difficult for two major reasons. First, one is *defined* at least partly in terms of the role. The greater one's role identification, the more that the role identity specifies one's very sense of self (at least within the organizational context that cues the identity). Furthermore, one is defined by others in the organizational context largely by the roles one plays. Individuals in organizations tend to meet initially in the capacity of role occupants while fulfilling their role obligations. Thus, inter*personal* relationships tend to be built on inter*role* relationships. Consequently, a role exit jeopardizes the very basis and understanding of the relationship. A major function of rites of separation is to foster a redefinition of the individual as an *ex*role occupant—providing a natural breakpoint for either severing a relationship or redefining it so that it may proceed on another basis.

Second, as noted, roles are seldom perceived by their occupants as universally good or bad. Roles are comprised of many attributes—social networks, tasks, rewards, and so on—that provide various costs and benefits. Moreover, as explored in chapter 7, in attempting to adapt to a given role, individuals tend to personalize their role enactment (i.e., make it more compatible with their own preferences) and often come to value whatever compensations may be found. Finally, as also noted, there is usually anxiety about what the future might entail. Thus, even when one is leaving a generally undesirable role, there are often mixed feelings. For example, Schmid and Jones (1993) found that prison inmates felt somewhat ambivalent about their impending release from prison.

The stronger one's identification with the role and one's cohesion with members of the role set and the more difficult and negatively valent the anticipated transition (see Fig. 4.1), the more likely that one will experience a deep sense of loss (Archer & Rhodes, 1995; Fein, 1990)—even if the exit is voluntary. Thus, models of grief and mourning may help explain the psychological and social utility of rites of separation.

According to Bowlby's (1980) stage model of grief, a significant loss triggers shock (involving numbness and disbelief), yearning and protest (involving pangs of grief, anger, and possibly guilt), despair (involving depression and social withdrawal), and readjustment (involving redefinition of oneself and one's situation; cf. Freeman, 1999; Kübler-Ross, 1969). The first two stages are most applicable to involuntary exits (although the precipitating events in voluntary exits may themselves trigger shock and yearning and protest), whereas the last two stages are applicable to both involuntary and voluntary transitions. Experiencing these stages allows one to come to terms with the loss and let go of the object of mourning—the role.[5] Rites of separation focus the attention of the exiter and role set members on the fact that the exiter is leaving, enabling them to jointly acknowledge the transition and express their sorrow (Jacobson, 1996). As Ebaugh (1988) found, a "last glance backward is necessary before actually taking the leap forward" (p. 143).

M. W. Kramer (1993) and Narváez (1990) provide good examples of rites of separation. M. W. Kramer found that individuals who were being transferred often underwent a "loosening process" where they received congratulations on the transfer and expressions of regret about leaving, relayed task-related information to stayers, talked about the future job and their excitement and anxiety as well as their unhappiness at leaving their friends, and expressed thanks and goodbyes. Finally, a farewell event was usually held. Narváez described in detail such events at one company. The focal individual is roasted through good-natured and humorous speeches, often focused on a retrospective summary of his or her career, a serious and laudatory speech then follows, capped with a collectively purchased gift and a card bearing coworkers' signatures. The individual then responds with a speech that also mixes humor and sentiment, extolling the virtues of coworkers and affirming solidarity.

---

[5]Typical stage models of job loss include shock at learning of the loss, optimism about finding a new job, pessimism if no new job is found, and finally resignation if joblessness persists and one comes to accept it as long term or permanent (see the review by Fryer, 1985). These stages are roughly consistent with Bowlby's (1980) grief model. However, when role or organizational identification is strong, grief models better capture the profound sense of loss. Because one identifies with a *particular* role or organization, the bond cannot be easily replaced by another role or organization; in a real sense, one must grieve the loss before one can move on and identify again (Archer & Rhodes, 1995).

It should be noted, however, that despite the popularity of stage models of grief and job loss, empirical assessments of the models have been inconclusive (cf. Archer & Rhodes, 1987; Freeman, 1999; Fryer, 1985).

Such ritualistic social exchanges and events clearly mark and signal a major change in roles and relationships, thereby facilitating the transition. These rites acknowledge and celebrate the transition, allowing both the exiter and role set members to recognize the gravity of the event and allowing the role set to bless the actual change in roles. Both the exiter and role set attain *closure* on the relationship. Thus, *by celebrating individual discontinuity, social continuity is preserved.* One indicator that rites of separation are as much for the organization's sake as the individual's is that such rites are typically extended even to individuals who are disliked by their colleagues—although the execution of the rites may have a cursory and insincere tone (Jacobson, 1996; McCarl, 1984).

Unfortunately, as Savishinksy (1995) documented, organizations often do a poor job of utilizing the rites of separation. Savishinsky studied retirement ceremonies and concluded that formal and official ceremonies were often clichéd and stilted, with pallid speeches and impersonal gifts, officiated over by individuals who did not know the retirees beyond the work role. (Conversely, private and informal ceremonies organized by friends were far more personalized and meaningful to the retirees.) Atchley (1991) further noted that retirement ceremonies, and presumably other rites of separation, focus on the past rather than on the transition ahead. However, Savishinsky (1995) concluded, "whether hollow or not, the rite was still an important form of closure these retirees preferred not to forego" (p. 247)— attesting to the yearning for closure that role exit fosters.

Degradation Ceremonies.   It should also be recognized that the rites of separation may be used to coerce an individual into submitting to an involuntary and socially undesirable transition. Garfinkel (1956) referred to such rites as *degradation ceremonies.* A graphic example is reported by Johnson (1990). He found that during the final hours of the deathwatch, condemned prisoners awaiting execution are required to box their worldly goods; to have their head, face, and right leg shaved; to shower and don fresh clothes; to be weighed and photographed; and then to wait in an empty cell. These rites clearly signal the impending execution, thereby draining the condemned of hope and rendering him or her more compliant. As one officer put it:

> When you get to the point of shaving the man's head, that usually will take just about all the strength a man has out of him. It's not long before he actually becomes a walking dead man. Because he knows that there is no more hope after that point. (p. 92)

A more prosaic and widespread instance of ritualistic coercion is the treatment of many older employees. As Sonnenfeld (1988) documented, older employees are often incorrectly believed to be less productive and more resistant to change than their younger counterparts. Accordingly, many organizations have institutionalized policies that implicitly signal lower confidence in their older employees such as restricting certain training and promotion opportunities to younger employees. These policies, as meaning-laden rites, tend to become self-fulfilling: The older employee finds less reason to remain actively engaged in the organization and may internalize the label of *over the hill* (Ashforth & Humphrey, 1995). Thus, this tacit rite of separation may nudge the older employee to accept a retirement package and exit quietly.

The function of degradation ceremonies is to *separate* the person from the role: To dramatize the casting out or *excommunication* (Willmott, 1993) of the person for their real or perceived shortcomings. Degradation ceremonies thus uphold the standards and sanctity of the role and allow members of the role set to close ranks against the deviant (Gephart, 1978; Trice & Beyer, 1984).

In sum, a turning point is the critical moment when an individual realizes that leaving is the most viable solution to his or her discontents. A turning point may reflect a variety of exit trajectories from a major epiphany to a series of small epiphanies. Rites of separation publicize and sanctify the decision to exit, allowing both the individual and members of his or her role set to conceive of the individual as an ex-role occupant.

STAGE 4:
CREATING AN EXROLE

The physical role exit does not complete the exit process. Exiters must still come to grips with their prior role occupancy. What did the role mean to them? What portions of the role identity should they retain and what should they attempt to forget? How should they present themselves to others—should they play up or play down their past? (See chap. 8, "Identity Narratives.") As Ebaugh (1988) noted, "the process of becoming an ex involves tension between one's past, present, and future. . . . To be an ex is different from never having been a member of a particular group or role-set" (p. 149).

Individuals generally desire to retain aspects of their prior role that are socially desirable, that are expected to facilitate subsequent role transitions or adjustment to life in general, and that are prized or fondly recalled for their own sake. Conversely, individuals generally desire to shed those aspects that are socially undesirable, that are expected to impair future transitions and adjustment, and that are disliked or conjure bad memories. An intriguing research question is whether memory can be *willed*: Can an individual deliberately forget that which is inconvenient to the present or future? This question is discussed in chapter 7 under "Selective Forgetting."

Factors Affecting the Ease of Creating an Exrole

For now, six factors that affect the ease of creating an exrole should be noted: Two situational factors, magnitude of the transition and visibility of the role or transition; and four individual difference variables, role identification, sentimentality, nostalgia, and coping resources. These factors are depicted in Fig. 5.2 as moderating the link between the turning point and the formation of an exrole identity.

Magnitude of the Transition. The magnitude of the transition may simultaneously ease and impair the creation of an exrole. As discussed last chapter, high-magnitude transitions such as a shift from clerical work to high school teaching are more difficult to accomplish because the gulf between the old and the new role identities and contexts is so wide. It is difficult to apply the lessons of the old to the new and to retain those aspects of the old that one values. Individuals must actively work to reaffirm valued features of the old role identity and to maintain social connections with members of the old role set (hence the popularity of alumni associations, veteran's groups, associations of retirees, etc.). By the same token, however, the wide gulf makes it somewhat easier to distance oneself from those aspects of the old role that one wishes to disavow. In a real sense, the individual is free to reinvent himself or herself.

Conversely, low-magnitude transitions such as a promotion from vice president to senior vice president are less difficult to accomplish and they make it easier to actively maintain valued features of the old role identity and contact with valued members of the old role set. However, the very overlap in role identities and possibly contexts that facilitates the transition may create some blurring of the roles. The overlap makes it more difficult to distance oneself from undesired aspects of the old role. For example, a newly promoted manager may find it difficult to deal with her former peers in a superordinate–subordinate relationship: She is constrained by her role history. The quote that opened this chapter conveys the angst that this distancing may entail.

Visibility of the Role or Transition. The more visible the prior role or the transition, the more susceptible is one to the judgments and intrusions of others. For example, Ebaugh (1988) found that former occupants of highly visible roles such as opera singer, astronaut, and professional athlete had a particularly difficult time extricating themselves from their former roles. Presumably, their celebrity status was highly salient to members of the public, leading to intrusive conversations and questions and making it difficult for these individuals to distance themselves from their former roles. The past owned the present. Generally, visible roles or transitions that have a celebrity quality (e.g., athlete), are counternormative (e.g., a minister becoming a politician), relatively unique (e.g., opera singer), stigmatized (e.g., convict), or otherwise intriguing arouse people's curiosity—and the visibility of the role or transition enables some people to conclude they have the requisite personal familiarity and social right to approach the individual and start invasive conversations.[6]

A common response to unwanted intrusions is what Goffman (1963) referred to as *passing*, where individuals attempt to conceal the former role and pass as someone who did not occupy the role. Individuals may disguise or change their appearance or fictionalize their work history to gloss over certain roles. Breakwell (1986) added that individuals may vehemently disparage others who occupy the disavowed role as a way of affirming their distance from the role. Ironically, it is precisely their vehemence that betrays their former role occupation and their fervent desire to be perceived by themselves and others as *not* like others who occupy the role (Ashforth & Humphrey, 1995). Such individuals may be said to "protest too much." Ebaugh (1988) found that about half of the exnuns she interviewed "went wild in regard to clothes, makeup, and behavior" (p. 162) to distance themselves from the stereotype of nuns.

---

[6]I once spoke with a local TV newscaster who said that strangers often approached her in public and started conversations as if they were old friends. A popular topic among these "virtual friends" was the newscaster's appearance: They often offered unsolicited advice on her hairstyle, make-up, clothing, and weight.

Role Identification.   It was argued earlier that role identification
may act as a brake on role exit. Regarding Stage 4, identification may ease
or impair the creation of an exrole, depending on the situational *specificity*
of the identity. The more specific the identity, the less readily one can generalize one's identification to other social entities. Thus, the experience of
exiting an occupation, work group, or organization with which one
strongly identifies tends to be traumatic; in a real sense, part of oneself is
being left behind (Sherman, 1987; Taylor Carter & Cook, 1995). In such
cases, strong identification may make it difficult to gracefully exit the
role, to relax one's grip sufficiently to relegate the role to the past (i.e., create an exrole) and get on with one's life. Cassell (1991) commented on the
reluctance of many surgeons to retire:

> Surgeons have invested too much in becoming and being surgeons to con-
> template giving it up with equanimity. ("I feel like an amputee!" confided
> a surgeon who had recently retired.) Many surgeons find it difficult to cut
> back, to operate less frequently, or to confine themselves to less interesting,
> less challenging procedures. And, as patience and judgment falter, a sur-
> geon's arrogance may fill the void. (p. 147)

It is often very painful for members of the role set to watch someone
"hang on too long," denying that which is apparent to all.

Conversely, the more *generic* the identity (e.g., worker, team member)
or the features of the identity with which one identifies (e.g., an exdoctor
who identifies with the caring orientation of medicine), the more readily
one can transfer one's identification to other roles. The transferability of
the identity greatly eases role exit by enabling one to continue to derive
fulfillment after exit.

Sentimentality and Nostalgia.   *Sentimentality* is the tendency
to retain emotional or tangible ties to one's past (e.g., memories, memorabilia, old friends), or both, and to derive pleasure from discussing or reliv-
ing one's past, whereas *nostalgia* is a longing for a fondly remembered
past (Davis, 1979; Mael, 1988; Mael & Ashforth, 1992).[7] Both concepts
suggest a desire to at least periodically reaffirm previous attachments
whether or not the attachments have elapsed (e.g., reminiscing about one's

---

[7]Mael (1988) argued that sentimentality is correlated with identification as the tendency to form
strong ties suggests a propensity to identify. In support, Mael and Ashforth (1992) found a significant
association between sentimentality and college identification in a sample of alumni.

high school days). In the short run, sentimentality and nostalgia may render one less willing to exit a role and may make an exit more painful once the decision to exit has been made. In the long run, however, sentimentality and nostalgia may serve as transition bridges by: (a) encouraging one to properly grieve the loss of the role, thus enabling one to move on, (b) providing a sense of continuity between the past and present, and (c) providing a sense of confidence for the future ("Since that self dealt successfully with life's complexities, it can and will continue to do so," Ebaugh, 1988, p. 174; Davis, 1979). However, it seems likely that if the role contrast is great, nostalgia (although not sentimentality) may represent more of a retreat into a bygone past than a source of confidence for the future (e.g., Davis & Olesen, 1963).

Coping Resources. Armstrong-Stassen (1994) defined *coping resources* as "psychological, social, and organizational resources . . . which influence whether a particular coping strategy can or will be implemented" (p. 599). Earlier, I mentioned resources that affect the seeking and weighing of alternatives. Here, I focus on resources that affect the ease with which one may create an exrole. For example, psychological resources may include self-esteem and optimism; social resources may include instrumental and expressive social support; and organizational resources may include outplacement and referral services (e.g., Armstrong-Stassen, 1994; Latack et al., 1995; Wanberg, 1997). Although these resources have been researched primarily in connection with involuntary role exit, they are also likely to buoy the voluntary exiter as he or she endeavors to construct an exrole identity that serves the unfolding identity narrative. For instance, an optimistic individual may be more inclined than a pessimistic individual to conclude that the role facilitated his or her development and to search for and construct features of the exited identity that appear consistent with a hoped-for self.

Liminality

Rites of separation lead to a *liminal phase* (van Gennep, 1960) or *liminality* (V. W. Turner, 1969), from *limen*, Latin for threshold (V. W. Turner, 1969). In the liminal phase, the role identity of the individual is ambiguous: Having disengaged from one role or possibly multiple roles (e.g., job holder, work group member, organizational member) and having not yet engaged in a new role(s), he or she is roleless *in that social domain*. I emphasize "social domain" because the individual retains a store of other roles and associated social identities (e.g., family member, parishioner, friend).

Thus, "liminal entities are neither here nor there; they are betwixt and between the positions assigned and arrayed by law, custom, convention, and ceremonial" (V. W. Turner, 1969, p. 95). I would add that liminality, framed as a psychological concept, refers to the *experience* of this betwixt and between state, of being roleless. As such, this experience is not tied explicitly to physical role exit. Ebaugh (1988) found that three fourths of her interviewees experienced "the vacuum" (p. 143), as she put it, "either right before the decision to exit or in some cases shortly after" (p. 184), when they realized that leaving was distinctly likely. Indeed, I would argue that liminality exists when one lacks or soon expects to lack an actual role in the given social domain, or has a role but lacks even a mod-icum of identification—or disidentification—with it and does not expect to identify or disidentify with it.[8] As such, liminality is the absence of a self-defining connection to a given social domain and is represented by the indifference quadrant in Fig. 3.3.[9]

The experience of liminality depends largely on the value one places on the relevant social domain and on what is expected to come next. Consistent with the boundary conditions of the book (see chap. 1), I will assume that one indeed values the domain (in the case of work organiza-tions, that one views work as a central life interest). If one anticipates the assumption of a new role within a personally and socially acceptable time frame, then liminality may actually be experienced very positively.

Regarding the personally acceptable time frame, sure knowledge of a future role tends to trigger—as we have seen—anticipatory identification and socialization. This anticipation provides a frame of reference for the future and helps structure the present: Time is bounded and tasks need to be done. Thus, one may use the time to prepare (e.g., taking courses, becoming "psyched up"), attend to other matters (e.g., selling one's house), or simply relax. The key point is that one continues to *have* a defined role in that social domain, albeit delayed. Even if the role transi-tion is perceived to be undesirable, knowing one will have a defined role helps, nonetheless, to structure the present.

---

[8]It may seem odd to add disidentification to the mix. However, in a backhanded way, disidentifi-cation provides some sense of self-definition: One is *not* what the role identity implies. Thus, the role becomes a foil for defining the self, providing a tie of sorts to the work setting.

[9]However, it is argued later that one may create a specific *ex*role as a means of maintaining an identity connection to the domain—and thereby forestall liminality.

Furthermore, as a suspension of normal role-related activities, liminality facilitates a psychological and physical shift from the old role and its context to the new. Liminality provides time and psychological space to come to grips with the old before having to fully embrace the new. Grossman (1995) noted that soldiers returning home from war typically undergo "purification rituals" that allow them to decompress and attain some psychological closure and distance from the horrors they have experienced. For example, World War II soldiers returned on long troopship voyages, enabling them to grieve for their lost friends, vent their stress, and receive social support from their fellow soldiers. On returning, they were often honored with parades and other civic tributes that reframed the horrors of war as a heroic duty. Conversely, soldiers returning from their tour of duty in the Vietnam War were flown home within days or even hours of their last combat, without their buddies, and were denied tributes. In the absence of purification rituals, many Vietnam veterans had a difficult time becoming reintegrated into American society (e.g., Figley & Leventman, 1990).

Regarding the socially acceptable time frame, if one anticipates the new role within such a time frame, then members of one's role set within that social domain will have a firmer basis for interaction. As discussed in chapter 2, roles serve as prominent identity badges, enabling others to locate one in the social domain and develop preliminary perceptions and expectations of one, and perhaps provide a basis for more personalized relationships. In the absence of defined roles, there is less reason or opportunity to interact in any given milieu and less basis for developing initial perceptions. If one anticipates a new role, then members of one's role set are able to relocate one in the social domain and, if they so choose, reknit their interrole and interpersonal relationships on that basis.

Conversely, if one does *not* anticipate assuming a new role within that social domain within a personally and socially acceptable time frame, then liminality may be experienced very negatively. As Ebaugh (1988) put it, "the experience is best described as 'the vacuum' in that people [feel] 'in midair,' 'ungrounded,' 'neither here nor there,' 'nowhere'" (p. 143). Absent anticipatory identification, one has no basis for locating or anchoring oneself—or for others to locate one—in the current social domain. One is no longer a member and has no role-related basis for interaction. Indeed, in the case of work-based roles, one has no role-related reason for remaining in the organizational context. Thus, the ongoing social affirmation process on which role identities depend tends to be disrupted (Burke, 1991). If the social domain remains highly valued, the result may be a sense of disorientation (loss of identity), meaninglessness, lack of control and belonging, and perhaps depression.

Shield (1988) described how some nursing home residents viewed their life in the home as a painful liminal phase. Having forfeited the autonomy, privacy, goals, status, and prized trappings (e.g., home, car, money) that had signified their social identity as adults, the "resident is perceived as 'other'—neither adult nor dead" (p. 22). Although supported financially by the local Jewish community, members of the community tended to avoid contact with residents. Moreover, because the topic of death was taboo, residents could not prepare for the eventual resolution of their liminality.[10]

In the work domain, the social-psychological dynamics of liminality are perhaps most evident in cases of retirement and job loss.

Retirement and Job Loss. Although usually voluntary, full retirement represents a loss of work role identity along with the daily structure, social network, and status and perquisites of employment. Sonnenfeld (1988) studied the retirement of CEOs, an occupational group with particularly strong work role identification, and found that for many, "leaving office means a loss of heroic stature, a plunge into the abyss of insignificance, a kind of mortality" (p. 3). Similarly, Erdner and Guy (1990) found that work role identification was negatively associated with attitudes toward retirement.

Job loss also represents a threat to one's work role identity and the everyday structure and taken-for-granted meanings of work and home life (Fineman, 1983; Leana & Feldman, 1992; McFadyen, 1995; Price, Friedland, & Vinokur, 1998)—a threat that is compounded by the usually involuntary nature of the exit (as the next section discusses). A strong refrain in qualitative research on job loss is the experience of shock, emo-

---

[10]It could also be argued that prisoners, hospital patients, refugees, commuters, and even students are in a liminal phase in that they are "betwixt and between" the everyday permanent roles that signify adulthood (e.g., Mortland, 1987; Tsuda, 1993). However, the difference between nursing home residents and members of these other groups is that the latter anticipate—given certain positive events—a return to everyday life, thus bounding the liminal phase and rendering it more tolerable. In short, prisoners, patients, and the rest occupy transitional roles (see chap. 3) and may conceive of their role identities as temporary identities (see chap. 2). Note that they are unlikely to regard their identities as transitional (i.e., as a partially formed understanding and enactment of the role; see chap. 3) because the identities are not ends in themselves—although the individuals may learn much that is relevant to their future roles of exconvict, well person, and so on.

tional distress, and the disruption of "normal" life. For example, Leana and Feldman (1992) quoted one unemployed worker:

> I never dreamed of the drastic changes that would occur: the money prob-
> lems, arguing problems, tension between husband and wife, tension
> between parents and children, me working nights—my wife working days,
> constant strain on relationships, tears, my kids probably will not see college.
> (p. 51)

Retirement and job loss may also change the very meaning of home life. Work and home are often stereotypically perceived as opposites on many dimensions, such as instrumental (work) and expressive (home). The power of opposites is that each pole helps define and impart value to the other. For example, as suggested in chapter 2, at least part of the appeal of leisure (home) is that it represents an earned time out from wage labor (work). In retirement and unemployment, the yin of work no longer exists to help render the yang of home meaningful. Reflecting on his retirement, Fitzgerald (1988) wrote: "Now that the demands, expectations, implicit rules—the pushes and pulls of organizational life—had been removed, I was curiously disabled. . . . Now the freedom was here, it was without content" (p. 99).

The psychological impact of retirement and job loss—and more gener-
ally, of liminality—largely depends on how the individual *frames* the role exit (cf. cognitive/discrepancy appraisal; Latack et al., 1995; Lazarus & Folkman, 1984; McFadyen, 1995). The issue is not the voluntariness of the exit per se (although the negative effects of liminality tend to be exacer-
bated by involuntariness) but what the loss is perceived to mean and what is expected to replace the old role. Hepworth (1980), for instance, found that some unemployed men "felt bitter that they had been 'thrown on the scrap heap' and were rather depressed, but others (who were nearing retirement age) welcomed job loss for all the free time they had to pursue leisure interests" (p. 143). Thus, rather than view retirement and job loss as a prelude to nothingness, one may view them as a chance for change, growth, rest, time with family, or any other potential boon. The discontinuity is framed as an opportunity rather than a problem. This frame is more likely to be invoked and sustained if the individual can conclude that closure with the role had been more or less attained (e.g., job or career goals had been met, there were few further learning opportunities), if the old role had salient sources of dissatisfaction, and if the individual has the necessary resources (e.g., financial, social, informational, psychological)

to support the frame (e.g., Beehr, 1986; Latack et al., 1995; Leana & Feldman, 1992).

However, there are three key provisos to sustaining a positive frame. First, because retirement is normatively expected and sanctioned whereas job loss is not and because job loss is usually involuntary, it tends to be more difficult to invoke and sustain a positive frame for job loss. As with any precipitating event, one has to make sense of what has occurred. If a person incurring a job loss attributes it to *internal* causes (e.g., ability, effort), the attribution may undermine self-efficacy; if the person attributes the loss to *external* causes (e.g., foreign competition, incompetent management), self-efficacy may be preserved but the attribution may provoke feelings of insecurity (e.g., Prussia, Kinicki, & Bracker, 1993). Either way, the person must cope with a threat to their motives for identity and control and perhaps meaning and belonging (Feather, 1982; Leana & Feldman, 1992)—a threat that may be exacerbated by the unprofessional manner in which many people are let go (e.g., no advance warning or explanation, impersonal notification, callous attitudes, no outplacement or counseling; Latack & Dozier, 1986).

A second proviso to sustaining a positive frame is that it is difficult to do so unless one engages in complementary behaviors and receives social support. For example, a person who frames a layoff as an opportunity to change careers may succumb to anxiety and self-doubt unless he or she soon engages in concrete steps to change careers *and* is reinforced for doing so (e.g., invited to interviews; Wanberg, 1997).[11] Third, the adverse economic impact often associated with retirement and particularly job loss may simply overwhelm one's efforts to construct either event as a positive experience. Brief, Konovsky, Goodwin, and Link (1995) found that economic deprivation mediated the impact of unemployment on subjective well-being, underscoring the importance of a paycheck to most employees. As Brief et al. put it, "although 'man does not live by bread alone' (Deuteronomy 8.3), people cannot live without bread" (p. 707).

Ultimately, if individuals do not harbor expectations of a return to similar employment, they may engage in *role realignment* (Mutran & Reitzes,

---

[11]Research generally suggests that the length of unemployment is negatively related to psychological health (e.g., Hepworth, 1980; Kaufman, 1982)—although, as Breakwell (1986) noted, the length of time is less important than what happens during this period. Inactivity or a lack of success prolong the liminal phase, making it difficult for the individual to sustain his or her work role identity and confidence to enact the identity if an opportunity should eventually arise (Latack & Dozier, 1986; Latack et al., 1995).

1981). That is, they may implicitly lower the ranking of the work role (in the case of retirement) or the specific job or organization role that was exited (in the case of job loss) on their hierarchy of subjective importance and assign greater weight to other roles and personal interests and activities. As part of the grieving process mentioned earlier, the presumed importance of work or the specific job/organization may simply atrophy over time.[12] First, just as one may begin to identify with an anticipated role, one may begin to deidentify (or even to disidentify) with a role that one anticipates leaving—a process of *anticipatory deidentification.* For example, it was noted earlier that individuals approaching retirement increasingly express discontent with their work role as a means of justifying their withdrawal (Ekerdt & DeViney, 1993).

Second, after exit, one may discover new activities or value known activities more highly (L. K. George, 1983). As discussed in chapter 3, individuals tend to be very adept at finding value where they can. Indeed, individuals may sublimate their general or specific work role identities in other somewhat similar roles and activities (e.g., volunteer work, retraining; Taylor Carter & Cook, 1995). Research strongly indicates that the discontinuity of role exit is buffered by active engagement in other activities, whether instrumental (e.g., job search) or valued for their own sake (e.g., hobbies; Eby & Buch, 1995; Feldman, 1994a). Furthermore, many retirees opt for part-time or less demanding jobs as a form of bridge employment to facilitate gradual role realignment and adjustment to eventual full retirement (Feldman, 1994a).

Finally, as a transition bridge, one may reconstruct the role as an exrole per se (e.g., ex-IBMer, school alumni, former lawyer; J. D. Brown, 1991; Ebaugh, 1988). For example, Rousseau (1998) described how Arthur Andersen runs outplacement programs for its professional employees, including those who quit voluntarily: "The end result was a network of loyal 'alumni,' many placed in firms that were present and future clients of AA" (p. 229). Thus, rather than relegate the exited role to the past, one may transform it into that of the historical insider, the loyal alumnus. The exrole may or may not entail active duties (e.g., fund-raising for one's alma mater) and a unique identity (e.g., goodwill ambassador). It is the conception that one is a member of a legacy that ties the present to the past, thereby affirming the identity even after one no longer lives it (L. K.

---

[12]Individuals may also engage in short-term "job [role] devaluation" (Kinicki & Latack, 1990, p. 345; sample item, "Remind myself that a job isn't everything") to temporarily distance themselves from the lost role and thereby minimize the emotional impact of the loss (Wanberg, 1997).

George, 1983). Various symbolic gestures such as war veterans' parades and honorific titles (e.g., professor emeritus) may even institutionalize the exstatus, keeping the role identity salient and possibly active.

Thus, research indicates that many retirees and unemployed persons, including portions of Sonnenfeld's (1988) sample of CEOs, are able to not only bypass much of the negative impact of liminality but to view the experience in very positive terms (e.g., Atchley, 1976; Beehr, 1986; Eby & Buch, 1995).

In sum, the creation of an exrole pertains to coming to terms with the role exit: Deriving meaning from the experience that enables one to let go of the role and move on to other challenges. Thus, the creation of an exrole, and the process of role exit more generally are intimately connected with the process of subsequent role entry (or role realignment, in the case of full retirement and permanent job loss).

EXPANDING
THE EBAUGH (1988) MODEL

I noted that the Ebaugh (1988) model pertains largely to the voluntary–push forces cell of the 2 x 2 matrix shown in Fig. 5.1. This final section expands the Ebaugh model by briefly considering involuntary role exit, pull forces, and the effects of role exit on those who remain.

Involuntary Role Exit

This section focuses on the involuntary–push forces cell of Fig. 5.1, leaving the voluntary/involuntary–pull forces cells to the next section. In the context of involuntary role exits, push forces refer to those factors indigenous to the role or its enactment that prompt an exit, such as poor performance leading to individual termination or an excessive number of role occupants—as perceived by management—leading to a layoff.

A speculative model of involuntary role exit is summarized in Fig. 5.3, incorporating only the revised ordering of Ebaugh's (1988) four stages for ease of exposition (cf. Breese & Feltey, 1996). As Ebaugh argued, much of the role exit process depicted in Fig. 5.2 for voluntary exits occurs *after* the physical exit for those who leave involuntarily. The notice of termination is the de facto *turning point* and beginning of the model. The notice triggers attributional processes as individuals attempt to make sense of what is happening. Given self-serving biases, individuals are predisposed to attribute blame more to external causes (e.g., incompetent management) than to internal (e.g., poor performance; Ashforth, 1992; Feather, 1982). Moreover, individuals are likely to attempt to distance themselves from the role—or at least the organization—as a means of controlling their distress at the loss. The upshot of these tendencies is the *escalation of doubts*. The fact of role exit (the turning point) in conjunction with escalating doubts may in turn galvanize individuals to *seek and weigh alternatives*. Figure 5.3 shows the turning point and doubts exerting independent effects because the exit may compel individuals to seek new roles regardless of whether they are experiencing retrospective doubts about their prior role or organization. Finally, the turning point in conjunction with the doubts and alternatives may help individuals in *creating an exrole*. The fact of exit, the growing retrospective doubts, and the consideration of concrete alternatives each help individuals to come to terms with their former role and the involuntary exit.

In addition to the revised ordering of Ebaugh's (1988) four stages, the model of involuntary exit differs in three key ways from that of voluntary exit. First, involuntary exits from push forces tend to be stigmatizing, creating the additional burden of coping with the weight of shame and other emotions (Ashforth & Humphrey, 1995). Second, involuntary exits often come with little or no advance warning, creating the burden of shock and distress (Fineman, 1983; Leana & Feldman, 1992), as noted earlier. Third, because of these two factors, individuals often must exit one role with no clear alternatives in sight, exacerbating the sense of discontinuity and liminality that often attends role transitions—particularly if the individuals are compelled to find work in other occupations or industries. The upshot of these three factors is that involuntary exit often constitutes a significant threat to one's identity and sense of meaning, control, and belonging.

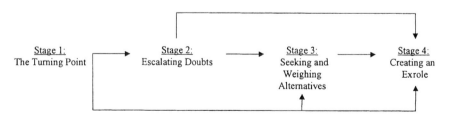

FIG. 5.3.   The phenomenology of involuntary role exit. (Note. It is assumed that role exit results largely from push forces.)

Consequently, as shown in Fig. 5.3, the impact of each stage on future stages of the involuntary exit process is not fully mediated by the intervening stages, as in the model for voluntary exit. For example, the turning point (Stage 1) exercises both direct and indirect effects on all subsequent stages. It was argued that in voluntary exits, individuals usually take a more reflective approach, moving more or less methodically from first doubts, to seeking and weighing alternatives, to the turning point, to creating an exrole.[13] However, in *involuntary* exits, the often unexpected displacement forces individuals to scramble to make sense of and adjust to their changed circumstances while simultaneously attempting to exit one role and enter another. This shock and truncation of time may create a cacophony of emotions and actions such that the impact of the four stages is telescoped and jumbled.

Pull Forces

In reality, most voluntary transitions are a combination of push and pull forces. As discussed, push forces foster a desire to seek and weigh alternatives, thus helping to pull one out of the role. As noted, only 6% of Ebaugh's (1988) sample exited without considering alternatives. Similarly, an initial set of pull forces, such as an unexpected call from a headhunter, may cause one to reflect on the status of the current role, fostering dissatisfaction and thereby galvanizing or pushing one toward role exit. Indeed, it could be argued that there is no such thing as a pure case of voluntary role exit caused by pull forces. Pull forces exert their pull precisely because they represent an opportunity not found in the current role: Thus, one's perception and evaluation of the status quo are at least implicit in every voluntary role exit.

In the case of *involuntary* transitions, however, pull forces provide little or no opportunity to remain in the current role. For example, turning down a promotion or transfer may imperil one's standing in the organization, and failing health may impair one's ability to perform effectively. There are two major sources of pull forces: Factors extrinsic to one's career, such as failing health or a spouse who is transferred, and factors intrinsic to one's career (but by definition, extrinsic to the current role per se), such as a promotion or role progression. The social-psychological dynamics for pull forces extrinsic to one's career are similar to those dis-

---

[13]Again, these are modal tendencies rather than universal principles.

cussed for involuntary transitions prompted by push forces except that the attribution of causality tends to be much clearer.

In contrast, involuntary exit prompted by pull forces intrinsic to one's career is considerably eased by three factors. First, the transition is usually socially acceptable if not desired. Thus, the sting of loss may be cushioned by the anticipated challenges and gain in status and perquisites. Second, the transition is likely expected (although the specific job and location may not have been), thereby allowing some anticipatory identification with the future role and anticipatory deidentification (and perhaps disidentification) from the current role. Lennox (1992) studied a 6-week, full-time police executive development program. Although the executives had developed strong cohesion during the program, as the end neared, they referred increasingly to their departures, their work at home, and their families. Third, given that the future role likely builds on the lessons of the current one, one's current role identification may generalize quite readily to the future role (although the loss of one's work group and other attachments may continue to cause distress). Thus, an apprentice mechanic may exit the apprentice role quite seamlessly.

Effects of Role Exit on Those Who Remain

Because roles are embedded in role sets and role-based relationships often become suffused with interpersonal affect, role exits also tend to affect those who remain. Exits trigger sense-making processes: "Why did she leave? Are the reasons relevant to me? If so, what should I do?" (Brockner & Wiesenfeld, 1993). A voluntary exit implicitly threatens the meaning and sanctity of the role identity precisely because the exiter has *chosen* to forsake the role—at least in that specific context.[14] The more that sense-making attributions center on aspects of the role, group, or organization

---

[14]The threat to occupants of *other* roles in the role set tends to be less marked because the differences between roles typically lessen the relevance of the comparison (Wood, 1989). For example, a secretary is likely to feel more threatened by the voluntary exit of another secretary than of an office clerk. A major exception occurs when the exiter is the manager (or more generally, occupies a relatively powerful position in the role set). Because one's manager essentially personifies the organization or subunit, is thought to have inside information about the future of the organization or subunit, has formal authority over the role set, and has the power to change the way the subunit and roles operate, managerial role transitions are usually scrutinized very intensely by members of the role set ("Is the department in trouble? How will the new manager differ from the old? Will I get along with the new manager? How might he or she change things?"; e.g., Ogawa, 1991).

rather than on idiosyncrasies of the exiter, the greater the threat. Under such conditions, factors that increase the relevance and salience of the exit to those who remain will further increase the implied threat. Consequently, the threat will likely be strong if: (a) the role identity is widely shared and deeply held by role occupants, (b) the role identity is perceived to be relatively unique, (c) the exiter is perceived to be similar to other role occupants or to personify the role identity, (d) the exiter played a central part in the network of roles and is well regarded (i.e., high status and well-liked), and (e) the actual exit is highly salient.

The greater the threat to the role identity, the more likely that role occupants will rethink their involvement in the role. Indeed, a highly salient and unpopular exit that seems to impugn the role, group, or organization may precipitate a rash of exits. Krackhardt and Porter (1986) found evidence of a *snowball effect,* where turnover in three fast food restaurants tended to occur in clusters. This is one more reason for the widespread use of organizationally sanctioned rites of separation: They facilitate the *control* of information—and thereby, attributional processes—by management ("Sue is leaving for health reasons"). Thus, rather than constituting a threat to the role identity, an exit may be framed as a *reaffirmation* of the identity ("Sue exemplified good performance"; Jacobson, 1996; cf. McCarl, 1984).

If a voluntary exit threatens the meaning and sanctity of the role identity, an *involuntary* exit threatens the security of the role itself and the tenure of those who remain. Once again, attributions are paramount. At one extreme, research indicates that if the survivors of a layoff attribute the cause of the layoff (the why) to managerial incompetence or misconduct or construe that the layoff process (the how) was handled unfairly (as noted earlier, no advance warning, impersonal notification, etc.), their trust in management—and thereby the safety and status of their own role in the organization—may be badly shaken (Brockner & Wiesenfeld, 1993). Survivors may worry about their own future and view it as less controllable. Ironically, although not surprisingly, it is precisely those survivors who identify most strongly with the role and organization that are most likely to feel threatened and become upset by perceptions of wrongdoing or unfairness (Brockner, Tyler, & Cooper-Schneider, 1992).

At the other extreme, it is likely that if layoff survivors attribute the cause to the failings of the laid off role occupants and perceive the process to have been fairly handled, their sense of security and faith in their role may remain intact. Bourassa and Ashforth (1998) reported that the role identification of novice fishers was initially *strengthened* by the selective firing of peers. The terminations appeared to reaffirm the norms and standards of toughness that were central to the fisher identity (Dentler & Erikson, 1959). Indeed, the fishers may have been eager to "blame the victims" of the firings to enhance their own sense of control over their destiny.[15]

Effects on Interpersonal Relationships. Whether voluntary or involuntary, role exits necessarily disrupt the pattern of interrole relationships. Earlier, I discussed how these disruptions give rise to rites of separation and liminality. Here, I would like to underscore that inter*personal* relationships in organizational settings are typically predicated on inter*role* relationships such that role exit imperils both. In the absence of an ongoing role-based reason for interaction and of the organization as a common ground for conversation, the physical and perhaps psychological distance created by role exit may cause people to drift apart—despite their best intentions. This *interpersonal drift* is most evident in high-magnitude transitions, particularly where: (a) one enters a role that is the foil or antithesis of the role that was exited, such as a line worker becoming a foreman (see the quote that began this chapter, and see chap. 8, "Role Reversals"), (b) there are major changes of locale or accessibility, making it difficult to sustain relationships, and (c) there are major changes in status and perquisites, creating a disparity between previously equal peers. Schmid and Jones (1993) discussed how

> [prison inmates'] estrangement from their outside social network . . . took place through a gradual process in which inmates and their families and friends, while trying to support or reassure one another, recognized that they were living in separate worlds, mutually withheld certain types of information, and eventually found that their communication was becoming increasingly constrictive. (p. 461)

In short, role transitions may strain interpersonal relationships so that individuals once defined as friends are seen less and less often and perhaps not at all (R. L. Kahn & Antonucci, 1980). Thus, role transitions can undo friendships as surely as they can make them.

---

[15]Ultimately, however, several seemingly capricious terminations caused the fishers to rebel against their captain. Consistent with Brockner et al.'s (1992) findings, it was the most senior fishers—and presumably the most strongly identified and loyal—who led the rebellion.

CONCLUSION

Much of the chapter focused on voluntary exits prompted by push forces because this tends to be the most phenomenologically complex exit process. Despite the complexity of the model in Fig. 5.2, the process boils down to a sense-making exercise where the individual seeks to resolve doubts that may emerge. The nature of these doubts depends largely on how well role-related events and the role identity appear to resonate with the individual's valued or hoped-for selves. However, the sense-making process is not necessarily a rational one. Individuals may display cues (deliberately or not) that become self-fulfilling, they may rely heavily on the views of social referents, they may face resource constraints, and—as they begin to resolve their doubts—they may seek to confirm rather than disconfirm their suspicions.

Given that social identities essentially tether an individual to a given social domain, a major challenge of role exit is to reconnect with the domain (if desired) and thereby resolve one's liminal status. Indeed, as will become more evident in the two chapters to follow, psychological exit often continues after physical entry into the next role, just as psychological entry usually begins before physical exit from the old.

6

Role Entry:
Situational Context

Sergeant Carey moves the platoon across the asphalt at a crawl, correcting hand movements, straightening arms, aligning files, enforcing forty inches of separation between each rank. The platoon finally arrives at the mess hall. There Sergeant Carey uses the wait in line to initiate [platoon] 3086 into another aspect of Marine boot camp's Zen-like fetish for minor details, in which not a single action is left to individual improvisation. The mess hall tray is to be held with arms flush at the side, bent ninety degrees at the elbow, he instructs. But there is more to it than that. "You will hold your tray this way: thumbs on the outside," he continues.
—at a U.S. Marine boot camp (Ricks, 1997, pp. 63–64)

My first night in the joint was spent mainly on kicking myself in the butt for putting myself in the joint. It was a very emotional evening. I thought a lot about all my friends and family, the good-byes, the things we did the last couple of months, how good they had been to me, sticking by me. I also thought about my fears: Am I going to go crazy? Will I end up fighting for my life? How am I going to survive in here for a year? Will I change? Will things be the same when I get out?
—a prison inmate (Schmid & Jones, 1991, p. 418)

These two quotes illustrate the theme of this chapter: The power of the situational context to influence not only one's role behavior but one's thoughts, feelings, and even one's self-concept. First, I revisit the notion of strong situations and discuss the potent effects that control systems may have on the newcomer. Second, I briefly discuss how entry shock predisposes newcomers to situational influence. Third, these discussions of strong situations and entry shock set the stage for a discussion of socialization tactics: It is argued that these tactics are largely responsible for galvanizing personal change. Fourth, I examine how rites of transition and incorporation facilitate role entry. Fifth, as a kind of chapter summary, I argue that strong situations also effectively normalize the extraordinary such that individuals may become capable of a wide range of behavior, including immoral acts.

149

These arguments are complemented by those in the next chapter. Chapter 7 continues the discussion of role entry but focuses less on the situation and more on the power of the individual as a proactive agent in his or her own role learning and innovation. Together, chapters 6 and 7 suggest that personal change and role innovation are a common and often *positively* correlated response to role entry.

A boundary condition of this chapter and the next is that newcomers remain in the role during the entry period. I recognize that newcomers who feel mismatched, are deemed by the organization to be inadequate, or who do not wish to pursue the various dynamics of role entry may simply exit the role (whether voluntarily or involuntarily). In short, role exit is an alternative to role entry dynamics, except for certain involuntary transitions (e.g., imprisonment).

STRONG VERSUS WEAK SITUATIONS

In chapter 1, a situation was said to be strong when there is a clear consensus on the right way and wrong way to behave. Strong situations demonstrate the potential power of the context to condition behavior, thought, and feeling—to condition the very way that individuals conceive of themselves.

Two Classic Illustrations

The power of the situation to shape incumbents' role identities is illustrated by two classic studies, one an experiment, the other a field study. The Stanford County Prison experiment is described by Haney, Banks, and Zimbardo (1973; Haney & Zimbardo, 1973). College students living in the Stanford University area were recruited for a study of prison life. Based on a battery of psychological tests, a sample of normal and healthy males was selected. Half were randomly assigned to the role of guard and half to that of prisoner. Local police arrested the prisoners at their homes and booked them at the local precinct. The experimenters transported the prisoners to a mock prison located at Stanford. Prisoners wore a stocking cap, a loose-fitting smock with an identification number on the front and back, and an ankle chain. Guards wore a khaki uniform and sunglasses and carried a whistle and night stick. The guards' task was to "maintain the reasonable degree of order within the prison necessary for its effective functioning" (Haney et al., 1973, p. 74), but minimal guidelines were provided.

The experimenters soon found that encounters between guards and prisoners tended to be negative, hostile, and dehumanizing. Guards relied on impersonal commands ("You there") and verbal aggressiveness, redefined prisoner's rights (e.g., eating and sleeping conditions) as privileges that had to be earned, engaged in petty and capricious behavior, and escalated their harassment of the prisoners over time—even after most prisoners had stopped resisting. The most hostile guards on each of the three shifts became leaders and role models. Norms of toughness quickly solidified, and guards who resisted these dynamics nonetheless never interfered with the actions of their more hostile peers. For their part, prisoners initially expressed disbelief and rebelliousness but soon became passive and isolated. Half became "extremely disturbed emotionally" (Haney et al., 1973, p. 95) and others became excessively obedient. Prisoners and guards alike became caught up in the moment as many "ceased distinguishing between [their] prison role and their self-identities" (p. 89). Indeed, "fully 90% of all conversations among prisoners were related to prison topics" (p. 86), and prisoners appeared to internalize the guards' negative attitude toward them, as 85% of the evaluative statements about fellow prisoners were uncomplimentary and deprecating.

Given that minimal behavioral guidelines were provided for the guards, it might seem odd to label this experiment an example of a strong situation. During postexperiment interviews, most guards said they were "'just playing the role' of tough guard" (Haney et al., 1973, p. 93). However, their initial stereotypic projections of the guard role quickly became the normative reality, shaping their behavior just as surely as the prisoners'. Abuse had become institutionalized.

In the second study, Lieberman (1956) surveyed the attitudes of factory workers toward the company and union in late 1951 and again in late 1952. In the interim, 23 workers had been promoted to foreman and 35 had been elected as union stewards. Lieberman found that whereas the attitudes of the 23 soon-to-be foremen were indistinguishable from those of the 35 soon-to-be stewards in 1951, there were marked differences in 1952 *after* the role transitions. The groups had polarized in opposite directions, with the newly promoted foremen becoming relatively more promanagement and the newly elected stewards becoming relatively more prounion.

Subsequently, a recession forced 8 of the 23 foremen to revert back to the worker role, and 14 of the 35 stewards returned as well to the worker role. Lieberman (1956) found that the foremen who remained foremen retained or increased their favorable attitudes toward management, whereas the attitudes of the demoted foremen reverted partially toward their prior level. However, the attitudinal changes among the stewards were less pronounced. The overall results suggest that the role changes triggered commensurate attitude changes. Lieberman attributed these effects to what he termed the *self-consistency principle* (self-coherence in the language of chap. 3), that is, the desire to attain congruence among the behaviors and attitudes implied by a role.

Although these two studies are cited here as examples of strong situations, two provisos are warranted. First, it should be noted that not all participants reacted alike. Thus, even in roles where strong norms and rewards and punishments prevail, there typically remains some latitude for individual discretion in the enactment of the norms.[1] The main point is that the stronger the situation, the less real latitude one has. Second, except for involuntary transitions, individuals *choose* to subject themselves to these situations: This implies some initial affinity for the implied role identity, if not for the situation that conveys it.[2]

Strong Situations: External and Internal Control

What accounts for the strength of the situations in these two illustrations and countless others? Newcomers encounter a strong situation to the extent that there are control mechanisms for imparting and reinforcing a clear conception of what is expected. Formal control mechanisms, particularly hierarchical (supervision), technical (machinery and operating procedures), and bureaucratic (policies, job descriptions, and rules) controls, can be characterized as *external* controls in that the individual is not required to believe in or internalize them as necessary and appropriate but

---

[1]Moreover, in attempting to coerce change, strong situations may provoke strong resistance. In effect, strong situations compel one to either capitulate or fight. Because of the constraints on overt resistance in organizations, *covert* resistance and both voluntary and involuntary turnover (where turnover is an option) are likely to be prevalent. However, Ashforth and Mael (1998), Goffman (1961a), and Kunda (1992) argued that it is precisely because individuals facing strong situations often engage at least periodically in covert resistance that they are more willing to overtly accept the status quo. Covert resistance reassures individuals and perhaps their peers that they are not management's patsies.

[2]I once spoke with a Canadian soldier who said his chief regret during basic training was that his drill sergeant had *not* been particularly ornery. The soldier had joined the army expecting the heavy dose of discipline for which armies are stereotypically known.

merely to conform to them. "Simply stated, the hands matter, but the head and heart do not" (Ashforth & Mael, 1998, p. 92). External controls are most likely to be found in entry-level positions within large bureaucratic organizations facing relatively stable and simple environments (Mintzberg, 1979)—such as insurance companies and conventional auto plants—because of the resulting stability, clarity, observability, and measurability of tasks and because large organizations are more likely to have invested in an infrastructure of formal control. Conversely, the further removed positions are from the entry level and the smaller and more organic the organization, the more ambiguous, dynamic, interdependent, and difficult to observe and measure the tasks tend to become—and the less applicable are external controls (Ouchi, 1980).

This discussion suggests two conclusions. First, newcomers to the world of work are more likely to encounter a strong situation in the form of external controls than are more experienced individuals undergoing, say, a promotion or transfer. Second, individuals in large or bureaucratic organizations are more likely to encounter external controls than are individuals in small or organic ones. However, both conclusions are subject to a huge proviso: Organizations are increasingly recognizing the efficacy of *internal* control mechanisms, also known as *cultural, social, concertive, unobtrusive,* or—henceforth—*normative* control (Barker, 1993; Bullis & Tompkins, 1989; Kotter & Heskett, 1992; Kunda, 1992; O'Reilly & Chatman, 1996; Willmott, 1993; see Fig. 6.1). Normative control is referred to as internal control because once internalized, it is experienced not as externally imposed but as freely chosen. Because normative controls may not only complement external controls but serve as a partial *substitute*

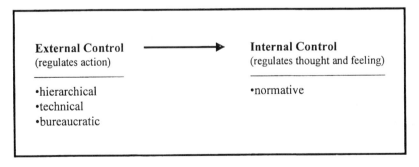

FIG. 6.1. External and internal control. (Note. The arrow signifies the growing use of internal control.) (Reprinted from B. E. Ashforth & F. A. Mael, in *Power and influence in organizations*, p. 93, copyright © 1998 by Sage Publications, Inc. Reprinted by permission of Sage Publications, Inc.)

for them (Barker, 1993; Kunda, 1992), they are amenable to a wide variety of organizational forms, including small and organic ones.

Normative Control. External controls tend to be difficult and expensive to institute and maintain. Furthermore, because they often enshrine the status quo, they are becoming less relevant to a dynamic world of protean organizations and individuals. Finally, they are likely to provoke the resistance noted in footnote 1 precisely because they are experienced as imposed rather than freely chosen. Ironically, however, normative control is potentially *more* invasive because it focuses on thought and feeling in addition to behavior, on the very way that an individual conceives of the organization and his or her role within in. Kunda (1992) defined normative control as "the attempt to elicit and direct the required efforts of members by controlling the underlying experiences, thoughts, and feelings that guide their actions . . . a sort of creeping annexation of the workers' selves" (pp. 11–12).

Normative control is imparted through the well-known practices of symbolic management, including mission statements, strategies, stories, rituals, advertising, physical setting, and role models (Ashforth & Mael, 1996; Cheney, 1991; Czarniawska, 1997; Pfeffer, 1981; Rosen, 1985; Rousseau, 1998). These practices, coupled with certain external controls (e.g., reward systems, information systems, budgets), convey the organization's identity—its central, distinctive, and enduring values, goals, beliefs, assumptions, and norms (Albert & Whetten, 1985).[3] Research suggests that individuals identify more strongly with entities that convey a relatively distinct identity (Dutton et al., 1994; Elsbach, 1999; Pratt, 1998; Wan-Huggins, Riordan, & Griffeth, 1998). For example, Iannaccone (1994) found that the more distinctive the practices of Christian and Jewish denominations (e.g., diet, dress, grooming, social customs), the more likely that members were to attend religious services, contribute money, choose friends from the religion, be less involved in competing activities, and describe themselves as strong members.

Research further suggests that individuals are more willing to identify with organizations that convey a relatively prestigious identity (Dutton et al., 1994; Elsbach, 1999; Pratt, 1998; Wan-Huggins et al., 1998). Thus,

---

[3]It should also be noted that normative control can form from the bottom up, particularly in new, organic, and turbulent organizations (Weick, 1996). For example, Barker (1993) described how members of self-managing teams improvised guidelines that soon came to be seen as strong norms. The team members had, in effect, constrained the very behavior that "self-management" ostensibly liberated.

Ashforth and Mael (1996) argued that organizational identities—and by extension, role identities—tend to selectively embody "transcendent moments [whether actual or hoped for] of exemplary service, competitive coups, major product innovations, and so on that represent the organization at its finest" (p. 31). Organizational members essentially collude in the promulgation of attractive role and organizational identities as a means of feeling good about their membership and themselves. As somewhat idealized claims to certain values and goals, the espoused identities may resonate with prospective members, attracting recruits and encouraging anticipatory identification.[4]

The impact of distinctiveness and prestige on identification is likely mediated by three mechanisms: (a) the motives for identity and meaning (see chap. 3), (b) the visibility of the identity, and (c) behavioral commitment (cf. Pratt, 1998). First, distinctive and prestigious organizational and role identities are more likely to address individuals' motives for identity (i.e., self-distinctiveness and self-enhancement) and meaning (i.e., meaningfulness). Moreover, following Schneider's (1987) attraction-selection-attrition model, distinctive identities act as a beacon, attracting and retaining those people for whom the practices and what they signify accord with personal needs. O'Reilly and Chatman (1996) further noted that cults, cult-like firms, religious organizations, and mutual help organizations[5] often select individuals who have similar values to the organization's or whose circumstances may render them willing to identify with the organization (e.g., lack of industry experience, undergoing a personal transition).

Second, the distinctiveness of the practices (e.g., wearing ringlets) creates a marked perceptual contrast between members and nonmembers, heightening the visibility of the identity. The social world becomes divided into insiders and outsiders, and neophytes see themselves—and are seen by others—as the former. As a result, "potential members are forced to choose whether to participate fully or not at all" (Iannaccone, 1994, p. 1188).

---

[4]Because attractiveness exists in the eye of the beholder, a given identity may well repulse many even as it attracts others. What matters for the organization and role is that the identity attracts a sufficient number of qualified people who, if necessary, can tolerate the disdain of others. Thus, organizations such as the NRA can achieve many of their legislative goals even while antagonizing much of the public (Davidson, 1993).

[5]O'Reilly and Chatman (1996) argued that the difference between these organizational types is not so much the techniques of normative control—the techniques are remarkably similar across these organizations—but the content or nature of the identities, the intensity of the indoctrination, the tolerance for deviation (at least on the means for realizing the identities), and the openness of leaders to dissent and change.

Third, the very act of engaging in the unusual practices further commits neophytes to the organization (Pratt, 1998; Salancik, 1977). Altering their social identity thus justifies and normalizes the behavior.[6] O'Reilly and Chatman (1996) noted that cult-like organizations use multiple recruiting and orientation steps (e.g., visits, interviews, training) to escalate individuals' commitment to the organization. Research on the foot-in-the-door phenomenon (e.g., Dillard, 1991) indicates that small, incremental, and seemingly innocuous decisions and actions—each intended to resolve a specific and immediate issue—can gradually lead one down a path that one would have strongly disavowed if one had truly realized the ultimate end (e.g., Milgram, 1974).

Normative Control and the Local Context. Because thought, feeling, and behavior tend to be shaped by proximal forces (i.e., immediate, pressing, and salient concerns) and proximal forces are in turn shaped by more distal ones, *the impact of control is largely mediated by the local context.* In particular, the actions of an individual's managers and peers tend to have an enormous impact on the experiences of the individual and the meaning he or she derives from them. Managers and peers *personify* and thus instantiate the organization; in a real sense, they *are* the organization.

In strong situations, control practices often unfold in a "social cocoon" (Greil & Rudy, 1984, p. 260) where: (a) managers and peers model the espoused role and organizational identities, (b) newcomers are encouraged to affiliate and form personal attachments with peers, (c) newcomers are subjected to a strong and consistent informational context such that doubts are resolved and mixed messages are absent—thus normalizing practices that may seem bizarre to outsiders, and (d) newcomers receive frequent social rather than pecuniary reinforcement (e.g., recognition, group approval) for displaying an acceptance and adoption of the espoused role and organizational identities (Cushman, 1986; O'Reilly & Chatman, 1996). The cocoon creates intense and relentless pressure to adopt the espoused role and organizational identities.[7]

---

[6]However, as discussed in chapter 3, there is likely to be an optimal level of distinctiveness for any given organization or role (Brewer, 1993; Iannaccone, 1994). That is, the organizational or role identity must be sufficiently distinct to attract certain individuals but not so distinct that too few are attracted to sustain the organization.

[7]The cocoon also reinforces the socialization of the change agents themselves. In extolling and modeling the virtues of the role and organizational identities, the agents are reminded of why the identities may matter to them and they become publicly committed to the identities (Feldman, 1994b; Sutton & Louis, 1987). Guimond (1995) referred to this notion that socializing others also socializes oneself as the "responsibility hypothesis" (p. 265).

Thus, normative control, as reflected in symbolic management and certain external controls and enacted locally, shapes how individuals make sense of the organization and their role within it. The stronger the normative control, the more that individuals are induced to accept the espoused identities as self-defining—that is, to identify with them and remake themselves in the image of the desired member. Normative control insinuates itself into one's workplace identity such that to resist it is to be at war with oneself (Ashforth & Mael, 1998; Kilduff, Funk, & Mehra, 1997; Kunda, 1992; Willmott, 1993).

It can be seen, then, that normative control addresses the four psychological motives of chapter 3: (a) for identity (by inducing a fusion of self and role and organization), (b) for meaning (by facilitating sense-making and, via goals and values, by providing a sense of meaningfulness), (c) for control (by inducing one to "choose" to internalize the role and organizational identities and consequently, by allowing one to experience as one's own the power and successes of the role's incumbents and predecessors as well as of the organization), and (d) for personalized and depersonalized belonging (by providing a cohort of similarly identified organizational members). It is this fusion of individual and organization that makes normative control so appealing to organizations (Ashforth & Mael, 1998). Moreover, as organizations continue to gravitate from bureaucratic to organic structures to cope with growing environmental complexity and dynamism, this form of control will become increasingly attractive.

In summary, external and—increasingly—internal controls are being used by organizations (and subunits and other collectivities) to fuse individual and role and organizational identities. The stronger the controls, the less latitude the individual retains for thinking, feeling, and acting—for conceiving of himself or herself as different and separate from the organization and role.

ENTRY SHOCK

As Bauer et al. (1998) noted, stage models of socialization are quite similar and tend to recognize three distinct stages: (a) anticipatory socialization, where individuals prepare for role entry, (b) encounter or accommodation, where individuals actually enter and confront organizational realities, and (c) metamorphosis, role management, or mutual acceptance, where individuals adapt to and modify their role (e.g., Feldman, 1976; Nicholson & West, 1988; Porter, Lawler, & Hackman, 1975; Schein, 1978; Van Maanen, 1975). Although evidence for distinct and fixed stages that generalize across various roles and organizations is mixed (Bauer et al., 1998; Fisher, 1986), the three-stage notion does provide a useful heuristic for the trajectory of role entry: Preparing, encountering, and innovating. The theme of encountering is pursued later, and that of innovating is picked up in chapter 7.

Unrealistic Expectations

The more socially desirable, voluntary, and irreversible a transition is perceived to be, the more likely that one will enter with high expectations. Social desirability fuels positive expectations, and the act of voluntarily engaging in an irreversible transition effectively commits one to the role and organization such that potential drawbacks are apt to be minimized or rationalized away to reduce cognitive dissonance (Vroom & Deci, 1971). Furthermore, the greater the magnitude of the transition and the less experience one has, the less likely is one to be knowledgeable about the new role and organization. Accordingly, one's initial expectations may be based on unreliable sources such as cultural stereotypes, the beliefs of friends and families, tangential experiences, and projected hopes and fears. Finally, recruiters tend to portray their organizations and available jobs in a positive light, contributing to high expectations.

The net effect of these tendencies is that newcomers to a role often have unrealistic—especially unrealistically high—expectations (Wanous, 1992). On the one hand, these expectations may create an initial *honeymoon effect* (Fichman & Levinthal, 1991; Helmreich, Sawin, & Carsrud, 1986; M. Kramer, 1974), where the desire to think well of the role and organization buffers one from less positive discoveries and where the realization of at least some of one's expectations produces a sense of delight and harmony. High expectations function much like trust in that one is motivated to give the benefit of the doubt to the role and organization to preserve the sense of harmony and the hoped-for relationship (S. L. Robinson, 1996).

On the other hand, the more unrealistic the expectations, the more difficult it is to minimize the discrepancy, provoking a sense of *entry shock* (also known as *reality shock* and *role shock*; Hughes, 1958; M. Kramer, 1974; Minkler & Biller, 1979). The more important a given expectation is to the individual and the greater the discrepancy, the greater the shock. Indeed, the experience of disappointment may fuel a sense of violation precisely because the individual initially trusted the organization to meet his or her expectations (Rousseau, 1995). Thus, positive expectations are double-edged: They make the role and organization attractive but if not met, they may ultimately undermine the individual–organization bond. Not surprisingly, then, research indicates that unmet expectations tend to erode newcomers' attachment to the role and organization (Wanous, Poland, Premack, & Davis, 1992). For example, Holton and Russell (1997) surveyed university students 1 year after graduation who reported that they were employed in a position appropriate for starting their career. The researchers found that individuals who felt their position was not what they had anticipated having (despite its career appropriateness) reported more stress and difficulty with the role transition and lower job satisfaction and organizational commitment. Conversely, Hom et al. (1998) found that realistic job previews (RJP) reduced voluntary turnover among nurses, and Buckley, Fedor, Veres, Wiese, and Carraher (1998) found that a RJP and an expectation-lowering procedure (ELP; where the likelihood and negative effects of inflated expectations are openly discussed) each reduced turnover among assembly line workers. The RJPs and ELP presumably deflated expectations so that they were more likely to be met.

It is important to note that despite the negative connotation of the term *entry shock* and the tendency in the literature to treat shock as necessarily undesirable, not all seemingly undesirable discontinuities are actually *experienced* as undesirable (see chap. 4, "Socially Desirable Versus Socially Undesirable Transitions"). For example, Suedfeld (1991) noted that solitary confinement in prisons has been roundly criticized based on faulty analogies from the literatures on social isolation and sensory deprivation. In actuality, convicts frequently find solitary to be a pleasant time-out from the constant dangers and demands of prison life. The defining feature of entry shock is the element of *surprise*—as Louis (1980a, 1980b) termed it—that is, the discrepancy between expectations and experiences. In terms of Lewin's (1951) model (see Fig. 1.1), either negative or positive entry shocks may unfreeze the individual, provoking sense-making processes and thereby the potential for learning and personal change.

Outsiders Versus Insiders. Most of the research on entry shock has focused on individuals moving into entry-level positions from outside the organization. Given that the magnitude of the transition contributes to the likelihood of unrealistic expectations, it is not surprising that outsiders often experience considerable shock. However, it is important to note that because roles differ in kind and not just degree, insiders are also likely to experience some degree of entry shock.

This argument is illustrated by L. A. Hill's (1992) research. She found that salespeople promoted to first-line management encountered major surprises in their first weeks on the job. Promoted because of their sales achievements, they had enjoyed relatively positive and nonproblematic relationships with their former managers. These experiences shaped their expectations such that they were surprised by the amount of time they had to devote to remedying poor subordinate performance.

L. A. Hill's (1992) study highlights several features of insider entry shock. First, role transitions initiated by management are often based on success in a former role(s). Managers often assume that success inheres in the person and is thus generalizable to new and often radically different situations. Because actual success is based instead on the interaction of person and situation, this may be a dubious assumption. Second, because promotions are usually offered to employees with superior performance, new managers may have little experience dealing with problematic performers—a major preoccupation of management. Third, individuals tend to draw inferences about a prospective role from the necessarily myopic perspective of their own role-bounded dealings with role occupants and from vicarious observation and information. As an observer looking in, the inferences and information may be unreliable and may fail to capture the visceral scope of the role. Finally, given that inside transitions are often encouraged via carefully graded ladders of status and perquisites, there is a tendency to glamorize the role. As noted last chapter, individuals are predisposed to see that "the grass is greener on the other side of the fence." Thus, L. A. Hill described how the salespeople fixated on the apparent power and autonomy of the managerial role identity but when they were promoted, they soon realized that managers are highly dependent on others and operate within considerable bureaucratic constraints.

The upshot is that insiders are often woefully unprepared for new roles: Entry shock is not the exclusive province of outsiders.

An Intellectual Versus Visceral Grasp of the Role. As noted earlier, one's preconceptions of a role may be based on vicarious learning. Although social learning theory clearly indicates that a great deal of learning occurs vicariously (Bandura, 1977), much of this learning must remain abstract and intellectualized until put into practice. It is very difficult to anticipate, in a realistic and visceral sense, the holism and immediacy of a rich and dynamic context and one's experience of it: An intellectual grasp is a necessarily pale imitation of an experiential grasp

(Fazio & Zanna, 1981).[8] Thus, even if one has a fairly realistic intellectual understanding of a role, one may be unprepared for the actual experience of the role.

Reed (1989) described the discomfort he felt as a hospital orderly when he first had to perform certain duties such as inserting a catheter in a patient's penis. Much of the discomfort occurred because Reed, as a newcomer, automatically imported his everyday interpretations of objects and events. Thus, as a heterosexual male, it was disconcerting to handle another man's penis. Only with experience and socialization did he come to internalize the occupational frame for making sense of and fully accepting his own behavior:

> The workers do not have to reconcile feeling one way about an event in the outside world and another way about an event within the work setting, since they become in fact different events. The workers do not have "ordinary" reactions, because they do not encounter "ordinary" events. (p. 79)

In short, experience facilitates a visceral understanding and acceptance of the role and its identity such that to cue the role identity is to cue a particular frame of reference that may be at odds with one's other less salient role identities.

Receptiveness to Personal Change

The upshot of entry shock is that individuals quickly learn that portions of their expectations and perhaps prior learning are invalid. As in the case of first doubts discussed last chapter, this shock triggers attributional processes as individuals search for reasons why the shock occurred and what to do about it. In short, entry shock predisposes newcomers: (a) to role learning and role innovation (the focus of chap. 7) as they attempt to make sense of the situation and, if possible, rework it to better suit their preferences, and (b) to personal change, discussed later, as they themselves are "reworked" to better understand and suit the situation. In short, unmet expectations may provoke *both* role innovation and personal change (M. West & Rushton, 1989)—although unmet expectations are not a necessary precondition for either.

---

[8]Hence the utility of internships, apprenticeships, interim positions, relief assignments, job rotation, and other means of allowing "real" experience in a protective (e.g., closely supervised, temporally bounded) atmosphere (e.g., Blau, 1988; M. S. Taylor, 1988).

SOCIALIZATION TACTICS

Socialization is the process through which individuals learn the values, beliefs, norms, skills, and so forth that are necessary to fulfill their roles and function effectively within the local context and wider organization (Fisher, 1986; Van Maanen & Schein, 1979). Socialization includes orientation, training, apprenticeship, buddy, and mentorship programs as well as more informal on-the-job learning.

The significance of entry shock to the socialization process is that it stimulates all four of the critical motives (and thus the willingness to be socialized): (a) to locate and learn one's role within the organizational context (identity), (b) to make sense of the situation and discern a purpose for being there (meaning), (c) to recover a sense of self-determination (control), and (d) to connect with others, particularly one's peers (belonging). The significance of situational strength to the socialization process is that the greater the use of external and internal controls in the process, the more regimented are early role experiences and the lessons to be drawn from those experiences. The remainder of this chapter focuses on how socialization and normalization processes affect role adjustment and identification and thus personal change (however, a discussion of individual differences that are relevant to personal and role change is deferred until the next chapter).

Strong Situations: Institutionalized Versus Individualized Socialization

Van Maanen and Schein (1979; Van Maanen, 1982) proposed that organizations—and by extension, subunits and occupational training schools—use at least six socialization tactics to shape experience and learning. Each tactic consists of a bipolar continuum, as depicted in Fig. 6.2. These six tactics subsume the various processes noted earlier—orientation, training, apprenticeship, and so on.

First, as noted in chapter 4, *collective (vs. individual)* socialization consists of grouping newcomers and exposing them to a common set of experiences rather than treating each newcomer individually and exposing him or her to more or less unique experiences. Management training programs often involve extended stays at a training center where trainees are grouped in classes. Second, *formal (vs. informal)* socialization is the practice of segregating a newcomer from regular organization members during a defined socialization period versus not clearly distinguishing a newcomer from more experienced members. Army recruits must attend boot camp before they are allowed to work alongside established soldiers. Boot camp allows recruits to make mistakes and learn in a relatively safe training environment. Third, *sequential (*vs. *random)* socialization refers to a fixed progression of steps that culminate in the new role, compared to an ambiguous or dynamic progression. The socialization of doctors involves a lock-step sequence from medical school, to internship, to residency before they are allowed to practice on their own.

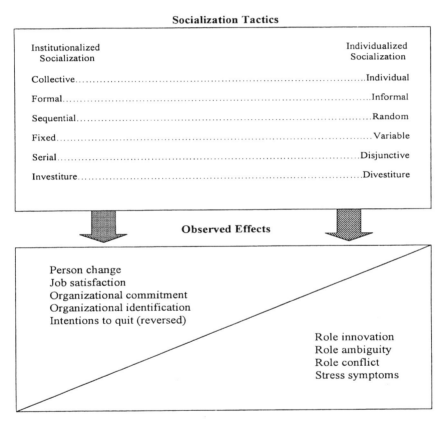

Socialization Tactics

Institutionalized Socialization	Individualized Socialization
Collective	Individual
Formal	Informal
Sequential	Random
Fixed	Variable
Serial	Disjunctive
Investiture	Divestiture

Observed Effects

Person change
Job satisfaction
Organizational commitment
Organizational identification
Intentions to quit (reversed)

Role innovation
Role ambiguity
Role conflict
Stress symptoms

FIG. 6.2. Socialization tactics and their observed effects on newcomers. (Note. Investiture [vs. divestiture] is negatively related to person change; although individualized socialization is positively related to role innovation, institutionalized socialization is not necessarily inconsistent with role innovation.) (Reprinted from B. E. Ashforth & A. M. Saks, 1996, "Socialization tactics: Longitudinal effects on newcomer adjustment," *Academy of Management Journal, 39,* 149–178. Copyright © 1996 by the Academy of Management. Reprinted by permission of the Academy of Management via the Copyright Clearance Center, Inc.)

Fourth, *fixed (vs. variable)* socialization provides a timetable for the assumption of the role, whereas a variable process does not. American university students typically spend 1 year apiece as freshmen, sophomores, juniors, and seniors. Fifth, a *serial (vs. disjunctive)* process is one in which the newcomer is socialized by an experienced member, whereas a disjunctive process does not use a role model. Mentorship programs pair a newcomer with a veteran so that the former can hopefully bond with the latter and learn an insider's perspective. Finally, *investiture (vs. divestiture)* refers to the affirmation of a newcomer's incoming global identity and specific role identities and attributes. Organizations use executive search firms because they wish to hire individuals with certain aptitudes and knowledge. Conversely, divestiture is the denial and stripping away of the newcomer's existing sense of self and the reconstruction of self in the organization's image. During police training, cadets are required to wear uniforms and maintain an immaculate appearance, they are addressed as "officer," told they are no longer ordinary citizens but are representatives of the police force, their behavior is closely scrutinized and regulated, and they are subjected to rigorous discipline (Rachlin, 1991).

Ashforth, Saks, and Lee (1997) argued that the collective, formal, sequential, fixed, and serial tactics (and at times the investiture tactic, see next section) provide a relatively *structured* program of socialization because they deliberately segregate newcomers from veterans, involve a well-defined series of stages that unfold according to a set timetable, and utilize a mentor or role model. In short, these tactics *are a major vehicle for both external and internal control* and thus facilitate a relatively predictable role transition. Indeed, Jones (1986) labeled these six tactics *institutionalized socialization* because the structuring of early experiences and their interpretation tend to encourage newcomers to passively accept preset roles and thus maintain the status quo. (However, as argued in chap. 7, institutionalized socialization can be used instead to convey a more innovative orientation to work.)

Conversely, at the opposite end of the continuum of tactics, individual, informal, random, variable, and disjunctive socialization (and perhaps divestiture, see next section) reflect a relative *absence* of structure and may occur more by default than by design (Ashforth, Saks et al., 1997). Thus, the contours of role transitions are relatively unpredictable. Jones (1986) labeled these tactics *individualized socialization* because the absence of structure encourages newcomers to question the status quo and develop their own approaches to their roles. Thus, Ashforth and Saks

(1996) found that individualized socialization was positively associated with both attempted and actual role innovation 4 months after role entry and actual innovation 10 months after entry.

A growing body of research indicates that compared to individualized socialization, institutionalized socialization is associated with lower role ambiguity, role conflict, and intentions to quit and higher job satisfaction, organizational commitment, and organizational identification (see Bauer et al., 1998, and Saks & Ashforth, 1997, for reviews). Thus, consistent with the argument in chapter 4 that newcomers prefer predictable transitions, newcomers appear to desire and respond well to the clear structure that institutionalized socialization provides. However, most of this research has focused on young people who are relatively new to the workplace. It is highly likely that experience in organizational settings and the knowledge and confidence it provides serve to some extent as substitutes for the external and internal control provided by institutionalized socialization. "Indeed, the welcome security that institutionalized socialization initially represented may come to represent smothering paternalism" (Ashforth & Saks, 1996, p. 172).

Two tactics, investiture (vs. divestiture) and serial (vs. disjunctive), are particularly relevant to how socialization affects newcomers' role identity and propensity to identify and are elaborated on next.

Investiture Versus Divestiture

Research generally indicates that with the exception of investiture/ divestiture, the socialization tactics tend to cluster as Jones (1986) predicted (i.e., collective, formal, sequential, fixed, and serial vs. individual, informal, random, variable, and disjunctive; Ashforth, Saks et al., 1997). Bourassa and Ashforth (1998) speculated that investiture is positively associated with the tactics of institutionalized socialization in most organizations (consistent with Jones, 1986) but *negatively* associated with institutionalized socialization in certain other organizations. Investiture affirms and builds on the incoming identities and attributes of newcomers and is thus favored by mainstream organizations because their proffered role and organizational identities tend to be more or less consistent with the newcomers' incoming identities. An insurance firm hiring a business school graduate from Jones' (1986) sample is presumably looking to utilize and reinforce the knowledge and skills learned in school rather than challenge them.

Conversely, organizations are likely to actively attempt to strip away newcomers' incoming identities if those identities contradict—or are at least radically different from—the role and organizational identities and newcomers appear unable or unwilling to divest themselves of those identities and their various "bad habits" in a timely manner. Divestiture facilitates both de- and disidentification such that these habits are not simply forgotten but *unlearned* (Hedberg, 1981).[9] The more central the habits are to the newcomers' incoming identities, the more assertive the divestiture. Thus, divestiture is prevalent in such distinctive settings as military boot camps, organized religion, and commercial fishing (Bourassa & Ashforth, 1998; Bruder, 1998; Ricks, 1997). At the level of the role, divestiture is also more likely to be prevalent where individuals are highly interdependent for safety and performance, as in construction and shop-floor teams (Collinson, 1992; Riemer, 1979), and for economic well-being, as in a union. Here, divestiture tends to focus on aspects of identity related to the interface between peers because peers need to know that they can count on one another to act a certain way.

Although divestiture is likely more prevalent in high-magnitude role transitions (because prior learning is not as helpful) and involuntary and socially undesirable transitions (because newcomers are more resistant to change), these are not necessary factors. Regarding magnitude, as discussed last chapter, disidentification is often needed where the magnitude of change is actually *low* (e.g., a professional athlete changing teams in midseason) because the newcomer may easily regress to his or her former role identity or feel little need to assimilate the new identity. In such cases, however, divestiture is likely to be focused on a narrow portion of the old identity because much of the identity will remain helpful—and can generalize—to the new role. Regarding voluntary and socially desirable transitions, many individuals may *want* to divest themselves of an incoming identity because they dislike it or recognize that it is incongruent with the current situation or hoped-for self but need guidance and support to do so. Indeed, an entire industry, that of mutual help, has arisen precisely because individuals often find that their identity reach—their hoped-for self—exceeds their grasp even when the identity is perceived to be highly desirable.

---

[9]It should be noted that many organizations practice divestiture for other reasons, particularly as a rite of passage ("paying your dues"), to instill respect for the role- and organization-specific knowledge of insiders, and to render the newcomer more receptive to further learning. However, divestiture may backfire and antagonize newcomers if they see the practices as unhelpful or excessive (see "Initiation," this chapter).

It should be noted that even in organizations practicing investiture, newcomers are typically encouraged to identify with the role and organization, that is, to overlay these situated identities on their incoming identities. Indeed, the tactics of institutionalized socialization facilitate a clear sense of what the organization purportedly represents and how one should construe events. This coherent sense of identity and meaning provides a clear referent for identification. Thus, Ashforth and Saks (1996) found that institutionalized socialization was positively associated with organizational identification.

Finally, it should also be noted that organizations may use investiture to reaffirm some portions of a newcomer's incoming identity while *simultaneously* using divestiture to shed other portions. For example, organizations hire engineers for their professional skills (investiture). Nonetheless, Schein (1978) found that managers arranged "up-ending experiences" to contradict newcomers' beliefs (divestiture) so that they would become receptive to further learning. One manager gave newcomers the task of analyzing a circuit that should not have worked. When newcomers said that it would not work, they were shown that it did. The experience quickly demonstrated to the newcomers that their education could not be fully trusted (Trice & Morand, 1989).[10] Thus, the use of divestiture was found to predict person change 4 and 10 months (Ashforth & Saks, 1996) and 12 months (Black & Ashford, 1995) after role entry.

Identity Transformation.   The literature on *identity transformation* (Frankel, 1989) suggests how divestiture works. Identity transformation encompasses a diverse array of applications including religious conversion, thought reform or brainwashing, psychiatric therapy, resocialization, status passage, social rehabilitation, and deprogramming. As Frankel (1989) observed, theories of identity transformation are generally consistent with Lewin's (1951) model of unfreezing-movement-refreezing (see Fig. 1.1). Consistent with the earlier discussion, the higher the magnitude and the more voluntary and socially desirable the transition, the more likely that newcomers will be predisposed to identity transformation. Furthermore, individuals experiencing the liminality described last chapter (e.g., from job loss, geographical dislocation, school graduation)

---

[10]The mixed message implied by simultaneous investiture/divestiture ("We like what you bring to the role"/"We want you to change") may also help account for the relatively weak reliability of investiture measures that position investiture and divestiture as opposing poles on a continuum (e.g., Ashforth & Saks, 1996).

may lack strong identity moorings and thus be more receptive to transformational experiences (O'Reilly & Chatman, 1996; L. J. West, 1993).
Finally, the desire for a sense of identity, meaning, control, and belonging
that is grounded in the organizational setting renders newcomers somewhat amenable to transformation.

Regardless of their predisposition, organizational newcomers undergoing divestiture are often *encapsulated* (Lofland, 1978; Moreland &
Levine, 1989), that is, temporarily isolated from outsiders who might:
(a) attempt to relate to the newcomers in terms of their disavowed identities, (b) challenge the legitimacy of the newcomers' claim to the new identity, or (c) challenge the legitimacy of the identity itself (e.g., a parent
contesting a child's membership in a cult). As Baumeister (1986) put it,
"remove the public self by isolating the person from all who have known
him, and the private self becomes surprisingly malleable" (p. 242). In
addition, it appears that acceptance of a radically new identity by the newcomers' existing social network is facilitated not by ongoing contact but
by a period of separation: The separation interrupts contact, allowing outsiders to more readily perceive any substantive change in demeanor or
other visible cues and to accept that something significant has happened
to the individual in the interim. Encapsulation tends to occur through
physical isolation (e.g., a distant training center), heavy work loads, after-
hours socializing, authoritarian control over activities, and injunctions to
restrict contact with outsiders during the transformation.

Encapsulation allows the organization to create the social cocoon mentioned earlier (Greil & Rudy, 1984). Within the cocoon, newcomers'
incoming identities are challenged via some subset of the following practices: Subtle reminders of shortcomings, confrontational verbal assaults,
reminders of hoped-for selves, intended or unintended failure experiences,
induced public confessions and personal stories, initiation events (discussed later), and other means that convey that the newcomers are not
ready to assume the new role and that induce dissonance and dissatisfaction with incoming identities. Often, the identities to be divested are
impugned as not merely inappropriate but as *morally* deficient, thus
undermining the values and goals on which the identities are predicated.
Newcomers may be induced to feel guilt and shame regarding their past
(Baumeister, 1986; Gecas, 1986). The intent of these practices is to motivate or, if necessary, coerce change by unfreezing identification with prior
identities (Schein, 1961). The relentless ridicule of U.S. Marine recruits
by drill instructors is a paradigmatic example of this process (Ricks,

1997). Pratt and Barnett (1997) found that encapsulation was effective even in relatively short Amway recruitment meetings where company distributors challenged the complacency of the audience and proffered a substitute identity (independent businessperson): Sufficient numbers of people respond to the divestiture to keep Amway profitable.

As the disavowed identities are divested, newcomers lose their comfortable moorings and cast about for surrogate moorings within the organizational context that will address their motives for identity, meaning, control, and belonging. The socialization agents are ready to extol and perhaps model the desired role and organizational identities, providing a salient contrast between the now-stigmatized incoming identities and the desired identities. As noted earlier, the latter tend to be expressed in idealized terms, perhaps supported by a simplified ideology that provides facile answers to criticisms of the identity and socialization process (what Lifton, 1961, termed *loading the language*). Newcomers are encouraged to interpret the rigors of the divestiture process as the price of becoming worthy of admittance. They are also encouraged to attribute any doubts or misgivings they may have to their own shortcomings rather than to the rigors of the process itself (Lifton: *doctrine over person*)—thus indicating that they need *more* shaping, not less—or to interpret their doubts as a natural by-product of their personal growth in the role.[11]

Newcomers may be led through a series of training experiences where the level of difficulty is gradually increased, enabling the newcomers to gain a sense of mastery and thus reinforce the attractiveness of the proffered identity. Although progress is reinforced, relentless pressure is still applied to pursue perhaps impossible standards so that recruits do not feel complacent or begin to backslide (Lifton, 1961: *demand for purity*). Moreover, the failure of any peers during this process provides a benchmark for the survivors' own progress, further stoking their sense of mastery and identification. Indeed, as each peer fails and leaves, so too does a portion of the survivors' previous identity, creating a growing sense of us (the successful recruits and their fellow role occupants) versus them (failed recruits and outsiders).

---

[11]Cushman (1986) noted that such a "self-sealing doctrine" instills in the socialization *agents* "an unshakable belief in the group [organization], a rigid self-confidence, and a rationale for using the ends to justify the means . . . (e.g., permission to use painful or humiliating tactics)" (p. 14). The actions of the agents are, *by definition*, for the greater good.

The intent of these processes is to provide a desired role and organizational identity around which the newcomer can refreeze his or her sense of self. Refreezing allows the newcomer to regain a sense of personal equilibrium—a sense of identity, meaning, control, and belonging—much like a trapeze artist swinging from one platform (incoming identity) to another (new identity).[12]

Going Native. The power of strong situations to remake identity is particularly evident when divestiture occurs *despite* the intentions of management and the newcomer. The phrase *going native* is often applied to anthropologists and sociologists studying a particular culture (or subculture) who come to identify with the members of that culture and sacrifice the espoused objectivity and neutrality of their identity as social scientists (e.g., Freilich, 1970). However, the central notion of forsaking one's social identity for another may apply to anyone in a boundary-spanning role who spends significant amounts of time with people outside the organization or subunit including police officers working under cover, social workers and psychiatrists working intensely with clients, foreign diplomats and expatriate workers, and company representatives working regularly at clients' premises (Black, Gregersen, & Mendenhall, 1992; Dorsey, 1994; Girodo, 1984). When one is transplanted from an identity-sustaining culture (in this case, one's own subunit, organization, or nation) to another culture for a protracted period, it becomes difficult to park one's psyche outside the latter culture—particularly if the role requires one to understand the "natives'" perspective. Empathy may turn to identification as the distant home culture recedes in salience, and one may act in ways that favor the natives rather than one's own subunit, organization, or nation.[13]

---

[12]If the entry transition is sufficiently intense, it may provoke a sudden or radical conversion (Bankston, Forsyth, & Floyd, 1981; Boyanowsky, 1977). Intense emotional experiences, perhaps coupled with strong social pressure and heightened suggestibility (via, for example, physical and mental exhaustion, hunger or thirst, drugs or alcohol, disorientation, chanting, or emotional contagion), occasionally prompt a breakthrough epiphany, leading to a major reconstruction of self. Sudden conversions appear to be relatively rare. However, even a gradual conversion can be characterized as a series of more or less sudden small epiphanies that ultimately amount to a radical change (Denzin, 1989; see "Turning Points," this chapter).

[13]Many organizations appear to be aware of the potential for their members to go native and have instituted precautions such as keeping outside visits short, punctuating long visits with regular reports or actual trips home, working and living in pairs or groups, formalizing rules that limit fraternizing with outsiders, displaying markers of organizational affiliation (e.g., a uniform), and inculcating pejorative stereotypes of outsiders (cf. *social encapsulation* and *ideological encapsulation;* Greil & Rudy, 1984).

Serial Versus Disjunctive Socialization

The second tactic, in addition to investiture (vs. divestiture), that is particularly relevant to the impact of socialization on newcomers' role identity is serial (vs. disjunctive) socialization. Serial socialization was defined earlier as the use of experienced organizational members as socialization agents. A provocative question is whether identification with a role model—such as a manager or senior peer—can generalize to the role itself or the organization. I believe it can. As noted, managers and peers may personify the organization for the newcomer. Similarly, a role model literally embodies the role, providing a flesh and blood instantiation of the identity and a ready referent for learning and social comparison (Weiss, 1977). The serial tactic therefore provides newcomers with role models to emulate as a means of resolving their liminality (Cushman, 1986), particularly if coupled with the disorientation of divestiture.[14] In identifying with the role model, one "attempts to be like or actually to *be* the other person" (Kelman, 1961, p. 63). It is then a small step from identifying with a role model to identifying with a more generalized representation of the role identity—or even with the organization as a whole (assuming some overlap in role and organizational identities).

Ibarra (1996) found that neophyte consultants and investment bankers often came to assimilate aspects of their new roles into their professional identity by observing role models and then experimenting with and refining what was most likely to work for themselves. The role models rendered the abstract and tacit more concrete, and by providing a social template of the role, they enabled the neophytes to more easily conceive of themselves as bona fide role occupants. Moreover, Ibarra found that perceived similarities between a role model and protegé facilitated the latter's role identification, presumably because the protegé could more easily conceive of himself or herself as being in the shoes of the role model (Bandura, 1977). Thus, identification with a role model(s) may function as a segue into identification with the role that the model(s) exemplifies.

---

[14]Research on *identification with the aggressor* and the *Stockholm syndrome* suggests that under certain extreme circumstances (such as the chronic stress, total dependence, and isolation experienced by a long-term hostage), one may identify with one's "keeper" (L. J. West, 1993). In so doing, one is transformed "from the person threatened into the person who makes the threat" (A. Freud, as cited in Kets de Vries & Miller, 1984, p. 140). Identification with the aggressor thus protects one from the anxiety of subjugation and provides a sense of secondary control (see chap. 3).

RITES OF PASSAGE:
TRANSITION
AND INCORPORATION

It was noted in chapter 1 that van Gennep's (1960) rites of passage consist of rites of separation (facilitating role exit), transition (facilitating the journey between roles), and incorporation (facilitating role entry). The rites of separation and the associated sense of liminality—of lacking a self-defining connection to the social domain—were discussed last chapter. It was argued that liminality tends to be aversive unless one anticipates a valued new role or set of activities within a personally and socially acceptable time frame.

Here, I discuss the rites of transition and incorporation. Collectively, these rites pertain to the processes through which newcomers seek, enter, and come to identify with (and be identified by) the new role. Where one set of rites stops and the next begins is somewhat arbitrary; I will denote rites pertaining to the period of preentry and early socialization (when role ambiguity—and presumably liminality—are still high) as rites of transition, and rites pertaining to late socialization (when role ambiguity and liminality are substantially reduced) as rites of incorporation.

Rites of Transition

Given this partitioning of rites, much of the socialization process can be regarded as a rite of transition in that it facilitates the psychological journey from the prior role (if relevant) to the current one.[15] The tactics of institutionalized socialization, in particular, represent a more or less formalized and often ritualized means of investing newcomers in their new roles. Segregating newcomers from veterans and subjecting them to well-defined developmental phases clearly marks the newcomers as neophytes who are not yet ready to assume the roles for which they were hired. Despite the implied liminality (newcomers are *in* but not really *of* the organization), newcomers often enjoy this period because they recognize its contribution toward their mastery of the role and their acceptance by more senior members. Thus, newcomers are often willing to tolerate low status, grunt work, and ritualistic debasement because they correctly

---

[15]Certain aspects of the period prior to physical role entry, such as a vacation and job search, can also be regarded as rites of transition. However, such rites are beyond the scope of this discussion.

expect it to cease or decrease after they have "paid their dues" and "proven their mettle" (e.g., Bourassa & Ashforth, 1998; Riemer, 1979).

By the same token, the more prolonged, open-ended, and uncontrollable the period of socialization and the less predictable the nature and sequence of developmental activities, the more difficult it is for newcomers to *anticipate* the resolution of their liminality. Ongoing liminality consigns the newcomer to a disembodied, almost nonperson status, and is therefore psychologically untenable. Mansfield (1972) described the angst experienced by recruits in an industrial firm who were subjected to a 4-week induction course, followed by a series of 2-week training rotations through various departments: In the absence of a permanent position with formal job responsibilities, they found it difficult to situate themselves in the organization. As one recruit put it, "I got fed up. . . . I felt unsettled—didn't know where I was going" (p. 80). A similar sense of disembodiment has been reported among temporary workers on open-ended engagements (Henson, 1996), prisoners awaiting trial (Gibbs, 1982), plateaued middle managers (Schrier & Mulcahy, 1988), and the children of members of the military whose fathers were frequently transferred (Wertsch, 1992).

Collective (vs. Individual) Socialization.   One socialization tactic that is particularly relevant to rites of transition is collective socialization. As discussed in chapter 4, collective transitions tend to be less difficult and more positively valent. The sense of disembodiment and the anxiety of role entry are mitigated somewhat when newcomers are socialized in groups. V. W. Turner (1967, 1969) noted the strong feeling of togetherness or *communitas* that participants in a rite of passage often share precisely because they lack other social referents and identity anchors and recognize in their fellow initiates common travelers in an otherwise stressful journey. With little to cling to in the ambiguous entry period, they cling to each other (Trice & Morand, 1989).

Furthermore, as noted in chapter 4, the involvement of peers can redouble the force of the learning. In socializing newcomers in batches, the organization implicitly encourages them to engage in social comparison and social construction processes and to learn vicariously from one another. In a real sense, the newcomers socialize themselves (Van Maanen & Schein, 1979). Thus, Banks et al. (1992) found that the collective context in which vocational training took place helped students change their perceptions of jobs for which the training was designed. For example, adolescent girls in a training program for providing institutional care found their training jobs to be far more physically and emotionally demanding than anticipated (e.g., cleaning up beds soiled by the incontinent, sitting with the dying, dealing with abusive patients). The collective context of occupational socialization helped them redefine their work as meaningful and worthy of pride. As argued in chapter 4, groups can often create and sustain beliefs that individuals alone cannot.

However, collective socialization carries a considerable risk for the organization. Despite the use of normative control, organizations cannot control the bulk of interactions between peers. Thus, as also noted in chapter 4, the same batch of fellow initiates who provide comfort may also provide interpretations of entry experiences that contradict those espoused by management. Moreover, the cohort may be susceptible to emotional contagion such that the angry or depressed few infect the many, as Davis and Olesen (1963) found among a group of neophyte nursing students. It seems likely that the less voluntary and socially desirable the transition, the greater the risk presented by socializing newcomers in batches. For example, Greil and Rudy (1984) contended that collective socialization largely accounts for the difficulty that prisons and psychiatric institutions have in rehabilitating inmates.

Turning Points.   Organizational life is experienced not as a smooth arc of continuous processes but as a series of more or less disjointed *episodes* embedded in rich contexts (Mintzberg, 1973). The nature of one's first major assignment, a chance remark overheard in the washroom, poor advice from a veteran coworker, the first invitation from a coworker to a social event, an unpleasant feedback session with one's supervisor, and so on have the potential to radically affect the trajectory of one's development and propensity to identify with the role and organization. Such episodes may serve as markers of progress (or setbacks) on the journey to full incorporation in the role and thus can be regarded as a melange of informal and formal rites of transition. Even in organizations that rely heavily on institutionalized socialization, such as the U.S. Marine Corps and teaching hospitals, the serendipity of everyday encounters plays a large role in newcomers' development (Marion, 1990; Ricks, 1997).

This episodic quality is reflected in some models of socialization that are loosely organized around formative events such as physical entry, job assignments, and performance appraisals (Wanous, 1992). Similarly, Bullis and Bach (1989) typified learning as a series of "socialization turning points"; Stohl (1986) noted that newcomers resolve ambiguity partly through "memorable messages" from trusted people; Gundry and Rousseau (1994) described how newcomers came to understand their organization's culture by decoding "critical incidents"; and I noted in earlier chapters Louis' (1980b) and Denzin's (1989) observation that learning occurs through decoding various surprises and epiphanies. For example, Bullis and Bach (1989) found that graduate students reported a diverse array of turning points during their first 8 months such as establishing a physical territory and becoming familiar with surroundings, establishing comfortable routines, participating in informal and formal social events, receiving informal and formal recognition, approaching and jumping hurdles, representing the organization, and handling disappointments. The turning points were associated with significant changes (generally positive) in organizational identification.

The concept of turning points suggests four implications for role entry. First, a given incident becomes a turning point when it raises, resolves, or marks an important issue for the individual. Thus, the *timing* and *nature* of the incident are very important: The incident must occur when the individual is emotionally receptive to the possibility of learning, change, or confirmation and must occur in a manner that bypasses normal perceptual and ego defenses and "hits home." For example, Stohl (1986) found that messages are more likely to be turning points (be "memorable") when offered early in one's career and in private settings. Second, the *sequence* of turning points will greatly affect the course of role entry and identification. Sharp criticism from one's manager during the first week of employment may devastate one's self-confidence, whereas such criticism 6 months later may be seen as constructive feedback from a gruff source (Saks & Ashforth, 1997).

Third, the pacing and content of learning will tend to vary across newcomers and over time such that *a given individual's arc of learning may appear erratic*—perhaps leading to misattributions about the individual's abilities and motivation (e.g., "She's progressing slowly" vs. "She's had few learning opportunities"). For example, L. A. Hill (1992) found that although most managers had similar experiences over a time frame of several months, it was impossible to predict precisely when a new manager might be exposed to a particular learning situation. Similarly, identification may be paced as much by the situation as by the individual. Fourth, research on socialization and work adjustment may profit from focusing less on individual-centered variables (e.g., job satisfaction, role clarity) at fixed points of time (e.g., 3 months after entry) and more on experienced events when they occur (Saks & Ashforth, 1997). However, the somewhat erratic sequence of turning points does not necessarily invalidate stage models of socialization and adjustment: Turning points may reflect micro changes (e.g., elation at receiving positive feedback from one's supervisor followed by disappointment at receiving negative feedback from one's coworker) within a smoother backdrop of macro patterns (e.g., a general concern with proving one's task competence; Bullis & Bach, 1989).

Transition Bridges. As discussed in chapter 4, the greater the magnitude of the transition, the greater the threat to one's sense of self-continuity—and possibly one's sense of meaning, control, and belonging. Certain transition bridges, beyond the turning points discussed earlier, may serve as rites of transition. In particular, treasured objects and comforting routines may facilitate role transitions by helping newcomers feel at home (Csikszentmihalyi & Rochberg-Halton, 1981). First, according to Belk's (1988) notion of the extended self, individuals regard their possessions as parts of themselves, thus helping define and symbolize their identity. As such, possessions may function as identity totems. Thus, mementos of one's "personal biographies—places, events, and social relationships" (Silver, 1996, p. 2) provide a sense of continuity during an unsettled period and may serve as props to affect how others categorize one. Second, following Ashforth and Kreiner's (2000) notion of ritualism, familiar routines may serve to normalize a situation—and may also express one's identity and provide a sense of control.

Consequently, arranging family pictures on one's desk, bringing a favored coffee mug from home, enacting familiar rituals such as reading the business section on arriving at work, and so on may help bridge the psychological distance from the old role to the new and shape the impressions others form of one. In helping one colonize the new role, such transition bridges may also serve as a buffer against anxiety and divestiture. Indeed, the more difficult the transition (e.g., high magnitude, irreversible; see Fig. 4.1), the greater the premium placed on such emotionally charged totems. For example, individuals moving from home to university (Noble & Walker, 1997; Silver, 1996) and individuals moving into a nursing home (Shield, 1988; Wapner, Demick, & Redondo, 1990) have been found to invest great care in selecting personal and social identity markers to accompany them. One woman moving into a nursing home talked about a favorite doll that she wished she had kept because it symbolized her childhood; giving away the doll was tantamount to giving away her past (Shield, 1988).

Conversely, individuals seeking a clean *break* from the past may abandon or reinterpret objects associated with disavowed identities. For example, McAlexander and Schouten (1989) and Schouten (1991) found that hairstyle changes and cosmetic surgery were sometimes used as catalysts for personal identity changes during nonwork role transitions such as a divorce or relocation.

Rites of Incorporation

Rites of incorporation serve to invest or institutionalize the individual in the new role, thus helping resolve—and marking the resolution of—liminality. Such rites test or sanctify, or both, the individual's readiness and worthiness to don the mantle of full-fledged role occupant. Rites of incorporation vary widely across occupations and organizations. D. T. Hall (1968) found that after passing their general examination, doctoral students' self-image became more similar to their conception of the professor role. D. T. Hall argued that the exam was a rite of passage in that the self-image changed along dimensions that were *not* reflected in the content of the exam: The medium was the message. Kadushin (1969) found that music students came to think of themselves as professional musicians rather than as students when they won talent competitions, began performing for pay, and joined the union. These events signaled that they were not only acting the part of the professional but doing so in a convincing manner. And for first-year medical students, anatomy lab and the dissection of cadavers is a major marker of their entry into medicine. As two medical students put it:

> Anatomy is *the* subject that says you're in medical school. . . . Your cadaver is like your first car. It's impressive, so that when you talk to other people about it they are taken aback. . . . Having done it [dissection], it sets you apart. It's one of the biggest symbols of medical school. (Hafferty, 1991, p. 53)

Initiation. The process of initiation or hazing is a particularly poignant rite of incorporation. The process ranges from informal harassment of newcomers to formal rituals in which newcomers attempt to prove their worthiness to the group or organization (Moreland & Levine, 1989). When used early in the socialization process, initiation serves as a form of divestiture and is thus more a rite of transition than incorporation. For example, newcomers to a trawler were addressed as "new guys" rather than by name, denied pillows and blankets, denied the shore leave that was granted to other crew members, and were required to do make-work tasks (Bourassa & Ashforth, 1998). The implicit message was, "You are not yet one of us." When used later, initiation serves more as a test of the newcomer's internalization of the new role identity and is thus more a rite of incorporation than transition.

Although the process of initiation has generally been found to predict increased attraction to and compliance with the group in both experimental and field settings (e.g., E. Aronson & Mills, 1959; Lodewijkx & Syroit, 1997), the precise causal mechanisms are unclear. An initiation may: (a) discourage newcomers who are unlikely to fit in, thereby increasing the likelihood of interpersonal compatibility and liking among those who remain, (b) induce cognitive dissonance in the newcomers ("Why have I allowed myself to be subjected to this treatment?"), thereby making the group more attractive as a means of resolving the dissonance ("I guess I must like the group"), (c) induce intense emotions and suggestibility, thereby rendering newcomers more receptive to the group's influence, (d) underscore newcomers' low status and dependence on the group, thereby rendering newcomers more receptive, (e) foster an in-the-same-boat consciousness among newcomers, thereby facilitating affiliation and cohesion, and (f) induce an afterglow of positive affect if the newcomers pass the initiation, thereby facilitating self-esteem and affiliation (e.g., Boyanowsky, 1977; Hautaluoma, Enge, Mitchell, & Rittwager, 1991; Lodewijkx & Syroit, 1997; Moreland & Levine, 1989; Schopler & Bateson, 1962). Direct comparisons of these causal mechanisms have been few in number. In one longitudinal study of the initiation processes used by two student organizations, Lodewijkx and Syroit (1997) found evidence for the fifth but little for the second.

Findings regarding the efficacy of *severe* initiations, where newcomers are subjected to particularly taxing situations (e.g., strenuous, embarrassing)—and cognitive dissonance is presumably maximized—have been somewhat mixed (Hautaluoma et al., 1991; Moreland & Levine, 1989). Perhaps severe initiations are double-edged. If newcomers perceive an initiation to be offensive ("to cross the line") or out of proportion to the presumed value of the group, tacit concerns with dissonance may be overwhelmed by revulsion or anger at the group that sponsored the initiation and perhaps by feelings of mortification, either of which may decrease the attractiveness of the group.

Similarly, Yoder and Aniakudo (1996) argued that initiations perceived by the newcomer to be exclusionary rather than inclusionary—as intended to repulse rather than welcome—tend to undermine a newcomer's solidarity with the group. Newcomers accorded marginal status (due, for example, to subpar performance or gender or race differences) are more likely to receive overtly exclusionary messages and to interpret equivocal messages as exclusionary (e.g., Sheffey & Tindale, 1992). Yoder and Aniakudo (1996) quoted a female firefighter who put it this way: "When hazing is directed against a person that can not become fully 'one of the guys' for whatever reason, the contract is broken. The hazing is nothing but harassment, pure and simple" (p. 265). Thus, what may have been intended to dramatize initiation may instead be construed by the newcomer as dramatizing degradation (see chap. 5).

In any event, the appeal of initiation to organizations is clear. In addition to the tendency toward increased attraction and compliance among those newcomers who remain, initiation processes provide critical information about the newcomers (are they sufficiently skilled, tough, and loyal to be trusted?).

NORMALIZATION

Much of the chapter can be summarized by revisiting the concept of normalization. As noted in chapter 1, role transitions are partly about normalization, that is, rendering the new and perhaps threatening more or less ordinary (Ashforth & Kreiner, 2000). Individuals must come to terms with the parameters of their new role and organization to feel comfortable and perform effectively. Normalization is most likely to occur under two conditions. First, normalization is likely if the newcomer is immersed in a local context that dominates time, action, and psychological processes. The context provides a social cocoon in which the newcomer's experiences are sharply regulated and a tightly coupled and invasive local culture is substituted for the outside world. The local culture situates the newcomer and offers a seductive ideology for understanding the status quo and his or her place within it. Less extreme forms of this cocoon are found in virtually all organizational socialization programs. The intent is to make the organization familiar and valued, to motivate the individual to succeed on whatever terms the organization prescribes; in short, to normalize the individual–organization interface.

Second, normalization is likely to occur if the individual is predisposed to becoming involved in the role and organization, that is, to make sense of the local reality, to meet or exceed normative expectations, and to fit in and gain acceptance. Given self- and organizational selection and the social dynamics of rites of transition and incorporation, newcomers are indeed typically motivated to internalize the lessons of the new culture.

The Making of a Torturer

The process and seductive quality of normalizing are most starkly revealed in circumstances that seem *beyond* normalizing. One such circumstance is institutionalized torture. How do nations that systematically practice torture—that routinely and deliberately inflict severe pain or discomfort— socialize individuals to become torturers? Given the near universal repugnance of people to torture, one might think that such nations would simply select those rare individuals who appear predisposed to torture; sadists, psychopaths, and others that might enjoy or not mind causing pain in others. In fact, such individuals are avoided precisely because their personal motives—their zeal—render them unreliable (J. T. Gibson, 1990; F. E. Katz, 1993). State torture is usually practiced for pragmatic reasons, to extract information and intimidate, and overzealous torturers cannot be trusted to calibrate their behavior with sufficient care.

J. T. Gibson and Haritos-Fatouros (1986) examined the official testimonies of 21 former soldiers who had systematically performed torture for the Greek military regime from 1967 to 1974, and Haritos-Fatouros (1988) interviewed 16 of them after their trials. The researchers concluded that the preferred prospects were basically normal and well-adjusted, with an antipathy to communists. The antipathy meant that the recruits were more likely to have negative attitudes toward their political victims. Other desired attributes of prospects were that they were obedient, loyal, and discrete.

Once selected, the behavior and attitudes of prospective torturers were gradually shaped through a series of small acts that led, incrementally, to the adoption of the role. To normalize both interpersonal violence and obedience to authority, Haritos-Fatouros (1988) reported that during the first day of military police training camp, from which torturers would be selected, recruits underwent an initiation beating and, while on their knees, swore allegiance to their commander in chief and the revolution. Recruits were not allowed to defecate for up to 15 days and had to obey degrading and illogical acts such as eating a burning cigarette. A daily routine involved running to exhaustion while being harassed and beaten. As one interviewee put it, "we had to *learn* to *love* pain" (p. 1116).

To shape and normalize torture in particular, recruits initially brought food to the prisoners and were occasionally ordered to strike them. Next, they observed veteran soldiers torture prisoners while they stood guard. Then they participated in the "standing ordeal" where they had to beat the prisoner each time he moved. Later, they were ordered to use a variety of methods of torture. Finally, to minimize time for reflection, they were "promoted" to chief torturer without warning.

As the theory of cognitive dissonance indicates, individuals need to make sense of seemingly voluntary acts that are discrepant with their prevailing attitudes and desires (Festinger, 1957). An overarching ideology is provided that justifies torture as a necessary means of realizing a valued end. Moreover, the appearance of voluntariness entraps the recruits, making them more receptive to an ideology that negates personal blame and glorifies their acts as furthering lofty social goals. To further cement this recasting of behavior, Haritos-Fatouros (1988) found that torturers were granted special status and privileges that enhanced their self- and social esteem.

Regardless of the social goals that are invoked, torturers are encouraged to devalue their victims, that is, to see them as less than human and therefore not privy to the same consideration, and to deindividuate their victims, to see them as representing an undifferentiated group rather than as individuals capable of arousing empathy. The daily indoctrination of the Greek torturers referred to prisoners as "worms" (J. T. Gibson & Haritos-Fatouros, 1986). Indeed, to further reduce personal inhibitions, torturers may be encouraged to engage in *self*-deindividuation—self-stereotyping in the terminology of chapter 2—by wearing a mask and uniform and to utilize jargon and euphemisms that lessen the salience of torture (Zimbardo, 1969).

Torture is often perpetrated in a group context, enabling torturers to gain a sense of belonging and social support from their peers. Through the means of collective socialization and the rites of transition and incorporation, the individuals may come to identify with the group and to subordinate their own values, beliefs, and desires to the will of the group. The group becomes the local mechanism for socializing newcomers. The allure of the group may be sufficiently strong that newcomers engage in torture primarily to gain acceptance and status regardless of whether they have internalized the espoused ideology. Indeed, groupthink may take root such that doubters self-censor their concerns, creating an illusion of unanimity (Janis, 1983). Haritos-Fatouros (1988), however, found that peers were induced to spy on one another so as to maintain fear and discipline.

Finally, the more that one engages in torture, the more normal it appears to become. Repetition may blunt the salience of otherwise repulsive acts such that one becomes desensitized to their effects (St. Onge, 1995). F. E. Katz (1993) discussed the diary of a physician who performed medical experiments at Auschwitz, the most notorious of the Nazi concentration camps:

> After his first two diary entries expressing horror about the murderous deeds, [he] never again mentioned a sense of horror. Step by step, incrementally, he became used to it. He routinely placed mention of taking part in "special actions" [mass executions, usually by gassing] alongside the things that really counted for him: the joys of eating, associating with high-ranking officers, being saluted by underlings, getting a tailor-made uniform. (p. 54)

Although the making of a torturer illustrates the power of normalizing, it should be noted that there are probably limits to *what* can be normalized (breadth) and *how thoroughly* something can be normalized (depth). Individuals vary in their susceptibility to normalizing, as shown by various laboratory studies of strong situations (e.g., Haney et al., 1973; Milgram, 1974), and may remain ambivalent about their involvement. Staub (1990), for example, noted the psychological problems experienced by some former torturers. In general, the more the subculture of the organization or role deviates from societal prescriptions, the greater the resistance to normalizing. Also, once a normalized individual is removed from the context that sustains the role identity, other identities may assume greater salience (e.g., recall the discussion of going native).

CONCLUSION

Given newcomers' motives for identity, meaning, control, and belonging, newcomers are predisposed to internalize organizational messages about what the role and organization are about. The stronger the use of normative control, via certain socialization tactics and rites of transition and incorporation, the more likely that the organization will present a prefabricated self for the newcomer to assimilate. Thus, socialization practices largely *mediate* the impact of the context on self and adaptation. This is an important point. Given that role contexts are often complex and overdetermined (i.e., designed to realize multiple purposes), the meaning(s) of a given context is inherently equivocal: Socialization renders certain aspects of the context more salient and meaningful by structuring early work experiences and facilitating accounts of those experiences. Thus, depending on the course of socialization, a given context can come to mean somewhat different things to newcomers. For example, Salzinger (1991) studied two cooperatives specializing in domestic worker placement. Although the work was equivalent, domestic workers in one agency were socialized to regard their job as unimportant and demeaning, whereas workers in the other agency came to regard their job as skilled and deserving of respect.

Omitted from this argument, however, is the other side of the coin: How does the *individual* navigate a new role and put his or her own stamp on institutionalized identities? Chapter 7 examines the pivotal role of the newcomer as a proactive agent in his or her own socialization.

7

Role Entry:
Individual Dynamics

I've been home three days and . . . I find things much different from the time I once lived here. But I think the difference is more in me than in the rest of the family. They go about their everyday business as if I were not a "hockey star"; they treat me for who I am and not for the job I have and it's nice. The last few days at home, I have found when shopping or running errands that people I once knew treat me now as John Tanner the goalie rather than John. It's like there is a newfound respect for me that I believe is silly; why would things be different just because I play hockey? On the other hand, I don't mind it—it makes me feel a little important. However, I usually end up "playing the role" and I feel silly for doing it as I act in a very airy manner and make things appear important and they aren't. . . . "You're John Tanner," they all yell, and against what I think I should feel, I experience a sensation of importance. Humility is gone and cockiness takes over. I talk like I make a million bucks rather than the eighteen [for weekly expenses].
                                    —a minor league hockey goalie (Olver, 1990, pp. 92, 96)

Chapter 6 examined the situational context affecting role entry. The current chapter examines the individual's perspective during role entry; how he or she addresses the psychological motives for identity, meaning, control, and belonging. The individual's perspective is becoming increasingly important. The trends outlined in chapter 1—the growing flux of individuals and organizations and the resulting boundaryless careers and need for meta-competencies—suggest that individuals can no longer rely on paternalistic organizations to shepherd them through carefully calibrated developmental experiences. In a dynamic world, a greater premium is placed on an individual's willingness and ability to learn, to innovate, and to change. Increasingly, the individual (together with his or her groups) rather than the institution is the fulcrum for organizational action and change.

The chapter spans six major topics. First, the dynamics of role learning are explored. I argue that newcomers are often highly proactive agents in their own socialization. Also, I consider the intriguing notion that newcomers selectively forget elements of their past that are inconsistent with their present role. Second, the dynamics of role innovation are explored and contrasted with the notion of personal change (identity transformation) from last chapter. Third, the impact of certain individual differences on role learning and innovation, as well as personal change, are discussed. Fourth, I then switch gears somewhat and focus more narrowly on the process of role identification. As presaged by the opening quote from the hockey goalie, I discuss affect, behavior, and cognition—the ABCs of role entry—as the starting points of identification. Fifth, it is argued that social validation helps cement emergent role identities. Finally, the relevance of stress to role entry is briefly considered.

ROLE LEARNING

Much of the literature on role entry has appeared under the labels of *work adjustment* and *socialization*. Many studies have focused on secondary or distal outcomes of entry such as job satisfaction, organizational commitment, performance, intentions to quit, stress, and person–job and person–organization fit. Far fewer studies have focused on primary or proximal outcomes such as role clarity, knowledge/skill/ability acquisition, social integration, motivation, personal change, and role orientation (i.e., the tendency to conform vs. innovate; Ashford & Taylor, 1990; Bauer et al., 1998; Saks & Ashforth, 1997). The primary outcomes are critical because they substantially mediate the impact of the situational context and unfolding events on the secondary outcomes (e.g., Bauer & Green, 1998). This section discusses how the process of role learning affects certain primary outcomes and, thereby, longer term adjustment.

Areas of Role Learning

The motives for identity, meaning, control, and belonging can only be addressed if the individual has a clear understanding of his or her role and the surrounding context. Thus, role learning is paramount to effective role entry. E. W. Morrison (1995) argued that newcomer learning centers on seven areas: (a) technical information about how to perform tasks, (b) referent information about role expectations, (c) social information about other people and one's relationships with them, (d) appraisal information about how one is evaluated, (e) normative information about the organization's culture (and presumably identity), (f) organizational information about structure, products/services, and procedures, and (g) political information about the distribution (and presumably the use) of power (cf. Chao et al., 1994; Comer, 1991; V. D. Miller & Jablin, 1991; E. W. Morrison, 1993a, 1993b; Ostroff & Kozlowski, 1992). In short, newcomers must learn about the nature of the role and the context within which it is embedded. Moreover, consistent with the argument that roles mediate much of the effect of organizational life on individuals, E. W. Morrison (1995) found that newcomers regard role-related information (i.e., technical, referent, and appraisal) along with political information as more useful than context-related information (i.e., social, normative, and organizational).

Proactivity

The traditional approach to role entry portrays individuals as relatively passive or reactive recipients of socialization practices (Bauer et al., 1998; Saks & Ashforth, 1997). In contrast, recent work portrays individuals as far more proactive in their learning—a change in focus that Major, Kozlowski, Chao, and Gardner (1995) characterized as a "paradigm shift" (p. 420) in socialization theory. The common denominator of research on information seeking, feedback seeking, proactive behavior, and self-management—in short, *proactivity*—is that individuals tend to be highly motivated agents in their own socialization.[1] Proactivity fosters role learning and thereby the knowledge and confidence to engage in role innovation and personal change (discussed later).

It is no accident that this paradigm shift is occurring. As noted, the rise of protean individuals and organizations is placing greater onus on the individual to navigate the shoals of change. Moreover, orientation and training programs often present an idealistic and stylized view of the organization, reflecting management's hopes more than coworkers' realities. And the information imparted via mentorship, apprenticeship, and buddy programs is tied to the necessarily parochial perspective of a limited number of individuals, no matter how wise and well-intended they may be.

Proactivity facilitates the acquisition of information from more diverse sources, enabling the newcomer to uncover diverse perspectives, conflicts, and contradictions. In turn, this diversity enables the newcomer to better triangulate on informed beliefs about the role and organization. Most

---

[1]However, as discussed later in this chapter under "Individual Differences," individuals vary widely in their propensity to be proactive.

important, proactivity enables the individual to learn *personalized* knowledge, skills, and abilities (Falcione & Wilson, 1988, p. 157); that is, to learn things that are more directly relevant to his or her role and longer term interests and aspirations.

There are numerous forms of proactivity. V. D. Miller and Jablin's (1991) model of information seeking included the tactics of overt questions, indirect questions, third parties (e.g., validating information from primary sources), testing limits (e.g., deliberately breaking rules), disguising conversations (e.g., using self-disclosure and jokes to draw someone out), observing, and surveillance (e.g., wandering around). Ostroff and Kozlowski (1992) added the tactics of trial and error and reading documentation such as manuals. Ashford and Black (1996) operationalized proactive socialization as networking with colleagues in other departments, general socializing (e.g., attending office parties), building relationships with one's manager, negotiating job changes, positively framing the situation (e.g., as an opportunity rather than a problem), and information and feedback seeking. And Manz's (1983) model of self-management included the practices of self-observation (i.e., reflecting on one's behavior and its causes), cueing (i.e., regulating behaviors by creating or altering cues, such as the arrangement of the work area), goal setting, self-reward and -punishment (i.e., administering sanctions for success and failure), and rehearsal (i.e., practicing desired behavior).

Reviews by Bauer et al. (1998) and Saks and Ashforth (1997) indicated that the relationships among these tactics, the sources of information (e.g., supervisor, coworker, documentation), and the specific content areas appear to be quite complex. For example, E. W. Morrison (1995) found that newcomers use more direct tactics (e.g., inquiry) to learn technical information but more indirect tactics (e.g., monitoring) for organizational information. Settoon and Adkins (1997) found that information seeking from family and friends (e.g, "When something happens to you on the job that is unexpected, how often do you ask your friends [family] outside work about it?," p. 511) was negatively related to work adjustment shortly after entry, whereas information seeking from supervisors and coworkers was positively related to adjustment 6 months after entry.

The reviews by Bauer et al. (1998) and Saks and Ashforth (1997) also indicated that the relationships between proactivity and both the primary and secondary outcomes are quite complex. For example, E. W. Morrison (1993a, 1993b) found that information seeking was positively related to task mastery, role clarity, social integration, job satisfaction, and job performance and negatively related to intentions to quit; conversely, M. W.

Kramer, Callister, and Turban (1995) found that information seeking did *not* predict organization knowledge, role clarity, job satisfaction, job performance, or intentions to quit. Thus, the bivariate associations between specific tactics and specific outcomes are as yet unclear and may well be moderated by information source, content area, and various individual differences.

What does seem more clear is that proactivity fosters role learning (as well as role innovation and personal change; again, see the later discussion) and thereby the attainment of both primary and secondary outcomes.

Factors Affecting the Ease of Role Learning

Learning is facilitated by three sets of factors: Role attributes, sources of support, and individual differences. (Individual differences are discussed later in a separate section.) Regarding role attributes, role complexity refers to work involving a variety of tasks and intricate skills and abilities (Kemp, Wall, Clegg, & Cordery, 1983). The more complex the role, the more difficult it is to learn. Indeed, education for certain highly complex roles is often outsourced to vocational, business, and professional schools and to internal training departments and formal socialization programs (where newcomers are sequestered; see chap. 6). Similarly, role ambiguity (where "priorities, expectations, and evaluation criteria are not clear to the employee," Rahim, 1996, p. 48), role overload (where "work demands exceed personal and workplace resources," p. 48), and role conflict (where attributes within the role or between multiple roles are inconsistent) may also inhibit learning (Brett, 1980). For example, Black (1988) found that role ambiguity (although not role overload or conflict) was negatively associated with work adjustment among American expatriate managers in Japan.

Regarding sources of support, abundant research indicates that the instrumental and expressive social support of peers, mentors, managers, and family and friends may greatly facilitate role transitions (e.g., Bauer & Green, 1998; Gerpott, 1990; Heppner, Multon, & Johnston, 1994; Louis, Posner, & Powell, 1983; Major et al., 1995; V. D. Miller et al., 1999; Moreland & Levine, 1989).[2] These sources may provide guidance

---

[2]However, as Settoon and Adkins' (1997) findings (noted earlier) suggest, extraorganizational sources may provide problematic advice. Lacking the nuanced knowledge of an insider and dependent on how the individual presents role-related events, they may provide poor advice—albeit well-intended.

that is tailored to the idiosyncratic concerns and learning styles of the newcomers. Indeed, Louis et al. (1983) found that informal and supportive daily interactions with peers and supervisors were reported by newcomers to be more helpful than formal orientation and training programs. Peers and supervisors may explain situations, validate emergent perceptions, clarify political realities, provide task guidance and feedback, help circumvent red tape, and signal social acceptance. Furthermore, interactions with peers are often spontaneous and unstructured as the newcomer asks and receives input as issues naturally arise.

More broadly, organizational support (Eisenberger, Huntington, Hutchison, & Sowa, 1986; Nicholson, 1987)—such as the institutionalized socialization programs discussed last chapter—may facilitate learning. Developmental opportunities, adequate resources, tolerance of mistakes, and so on contribute to a *climate for learning*—a nurturing atmosphere within which newcomers can experiment with their nascent role identities. For example, Ibarra (1996) found that opportunities for trial and error enabled neophyte consultants and investment bankers to explore possible selves, learning about their role and how to enact it in a way that reflected their preferences.

Selective Forgetting

Part of the challenge of learning a new role is in *un*learning goals, values, beliefs, and norms that are antithetical to the new role, attaining and displaying a certain distance or progress away from earlier roles (cf. Hedberg, 1981). This is particularly true of roles that serve as foils for one another, such as subordinate and superordinate, where the yin of one is meant to complement the yang of the other (see chap. 8, "Role Reversals").

L. A. Hill (1992) found that new sales managers had to unlearn their previous identity of individual performer to internalize their new identity of manager, that is, as one who performs via a network of subordinates and peers. The previous focus on the tactical and technical issues involved in sales had to give way to a longer run, more strategic focus on the organization and the development of subordinates. To be sure, knowledge and skills learned previously proved very useful; however, in a real sense, the identity of individualist had to be subordinated—if not forgotten—relative to the new identity of facilitator. The change was *visceral*, cutting to the core of the new managers' self-definition, with its attendant values, beliefs, and norms.

Initially, L. A. Hill's (1992) new managers experienced their own managers' expectations of them to be inconsistent, ambiguous, and unrealistic. With time, however, the new managers were able to distill those expectations into the message that they were expected to be businesspeople rather than salespeople. The label and attendant identity of *businessperson* provided an organizing framework for the previously incomprehensible set of messages (Ashforth & Humphrey, 1997). As they gradually "forgot" one role identity (salesperson) and learned the other (businessperson), they came to realize that managing conflict, uncertainty, and overload was the essence of the businessperson role.

In dialectical terms, it could be argued that the thesis of the exited role has to be reconciled with the antithesis of the entered role, resulting in a synthesis of sorts. However, the more that two roles are structured as foils, the more one is forced to move from the yin to the yang or from one extreme to the other as one changes roles. A person who enacts the role of manager as if it were a compromise between subordinate and superordinate is apt to be ineffective.

However, the process of selective forgetting is likely far from smooth. Following chapter 5, the more that a person identified with and derived satisfaction and pride from the exited role, the more likely that he or she will resist forgetting the role. Similarly, the more that members of the role set associate the person with the exited role, the more likely that he or she will have a difficult time becoming detached from the role. At the same time, memories of—and lessons derived from—the exited role may serve as a transition bridge to the newly entered role. Thus, L. A. Hill (1992) found that the new managers fondly reminisced about their previous role of individual performer and would draw confidence from these temporary retreats during times of crisis. An occasional *role relapse*—brought on by nostalgia (see chap. 5)—where one immerses oneself in a prior identity may simultaneously facilitate the process of letting go and the process of engaging in the new role by enabling one to draw comfort and sustenance from past glories.

Double Standards and Hypocrisy. Laurent (1978) observed that managers tend to believe that they keep their subordinates informed and yet tend not to believe that their own managers keep them informed: "The same people perceive . . . very differently the same events depending upon which hierarchical glasses they are invited to wear: proud masters or frustrated servants" (p. 221). Similarly, Menzies (1960) found that senior nurses believed they were denied a sense of responsibility by their unnecessarily strict superiors and yet were viewed precisely the same way by their own subordinates.

In selectively forgetting aspects of the exited role identity that contradict those of the new role identity, a person becomes vulnerable to accusations of having double standards and being hypocritical, of "turning their back" on their past and their former role set members (Ashforth & Mael, 1989). Although the role set members may understand intellectually that the person has changed roles and thus has adopted different responsibilities, they may nonetheless expect—at a more visceral level—that he or she will continue to share their necessarily role-bounded perspective on the organization and act much the same as before. Thus, it may come as an unpleasant shock when, say, one's former peer acts like a typical manager.

The larger point is that when individuals switch roles, they switch lenses for perceiving reality. This malleability is vividly illustrated by the Panalba role-playing experiment (Armstrong, 1977). At issue is a medical product considered by experts to be potentially dangerous. Participants must weigh the health risks (and associated damages to the firm) against the likely economic loss if sales are curtailed or discontinued. When presented as a problem in social responsibility to students, faculty, and managers, 97% stated that continuing to market the product and attempting to prevent the authorities from banning it would be irresponsible. In contrast, when participants instead played the role of the firm's board of directors, 79% of the boards chose precisely this course of action. Role players adopted the frame of the board of directors, and the ambiguity regarding the risks and losses permitted what less partial observers saw as irresponsible action. Derry (1987) suggested that because managers are primed to focus on efficiency and effectiveness as worthwhile values, they may use different moral yardsticks at work than at home. A preoccupation with efficiency and effectiveness may induce an individual acting in the capacity of manager to not perceive the same moral dimensions of an issue that he or she would readily perceive when acting in a nonwork capacity. As suggested throughout the book, to change roles is to change selves.

Can Memory Be Willed?   In answer to the question raised in chapter 5—can memory be willed, can one deliberately forget that which is inconvenient to the present or future?—I would offer a tentative yes. In "trying on" and possibly internalizing a role identity (see "The ABCs of Role Entry," later in this chapter), individuals redirect their attention from the old role to the new. As in a shell game, they may lose sight of the old— despite their best intentions—as they struggle to keep pace with the new.

And the greater the magnitude of the role transition, the easier it is to forget the old identity because of the loss of the sustaining context with its identity cues and reinforcements (see chap. 4).

However, direct incongruities and contradictions between the old and new are likely to be highly salient and cause dissonance (at least initially; see chaps. 8, "Identity Narratives," and 9, "Role Transitions Over Time"). The new role identity may provide rationales that reconcile or dismiss the incongruities (particularly if the sequencing of roles is normatively expected; e.g., subordinate→superordinate), and the felt pressure to adopt the new may predispose newcomers to seek and accept such rationales. Abravanel (1983) referred to rationales that reconcile contradictions as *mediatory myths*. For example, L. A. Hill's (1992) new sales managers learned that the role identity of businessperson meant adopting a broader perspective than that of salesperson: Selectively forgetting the aggressive individualism of sales was said to be a sign of their growing maturity. Thus, mediatory myths are yet another form of transition bridge, enabling individuals to let go of old roles in favor of new ones.

If the mediatory myths prove inadequate, however, unresolved incongruities may threaten newcomers' acceptance of the role. To the extent that newcomers have begun to identify with the new role, they may be motivated to actively suppress such incongruities. Just as people routinely suppress unwanted thoughts about events both real (e.g., a spouse's death) and imagined (e.g., jumping off a building; Wegner, 1989), so they may actively suppress elements of old identities that contradict the current identity. This may involve consciously or unconsciously turning their back on their past, as noted earlier.

For example, Granfield (1991) described how working-class students in a prestigious law program came to regard their backgrounds as burdens and sought to conceal their origins and pass (Goffman, 1963) as typical freshmen. They imitated the dress and diction of their classmates, avoided discussions of their backgrounds, and overcompensated for their self-perceived drawbacks by working diligently. However, given the set of deeply embedded values, beliefs, mannerisms, and so forth that family and class origins represent, Granfield's working-class students felt a pronounced "identity ambivalence" (Goffman, 1963, p. 107). As echoed in other studies of working-class individuals who have experienced upward mobility (Ryan & Sackrey, 1984; Steinitz & Solomon, 1986), they felt somewhat fraudulent and some felt as if they had "sold out." The students generally attempted to resolve this ambivalence by harnessing their ideals to the law school culture's definition of career success: They concluded that they could serve the less privileged better by working as role models and change agents within the network of elite law firms and corporations and by doing pro bono work than by working as outside activists and public interest lawyers. To bolster this somewhat shaky rapprochement, some avoided peers who reminded them of the forsaken road. As a third-year student said:

> It's taken for granted here that you can work for a large firm and still be a good person. The people who don't reinforce that message make me uncomfortable now. Frankly, that's why I'm not hanging out with the public interest people. They remind me of my own guilt. (Granfield, 1991, p. 346)

Thus, in a real sense, some students sought to forget their origins.[3]

However, if repression proves as difficult or inadequate as the mediatory myths, individuals may withhold commitment or even forsake the new role for something more consistent with the old. As suggested by the discussions of self-coherence and self-continuity in chapter 3, deeply internalized role identities tend to exert a gravitational tug on future identities.

In sum, role learning—coupled with selective forgetting—enables newcomers to understand their role and its relationship to the wider organizational context, thus providing an informational base for the potential realization of the motives for identity, meaning, control, and belonging.

ROLE INNOVATION

If role learning provides information, *role innovation* provides personal space. Nicholson and West (1988) defined role innovation[4] as "moulding the new role to suit the requirements of the mover, ranging from minor initiatives such as variations in work schedules, to more dramatic role innovations such as changes in the main goals of organizational work" (p. 106). Thus, role innovation varies from the minor to the momentous,

---

[3]However, Wegner (1989) noted that sometimes "traversing the thin line from suppression to obsession takes only a single step" (p. 31). Like an alcoholic "falling off the wagon," an inadvertent cue may cause an otherwise suppressed identity to return with a vengeance—particularly if the identity was well-learned and positively valent. Thus, "forgotten" role identities may exist as more or less latent capacities, compartmentalized in the mind, awaiting something to open the door.

[4]Role innovation is also known as *role change, role development, role negotiation,* and *role making.*

involving the ends for which the role is designed, the means by which the ends are realized, the evaluation of performance, or all of these.

As Staw and Boettger (1990) argued, role innovation can be functional or dysfunctional for the organization. Generally, role innovation is more likely to be functional—and necessary—if: (a) the role is new, (b) the means or ends are incompletely or incorrectly specified, (c) creativity is normatively expected, (d) the context is dynamic, (e) individuals are accountable for outcomes and empowered to attain them, and (f) individuals identify with the organization and have the requisite experience or knowledge, skills, and abilities to innovate effectively. The notion of innovation is particularly germane to organic organizations with their fluid tasks and to managerial and professional work where the ends may be clearer than the means.

However, role innovation is relevant to *every* role regardless of how rigorously and effectively specified the ends and means may be. This is because role enactment is necessarily a function of the specific person in the role. Roles are flat abstractions until they are given life by a unique individual. Short of automation, it is the individual who must interact with a customer, inspect a product, participate in a team meeting, and so on— in short, it is the individual who interprets and makes ongoing adjustments to the flow of activity. Because no two people are alike, no two role enactments are alike except in extremely strong situations.

To role innovate, then, is to *personalize* or *individualize* the way a role is enacted to suit one's judgment and idiosyncrasies. In addition to being a necessity, personalization enables one to put their stamp on the role (Harré, 1983)—marking it as theirs—so as to express valued personal identities and to accommodate one's preferred operating methods. As such, role innovation conveys one's uniqueness both to oneself and to members of one's role set, differentiating one from other role occupants and predecessors. Thus, role innovation may address the identity motives of self-distinctiveness, self-expression, and self-continuity (by enabling one to project oneself into the new role) as well as the motives for meaning (by enabling one to impute purpose into the role) and control (see chap. 3).

Also, because roles are necessarily embedded in interdependent role sets, role innovation has implications for how others enact their own roles. Consequently, role innovation is often characterized as a process of negotiation or social influence between an individual and members of his or her role set (Fondas & Stewart, 1994; Graen, 1976). For instance, Bauer et al. (1998) argued that innovation attempts may be resisted by the role set if they are done in an arrogant or condescending manner.

Role Innovation Versus Personal Change

Nicholson's (1984; Nicholson & West, 1988) work-role transitions theory focuses on two adjustment processes: Role innovation and *personal change* ("personal development"), also referred to as *accommodation* and *assimilation* (Nicholson, 1987). Personal change involves "reactive change in the individual, ranging from minor alterations in daily routines and habits, to major developments in relationships and self-image" (Nicholson & West, 1988, p. 105). (Identity transformation, discussed last chapter, would obviously be considered a major development.) Simply put, whereas role innovation entails adapting the role to fit oneself, personal change entails adapting oneself to fit the role. However, as argued shortly, personal change may also involve proactive change and entail broader revisions to self than implied by person–role/organization fit (Fournier, 1995).

Some perspectives on work adjustment either explicitly or implicitly view adjustment as a *compromise* between the demands of the person and the demands of the organization, as if role innovation and personal change exist on a single continuum such that more of one necessarily means less of the other (e.g., Brett, 1984; Dawis & Lofquist, 1984). However, research suggests that these constructs tend to be weakly correlated (Ashforth & Saks, 1995; Black & Ashford, 1995; M. A. West, 1987) rather than negatively correlated. Closer to the mark, then, may be Nicholson and West's (1988) contention that role innovation and personal change are "independent but not mutually exclusive dimensions" (p. 113).

Crossing high and low levels of role innovation with high and low levels of personal change yields the four modes of work adjustment considered in work-role transitions theory and depicted in Fig. 7.1: (a) *replication* (low role innovation and low personal change), where one "performs in much the same manner as in previous jobs and also in much the same manner as previous occupations" (Nicholson, 1984, p. 176), (b) *absorption* (low role innovation and high personal change), where "the burden of adjustment is borne almost exclusively by the person" (p. 176), (c) *determination* (high role innovation and low personal change), the opposite of absorption, where the burden of adjustment is borne by the role, and (d) *exploration* (high role innovation and high personal change), where there is simultaneous change in role and personal attributes.

There are solid theoretical reasons for predicting both positive associations between role innovation and personal change (as in replication and exploration) and negative associations (as in absorption and determination) depending on the interaction of situation and individual. First, following Nicholson's (1984) theory, situational factors and individual differences may underlie each of the four configurations of role and personal change such that each configuration represents a more or less integrated response to role entry (see "Individual Differences," later in this chapter).

Second, role innovation may obviate the need for personal change and vice versa. For example, altering the role to suit one's preferences precludes the need to adapt one's preferences to the role; conversely, internalizing the proffered role identity may foster contentment with the status quo. This argument is obviously consistent with the notion that role innovation and personal change represent a compromise. However, if role innovation and personal change do *not* lie on a single continuum (as the compromise perspective implies), then one does not necessarily obviate the other: There may be times when they occur independently and other times when they occur synergistically.

Third, regarding synergism, some personal change may *facilitate* role innovation (and vice versa). Feij, Whitely, Peiró, and Taris (1995) studied young machine operators and office technology workers and found that skill development measured at 3 to 9 months was positively correlated with job content innovation 1 year later. Thus, self-development may create the ability, willingness, and credibility to modify one's role.

Finally, following personal construct psychology (Kelly, 1955), some personal change may reflect a proactive rather than merely reactive

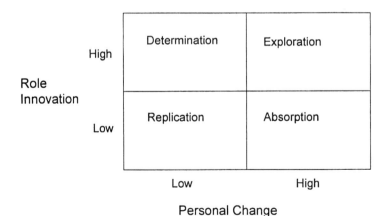

FIG. 7.1. Modes of work adjustment. (Reprinted from N. Nicholson, 1984, "A theory of work role transitions," *Administrative Science Quarterly, 29,* 172–191, by permission of *Administrative Science Quarterly.* Copyright © 1984 Cornell University.)

orientation to role entry such that personal and role change reflect two sides of the same coin. Like role innovation, personal change may represent an ongoing and somewhat idiosyncratic process of exploration and interpretation where the newcomer develops wholly new ways of regarding himself or herself. Thus, Fournier (1995) found that although some organizational newcomers internalized the proffered role identity, some reacted against it and defined themselves in opposite ways ("That is not who I want to be"), and others developed idiosyncratic role identities (e.g., success means self-fulfillment rather than promotions). Fournier added that one's extant social and personal identities influence what is attended to and assimilated.[5]

Predictors of Role Innovation

Chapter 6 focused on the situational forces that facilitate personal change. In contrast, role innovation is facilitated by four factors: Necessity, autonomy, unmet expectations, and individual differences. (Once again, individual differences are discussed later in a separate section.) Regarding necessity, role innovation often occurs because it must. As noted, roles are abstractions that can only be fleshed out through enactment. Thus, much role innovation occurs through incremental and unheralded concrete acts as individuals feel their way through their new roles. As noted last chapter, individualized socialization tends to be positively associated with role innovation (e.g., N. J. Allen & Meyer, 1990; Ashforth & Saks, 1996; Jones, 1986). This may occur more by default than design as newcomers are left to "sink or swim": Lacking guidance, they reinvent the role as they see fit. Indeed, a role can evolve into something quite different than originally anticipated by organizational planners and role occupants—without conscious intent or formal negotiation (Quinn, 1980).

However, Ashforth and Saks (1996) argued that although institutionalized socialization (the opposite of individualized socialization) tends in practice to be negatively associated with role innovation, it need not be. Whether a given socialization tactic results in high or low innovation

---

[5]In chapter 3, I noted Rothbaum et al.'s (1982) contention that primary control involves "bringing the environment into line with [one's] wishes," whereas secondary control involves "bringing [oneself] into line with the environmental forces" (p. 5). Secondary control was described as compensatory, a fall-back option if primary control is absent. However, as the current discussion suggests, personal change should not be regarded simply as a failure to role innovate: Individuals can seek and profit from personal growth and role and organizational identification.

depends not on *how* it is taught (the process) but on *what* is learned (the content). For example, a mentor (the serial socialization tactic) can impart norms of role conformity *or* role innovation.

Regarding autonomy, Nicholson (1984) argued that discretion determines the scope for role innovation: The higher the discretion, the greater the scope. Indeed, Nicholson argued that high-discretion jobs *necessitate* role innovation because "newcomers lack adequate data on which to base conformity" (p. 178). Thus, much as proactivity enables individuals to learn about their roles, autonomy enables individuals to modify their roles. Research has generally but not always supported the autonomy–role innovation relationship. For example, support has been obtained in samples of managers changing jobs (Nicholson & West, 1988), nursing students (M. West & Rushton, 1989), and recent business school graduates (Ashforth & Saks, 1995), whereas no support was obtained in a sample of relocated employees (Munton & West, 1995). In one provocative study, Black and Ashford (1995) did not find direct support but did find a significant post hoc interaction indicating that autonomy is more likely to be exercised if the person–job fit is relatively poor.

However, the exercise of power in social systems often requires at least the implicit consent of role set members—especially where task (and resource) interdependence is high. In highly interdependent roles, individuals tend to evolve patterned ways of interacting that come to be seen as normative, thereby assuming moral overtones (the "right" way) and becoming resistant to change (R. H. Turner, 1962; Weick, 1979). Thus, there are typically real constraints on the use of autonomy. If one's innovations are thought by others to deviate too far from the familiar and normative, then various social sanctions may be applied, from rebukes to ostracism. The higher the perceived costs of exercising autonomy, the more likely that one will withdraw psychologically from the role (Ashford & Taylor, 1990; Hirschman, 1970).

Regarding unmet expectations, reactance theory holds that denying a person something that is desired or expected induces him or her to value it even more highly and to attempt to reclaim it (Brehm, 1993). Given the entry shock discussed last chapter, it is likely that many newcomers will feel motivated to reshape the status quo more to their liking. Similarly, role innovation may be a means of coping with work-related stressors. However, Ashforth and Saks (2000) did not find that unmet expectations of control at 4 months predicted attempted role innovation ("problem-focused reactance") occurring between 4 and 10 months. They *did* find that unmet expectations predicted helplessness and poor work adjustment at 10 months. This led Ashforth and Saks to speculate that newcomers may well have reacted against the control system prior to the 4-month anniversary but that after that time, they essentially resigned themselves to an apparently impassive status quo. If accurate, this interpretation raises provocative questions about the *timing* of role innovation.

When Does Role Innovation Occur?

Individuals with knowledge, skills, and abilities that are relatively unique and valued by the organization may have sufficient power to negotiate the contours of their role *prior* to entry (Ashford & Taylor, 1990). Indeed, such individuals may be empowered to essentially define their role. Thus, Ashford and Taylor (1990) conjectured that "negotiations conducted around transition points will tend to be formal and direct," whereas "at other times, negotiations are likely to be informal and indirect" (p. 21).

As noted in chapter 6, stage models of socialization differentiate between encounter (early role entry) and metamorphosis (late role entry), arguing that role innovation tends to be delayed until the latter stage. Role innovation upon role entry may be muted (unless necessitated by individualized socialization) as newcomers typically need to assess the status quo via role learning (e.g., what is expected, how elastic is the role) and to accumulate sufficient *idiosyncrasy credits* (i.e., trust and credibility; Hollander, 1964) before they can venture significant changes. Furthermore, given the honeymoon period noted last chapter, newcomers may feel no need or desire to enact changes shortly after role entry.

That said, some research indicates that role innovation efforts tend to occur shortly after any such latency period—particularly if the newcomer is familiar with the job or organization (as when an experienced person is hired, promoted, or transferred). For example, Graen, Orris, and Johnson (1973) studied primarily clerical and secretarial positions and found that incumbents engaged in role innovation efforts within weeks of starting and maintained a relatively constant level of innovation during the 16 weeks of the study.[6] Similarly, Feldman and Brett (1983) reported that new hires and job changers were engaging in role innovation when assessed at 3 months. Initially, however, innovation may be largely focused on role means rather than role ends or the criteria for evaluation.

---

[6]As reported by Graen (1976): Graen et al. (1973) did not provide specific results for role innovation.

Also, it is very likely that role innovation varies widely across roles (given the conditions noted earlier) and individuals (given the individual differences described next).

A range of role innovation trajectories is possible over the long run. At one extreme, innovation efforts may produce substantive changes in the role such that the need for innovation tapers off. At the other extreme, innovation efforts may be discouraged before the fact, punished after the fact, or otherwise rendered ineffective, inducing the helplessness and withdrawal noted by Ashforth and Saks (2000). Indeed, with the passage of time, what may have once seemed intolerable may come to seem normal, fostering a congruent role identity (Ashforth & Mael, 1998). Shield (1988) described how nursing home residents were inadvertently made to feel dependent and useless, undermining their identity as efficacious adults and their willingness to assert themselves.

Short of either extreme, individuals and their organizations are apt to muddle toward a revised psychological contract where the role reflects a mutual accommodation. Over the long run, role innovation may resemble a punctuated equilibrium model (Gersick, 1991) where the pattern of accommodations is temporarily disrupted by emerging issues and shifting preferences, prompting new rounds of role innovation (Weiss et al., 1982).

In sum, the literatures on role innovation and role learning clearly indicate that newcomers are far more than straws in the wind. They are frequently willing and able to exercise some control—and to some extent *must* exercise control—over the contours of their roles and role identities.

INDIVIDUAL DIFFERENCES

Role learning/unlearning and innovation pertain to how individuals negotiate their roles. As such, it is likely that the inclination to engage in these processes and the pace and intensity of learning and innovation are strongly influenced by a set of individual differences.

Previous Work Experience

Socialization largely involves making sense of the surprises and contrasts one encounters during role transitions (Louis, 1980a, 1980b). Thus, experience affects *what* is seen as noteworthy and *how* one makes sense of it. Previous work experience provides interpretive schemas for perceiving and deciphering current experiences. The more diverse one's experiences, the more diverse and possibly complex the schemas for making sense of a new role (see chap. 8, "Between-Role Transition Styles"). Also, the more similar one's current situation appears to be to one's previous experience, the fewer the surprises, the greater one's confidence, and the more likely that one will reflexively invoke familiar schemas.

However, empirical support for the utility of previous experience has been somewhat mixed. For example, Shaw, Fisher, and Woodman (as cited in Fisher, 1986) found that U.S. Air Force personnel that were transferred to a new job adjusted to the technical and social aspects in about half the time if the new job was similar rather than dissimilar to the old job, and Black (1988) found that previous overseas experience was positively associated with the work adjustment of American expatriate managers in Japan. Conversely, Zahrly and Tosi (1989) found that previous experience with factory and shift work did not affect the adjustment of workers to a new plant start-up, and Pinder and Schroeder (1987) found that the number of previous transfers did not affect the time to proficiency of transferred employees. As Ashford and Taylor (1990) concluded, "adaptation is not a process that necessarily gets easier with experience" (pp. 26–27).

One possible reason for the mixed findings is that experience carries a considerable risk; namely, that the similarities between previous and current circumstances may be more apparent than real such that one's schemas are outmoded and one's expectations are no longer realistic. For example, Adkins (1995) found that the effect of previous experience on the adjustment of mental health specialists was minimal but that the general pattern of results suggested that experience *inhibited* adjustment. She speculated that this was attributable to a "false confidence" effect whereby prior experience in a similar setting induced newcomers to be "less attentive to formal instructions and organizational cues" (p. 856).

Perhaps, then, previous experience is most likely to be misapplied in situations of *moderate* change. The smaller the magnitude of the transition, the more likely that one will reflexively—but effectively—apply prior schemas. Thus, research comparing new hires to job changers within the same organization suggests that the local experience of the latter reduces their need for information and reliance on others (e.g., Feldman & Brett, 1983; M. W. Kramer et al., 1995). Conversely, the greater the magnitude, the more likely that one will recognize that the reflexive application of prior learning is inappropriate, thereby stimulating receptiveness to new learning (what Argyris & Schön, 1978, term *double-loop* rather than *single-loop learning*).[7] Thus, individuals undergoing an overseas transfer are likely to be more receptive to change than individuals undergoing a domestic transfer (cf. Black et al., 1992). However, in a transition of moderate change, the similarities in roles may induce the false confidence effect—particularly if the transition was unexpected and of minimal duration, therefore undermining preparation and inducing a reliance on familiar schemas.

Previous experience may also stimulate the learning of certain meta-competencies or skills for sense-making, coping with change, and role innovation. As alluded to in chapter 2, *meta-competencies* refer to learning how to learn (a process emphasis) and thereby manage change rather than to extrapolating prior views of the world (a content emphasis; D. T. Hall, 1986, 1996). For example, Nicholson (1987) cited evidence that managers were cushioned against the novelty of new work roles by the transferability of their generalist skills and the confidence this conferred, whereas young university graduates felt inexpert and lacked confidence when they entered new work roles. And M. A. West (1987) found that role innovation in previous jobs predicted innovation in current jobs.

In sum, previous experience may generate: (a) role-specific learning that generalizes to roles that appear to be similar and (b) meta-competencies for sense-making, coping, and innovation that generalize to any new role.

Personality Traits

To the extent that the following attributes are more or less stable across situations and over time, they can be described as traits. However, it should be noted that all have state-like qualities in that they may be primed and altered somewhat by environmental influences. For instance, identity resolution (discussed next) can be increased by developmental efforts (e.g., Chao et al., 1994) or decreased by the up-ending practices discussed last chapter.

Identity Style, Identity Resolution, and Self-Esteem. Building on Marcia's (1966) model of identity statuses, Berzonsky's (1990, 1992) research on *identity style* indicates that individuals differ in their receptiveness to the potential identity implications of their activities

---

[7]However, the high stress that is often associated with major change (see "Stress," later in this chapter) may induce a "threat-rigidity effect" (Staw, Sandelands, & Dutton, 1981) whereby some individuals alleviate the stress by enacting familiar—although ineffective—behaviors. Minkler and Biller (1979) referred to this tendency, in the context of entry shock, as "reverting to past roles" (p. 131).

and roles. Individuals with an *information orientation* actively seek out and use self-relevant information, developing complex, differentiated, but relatively coherent views of themselves. Other individuals follow a *normative orientation* and conform to the expectations of significant others, defending against and distorting information that threatens their idealized identity(ies). The result is a fairly rigid and undifferentiated sense of self. Finally, individuals with an *avoidant orientation* avoid dealing with personal problems and identity issues, resulting in a fragmented sense of self.

An important qualification to Berzonsky's typology is that the impact of identity style on information processing is moderated by commitment to a given identity such that commitment reduces the impact of style (Berzonsky, 1992). Consistent with Ruble's (1994) model of role transitions and Swann's (1990) research on self-verification, it seems likely that at least information- and norm-oriented individuals would become increasingly committed to their emerging sense of self and thus less amenable to change over time. As with any journey, the initial steps largely shape the direction of subsequent ones and perhaps diminish receptiveness to alternative paths.

Related to identity style is the notion of identity resolution, defined in chapter 5 as awareness of one's own abilities, values, and interests (S. Gould, 1979; D. T. Hall, 1976). S. Gould (1979) found that identity resolution was positively correlated with self-esteem, adaptability, and an internal locus of control and that these variables were positively correlated with career involvement and a tendency to engage in career planning. Chao et al. (1994) found that identity resolution was positively correlated with income, career involvement, adaptability, and job satisfaction. Similarly, the more subjectively important a given identity, the more likely that one will seek opportunities to enact the identity and perceive a given situation as such an opportunity (see chap. 3; Swann, 1990). People tend to seek out roles consistent with their identities, attempt to mold roles to suit those identities, and use these roles to express themselves (Semmer & Schallberger, 1996).

The implication for role learning and innovation is that individuals with an information orientation are more likely to be both proactive and receptive to situational cues, suggesting the exploration cell of Nicholson's (1984) work-role transitions model (see Fig. 7.1), whereas individuals with an avoidant orientation are less likely to be either proactive or receptive to learning, suggesting the replication cell. Conversely, the conformist stance of norm-oriented individuals suggests that they are likely to gravitate to the absorption cell, whereas individuals with high identity resolution may gravitate to the determination cell because they seek opportunities to personalize their roles to suit their firmly held identities. Clearly, however, these arguments are speculative.

Finally, *self-esteem* is one's evaluation of one's worth. High self-esteem may give one the confidence to explore various role identities and engage in risk taking (Grotevant, 1987). Thus, over time, individuals with high self-esteem are more likely to have engaged in role learning and innovation, to have adopted a diverse array of identities, and to ultimately find identities that are more consistent with their preferences. In support, Brockner's (1988) review of self-esteem in work contexts suggests that persons with high self-esteem tend to have a more firmly established sense of who they are and what they value. Consequently, individuals with high self-esteem are more likely to express their identities at work and to behave in a manner consistent with them (Shamir, 1991). For example, Munton and West (1995) found that the self-esteem of relocated employees predicted role innovation. High self-esteem also helps insulate one against threats to one's claim to a value identity (e.g., C. M. Steele et al., 1993).

The implication for role learning and innovation is straightforward. The willingness of high-self-esteem individuals to assert themselves suggests a proclivity for high role innovation, and to the extent they are also exploring identity options, a proclivity for exploration over determination.

Control Beliefs and Desires.   Organizational researchers have investigated a set of personality traits that reflect a *belief in one's capacity to exert control.* These traits include internal locus of control, self-efficacy,[8] and confidence. Individuals with strong control beliefs are likely to be highly motivated to master and personalize their roles. Thus, control beliefs are likely to be positively associated with role learning and innovation. For example, Ashforth and Saks (2000) found that generalized self-efficacy measured prior to university graduation predicted attempted role innovation ("problem-focused reactance") 10 months after role entry. And Heppner et al. (1994) found that two dimensions from their Career

---

[8]Self-efficacy has been referred to as both a motive and a belief (Erez & Earley, 1993; Gecas, 1986). To avoid confusion with the motive for control (see chap. 3), I reserve the term *self-efficacy* for generalized *beliefs* or state-like beliefs that one can successfully perform necessary and desired behaviors.

Transitions Inventory, confidence (e.g., "I feel confident in my ability to do well in this career transition process") and control (e.g., "Luck and chance play the major role in this career transition process" [reversed]), were positively correlated with a sense of progress and hope as well as a clear vocational identity among individuals undergoing a task, position, or occupation change.

Closely related to beliefs in control is the *motive, need,* or *desire for control,* defined in chapter 3 as a motive to understand and to exercise influence over subjectively important domains. Given the importance of this construct to Nicholson's (1984) work-role transitions theory, it is included here as an individual difference variable. Nicholson argued that individuals with a desire to master their task environment are more likely to engage in role innovation. In support, Ashford and Black (1996) found that the desire for control, assessed among MBA graduates 2 to 3 months prior to organizational entry, was positively associated with a number of proactive behaviors at 6 months: Information seeking, general socializing, networking, negotiating job changes, and positively framing situations. (However, the desire for control was not significantly related to feedback seeking or building a relationship with one's boss.) Furthermore, the desire for control was associated with proactive coping among a sample of newly transferred managers (Nicholson & West, 1988) and with both role innovation and personal change among nursing students in a training environment (M. West & Rushton, 1989). However, the desire for control was unrelated to role innovation among samples of recent graduates of undergraduate and MBA programs (Ashforth & Saks, 1995; Black & Ashford, 1995).

Growth Need Strength, Need for Achievement, and Conscientiousness. Growth need strength is a desire for personal accomplishment, learning, and self-development (Hackman & Oldham, 1980). Similarly, *need for achievement* is a desire to excel at challenging tasks (McClelland, 1985), and *conscientious* people tend to be careful, thorough, organized, and tend to plan and persevere (Barrick & Mount, 1991; Tokar, Fischer, & Subich, 1998). These attributes suggest a predisposition toward the self-development attained through role learning and for the mastery suggested by role innovation. Thus, these attributes predict the exploration cell of Fig. 7.1. For example, Nicholson and West (1988) found that need for growth predicted both role innovation and personal change among managers.

Self-Monitoring and Desire for Feedback. *Self-monitoring* is one's sensitivity to situational cues as guides to behavior, concern for displaying appropriate behavior, and effort to display such behavior (M. Snyder, 1987). The higher the self-monitoring, the more likely that one will conform to situational cues. Thus, high self-monitors are likely to display more variability in their projected identities across diverse social contexts than low self-monitors. The implication is that self-monitoring should facilitate role learning by enabling individuals to better read their social environments and respond accordingly. For example, based on a sample of managers, Church (1997) found a positive correlation between self-monitoring and one's knowledge of how one's subordinates perceived one's behavior. Chatman (1991), however, did not find that self-monitoring predicted changes in person–organization fit among entry-level auditors; she cautioned that the behavioral change associated with self-monitoring may not translate into value change.

Similarly, individuals with a *motive, need,* or *desire for feedback* "will be attuned and responsive to the influences, communications and needs of others, and to the perceived demand characteristics of the work situation" (Nicholson & West, 1988, p. 108). According to work-role transitions theory, such individuals will take their cues for "appropriate" role behaviors from others (Nicholson, 1984). Thus, desire for feedback should predict personal change. Support was obtained by Black and Ashford (1995) and Ashforth and Saks (1995; for 4 months after entry but not for 10 months) among samples of business school graduates but not by M. A. West et al. (1987) or M. West and Rushton (1989) among samples of managers and nursing students (however, M. West & Rushton attributed the finding to a restriction of range in the desire for feedback).

Positive and Negative Affectivity. Individuals with high *positive affectivity* (PA) are predisposed to experience positive or pleasant affective states over time and across situations (J. M. George, 1992; Watson & Clark, 1984). Their view of themselves and their world is generally positive and optimistic. Conversely, individuals with high *negative affectivity* (NA) are predisposed to experience negative or unpleasant affective states over time and across situations and they generally hold a negative view of themselves and their world (J. M. George, 1992; Watson & Clark, 1984). PA and NA tend to be relatively independent.

Individuals with high PA may be more likely than those with low PA to view a given role transition with optimism—as an exciting opportunity.

This suggests a willingness (even eagerness) to engage the role proactively and to embrace personal change. Thus, high PA predicts the exploration cell of Fig. 7.1. Conversely, those with high NA, relative to those with low NA, may be more likely to view a transition pessimistically and to experience distress. This suggests a tendency to hunker down and avoid both role innovation and personal change—the replication cell of Fig. 7.1.

Moreover, affectivity may interact with role learning and innovation in that individuals with high PA may be more pleasant to be around and attract more opportunities for interaction and mentoring and be less likely to have their innovation efforts rebuffed (Bauer et al., 1998). Each affective orientation is likely to prove self-fulfilling as eagerness and proactivity engender role learning and innovation, whereas negativity and distress dampen learning and innovation. For example, Braithwaite, Gibson, and Bosly-Craft (1986) found that a very negative attitude to retirement was correlated with poor adjustment to retirement.

A Cautionary Note

Despite this lengthy list of individual differences, it may well remain difficult to predict role learning and innovation. This is because of the notion of dynamic interactionism discussed in chapter 1. Individuals and roles may evolve *interactively* such that a new synthesis is achieved that is more than simply a compromise between static role demands and static individual traits. A newly promoted manager may define and enact her role in a manner that is consistent with her character but somewhat idiosyncratic to the organization. Certain aspects of her role performance may be reinforced by members of her role set and be experienced as gratifying, whereas other aspects may be punished and experienced as ungratifying. These external and internal responses may induce modifications in her role identity and role enactment and, over time, her global identity. Consequently, the role and the individual *coevolve* over time such that the exploration cell of Fig. 7.1 becomes a common adjustment mode—at least, in the long run (Ashforth & Saks, 1995; Barley, 1989). For example, Ibarra (1996) found that neophyte consultants and investment bankers experimented with how they enacted their roles, leading to a process of self-discovery and refinement of their roles. The implication is that it may be impossible to strongly predict role innovation or personal change from a static set of antecedents (except in very strong situations) no matter how comprehensive they are.

With role learning, role innovation, and personal change under our belt, the remainder of the chapter focuses more narrowly on an important facet of personal change, the process of role identification. Whereas chapter 6 considered the situational context, the focus here is on individual dynamics.

THE ABCs
OF ROLE IDENTIFICATION

Much of the literature on identification treats the phenomenon as more or less static, focusing more on what predicts a given level of identification or on what outcomes stem from a given level. Identification, in short, is treated more as a noun than a verb. The purpose of this section is to explore the *process of becoming*: How the ABCs of role entry—*affect*, *behavior*, and *cognition*—interact to influence the dynamics of role identification (Ashforth, 1998; Harquail, 1998). An overview of the argument is presented in Fig. 7.2.

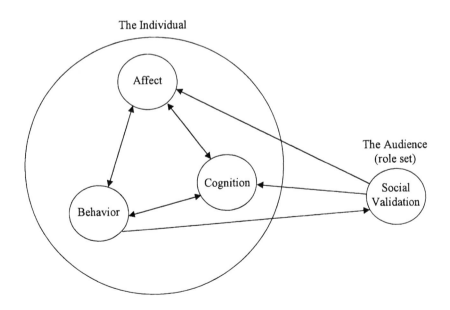

FIG. 7.2. The ABCs of role entry.

Affect and Cognition as First Movers

Identification was defined in chapter 1 as the sense of oneness with a group or role, entailing the perception (cognition) and valuing (affect) of that oneness. Rather than delve into the intricacies of whether affect *or* cognition comes first (cf. Lazarus, 1984, vs. Zajonc, 1984), I will discuss them as a relatively tightly coupled set of psychological forces and argue that identification may begin with affect *and* cognition rather than behavior (Harquail, 1998).

SIT contends that individuals can identify with a *psychological group*, defined by J. C. Turner (1984) as "a collection of people who share the same social identification or define themselves in terms of the same social category membership" (p. 530). A member of a psychological group does not need to interact with, like, or even know other members or be liked and accepted by them. It is his or her sense of sharing an affective and cognitive affinity with the group (e.g., being a loyal sports fan) that is the basis for identification. The individual credits the group with a psychological reality apart from any relationship he or she may have with its members (Ashforth & Mael, 1989; J. C. Turner, 1984). This argument implies that an individual can identify with a role without having met any of its occupants or enacting the role identity—without *behaving* as if he or she identifies with the role.[9]

In an organizational context, a new recruit may enter the role with high anticipatory identification based on little more than his or her stereotypic beliefs about what the role entails, perhaps supported by imaginary role rehearsals (see chap. 5). For example, Mael and Ashforth (1995) found that many U.S. Army recruits entered the Army with fairly high levels of

---

[9]Indeed, this argument raises the intriguing question of whether one can identify with a psychological group without *ever* actually enacting the identity (Harquail, 1998). I contend that the answer is a qualified yes. *Yes* because research on stigmatized identities, such as homosexual, suggests that individuals can remain "in the closet"—that is, aware of their leanings—without acting on them (e.g., Woods & Lucas, 1993). Similarly, one may consider oneself an environmentalist, Democrat, or atheist without displaying it. And *qualified* because it is very difficult to sustain strong identification in the absence of private or public behavior that expresses the identity. As the discussions of the self-expression motive in chapter 3 and of social validation (following) indicate, individuals feel a need to affirm their valued identities both to themselves and to members of their role set. As with love, identities that are continuously denied expression tend to wither for lack of affirmation. Moreover, as suggested by the discussion of selective forgetting, it is simply difficult to repress a latent identity if identification is indeed strong.

However, this argument regarding whether behavior is necessary for identification is less relevant to organization-based role identities because organizational imperatives require that most roles be routinely enacted and often publicly so.

organizational identification despite having no direct experience in soldiering. In addition to addressing the motive for identity, anticipatory identification may address the motives for meaningfulness (in that the identity may convey purpose and a perspective for understanding the world), secondary control (in psychologically yoking the individual to the role, identification enables him or her to share in the power and status of the role and the legacy of achievements), and depersonalized belonging (in that one becomes part of a community of like-minded and similarly labeled people).

Affect/Cognition→Behavior. The motive for self-expression indicates that individuals seek to enact their desired identities for the intrinsic pleasure of "being themselves." Similarly, Heise's (1977) affect control theory indicates that self and situational definitions connote certain "fundamental sentiments" (p. 164) that one seeks to experience (and thereby confirm) through one's behavior. For example, a manager who defines her role in a meeting to be that of a critic may act in ways that display and affirm her detachment and skepticism. Indeed, Heise argued that the identity–affect link is so strong that if the expected sentiments cannot be confirmed, the individual may select a new identity that better matches the situation. The upshot of these tendencies is that the affective and cognitive facets of role identification give rise to behaviors that are intended to affirm the role identity and its prevailing sentiments (see the outcomes of identification discussed in chap. 3). As such, identification tends to be self-fulfilling.

Behavior as the First Mover

Just as affect and cognition tend to foster behaviors that reflect the affect and cognition, so behaviors tend to foster congruent affect and cognition. Regardless of newcomers' level of anticipatory identification, they are typically required to enact the role—even if only in training simulations—before they actually feel comfortable in the role. Indeed, in many cases, comfort may only develop as newcomers attain behavioral mastery of the role. As stated in footnote 9, organizational roles often must be routinely and publicly enacted such that behavioral displays comprise a large component of the role identity. Anticipatory identification may remain tentative unless it is validated through such displays. This is likely to be particularly true for roles where performance: (a) is predicated on behavior-intensive activities (e.g., taxi driver), (b) requires complex behavior-based skills (e.g., surgeon), and (c) involves a critical audience (e.g., salesperson). Furthermore, because behavior is inherently more malleable than other facets of social and personal identities (e.g., values, goals, beliefs, traits), it represents an accessible means of fostering identification. Behavioral change creates a certain momentum in the self-system that may foment deeper personal change.

Ashford and Taylor (1990) framed behavioral learning in terms of the self-regulation literature (akin to Manz's, 1983, notion of self-management discussed earlier). First, newcomers and their socialization agents must *monitor* the newcomers' behavior. Second, they must *evaluate* the behavior in terms of the role's proficiency standards. Third, they must *reinforce* movement toward those standards. Ashford and Taylor noted that attention and sanctions are applied initially to successful role performance, but as the newly acquired behaviors become habitual, attention and sanctions are instead applied to *un*successful performance (management by exception). In short, the newcomer is taught to act out the role.

Behavior→Affect/Cognition.   Chapter 3 discussed how individuals seek a more or less internally consistent (self-coherence) and stable (self-continuity) sense of self across situations and over time. Similarly, research on self-justification and cognitive dissonance indicates that one's behavior must make sense to oneself—it must appear rational and consistent with what one thinks about oneself (Festinger, 1957; Staw, 1980). External attributions (e.g., "I'm working for the paycheck," "I need to get experience") may justify role enactment, but it is difficult to think about such externalities 8 hours a day, 5 days a week—particularly over the long run. Also, if the enactment remains devoid of positive internal attributions (e.g., "I enjoy this job," "I'm learning"), some dissonance may linger because one is, after all, investing massive amounts of time in a joyless enterprise. Thus, as one enacts a role, one feels pressure to identify with the role as a means of more fully justifying one's involvement (Ashforth & Humphrey, 1993).

Self-perception theory adds that individuals infer their attitudes toward something in part by interpreting their own behavior (Bem, 1972). A person's behavior may serve a signaling function regarding the person's nature if the behavior: (a) is perceived to be volitional (i.e., it occurs in the absence of a strong situation), visible, explicit, and irrevocable (as alluded to in chap. 2) and (b) relates to a facet of the self-concept that is not strongly developed or accessible or is only slightly discrepant from a facet that is (Fazio, 1987; Salancik, 1977; Schlenker & Trudeau, 1990).

Whether rational or irrational, spontaneous or considered, freely selected or subtly coerced, one's behaviors tend to *commit* one to a certain self (see chap. 6). Thus, voluntarily entering a role and complying with behavioral norms may predispose one to construe that one has some affinity for the role.[10] For example, Callero (1985) surveyed blood donors and concluded that identification with the donor role was "both a cause and consequence of donating blood" (p. 213): The act of donating blood—which may have reflected a spur of the moment decision—facilitated identification, which in turn predicted subsequent donations.

Moreover, enacting a new role identity fosters the role learning, role innovation, and personal change processes discussed earlier. In simulating the behavior of a bona fide role occupant and experimenting with the parameters of the role, one *experiences* the role phenomenologically. The act of *doing* the role necessarily engages one psychologically such that one is simultaneously *thinking* about and *feeling* the role. Thus, an abstract and intellectual understanding of the role becomes concrete and visceral. And as one experiments with one's enactment and learns, the articulation of self and role is refined such that the fit of self-*in*-role improves.[11]

The more that the emergent role identity resonates with the individual's hoped-for self—or evokes such a self—the more intense and meaningful the engagement will be. W. A. Kahn (1990) argued that "it is likely . . . that a hierarchy relates increasing depths of engagement to the investment of the self along physical, then cognitive, and finally emotional dimensions" (p. 719). Individuals who are physically, cognitively, and emotionally engaged in their roles are said to have achieved flow (Csikszentmihalyi, 1990)—a total immersion in the experience of enacting their roles.

Indeed, so powerful is the cognitive and affective tug of behavior that it is difficult to remain psychologically detached over time from *any* role that one continually enacts—especially if the role requires one to display strong emotions (Ashforth & Humphrey, 1993). In *acting* the part, one

---

[10]Involuntary entry into long-term roles (e.g., patient, prisoner, nursing home resident) may ultimately induce identification of a different sort—with the very dependency of the role ("I have no control over what happens," "I am a victim," and "I am a pawn"). T. Parsons (1951) referred to this internalized dependency as the *sick role.*

[11]This holistic involvement of affect, behavior, and cognition is the means by which role plays (i.e., simulated and short-term role enactments) foster personal change. For example, Baesler (1995) found that conditions that fostered greater involvement in a disability role play experiment also fostered greater change in beliefs about disabled people.

eventually tends to *become* the part. Military drill instructors are required to personify military standards for new recruits. This entails exceedingly long days at the barracks, rigorous attention to detail and discipline, and the cultivation of a relentlessly demanding demeanor (P. Katz, 1990). One effect of this comportment is that drill instructors often have a difficult time separating themselves from their role. A daughter of one U.S. Marine sergeant said, "the kind of menace a drill instructor needs to have was something he acquired on the drill field and was unable to let go of once he came home" (Wertsch, 1992, p. 21). As Haney and Zimbardo (1973) put it, "we are rarely aware of the co-optation of self by role" (p. 42).

Making It by Faking It.   In short, behaving as if one is a bona fide exemplar of the role may lead one to think and feel as if one *is* a bona fide exemplar—a process that Granfield (1991) termed "making it by faking it" (p. 331). Ibarra (1996) described how neophyte management consultants and investment bankers masked their initial feelings of immaturity with bravado. They adopted and refined the behaviors displayed by senior role models, winning approval from clients and colleagues. As members of their role set began to treat them as bona fide professionals, they began to view themselves as such. Individuals who experienced success dealing with clients began to shift their reference groups from inside the firm to outside and began to conceive of themselves as client account managers. Conversely, those who experienced difficulty cultivating client relationships focused more on internal team management.

Similarly, studies of law students (Granfield, 1991), medical students (Haas & Shaffir, 1982; Huntington, 1957), and camp counselors (Waskul, 1998) indicate that simulating and experimenting with a role identity facilitates internalization of the identity—that "behaving inauthentically is necessary for achieving an authentic identity" (Ibarra, 1996, p. 8). Like good actors, organizational members must offer convincing performances. Affirmation indicates that the credibility gap between the individual and the claimed role identity is narrow, instilling confidence for even more credible role enactments.

Newcomers are particularly likely to "fake it" if: (a) the role is complex, dynamic, or ambiguous such that they must learn by doing, (b) the organization does not use institutionalized socialization (particularly role models) such that newcomers must essentially sink or swim, (c) the role is enacted before critical audiences, (d) the duration of the transition period is short such that newcomers are expected to display proficiency with minimal lead time—and support, and (e) newcomers have little relevant experience to draw on. All five conditions prevailed in L. A. Hill's (1992) study of new managers such that "the managers had to *act* as managers before they understood what that role was. Only by acting would they know what their new assignment entailed" (p. 47).

In summary, individuals can think, feel, or act their way into a new role. Role entry triggers social-psychological processes that may ultimately lead to internalization of the role identity as a representation of self. The ABCs of role entry—affect, behavior, and cognition—are mutually reinforcing such that affect and cognition (as through anticipatory identification) tends to engender congruent behaviors, and role-based behaviors tend to engender congruent affect and cognition. These ABCs may be cemented through social validation, which is explored in more detail next.

SOCIAL VALIDATION

Identity theorists from a variety of disciplines argue that one's sense of self is largely grounded in the perceptions of others (Burke, 1991; Landfield, 1988; Mead, 1934; Schlenker, 1986; Stryker, 1980). As noted in chapter 2, through social interaction and the internalization of collective values, meanings, and standards, individuals come to see themselves somewhat through the eyes of others and construct more or less stable self-definitions (e.g., reliable coworker, loving spouse). This is particularly true of role identities because they are necessarily embedded in systems of interlocking roles, thus implicating others in the definition and performance of the self-in-role. Arnold and Nicholson (1991), for example, found that organizational newcomers saw themselves much the same as they believed others saw them (although these sets of perceptions did not converge more over time).

Role set members essentially conspire to sustain the definition of the situation (Goffman, 1961b), and role identities are reinforced—are *socially validated*—when valued members of one's role set begin to perceive and treat one as a bona fide exemplar of the role. For a student giving her first public speech, a catcall from the audience can prove devastating as it destroys the veneer of serious professionalism that she is attempting to establish. Individuals who are unable or unwilling to play their part threaten the integrity of the encounter and the espoused role identities by breaking the socially constructed frame. Conversely, social validation normalizes one's role identity in the sense that it helps enable one to feel comfortable or natural in the role and to enact it less self-consciously. Validation, in short, helps enable one to *own* the role. As such, validation also helps address the motives for identity, meaning, control, and belonging,

Validation can be expressed or signaled directly—via positive feedback and reinforcement—as in the rites of incorporation discussed last chapter. Validation can also be expressed more indirectly. For example, given the desire of newcomers to pass as bona fide role occupants, simply interacting with them as if they were indeed bona fide occupants is often sufficient to convey validation. Bourassa and Ashforth (1998) found that new fishers working on a trawler felt validated when the veterans referred to them by name rather than by the generic label of *new guy*. And Hafferty (1991) described how medical students welcomed tours of their anatomy labs (where cadavers were being dissected) by outsiders because the visits served "as an excellent opportunity for medical students to reinforce their own sense of emotional detachment by contrasting it with the apparent discomfort of these neophyte visitors" (p. 74).

The strong desire for social validation is most clearly revealed by the lengths individuals often go to in order to obtain it. Ouellet (1994) reported that a truck driver's training tends to be short and that he or she drives alone. The question thus arises: How do truck drivers validate their driving skills and desired social identity of modern-day cowboy or outlaw? The answer is that they rely heavily on questionable surrogate signals of proficiency (e.g., a clean and well-appointed truck), indirect probes (e.g., telling a fellow trucker about how one handled a snowstorm to see how he or she reacts), and positive cues from external audiences (e.g., an approving nod from a motorist). In short, individuals seek and find validation where they can.

It is important to note that only *observable* indicators of a role identity can be validated by others; values, beliefs, and so on can only be inferred.[12] Observable indicators include behavior, performance outcomes, and identity markers. Behavior refers to how one enacts the role identity and includes task behaviors, conformity to expressive norms (e.g., show respect for veterans, be courteous to customers), and organizational citizenship behaviors (i.e., efforts that are not formally prescribed but show devotion to the role and organization such as talking up the organization to outsiders). Performance outcomes speak to one's competence

---

[12]To be sure, one can verbalize intent to hold or master a role (e.g., a waiter who describes himself as an aspiring writer) and can verbalize values and beliefs that are consistent with the role and be socially reinforced for doing so. Ultimately, however, "talk is cheap" and may wear thin for one's social referents unless buoyed by concrete actions to enter and enact the role.

and motivation and typically include the quality and quantity of output, role innovations (if socially desirable),[13] and low absenteeism and tardiness. Identity markers signal role occupancy and include role-related attire, accessories (e.g., a doctor's stethoscope), grooming, mannerisms, use of jargon, physical location, office or workspace artifacts, and proximity to and association with other role occupants and members of the role set (e.g., Rafaeli & Pratt, 1993; Riemer, 1979). "To have is to be," according to the subtitle of Dittmar's (1992) book. Thus, individuals who feel insecure in a role often engage in *symbolic self-completion* (Wicklund & Gollwitzer, 1982) by adopting identity markers as signals of their legitimacy (Swann, 1990). For example, as the discussion of making it by faking it suggests, newcomers often make earnest efforts to adopt the trappings of their new roles (e.g., Haas & Shaffir, 1982).

Furthermore, the motive for self-expression discussed in chapter 3 suggests that enacting, succeeding at, and marking a valued identity enables one to affirm that identity to *oneself*. As noted, a valued identity assumes a moral cast such that to deny expressing the identity is to court feelings of guilt and hypocrisy. Thus, Loseke and Cahill (1986) attributed the difficulty that social work students had in identifying with the social worker role to a discontinuity between academic training and actual fieldwork, an unappreciative audience of other professionals and clients, a lack of unambiguous markers of the identity, and an absence of rites of incorporation: The students had no compelling way of affirming their role identity.

It should also be noted that there is usually some slippage in the validation process (Felson, 1992). Although individuals are generally accurate in their perceptions of how others perceive them and there is a strong correlation between others' perceptions and self-perceptions (Kenny & DePaulo, 1993), there is much room for error. Others may disagree among themselves and thus offer conflicting feedback, may lack opportunities to observe the individual, may misconstrue what they observe, and may be unable or unwilling to offer unequivocal feedback (particularly negative feedback and particularly where the relationship is of short duration and lacks intimacy and therefore trust). Also, given desires for self-verification

---

[13]However, role innovation may jeopardize validation if the innovations contravene significant expectations about what a role occupant should look and act like. Santino (1990) noted that a flight attendant is often viewed by passengers as "a waitress in the sky" (p. 322) and is expected to display cheerfulness and deference. Consequently, a flight attendant who opts to enact her role in a more somber or assertive manner may encounter resistance. This threat of *in*validation is why I argued earlier that innovation may be muted until a newcomer has established some trust and credibility with role set members.

(see chap. 3), individuals may misconstrue feedback, attribute negative feedback to deficiencies in the source rather than oneself ("You're saying that because you're jealous"), and project their self-perceptions on others and hear what they wish to hear.[14] Such sources of error in the validation process help explain how individuals who deviate significantly from organizational norms—from bullies to deadwood—may construe that all is actually well. Ironically, it is often those individuals most in need of feedback who are least receptive to it.

Projecting the Role onto the Person

Validation is also not necessarily a benign process. Behavior is such a potent cue for inferring identity that *members of a role set may believe that the person and the role are synonymous.* Humphrey (1985) randomly assigned subjects to the roles of clerk and manager in an experimental simulation of office work. Following the simulation, the clerks rated the manager as higher on such role-related attributes as leadership ability, intelligence, talkativeness, and motivation but as no different on such role-*un*related attributes as humorousness and friendliness. Behaviors required of the role had been projected onto the role occupants.[15] R. H. Turner (1978) referred to this phenomenon as the *appearance principle*: "In the absence of contradictory cues [such as behavioral inconsistencies over time], people tend to accept others as they appear" (p. 6).

It seems likely that an observer will use the appearance principle to form an impression of an actor to the extent that: (a) the actor and observer interact only within the context of a single role dyad (fostering behavioral consistency; e.g., buyer and supplier), (b) the situational constraints on the actor's behavior are not highly salient but allow only some personalization of the role (fostering consistency and the perception of discretion; e.g., police officer), (c) the actor and observer roles are highly differentiated

---

[14]Indeed, Felson (1992) and Kenny and DePaulo (1993) argued that self-perception and self-verification processes are more important than social feedback for validating the self—at least among adults with relatively stable self-concepts. However, typical person perception studies focus on personality traits and abilities, where the focal individual has a great deal of self-knowledge to draw on. Conversely, role transitions focus on self-*in-role*, where the individual may have far less self-relevant knowledge—particularly in high-magnitude transitions. Furthermore, role entrants are often motivated to learn and fit in and are dependent on others for important outcomes. Thus, social feedback is likely to be far more relevant to role transitions than to the typical person perception study.

[15]Consistent with the dissonance and self-perception arguments advanced earlier, it may not come as a surprise that the managers also projected the role onto themselves.

(fostering between-role distinctiveness; e.g., doctor–patient), (d) the actor has higher power and status (fostering the perception that he or she has behavioral discretion; e.g., manager–subordinate), (e) the assumption of the actor's role is presumed to have been difficult (suggesting a personal investment in the role; e.g., politician), (f) the actor's task requires behaviors that contravene social norms (fostering distinctiveness; e.g., a bill collector's displayed impatience), and (g) the observer lacks the motivation and resources (particularly time) to pursue more individuated perceptions (e.g., a customer observing a sales clerk; Fiske & Neuberg, 1990; Kelley, 1971; R. H. Turner, 1978). These predictors are likely to be additive such that the more that apply, the more likely that role behaviors will be attributed to personal predispositions. Thus, to some members of one's role set, one may be no more than an embodiment of the role.

This blurring of actor and role may constrain the actor such that he or she may find it difficult to act "out of character." Research on labeling theory indicates that labels such as *leader*, *troublemaker*, and *star performer* can alter interpersonal interaction (by affecting how the observer perceives and thus treats the actor), lead to the formation and polarization of ingroups and outgroups (by inducing similarly labeled individuals to cluster together for mutual support), and social identity change (by inducing the actor to internalize the label as a representation of self; Ashforth & Humphrey, 1995). The discussion of self-continuity in chapter 3 provides the final link in the chain. Even if the role identity is not positive, the desire for self-continuity may trigger self-verification processes that further solidify the identity. Thus, a label may become self-fulfilling as the actor is induced by external and internal pressures to act out and thereby confirm the label.

A classic example of a virtuous circle caused by labeling is R. Rosenthal and Jacobson's (1968) study of the *Pygmalion effect* (see Eden, 1990, for a review). Teachers were led to believe that some randomly selected students had very high potential for achievement. At the end of the school year, the students showed more improvement than did their nonlabeled peers in test scores administered by the researchers, suggesting that the teachers had imparted their differential beliefs to the students. Conversely, a classic example of a vicious circle is R. A. Scott's (1969) study that contrasted the ideologies of some agencies for the blind with that of the Veterans' Administration. The former implicitly viewed blindness as a debilitating and lifelong handicap that makes one incompetent and dependent, whereas the latter viewed it as a temporary setback that requires retraining so that one may resume a relatively normal existence.

As a result, blind people treated by the former were far more likely to become isolated from the community and dependent on the agencies.

In sum, an individual's claim to be a legitimate exemplar of the role may be cemented by social validation as members of the role set signal their acceptance of this claim. However, so eager are individuals for validation that they may see affirmation when there is little. Conversely, individuals risk being seen as synonymous with their role.

STRESS

It is frequently hypothesized that role transitions are very stressful (R. Katz, 1985). Indeed, the loss of a familiar role or the adoption of an unfamiliar one are typically regarded by scholars as among the most stressful of life experiences, capable of engendering tremendous emotional turmoil and depression (e.g., G. W. Brown & Harris, 1989). The social-psychological challenges of role exit and entry described over the last three chapters provide ample ammunition for this contention.

However, research has produced mixed findings. Reviews by Bruce and Scott (1994) and Nicholson and West (1989) suggest that the stress associated with the anticipation and experience of a transition is often not pronounced or fades relatively quickly after entry. Nicholson and West (1988) even found that stress and satisfaction were *positively* correlated in a sample of managers who had undergone a job change and suggested that the managers sought and were pleased with the challenge of upward moves. Based on their review, Nicholson and West (1989) concluded that there is "little support for generality of the stress model; people actively seek out the 'stress' of desirable moves" (p. 185).

Perhaps, then, it is more accurate to say that role transitions are associated with *arousal*, and whether this arousal is experienced as aversive depends on the interpretation or *primary appraisal* (Lazarus & Folkman 1984) of the situation (Ashford & Taylor, 1990). Interpretations likely depend on the interaction of person and situation. For example, individuals with high positive affectivity are probably more likely than individuals with high negative affectivity to frame a high-magnitude transition as an exciting and manageable opportunity rather than as a threatening problem.

Where arousal is construed negatively, a *secondary appraisal* assesses one's ability to cope with the situation (Lazarus & Folkman, 1984). Coping responses may be problem focused (i.e., the role learning, role innovation, and personal changes noted earlier) or symptom focused, or both. Ashford and Taylor (1990) and Ludwig (1997) described various symptom-focused responses to role transitions. For example, individuals may seek expressive social support, vent negative feelings, compartmentalize or psychologically wall off role identities so that the stress does not spill over into other social domains, and adopt a temporary identity (see chap. 2) that psychologically distances them from the role.

Finally, the stress engendered by a role transition tends to be transient (or at least less acute over time). The notion of normalization suggests that even undesired roles tend to become familiar and more acceptable in time as one learns about and attempts to cope with their demands. However, even a normalized role may remain a carrier of the stressors that are conventionally studied in organizational behavior: Role ambiguity, role conflict, role overload, and factors specifically associated with burnout (Jackson & Schuler, 1985; R. T. Lee & Ashforth, 1996).

Coping with Negatively Valent Transitions

An intriguing issue is how individuals cope with transitions that they regard as particularly undesirable. The concept of hope may provide an answer. *Hope* is defined by C. R. Snyder et al. (1991) as *"an overall perception that goals can be met"* (p. 570), entailing beliefs that paths are available to one's goals (*pathways*) and that one can successfully navigate those paths (*agency*). A sense of hope is thought by many scholars to be vital to psychological health (e.g., Abramson, Alloy, & Metalsky, 1995; Farran, Herth, & Popovich, 1995).

Highly undesirable transitions, particularly involuntary ones, may threaten hope by curtailing both pathways and agency. Yet, as noted in chapters 3 and 4, many examples can be adduced of individuals finding hope in organizational contexts where, objectively, there is little or none— from hospice patients to concentration camp inmates to prisoners on death row (e.g., Des Pres, 1976; Herth, 1990).

What is the source of hope in such "hopeless" contexts? Qualitative research on the elderly reviewed by Farran et al. (1995) suggests two sources: Particularized hope and generalized hope. The former is "the expectation that what exists in the present can be improved or achieved [and] is concerned with a hope object such as a valued outcome, good, or state of being" (p. 182). Individuals assailed by a grim and unremitting future may take refuge in the present, truncating their temporal purview and finding desires in the moment. The latter "is a sense of something beneficial in the future that casts a positive glow on life and protects against despair; it extends beyond the limits of time and provides an overall motivation to carry on with one's life" (pp. 181–182). Individuals may reframe their future more positively, may vest their hopes in an afterlife, or may vest their hopes in the betterment of loved ones or society as a whole. It seems likely that hope is strongly influenced by individual differences, notably positive and negative affectivity and previous experience with difficult situations.

An illustration is provided by Zamble and Porporino's (1988) study of male prison inmates. Given a threatening prison environment, inmates often focused on the present and the needs of the moment. As one inmate put it, "How often do I think about the future? If I get through this day, I have 5,000 more exactly like it ahead of me. I just try to survive each hour" (preface). Moreover, most of the inmates were resentful and critical about their experiences with the penal system. Nonetheless, they remained optimistic about their future, especially their chances for reform and success after their release—despite the fact that the "great majority" (p. 88) had only vague or unrealistic plans. As F. Crosby (1984) found, individuals often believe that they will fare much better than their peers, even when their peers are in the same situation and have the same resources. Apparently, hope may indeed spring eternal.

CONCLUSION

Role entry is about how newcomers navigate new roles to realize their motives for identity, meaning, control, and belonging. Newcomers must reconcile their motives with the very real pressures and constraints of the situational context discussed in chapter 6. However, given an increasingly dynamic world, greater emphasis is devolving to the individual to learn about, master, and change the self and the situation.

Newcomers may use a host of proactive behaviors to learn about their roles. Through role learning, often coupled with role innovation and personal change, individuals enact and may come to internalize a role identity that reflects a meld of institutionalized expectations and idiosyncratic refinements (Ibarra, 1996). Individuals may act, think, or feel their way into a role, experimenting with its parameters and content such that they may personalize the role even while it institutionalizes them. However, it is difficult for a role identity to stick unless its enactment is validated by valued members of the role set. Furthermore, role identification and performance may be abetted by selectively forgetting elements of exited roles that contradict the new role. The role entry process tends to be strongly influenced by an array of individual differences from previous experience to self-esteem to negative affectivity.

8

Role Transitions
and the Life Span

With Mel Fugate
Department of Management
Arizona State University

Most people think of work as what they do for a living, yet perhaps only in retirement they discover it is much of whom they have become. When we abandon work,
or it abandons us, we always leave part of ourselves behind; but if we have allowed
work to absorb most of ourselves and our days, we leave even more. The problem
then is this: Do we simply continue as a "former manager" or do we decide to go
on and become something else?

—a retired executive (Fitzgerald, 1988, p. 102)

In an undergraduate term paper, Sobel (1989) described his experience of
burnout when he was a camp counselor. What was provocative was not the
creeping exhaustion and depersonalization that are typical of burnout but
that the entire process unfolded in a matter of weeks rather than months
or years. As Sobel himself suggested, it was as if his experience was compressed so that he lived a span of many months in just a few weeks.

We argue in this chapter that the expected duration of time in a given
role, or in a series of related roles, or over the career frames one's experience such that one lives through a certain developmental or *transition
cycle* (Nicholson, 1987) during the course of each role, each set of similar roles, and the career. *Career* means the total "sequence of work roles"
(R. F. Morrison & Holzbach, 1980, p. 75) occupied during one's life
course regardless of whether the roles are tightly coupled or even similar.

Our basic point is that the experience of a given role identity and role transition plays out against a backdrop of a life cycle and an envisaged career. The experience of now is shaped by one's understanding of the past and by one's hopes and expectations for the future. In short, role transitions are necessarily embedded in a personalized historical context. Thus, a role change at age 19 may have vastly different connotations for oneself and one's role sets than a similar change at age 49.

The chapter is divided into four parts. First, we briefly discuss the transition cycle that represents the experience of a given role. Following Nicholson (1987), we note that individuals often move through phases of preparation, encounter, adjustment, and stabilization. Second, we argue that this within-role transition cycle may be embedded within an overarching transition cycle tied to a sequence of similar or integrated roles, such as supervisor→middle manager→executive. Just as a person must prepare for, encounter, adjust to, and stabilize her new role as supervisor, so too must she prepare for, encounter, adjust to, and stabilize her anticipated between-role arc of supervisor to executive. Furthermore, individuals craft identity narratives that foster a sense of coherence and progress as they journey through various and possibly diffuse roles over time. Third, we argue that the within-role and between-role transition cycles are in turn embedded within an overarching transition cycle tied to one's career (Reilly & Orsak, 1991; Super, 1990). Even if an individual's work roles are disjointed, so-called life cycle models suggest that the notions of preparation, encounter, adjustment, and stabilization provide a useful heuristic for the developmental challenges faced by an individual over the life course. Figure 8.1 summarizes the basic model articulated in the first three parts of the chapter. Finally, we close with a brief discussion of certain age dynamics, that is, the notions of social age and social clocks and the link between chronological age and transformational events.

WITHIN-ROLE
TRANSITION CYCLES

It was noted in chapter 6 that stage models of socialization tend to include the phases of anticipatory socialization (where individuals prepare for role entry), encounter (where individuals enter and confront organizational realities), and metamorphosis (where individuals adapt to their roles;

Bauer et al., 1998; Fisher, 1986). Nicholson (1987; Nicholson & West, 1988, 1989; cf. Ruble & Seidman, 1996) elaborated on this work to develop a model of the transition cycle that occurs within a given role. The first phase, *preparation*, is analogous to anticipatory socialization and involves developing realistic expectations, a positive orientation toward change, and an awareness of one's feelings toward the role. The second phase, *encounter*, mirrors the encounter stage of socialization and involves exploration and sense-making. The third phase, *adjustment*, is analogous to metamorphosis and involves role innovation and personal

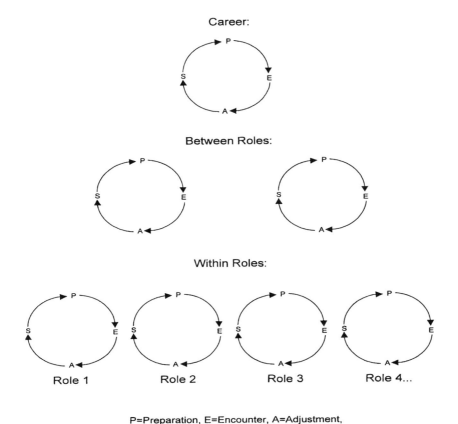

FIG. 8.1. Transition cycles within roles, between roles, and over the career.

change as well as relationship building. The more novel and complex the role and the less relevant experience the individual has, the longer the encounter and adjustment phases. The final phase, *stabilization*, is the aftermath of metamorphosis and involves personal and organizational effectiveness. Nicholson (1987) added that movement is continuous and that "even the most stabilized conditions contain the possibility of future change" (p. 179) such that the stabilization phase in turn helps prepare one for future roles and reiterations of the transition cycle.

The transition cycle is a normative model in that each phase is described in terms of the challenges it presents for the newcomer and each phase is predicated on more or less successfully addressing the challenges of the previous phases (Nicholson, 1987). For example, effective preparation smoothes the way for a successful encounter and adjustment such that "success breeds success" (D. T. Hall, 1976, p. 142), leading to the success spiral—or *success syndrome* (D. T. Hall & Nougaim, 1968)—noted in chapter 4. Conversely, poor preparation (e.g., unrealistic expectations) may ultimately impair adjustment such that failure is compounded, leading to a *failure syndrome* (Nicholson, 1987).

However, the phases are probably far more fluid than Fig. 8.1 suggests: Each phase shades greyly into the next; a newcomer may move fitfully through the phases, experiencing periods of inertia punctuated with rapid movement (e.g., Gersick, 1991); the phases may overlap such that a newcomer is simultaneously engaged in various stages of development (e.g., learning about coworkers [encounter] as one attempts to build relationships with them [adjustment]); different features of the role identity may have their own transition cycles of varying duration; and an emergent issue (e.g., new technology, new supervisor, poor performance appraisal) may cause one to recycle through the phases. Thus, the transition cycle should be regarded as a heuristic that describes the primary concerns of the newcomer over time as he or she settles into a role.

As discussed in chapter 2 and consistent with models of vocational choice (e.g., Holland, 1985), the individual's global identity and identity goals may inform the selection of roles. The individual seeks roles that will likely enable him or her to realize: (a) subjectively important aspects of the global identity (e.g., achievement orientation), (b) subjectively important role identities (e.g., a person who identifies with consulting pursues jobs within the consulting profession), and (c) subjectively important future selves (whether as a pull toward a desired self or as a push away from a feared self). For example, Breese and O'Toole (1995) interviewed female university students who were 28 or older and found that their pre-existing identities exerted a strong influence on their choice of academic major and their involvement in campus activities (e.g., "My role as a care-giver has greatly influenced my choice of nursing as a major"; "I chose Social Work because I associate well with other people, I have 'been there' so I can relate to battered women, welfare recipients, etc.," p. 18).

Once in a role, the psychological motives for identity, meaning, control, and belonging (see chap. 3) are manifested throughout the transition cycle. The motives are likely to be most salient early in the transition cycle as the newcomer endeavors to situate himself or herself in the role, to develop a salutary sense of meaning and control, and to feel accepted. As the newcomer settles in, the motives are likely to become less salient so that by the fourth phase he or she is reaping the benefits of effective adjustment. As chapters 6 and 7 showed, effective adjustment represents a meld of role innovation and personal change, with the nature and extent varying across individuals and situations.

As the individual learns about himself or herself, the global identity may be modified in myriad ways. For example, a new manager may dis-cover that she has a propensity for risk taking and decisiveness and revise her global identity accordingly. Indeed, if the individual comes to identify with the role itself, then the role identity may be imported en masse into the self-concept. For example, the new manager may come to think of her-self as not merely a decisive risk taker but as a "manager"—including whatever core and peripheral features the identity conveys to her.

The attributes of role transitions (see chap. 4) render a transition more or less difficult and therefore negatively valent. Specifically, a high-magnitude, socially undesirable, involuntary, unpredictable, individual, short duration (of the transition period), and irreversible transition is inherently difficult such that the motives are less likely to be met and the transition cycle is less likely to unfold smoothly. Indeed, an individual may become mired in the encounter and adjustment phases and never reach the stabilization phase.

Time Compression

Most discussions of socialization and work adjustment implicitly assume that the newcomer will be in the role and perhaps the organization indefi-nitely. Under such conditions, newcomer adjustment is paced by develop-mental needs and activities (e.g., Reichers, 1987). Although relatively quick adjustment is preferred by both the newcomer (to resolve liminality) and the role set (to enhance performance), the phases of the transition cycle may nonetheless be open-ended to ensure effective adjustment because the newcomer is expected to remain in the post indefinitely.

However, given the trends noted in chapter 1, fewer individuals are remaining in a given role or organization indefinitely. The rate of change appears to be escalating such that traditional notions of stable jobs and careers are being replaced by notions of the boundaryless career (Arthur & Rousseau, 1996b). For example, Nicholson (1987) found that most managers participated in a work role transition every 3 years and that newcomers in some large organizations initially changed jobs more than once per year. Moreover, the rapid growth in the contingency workforce (Fierman, 1994), where individuals work with an employer on specific assignments for a limited period, coupled with the trend toward transactional rather than relational contracts suggests that many newcomers must manage their own long-term developmental needs.

These trends suggest that in place of the long-term relational contract between individual and organization, the individual may expect frequent role transitions—often across organizational boundaries—and therefore shorter periods of role and organizational occupancy. The individual may enter with an implicit if not explicit idea of how long the occupancy will last.

This notion of truncated role and organizational engagements has interesting implications for the experience of role entry and adjustment. According to Parkinson's (1983) famous "law," work expands to fill the time available for its completion. When the amount or nature of work is not predetermined, people establish proximal and distal goals and calibrate their progress according to how much time they have available. Time is essentially a resource that is invested in developmental tasks and thereby frames the trajectory of one's role occupancy. However, the perception that time is finite or fixed renders distal goals more proximal, creating a sense of urgency (Locke & Latham, 1990). For example, Gersick (1988) studied organization-based teams with project deadlines ranging from several days to several months. She found that teams tended to pace themselves according to their deadline. The midpoint, whether it fell at 2 days or 2 months, was a particularly critical juncture because it signaled to participants that their time was ebbing. Thus, groups that had drifted into inertia were inclined to rethink their approach in ways that galvanized progress.

Similarly, individuals entering a role may frame their developmental tasks—the transition cycle—by the expected duration of their role occupancy. As Weick (1996) put it, "a lifetime of development is compressed into the lifetime of a project" (p. 50). A medical intern understands that she has a year to master her role before becoming a resident, whereas a camp counselor frames his adjustment in terms of weeks. The shorter the expected duration of role occupancy, the more compressed the transition cycle (see chap. 2, "Temporary Role Identities"). Thus, an individual's progression through the cycle may be dictated less by mastery of the role and more by the calendar. As suggested by the discussion of making it by faking it in chapter 7, newcomers may be prematurely thrust into the breach and forced to learn as they go. The upshot may be incomplete role learning and personal change, ill-advised role innovation, high stress, and poor performance.

However, this is not to say that a long role occupancy guarantees a leisurely apprenticeship. The more difficult the role transition (again, see the seven transition attributes in Fig. 4.1) and the greater the role complexity, ambiguity, conflict, and overload, the more difficult the developmental process. Thus, medical interns frequently report that a year-long training period is insufficient (recall the opening quote of chap. 2; Marion, 1990). And the less effective the developmental process, the less likely that a newcomer will progress through the complete transition cycle—at least in the prescribed normative manner.

In sum, the notion of time compression suggests that the transition cycle may be paced not only by developmental needs and activities but by the expected duration of role occupancy. Thus, the camp counselor mentioned earlier may have burned out in a matter of weeks because he experienced his entire anticipated career as a counselor in that short time: Like a sprinter, he paced his energy to the time frame of the task.

Conclusion

Nicholson's (1987) notion of a transition cycle that consists of preparation, encounter, adjustment, and stabilization provides a useful heuristic for understanding the developmental tasks that face newcomers to a given role. The relative success of one phase strongly affects the relative success of the next. However, an individual's progress through the cycle may be paced more by the expected duration of his or her role occupancy than by the developmental tasks.

BETWEEN-ROLE
TRANSITION CYCLES

In the traditional notion of a career, role progression plays out over decades such that a single overarching transition cycle captures the totality of one's work roles. In such a career, chronological age is strongly correlated with one's position in the transition cycle. However, with the changing nature of work, the need for continuous learning, and the high frequency of role transitions, the overarching transition cycle is giving way to a series of shorter cycles (D. T. Hall & Mirvis, 1995).

Thus, a between-role transition cycle refers to the arc of preparation, encounter, adjustment, and stabilization that typifies the experience of a series of related or integrated roles. The transition cycle is tied to one's anticipation of both the nature and the duration of occupancy of the series of roles. The more similar or integrated the roles, the more apparent the between-role developmental progression and transition cycle. Returning to the sprinter metaphor, if the within-role transition cycle can be likened to a sprint (short race), then the between-role transition cycle can be likened to a middle distance event, and the career transition cycle to a marathon.[1]

However, the same turbulence that is generating multiple between-role transition cycles is also making it difficult for individuals to address their identity motives for self-coherence (internal integration and consistency) and self-continuity (stability over time; see chap. 3). This quandary is described in the following sections in terms of the link between proteanism and identity narratives.

Proteanism

As discussed in chapter 1, the protean world is one of flux and perpetual change, and the protean person actively experiments with diverse roles and identities. Indeed, "the key issue determining a learning stage will not be chronological age (in which the 40s and 50s were 'midcareer') but *career age*, where perhaps 5 years in a given specialty may be 'midlife'

---

[1]If one's career is comprised *only* of highly disjointed roles, then the between-role transition cycles will be far less apparent. However, the notion of identity narrative, discussed later, suggests that individuals are motivated to construct synergies (either prospectively or retrospectively) from otherwise eclectic experiences.

for that area" (D. T. Hall & Mirvis, 1995, p. 277). Chronological age will become far less relevant as an index of role learning, adjustment, and organizational status. For instance, Bedeian, Ferris, and Kacmar (1992) found that tenure (whether organization, job, or time with supervisor) was a more stable predictor of job satisfaction than age.

The notion of proteanism suggests that a diverse repertoire of role identities may increasingly prove adaptive in organizations (cf. meta-competencies; D. T. Hall, 1986, 1996). Beyer and Hannah (1996), for example, studied engineers and other professionals in the semiconductor industry who were assigned to a consortium. Beyer and Hannah concluded that individuals with longer and more diverse work experience retained more diverse latent identities, which expedited adjustment to the consortium: Their self-definitions contained more hooks on which to hang their new roles.

However, the notion of proteanism raises intriguing questions about identity narratives—about how individuals make sense of their between-role history and present it to others (and themselves) as a more or less coherent story.

Identity Narratives

It was briefly discussed in chapter 3 that individuals construct identity narratives to provide meaning and continuity as they enter and exit various roles over time. Narratives highlight and organize certain events into a meaningful whole where the events both "contribute to the meaning of the story, and derive their meaning from the whole" (Widdershoven, 1994, p. 109). As the discussion of turning points in chapter 6 suggests, events generally mark a change in direction (what McAdams, 1992, called an "episode of change," p. 345) or progress along a given path (an "episode of continuity," p. 345), and may be seen as positive or negative.

With regard to role transitions, Zurcher (1979) argued that individuals offer a "vocabulary of motives" (Mills, 1940) to explain their movements to themselves and others. Whether these motives are offered prospectively (where one deliberately chooses a role to enact a desired self) or retrospectively (where one constructs post hoc reasons), the transitions are framed within the unfolding narratives. The notion of retrospective narration is particularly intriguing because it suggests that history is continually subject to rewriting: Prominent storylines may be discarded or forgotten, and seemingly minor events may be recast as central in new storylines.

Like identities themselves, individuals may have multiple identity narratives that vary in subjective importance and situational relevance (i.e., salience). Narratives may also vary in the themes that are expressed (e.g., achievement, affiliation, power), the desired and feared selves that are invoked, and the affective tone, from optimistic (comic or romantic) to pessimistic (tragic or ironic; McAdams, 1992; McClelland, 1985). Indeed, a given event may be recast in multiple ways depending on the forms of the narratives. This multiplicity of ongoing stories provides versatility or *requisite variety* (Ashby, 1960) for embracing and profiting from a range of roles and situations. Multiplicity enables individuals to shift storylines as circumstances warrant—putting on hold or rewriting those that are thwarted or not situationally relevant while activating others—and thus remain engaged in a particular role. Some narratives may be tightly coupled (e.g., poor kid who makes good–aspiring professional) and others loosely coupled (e.g., aspiring professional–dedicated mother) and even contradictory. And some may be quite specific (e.g., learning from a mentor) and others quite general or global (e.g., seeking knowledge); just as global identities can serve as overarching frameworks for diverse role identities, so global narratives can serve as overarching rubrics for diverse storylines.

Society provides archetypical narratives—and identities—that individuals can invoke to legitimate certain choices (McAdams, 1987). Examples include the budding entrepreneur (justifying long hours), the aspiring professional (justifying lengthy schooling), the struggling artist (justifying low-paying jobs), and the conscientious objector (justifying opting out of some conventional career path). Generally, social norms require the appearance of rationality, ranging from a clear and logical sequence of choices leading to the attainment of a valued goal (what Widdershoven, 1994, called a "closed" narrative, p. 111) to a pattern among possibly disparate events that may or may not crystallize in a specific role (an "open" narrative, p. 112). The power of these norms is evident in the careful construction of resumes and the strategic presentation of self in job interviews and many other social contexts. Indeed, constructing an identity narrative is often an exercise in creative writing. For example, Snow and Anderson (1993) discussed the accounts offered by homeless people to justify their current status, and Goffman (1961a) discussed how inmates of a psychiatric hospital exchanged "sad tales" to rationalize their hospitalization.

Identity narratives tend to be easiest to articulate where roles represent a clear and sequential progression of learning such as a manager promoted upward through an organizational hierarchy, an undergraduate student who moves on to graduate school, and a junior auditor promoted to senior status. In such cases, the institutionalized sequence of role transitions— role progression in chapter 5—signals one's movement through the overarching transition cycle. The accounting student studies for an auditing position (preparation); she becomes a junior auditor and confronts the realities of audit work (encounter), taking direction from her more senior peers; she becomes a senior auditor and is given more latitude to manage clients as she sees fit (adjustment); and she becomes a partner and assumes a more strategic perspective in her firm (stabilization).

Accordingly, identity narratives become more difficult to articulate if the sequential progression does not unfold as planned. Role transitions may be heavily influenced by emergent and unforeseeable events, necessity, social pressure, luck, misconceptions about the self or roles, and ineffable motives. T. Baker and Aldrich (1996) interviewed 82 people in fairly dynamic industries and occupations (e.g., computer training) and found that only 1 person with more than 7 years experience said "that her work history has been faithful to her vision of how she wanted to build her career" (p. 143). Similarly, Nicholson, West, and Cawsey (1985) asked managers to predict the likelihood of a role transition within the coming year and found that only about half who were promoted or changed employers had predicted it and less than a third of those who had predicted such a transition actually experienced it.

Given the vagaries of life, individuals tend to move somewhat opportunistically from role to role, attempting to marry their current desires and qualifications with available choices or delaying role transitions until a better marriage can be attained. The aspiring manager may grow impatient with his employer and pursue a vacancy in an industry he had never considered, and the junior auditor may suddenly decide to take a year off to have a baby. Chance and opportunistic moves are particularly likely outside of the large and relatively stable organizations—with their institutionalized role progressions—that have been heavily favored in past organizational research (Nicholson & West, 1989).

Identity narratives also become more difficult to articulate if this opportunistic sequencing of roles diverges from seemingly rational and socially acceptable career trajectories.[2] Donahue et al. (1993) found that women who had gone through many role transitions in their 20s and 30s, such as

---

[2]Because norms vary across occupations and industries, what may be acceptable in one field may be unacceptable in another. For example, taking a year-long sabbatical may be viewed positively in the software design industry but negatively in the insurance industry.

job changes, marriage, and divorce, had much higher self-concept differentiation across various roles in their 50s. Self-concept differentiation was associated with emotional distress, interpersonal difficulties, and lower self-esteem and well-being: It appeared that the women were unable to articulate a personally and perhaps socially acceptable narrative to account for their role changes and to harmonize their self-concepts.

Similarly, identity narratives may be hard to articulate in protean careers where diverse roles are occupied. For example, an individual may hopscotch opportunistically from job to job, attempting to build a repertoire of role identities for later self-employment. Indeed, there may be a touch of randomness to the role transitions as the individual engages in identity exploration, perhaps "discovering" a narrative in hindsight. For example, Wiener's (1996) interviews with Hollywood stunt people reveal that many essentially stumbled into stunt work despite the highly skilled nature of the profession. An assortment of odd jobs, from crop dusting to rodeo riding, enabled the future stunt people to unwittingly amass the diverse skills needed for stunt work. As the world becomes ever more turbulent and the future uncertain, identity narratives will increasingly reflect retrospective and highly creative sense-making.

Furthermore, in protean careers, the overarching transition cycle may move fitfully through a series of encounters and adjustment phases, with little time for preparation or stabilization (Nicholson, 1987). The absence of the seemingly smooth arc of the transition cycle may make it difficult to articulate a personally and socially acceptable underlying rationale for the various role transitions.[3] As suggested in chapter 7, talk is cheap: Members of the role set may discount narratives that do not appear to resemble the culturally sanctioned accounts—the archetypical plotlines. However, as protean careers become more widely accepted as a means of building diverse knowledge, skills, and abilities, the normative restraints on alternative role histories will likely relax. Indeed, diversity and change *per se* may become major identity narratives.

Proteanism and the Perils of Normalizing. In a protean world of potentially eclectic roles, one needs a certain psychological distance from a given role, abstracting generalizable identity features and les-

---

[3]Recall that an assumption throughout the book is that work constitutes a fairly central life interest for the individual. In cases where work is a more peripheral interest, the individual will feel far less of a need to articulate a compelling identity narrative—although the social pressure to do so may remain strong.

sons without becoming wedded to the idiosyncrasies of the role. However, it was noted at several points in the book that newcomers seek to normalize their roles—to render them understandable, familiar, and acceptable. Each role connotes a necessarily grounded and specific identity embedded in a necessarily rich context. In essence, each role is at the center of its own somewhat idiosyncratic universe such that "normal" must be defined anew with each role transition.

The risk, then, of normalizing a role is that one may overlearn or over-adapt to the role. The more thoroughly one has internalized a role's idiosyncrasies, the more difficult it may be to exit the role, to separate generalizable identity features and lessons from the particularistic, and to selectively forget any features and lessons that are inconsistent with future roles (see chap. 7). Thus, Johl (1989) described how a bank auditor was transferred to a large bank branch to head a department. As an auditor, she had been socialized to regard bank rules as ends in themselves and view conformity as necessary and good. However, department heads were compelled by practical exigencies to relax rule enforcement. Thus, in her new role, she needed to temper or essentially forget a central value of auditing. She was unable to do so and developed a reputation as a martinet, resulting in reduced departmental efficiency and a dissatisfied staff.

Older workers are likely to be particularly susceptible to the perils of normalizing. Having come of age in a time of bounded rather than boundaryless careers, older workers may well have internalized personal identities (e.g., loyal) and social identities (e.g., organizational member) that encourage normalizing but discourage switching employers and jobs when needed. T. Baker and Aldrich (1996) added that the stress occasioned by the dynamism of modern times may encourage such workers to redouble their commitment to the principles that have served them well in the past—hard work and loyalty: "We then have the sad specter of employees who are emphasizing loyalty at the very time their employers are devaluing it" (p. 144).

Identity narratives in the context of between-role transition cycles have other intriguing implications beyond proteanism. Narratives may trigger self-fulfilling prophecies and role foreclosure, and may shape the perception of the status quo.

Narratives as Self-Fulfilling Prophecies.   It was argued in chapter 2 that global identities tend to be self-fulfilling, and last chapter, that behavior commits the individual to a certain identity, triggering psychological processes that facilitate internalization of the identity as a partial definition of self. Similarly, Krau's (1989) research on the *accentuation phenomenon* indicates that occupational choices build on and reinforce initially held values, rendering certain future options more attractive and others less so. Banks et al.'s (1992) research on British teenagers further suggests that occupational perspectives develop to legitimate occupational choices. The accentuation phenomenon is strongly reinforced by organizational selection procedures that routinely favor applicants with certain identity markers (e.g., credentials, appearance) and career trajectories thought to indicate good person–role fit.

The implication, then, is that whether an identity narrative is constructed prospectively or retrospectively, individuals tend to become committed to their espoused narratives such that the narratives influence future role selection. However, the more broadly constructed or abstract the identity narrative, the broader the role options. An individual who espouses an identity narrative of *creative* will have more options than one who espouses a narrative of *advertising executive*. Indeed, a narrative may enshrine novelty and personal change as guiding principles (e.g., *thrill seeker*), thus justifying a very eclectic selection of roles.

Although identity narratives tend to be self-fulfilling, they are not necessarily so. An individual may be unable to enter a desired role, may face a strong situation that constrains his or her desired enactment of the role or induces change in the narrative, may confront a life-altering trauma, may learn that the anticipation of role occupancy was more satisfying than the reality, may mature and "grow out" of a narrative, may have mutually exclusive narratives, and so on. Alternatively, the individual may live out and fulfill the narrative, attaining closure and moving on to a new narrative.

Identity narratives are also subject to refinement and reinterpretation over time. An adolescent desire to do good may lead to a job in a hospice. Later, doing good may mean mentoring new employees and doing volunteer work in the community. In short, narratives may be rewritten over time as desires are clarified and opportunities arise. History, as a personal and social construction, is never fixed.

Narratives and Role Foreclosure. Just as identity narratives tend to become self-fulfilling, they tend to preclude certain roles. As Ludwig (1997) wrote:

> Early in our lives . . . the potential is greatest for us to become any one of many different selves. With more and more decisive experiences and more inflexible ways of interpreting them, our options for deviating from our par-

ticular course progressively diminish . . . our self-system becomes more and more self-confirming and limits our access to other potential selves. (p. 237)

Individuals may be labeled by their life histories and narratives and may not have developed the requisite skills and networks to exploit opportunities to explore other narratives. For example, Westby (1960) described the career trajectories of symphony musicians. Their training requires a great investment of time, effort, and money, and often begins at an early age. The training regimen effectively forestalls other potentially competing occupational identities. Also, most attend conservatories where the curriculum is devoted to grooming musicians, thus restricting the development of one's social network to people with similar aspirations and impairing exposure to other occupational choices and the development of other occupational skills. Finally, because prestigious symphonies are few in number and geographically dispersed, the aspiring musician must remain highly mobile— thereby inhibiting the development of a social circle and community roots. The upshot is *role foreclosure* where certain actions (or nonactions) set in motion a chain of events that preclude certain roles.

Role foreclosure is particularly likely to occur in cases where: (a) one is labeled and stigmatized by occupancy of another role (e.g., Henson, 1996, reported that female temporary workers—unlike their male counterparts— became typecast as clerical workers and ended up in secondary labor market positions),[4] (b) recruitment is restricted to a certain cohort such as people who are young or have not yet been "tainted" by other organizations, (c) assumption of a role is dependent on a series of developmental roles or experiences (role progression; e.g., becoming a doctor) such that one is expected to commit to the sequence by a certain age, (d) assumption of a role (e.g., senior management) is arranged as a tournament (Cooper, Graham, & Dyke, 1993; Nicholson, 1993) such that those who are passed over are effectively dropped from future consideration, and (e) one defines one's identity narrative so narrowly that otherwise feasible alternatives are not even considered (e.g., a laid off advertising manager fails to consider public relations as an option).

In sum, if a journey does indeed begin with a single step, that first step both enables (self-fulfilling prophecy) and constrains (role foreclosure) the selection of the second and subsequent steps.

---

[4]The labels need not be derogatory. For example, a person may be branded as overqualified for a post by virtue of his or her previous experience or education or may have occupied a highly visible role (e.g., politician, athlete) such that it is difficult to be seen as an individual separate from the role (see chap. 5, "Visibility of the Role or Transition").

Narratives and the Status Quo.   Identity narratives may also frame how one perceives the status quo and thus has provocative implications for role-based attitudes. Research on job satisfaction and organizational commitment focuses largely on one's perception and evaluation of particulars of the status quo (e.g., pay, job design, coworkers, working conditions) in absolute terms (the better the particulars, the more favorable the attitude) and relative to one's expectations (the better the match, the more favorable the attitude; Brief, 1998). However, satisfaction and commitment are strongly affected not only by present conditions but by how one regards the present *in the context of one's past experiences and future aspirations and expectations.* In short, the meaning of the present—and of a given transition to a new role—is strongly affected by its position in the arc of one's identity narrative.

For example, an assignment to a AAA baseball team is cause for celebration for a teenager arriving from AA baseball but a cause for sadness for an aging major league player who has just been demoted. For the former, the assignment is consistent with his identity narrative of major leaguer and represents an improvement over the job conditions prevailing in his former role. For the latter, the assignment is inconsistent with his narrative of major leaguer and represents a decline in job conditions. Thus, although the two individuals face the same objective job conditions, their different transition trajectories (one up, the other down) radically affect their subjective reading of the conditions. In short, role-based attitudes are based largely on the *meaning* of the role in the context of one's identity narratives.

Narratives and Nostalgia.   We close the discussion of identity narratives by considering the role of nostalgia. Nostalgia was defined in chapter 5 as a longing for a fondly remembered past. Davis (1979) argued that nostalgia is a response to discontinuities in one's life. Nostalgia helps one adapt by conferring a sense of personal continuity in the face of change. One reinterprets past experiences in a more positive light and establishes highlights in the identity narrative. By viewing or endowing the past with a positive light (through "rose-colored glasses"), one gains a temporary respite from current anxieties and may find continuities that connect the present to the past. As one adjusts to the new role, anxieties tend to fade, and nostalgic recollections become less frequent. Nostalgia thus functions as a transition bridge between roles.

Nostalgia is particularly functional for undesired change, that is, for changes that are inherently difficult to reconcile with one's desired selves and unfolding identity narratives. However, as argued earlier, even a transition from an undesired role tends to be laced with some ambivalence because people are adept at adapting to—and finding salutary meaning in—even the most taxing situations and because all transitions are at least somewhat anxiety provoking. For example, Mellon's (1990) compilation of interviews with exslaves reveals that many slaves spoke of their years in slavery with some wistfulness: Their relief and pride at gaining their freedom were tinged with nostalgia for the loss of what had been, after all, their only home.

The prevalence of nostalgia in role transitions is difficult to predict. On one hand, *denial of the past* seems possible. As noted in earlier discussions of selective forgetting (chap. 7) and dissonance reduction (chap. 5), individuals often affirm a transition by denigrating the past and edifying the present. Thus, a felt need to justify a transition may be negatively correlated with the frequency and severity of bouts of nostalgia. The more socially desirable a previous role and the greater the risk that a voluntarily selected new role may not pan out, the more difficult it is to justify the move to oneself and others. In such circumstances, individuals may feel a need to distance themselves from the past by focusing on the negative aspects of the prior role and the positive aspects of the current role. Ironically, then, nostalgia may at times be greater for *less* desirable past roles precisely because they represent less of a threat to one's need to appear rational.

On the other hand, *edification of the past* also seems possible. Here, the difficulty of securing positive meaning from a new role may be positively correlated with the frequency or severity of nostalgic bouts. The more problematic the current role, the more frequently one may take psychological refuge in rose-colored recollections of a more pleasant time. This scenario parallels research on regret theory that suggests that individuals may dwell on foregone alternatives and rue their decisions (e.g., Larrick & Boles, 1995).

Perhaps these crosscurrents of denial and edification of the past exist simultaneously, with one or the other more salient at any given time, because they reflect the two poles of ambivalence—the desire to look forward and the desire to look backward. When one is mustering the psychic resources to look forward and make sense of the new role, one does not need the doubts that thoughts of the prior role may occasion; conversely, when one is periodically overwhelmed by the demands of the new role, one may need the respite that edification of the past allows.

Conclusion. In an increasingly dynamic world, the career becomes less of an orderly progression of clearly linked roles and more of an opportunistic sampling of often diverse and diffuse roles. Identity narratives serve as a transition bridge between roles by stitching a more or less coherent and salutary story out of these diverse and diffuse threads. Thus, narratives may not only yoke similar roles (e.g., the narrative of expert provides coherence and continuity to the progression of student→ apprentice→craftsperson) but dissimilar roles (e.g., the narrative of exploration provides coherence and continuity to a series of odd jobs).

Before leaving between-role dynamics, we wish to briefly explore a particularly intriguing role transition: The role reversal.

Role Reversals

"It's a weird feeling. You come to hate this team, and now you have to be best pals with them"—a National Hockey League player who signed with a rival team and had to play his old team in the first game of the season ("Slap Shots," 1999, p. C8).

As discussed in chapter 1, roles are embedded in role sets such as the organizational grouping of occupational, departmental, and hierarchical positions and the familial grouping of parents and children. Within these networks of roles, roles typically exist in complementary relationships such as marketing–production and parent–child. A *role reversal* occurs when a person exits one role and enters the complementary role, whether temporarily or permanently. For example, as part of a training program for general management, a person may be transferred or rotated among complementary departments. Whereas the person may have once been defined as a marketing role occupant dealing with production people, he or she may now be defined as a production role occupant dealing with marketing people.

What makes role reversals intriguing is that they potentially invert the between-role narrative; the marketing employee is now a production employee, the child is now a parent, and the elected official is now just a voter. Given the relational and comparative nature of social identities, role reversals are likely to be a particularly disconcerting form of role transition and may challenge one's ability to articulate a personally and socially desirable story. Individuals must inhabit and make sense of precisely those roles against which they may have defined and evaluated themselves. This often means learning and accepting those goals, values, beliefs, and norms that were previously regarded as a foil for the former role or perhaps even impeded the execution of the former role. At a minimum, it typically means confronting former stereotypes of the role and its incumbents. Indeed, this is why training and development specialists often advocate role reversal exercises and cases as a means of reducing interpersonal and intergroup conflict (e.g., Watkins, 1986).

A search of the psychological, sociological, and business literatures for research on role reversals yielded little beyond a handful of articles in the field of gerontology regarding child–parent reversals (e.g., Berman, 1993). However, we speculate that role reversals are especially disconcerting, and therefore problematic, under four conditions:

1.   The complementary roles exist in a dependency relationship such as when a subordinate becomes a manager and an adult daughter gives birth to her own daughter. However, in the absence of a prior interpersonal relationship between role occupants (see Condition 2), it is likely that the person moving to the higher status role will more or less invert the pattern of interrole behavior learned previously (e.g., expecting deference instead of offering it). An extreme example is a victim of child abuse who as an adult reproduces the overlearned pattern with little reflection and becomes an abuser in turn (e.g., Higgs, Canavan, & Meyer, 1992).

2.   The role reversal is mutual such that occupants in complementary roles essentially switch positions, as when a subordinate leapfrogs over her manager to become her manager's manager and an adult child becomes the "parent" of a no longer competent parent. Such reversals are extremely difficult because the participants have a *personalized* relationship based on no longer applicable role identities. In addition, if a reversal of status is involved (as in these two examples), both parties must cope with the potential embarrassment caused by one party's loss of face.

3.   The reversal is counternormative, as when a foreman is demoted to line worker. By definition, such transitions are out of the ordinary and thus evoke surprise and attributional processes. Precisely because the event is counternormative, observers are likely to attribute causality to the focal individual, prompting a loss of face.

4.   The reversal is sudden and public. Under such conditions, the individual has little time to prepare for the transition and yet his or her reaction is likely to be closely scrutinized. If the reversal is considered socially undesirable, the individual most also cope with the sudden loss of face. Some reversals are sufficiently dramatic that they are found on best-seller lists, such as the account of a judge becoming a convict (Wachtler, 1997) and an evangelist becoming a sinner (L. Wright, 1993).

Home/Work.   In an interesting twist on the concept of role reversal, Hochschild (1997) argued that for many working parents, home life has become more like traditional notions of work life and work life more like traditional notions of home life. Based on an ethnographic study of the home–work interface experienced by the employees of one large company, Hochschild concluded that home life is often rigorously planned and segmented (e.g., day care, soccer practice, dinner, bedtime story) and regimented by the clock. Efficiency becomes the watchword as harried parents attempt to pack as many activities as possible into a limited amount of time. There is little time for indulgent play, spontaneity, and calm reflection and little sense of autonomy. Indeed, parents often feel that their home lives are somewhat out of control and that there is little appreciation of their efforts. Conversely, Hochschild cited survey research suggesting that employees often feel more competent, appreciated, and relaxed at work and have more close friends at work. For some parents, work is seen as a welcome refuge from the demands of home. Hochschild estimated that this role reversal was a "predominant pattern" for about a fifth of the families of the company she studied and an "important theme" (p. 45) for more than half.

Repeating Past Mistakes.   An intriguing mystery is why people so often disavow certain behaviors in others ("I would never do that") but when they assume the same role, they behave in much the same way. Why don't they practice what they preached? Why can't they translate their learning into behavior? For example, a person who was physically abused as a child is far more likely to be abusive as a parent than someone who was not abused—despite evidence that physically abused adults are more likely to disidentify with their parents (Rosenberg, 1997).

Perhaps part of the reason for this institutionalization of pathology is because people are often not aware of the situational constraints operating on role occupants and so tend to assume the occupants have more latitude than they do. In effect, observers make the fundamental attribution error (Ross, 1977) and personalize the causes of role occupants' behavior (see chap. 7, "Projecting the Role Onto the Person"). Thus, a manager's seemingly petty attention to detail may reflect strong directives from the head office.

Perhaps it is also because people tend to internalize and mimic what they see. As discussed last chapter, role learning and enactment tend to draw heavily on social learning (Bandura, 1977), particularly observation of others (notably role occupants). Thus, poor performers may model poor behavior. To break with the past requires that one: (a) discern functional behaviors from dysfunctional, (b) remember the difference once one assumes the role (i.e., resist selective forgetting), (c) be willing and able to enact only the functional behaviors, and (d) have sufficient resources and role latitude to do so. All four conditions may be problematic, particularly for inexperienced and low-status newcomers. Thus, dysfunctional behavior patterns may be inadvertently replicated in an organization—and in extreme cases, become institutionalized.[5] What cements such a vicious circle is that the carrier (e.g., the manager that inflicts the same abuse that he himself sustained as a subordinate) may be oblivious to the damage caused or may rationalize that it serves higher goals (e.g., instill discipline).

In sum, the notion of role reversals suggests that a role that may have once been a foil for defining one's role identity is now the identity itself. Thus, role reversals may challenge one's ability to articulate a seamless between-role narrative.

Conclusion

Just as there is a transition cycle of preparation, encounter, adjustment, and stabilization within roles, so too is there a transition cycle between similar or integrated roles. Individuals attempt to construct identity narratives to lend a sense of coherence and consistency to transitions not only between similar or integrated roles but between seemingly dissimilar roles as well.

CAREER TRANSITION CYCLES

And just as a transition cycle plays out within a role and between similar roles over time, so it plays out over a career. Indeed, Nicholson's (1987) transition cycle is generally consistent with prominent life cycle models. We discuss three such models—Super's (1990; Super et al., 1957), E. H. Erikson's (1963, 1968), and Levinson's (1986; Levinson, Darrow, Klein, Levinson, & McKee, 1978)—and how they are relevant to one's career transition cycle.

---

[5]Fein (1990) added that people often develop characteristic styles of interaction and reflexively apply them to situations that are inappropriate. Thus, functional behaviors learned in one social domain may be overgeneralized and become dysfunctional behaviors in another domain (e.g., a manager who attempts to boss his children).

Life Cycle Models

Super.   Super et al.'s (1957) seminal work divides the life span into five stages. The first stage, growth, extends from birth to about age 14. During this stage, individuals focus on fulfilling basic needs, developing their self-concept, participating socially in the surrounding world, and testing reality. The second stage, exploration, lasts from ages 15 to 24. Here, individuals undergo self and occupational exploration, try a variety of leisure activities, and begin to seriously consider career alternatives. According to Super, it is during this stage that one's career is first set in motion, with the trial of both part- and full-time work. The third stage, establishment (25 to 44), is where the majority of one's career is played out. Although individuals may try out various occupations, they ultimately identify a suitable career and work at establishing themselves within it. In the fourth stage, maintenance (45 to 64), individuals focus on preserving what they have attained during the previous stage. Finally, Super described the decline stage (65 and older) in which individuals "decelerate" (p. 41) in their careers and ultimately retire completely from the workforce. He characterized this stage as a switch from "participant" to "spectator" (p. 41), requiring one to assume new identities.

In his 1990 treatise, Super conceptualized the movement through these stages as a "maxicycle" (p. 206) that spans the life course. Each stage is separated by 5 to 7-year "transitional periods" that overlap the end of one stage and the beginning of the next. Consistent with Nicholson (1987), Super (1990) added that within each stage an individual also experiences "minicycles" (p. 206) of growth, exploration, establishment, maintenance, and decline.

E. H. Erikson.   E. H. Erikson (1963, 1968) proposed a model of development comprised of eight stages that play out over the life span. This model is truly developmental in that psychosocial crises in each stage must be overcome to advance to the next stage. The first four stages are associated with childhood, whereas the fifth begins with adolescence. The psychosocial crisis here is identity versus identity confusion.

> The young person, in order to experience wholeness, must feel a progressive continuity between that which he has come to be during the long years of childhood and that which he promises to become in the anticipated future; between that which he conceives himself to be and that which he perceives others to see in him and to expect of him. (E. H. Erikson, 1968, p. 87)

In other words, the individual must integrate personal and social identities into a socially validated global identity. Failure to do so leads to "role confusion," possibly prompting temporary overidentification "with the heroes of cliques and crowds"—"to the apparent complete loss of identity" (E. H. Erikson, 1963, p. 262).

The resolution of identity confusion is attained through a mix of identity exploration and identity commitment (see chap. 2). As noted, however, one may become committed to an identity without active exploration by uncritically internalizing conventional notions of self or the template modeled by one's parents or other social referents. Marcia (1994) noted that such foreclosure is functional only if the context does not change: Having not explored alternatives, the foreclosed individual has difficulty coping with unfamiliar situations.

Success at establishing a sense of self leads to the sixth stage, young adulthood, where the crisis is intimacy versus isolation. The individual becomes "eager and willing to fuse his identity with that of others" (E. H. Erikson, 1963, p. 262), to develop intimate relationships. Failure to do so leads to isolation and avoidance of others.

The psychosocial crisis of the seventh stage, adulthood, involves generativity versus stagnation. "Generativity . . . [is] the concern in establishing and guiding the next generation" (E. H. Erikson, 1963, p. 267) and includes productivity and creativity. If unsuccessful at developing generativity, one stagnates and becomes self-focused and self-indulgent. The final stage, which not everyone attains, is late adulthood. Here, the crisis concerns ego integrity versus despair, where one reflects on and evaluates one's life. Ego integrity essentially describes an appreciation and acceptance of the sum of one's life, "an emotional integration" (p. 269). If integrity is not established, feelings of despair and a fear of death ensue as the individual realizes that it is too late to start over.

Levinson.   Levinson (1986; Levinson et al., 1978) argued that the life cycle is divided into four eras or seasons, each lasting approximately 22 years and encompassing a broad range of biological, psychological, and social aspects. Each stage begins and ends at "a well-defined modal age" (Levinson, 1986, p. 5), whereas adjacent stages overlap in "cross-era transitions" (p. 5) that last approximately 5 years.

The first season, childhood and adolescence (ages 0 to 22), represents a period of "rapid biopsychosocial growth" (Levinson, 1986, p. 5). The next season, early adulthood (17 to 45) is, according to Levinson, perhaps the most dynamic of one's life. Tremendous development occurs on many fronts: One reaches physical and emotional maturity, raises a family, and establishes relatively stable adult and professional identities "that define his place in the adult world" (Levinson et al., 1978, p. 22). Furthermore, many of life's most valued relationships are established and evolve during these years. As such, this season "can be a time of rich satisfaction . . . [but also] crushing stresses" (Levinson, 1986, p. 5). Levinson added that individuals must make vital choices regarding marriage, family, work, and lifestyle before they have the maturity to choose wisely.

The third era, middle adulthood, encompasses ages 40 to 65. The era is ushered in by a midlife transition (40 to 45), "among the most controversial aspects" (Levinson, 1986, p. 5) of the model. For most individuals, physical and mental acuity remain intact in the early years of the third season. Socially and occupationally, interests and skills mature to higher levels of proficiency and satisfaction. One is regarded as a senior member, replete with responsibilities for grooming the current generation of young adults, and realizes the "fruits of [one's] youthful labors" (Levinson et al., 1978, p. 30). However, sometime after age 40, many compare their accomplishments with their goals and expectations: They become motivated to make their mark if the comparison falls short and to solidify their mark if the comparison is favorable. Middle adulthood is also the season when many choose to explore, to venture out on their own and realize professional dreams (e.g., starting one's own company).

Near the end of the middle adulthood season and continuing into the late adulthood (60 and older) transition is prime time for many to begin focusing on retirement. Consistent with the discussion of role exit in chapter 5, this focus is often prompted by noticeable physical changes or specific events (e.g., illness, death of a loved one, retirement). It is during late adulthood that one begins to reduce responsibilities and relinquish roles of formal authority.

The Life Cycle Heuristic

Although Super's (1990; Super et al., 1957) maxicycle of growth→exploration→establishment→maintenance→decline most clearly resembles Nicholson's (1987) transition cycle of preparation→encounter→adjustment→stabilization, all three life cycle models speak to a sense of growth, trial, discovery, and mastery. Also, these themes are echoed in the career stage models of D. T. Hall and Nougaim (1968; prework→establishment →advancement→maintenance→retirement) and Dalton and Thompson (1986; apprentice→independent contributor→mentor→director).

However, several questions have been raised about the validity of such life cycle models when applied to organizational life. Two in particular are of concern here. First, given D. T. Hall and Mirvis' (1995) notion of career age versus chronological age, it is perhaps not surprising that Levinson's strict age grading has not received strong empirical support (e.g., Ornstein, Cron, & Slocum, 1989; Smart & Peterson, 1994). If protean careers are indeed increasingly holding sway, then the within-role and between-role cycles discussed earlier may affect role-related variables (e.g., job satisfaction, intent to quit, performance) more strongly than does an overarching career cycle. The career transition cycle may become a background to the foreground of the current role and how it differs from what has gone before. Conversely, the career cycle may remain more relevant to certain deep life or phenomenological variables (e.g., global identity, awareness of global identity, contentment, angst, wisdom, anomie, hopes, fears, dreams).

A second concern with life cycle models is that individual differences in role trajectories become more pronounced over time such that universal developmental sequences are suspect (Lawrence, 1996a; Spenner, 1988; Sterns & Miklos, 1995). Because early role choices and experiences strongly influence later role choices and because experience represents a dynamic interaction of situation and person, two individuals will tend to diverge over time in their global identities, their desired selves, and their role trajectories. Similar to a decision tree, the result across a cohort of individuals is an ever-expanding range of trajectories (L. E. Wells & Stryker, 1988). For example, as Lawrence (1996a) noted, diverse patterns of work and retirement are observable for people older than 60: Some retire permanently, some return to work full-time or part-time, and some enter and exit the workforce repeatedly. Thus, it is not clear that all individuals necessarily experience the same developmental issues and sequences.

Because of such concerns with life cycle models, we view the models as a heuristic for broad developmental issues over one's worklife rather than as universal developmental sequences (L. E. Wells & Stryker, 1988). Five issues in particular are relevant here.

Age Grading. First, the models suggest that certain high-magnitude role transitions—including nonwork roles (particularly spouse and parent) —are more or less age graded. Although it appears that there is increasing variance in individual life trajectories and that *age norms* (i.e., the socially appropriate or normal age range for engaging in an activity; Lawrence, 1996b; Neugarten, Moore, & Lowe, 1965) are becoming more elastic, individuals nonetheless tend to land their first full-time job and to explore different occupations in their teens and 20s, to get married and begin families in their 20s to 30s, to assume senior member roles in their 30s to 50s, and to retire in their 50s to 70s. This crude age grading allows inferences about certain role transition dynamics, particularly: (a) what identity narratives may be invoked (e.g., a job change at 25 may be justified as exploration), (b) what role sequences and role conflicts are likely (e.g., individuals in their 30s may face pronounced work–family conflicts), (c) what transition bridges may be invoked to facilitate movement (e.g., a retiree may rely on nostalgia more so than a college student), and (d) what historical effects may be prevalent (e.g., contemporary newcomers to the workforce have generally experienced childhood in a particular decade, suggesting certain formative events and career and family expectations that may differ from those of their parents and grandparents).

Success and Failure Syndromes.   Second, the models suggest that each life cycle stage is associated with specific developmental tasks. If successfully fulfilled, the individual is equipped for the next stage in a process of incremental maturation. Conversely, if the tasks are not fulfilled, then subsequent adjustment will likely be impaired. For example, using Super et al.'s (1957) model, inadequate exploration may lead one to settle prematurely on an occupational choice for which one is ill-suited, and inadequate establishment may lead one to jump fitfully from job to job with little sense of continuity, self-definition, or growth. Similarly, Dalton and Thompson (1986) found that the transition from apprentice to independent contributor was predicated on technical ability, supportive peer relationships, and independence. Thus, consistent with the earlier discussion of the success syndrome and failure syndrome, the models place a huge premium on the early stages.

Stability and Flux.   Third, the notion of transitional periods suggests that personal development is not a smooth linear process: Periods of stabilization alternate with periods of flux throughout the worklife. Indeed, role transitions may both reflect individual flux and reinforce it as individuals experience the push and pull forces described in chapter 5, pursue their desired selves, and play out plotlines in their identity narratives. As noted in chapter 1, organizational life is increasingly about transitioning rather than stabilization. Thus, role-specific variables such as job satisfaction may show particularly marked fluctuations over the career.

Conversely, the notion of a career maxicycle suggests that these periods of stability and flux play out against a backdrop of growing stabilization. The career cycle may function as a keel for certain role- and age-based fluctuations, providing deep stability in the midst of more superficial change.

Self-Reflection.   Fourth, the argument that individuals tend to take stock of their life, whether in middle (Levinson) or late adulthood (E. H. Erikson), extends the notion of time compression to the career cycle. Just as knowledge that one's time in a role is ebbing may cause one to reframe the development cycle, knowledge that one's time in a career is ebbing may cause one to reflect on the road taken and what may lie ahead. Thus, self-reflection may be triggered not only by the passage of time (the past) but by the knowledge that the time ahead is fixed and dwindling (the future; Riverin-Simard, 1988). In the words of R. L. Gould (1978), "the sense of timelessness in our thirties is giving way to an awareness of the pressure of time in our forties. . . . [Time] makes existentialists of us all" (pp. 217–218).

An example is provided by C. P. Williams and Savickas' (1990) study of employees aged 35 to 64 years. C. P. Williams and Savickas found that individuals in the 35 to 44 age group were more likely to question their future direction and goals than were individuals older than 45. C. P. Williams and Savickas speculated that this questioning may lead to one of three responses: (a) reaffirming one's commitment to one's role, (b) altering one's lifestyle to better reflect the subjective importance of work and nonwork roles, or (c) changing one's occupation.

Indeed, a negative evaluation of one's work and nonwork life may precipitate the so-called midlife crisis and quite radical role transitions (e.g., D. O'Connor & Wolfe, 1991). An illustration is provided by an exteacher:

> I passed my fortieth birthday. . . . It was a traumatic time in my life. Everyone, in my mind, has certain ambitions, certain ideas about what they'd like to do, what they'd like to become. And I thought to myself if you want to be a teacher forever, great, but if you ever want to stick your neck out you'd better do it right now or it's going to be too late. So, I knew a little about real estate and decided to stick my neck out and did so. And left teaching. (Ebaugh, 1988, p. 129)

It is important to note, however, that the proportion of people who experience such a full-blown crisis and radical transition may be much smaller than popular conceptions suggest (Ebaugh, 1988; Lawrence, 1980).

Generativity.   Finally, E. H. Erikson's (1963) notion of generativity suggests that with maturity, many individuals become less self-centered and more concerned with supporting the occupation and organization per se, perhaps mentoring new members and immortalizing the lessons of their worklife (cf. Dalton & Thompson, 1986; Kegan, 1982). McAdams (1992) noted that "the ending of a story shapes all that comes before it" (p. 358) but that individuals do not really want their life story to end: One solution is generative acts that simultaneously round out an identity narrative and leave a legacy that survives the individual. Thus, individuals may embrace a more expansive or inclusive set of social identities (e.g., from role to organization or from home to community) such that the *I* extends further outward. Alternatively, the meaning of a given role identity may change even if the level of identification remains the same (L. E. Wells & Stryker, 1988). For example, to a 25-year-old employee, a dedicated organizational member may mean someone who does their job diligently and stays abreast of critical developments, whereas to a 50-year-old, it may mean someone who actively mentors junior members and acts with the best interests of the organization at heart.

Conclusion

As a heuristic, the notion of life cycle models nicely complements Nicholson's (1987) transition cycle. The developmental challenges inherent in certain prominent life cycle models suggest that transition dynamics are partially age graded, that early success or failure strongly affects the likelihood of later success and failure, that stability and flux are a normal part of maturation, that many individuals engage in pronounced self-reflection as they realize that their careers are temporally bounded, and that many individuals manifest a generativity motive in later adulthood— a desire to shepherd the next generation and "give back" to the society and institutions that have nurtured them.

AGE DYNAMICS

We close this chapter with a brief discussion of the notions of social age and social clocks and of the link between chronological age and transformational events.

Social Age and Social Clocks

Numerous studies have examined the relationship between chronological age and various role-related variables including abilities, performance, and satisfaction. As Lawrence (1996a) concluded, "the direction and size of the effects varies" (p. 27). Part of the reason for these inconsistencies is D. T. Hall and Mirvis' (1995) concept of career age, that time within a role or related roles may affect adjustment more strongly than chronological age per se. And part of the reason is that barring illness, the dramatic changes in biology associated with aging tend to be confined to the periods before and after the typical period of adult employment.

Another reason is that age and time are not merely temporal yardsticks but *social constructions*. Like gender and race, age tends to be a highly visible and universally used means of categorizing people—a *primary category* (Brewer, 1988). Although age is more of a continuous variable than either gender or race, individuals nonetheless sort people into "fuzzy sets" such as infant, child, teenager, young adult, middle-aged, older adult, and elderly according to how well they match prototypic images (Brewer, 1988). This occurs so frequently and consistently that it is relatively automatic, and individuals may react to others on the basis of their perceived age category without even being aware of it.

Like any social category, age connotes certain socially constructed meanings or stereotypes. For example, Sterns and Miklos (1995) noted that older workers are often seen as harder to train, more accident prone, more conscientious, and more knowledgeable. Higher age also tends to connote higher status in many social domains, particularly when roles are age graded (e.g., high school freshman vs. sophomore). A laboratory study by Cleveland and Hollmann (1990) found that managerial job descriptions that included tasks that are stereotypically associated with older workers were rated as having more value and prestige than job descriptions with tasks associated with younger workers.

Furthermore, occupational and organizational roles may have certain age norms, defined earlier as the "appropriate" or normal age for being a member. Finding a permanent job, obtaining significant promotions in a role progression, retiring, and so on may each have an expected age range. However, age norms may differ widely across occupations, organizations, industries, and nations and may change over time (L. K. George, 1993; Lawrence, 1987; Warr & Pennington, 1994). For example, Gordon and Arvey (1986) asked individuals to provide their "best estimate of the average age of all workers in a particular occupation" (p. 22) and found a range of 24.4 years (file clerk) to 45.8 years (mayor) across 59 occupations.[6]

Individuals use age norms to gauge their own progress and that of others through between-role and career transition cycles. People who deviate from this *social clock* (Neugarten, 1977) may incur social penalties and self-recrimination. As individuals strive to "act their age" (Lawrence, 1996b)—to conform with age norms or at least not arrive late—and are reinforced for doing so, the norms become self-fulfilling. The expected age distribution is reproduced, thereby validating the norms.

Age norms become insidious when they artificially compress the age distribution within a role. At one end, an individual may enter a role prematurely so as not to fall behind, whereas at the other, an individual may exit prematurely so as not to overstay his or her welcome. For example, it was noted in the discussion of degradation ceremonies in chapter 5 that many organizations implicitly signal ebbing confidence in their older employees by restricting access to developmental opportunities. Indeed, "some of the actions most limiting to older people are undertaken with the kindest intent and are rooted in concern for older people's well-being" (Greller & Stroh, 1995, p. 235).

As noted earlier, the rise of protean careers suggests that age norms are becoming more diluted in many occupations, organizations, industries, and nations. However, even where norms and sanctions are not strong, the mere distribution of age may affect how a given individual is perceived by others and himself or herself (Lawrence, 1996a). The impact of deviations from an age distribution can be quite complex, perhaps accounting for the seemingly inconsistent effects across studies (Cleveland & Shore, 1992). For example, individuals who are significantly younger than the mean age for a role may be perceived as exceptional and thus enjoy high status and feel positively toward their roles and role trajectories. Nicholson (1993) found that managers who were young relative to others in their role displayed higher satisfaction with their career and future prospects. (However, managers who were older relative to others did not display negative outcomes.) Conversely, the discrepancy in ages between such individuals and their peers may inhibit trust, open communication, and cohesion because of the perceived dissimilarity and the perceived threat to

---

[6]Interestingly, Gordon and Arvey (1986) also found a rank order correlation of $r = .75$ between the estimated ages and the actual median ages of workers, suggesting substantial accuracy.

the older peers (cf. Harrison, Price, & Bell, 1998). Moreover, insofar as age is correlated with status, youthfulness may partially mitigate the status of being a fast climber.

In sum, age matters in organizations largely because—rightly or wrongly—people *believe* that it does. Individuals are routinely categorized by age, and various social stereotypes may be implicitly projected onto them. Age norms may define the socially appropriate age range for role membership. And even in the absence of age norms, an individual's age relative to the age distribution of other role occupants may foster certain inferences about the individual. In short, the social construction of age may matter much more than the physiological and psychological changes associated with aging.

Chronological Age and Events

Chronological age is a marker for the passage of time and therefore the accumulation of experience. And just as socialization was argued in chapter 7 to be anchored in specific episodes, so too are the lessons that come with age.

The life events framework (e.g., Brim & Ryff, 1980) suggests that certain events may be transformational such that the fact that they have occurred may predict various identity-related processes and adjustment patterns better than mere age. For example, Rossan's (1987) longitudinal study of pregnant women revealed that many of them discovered somewhat unexpectedly that on the birth of their child, their occupational role identities no longer seemed important. And Lowenthal, Thurnher, Chiriboga, and Associates' (1975) cross-sectional study of men and women at four life stages (high school seniors, newlyweds, middle-aged parents, and preretirees) found that individuals facing a given stage encountered many of the same issues regardless of their age; thoughts of retirement, for instance, provoked certain concerns whether one was 50 or 70 years old.

Whether a given event is the result of careful planning or happenstance, it may become a symbolic and substantive milestone in one's life: *Symbolic* because society and the individual read much into the associated roles (e.g., parent, occupation) such that one becomes labeled by them (Ashforth & Humphrey, 1995); and *substantive* because the roles carry obligations, opportunities, and constraints that significantly shape future choices. Thus, considerable prospective and retrospective sense-making tends to surround such milestones as the individual endeavors to incorporate them into his or her unfolding identity narratives.[7]

In short, research on the nature and sequencing of role- and non-role-related events, and the meanings that are derived from them by the individual and by members of his or her role sets, may help decode the associations between age and role-related variables.

Event Absences. Danish, Smyer, and Nowak (1980) defined an *event absence* as the nonoccurrence of an expected or normative life event such as not having children after marriage. In the realm of organizations, examples of event absences may include not starting a new job after college or occupation-specific training, not being promoted, not exiting a job in industries where rapid turnover is expected (e.g., fast food), not going abroad in industries where cross-cultural experience is expected, and never retiring. If the event absence is not volitional (i.e., one wishes to transition but cannot), the nonoccurrence of the transition may be far more negatively valent than the transition itself would have been because it derails one's identity narratives. However, even if the event absence *is* by choice, the failure to progress as expected may lead observers to make various attributions that may undermine one's status (e.g., unlucky, off-beat, naive, untalented) and create social tension (e.g., Menaghan, 1989). Thus, the nontransitioner may be compelled to offer legitimating accounts or carry through with a transition that he or she abhors.

Once again, however, it is important to note that the rise of proteanism suggests that such normative pressures will relax somewhat over time.

CONCLUSION

The transition cycle of preparation, encounter, adjustment, and stabilization plays out within a role, between similar or integrated roles, and over the career. These intersecting cycles of adjustment suggest that flux and stability are experienced not only throughout the career but perhaps simultaneously. A 25-year-old may become settled in his first job even while he is mulling over a major occupational change, and a 60-year-old may struggle with a recent promotion although her career has been a succes-

---

[7]As discussed in chapter 2, an individual tends to regard some roles as more subjectively important than others. Thus, the individual's identity narrative may eagerly embrace some role-conferring events, may labor to accommodate others, and may simply reject still others.

sion of successful appointments. The notion of time compression suggests that individuals calibrate their transition cycle to match the expected duration of role occupancy: A medical intern may take a year to adjust because she *has* a year to adjust, and a camp counselor may burn out after a summer because he paces himself to last but one summer.

Part of the challenge of adjustment, particularly in this age of protean organizations and people, is to construct personally and socially acceptable identity narratives that weave one's role trajectory into a coherent and meaningful story. Individuals appear to be quite facile at prospectively and retrospectively constructing order and meaning from the healthy disorder that increasingly constitutes careers. Another part of the challenge of adjustment is that age itself is a social construction that imposes stereotypes and normative constraints on individuals as they move through the life course. Role entrances and exits may be tied to social clocks rather than personal needs and preferences: Individuals must write their identity narratives while "acting their age."

The essential argument is that the foreground of role transition and enactment is necessarily embedded in a background of life cycle dynamics and career concerns. Indeed, a focus on the larger promise of the background may at times dictate otherwise undesirable roles and role transitions; that same promise, however, may render an undesirable present far more tolerable.

9

Micro Role Transitions[1]

With Glen E. Kreiner
Department of Management
Arizona State University

Mel Fugate
Department of Management
Arizona State University

Scott A. Johnson
Organization & Management Department
San Jose State University

When I get to work, I immediately enter the shoes of a very defined role. Noah at home is not Noah at work. When I am at work, I don't allow myself to express emotions. I can show some empathy, but even this is not necessarily true; I act.
　　　—a counselor at a psychiatric facility (Yanay & Shahar, 1998, p. 359)

Because we work in the same space, a space that also happens to be our home, all of our marital presumptions are now in the workplace and all of our workplace presumptions are now in the home. . . . when you sit across from your partner at a home business meeting in your jammies, the wrong presumptions may be made.
　　　—a home-based worker (Petrick, 1999, Section 3, p. 13)

In chapter 1, it was argued that organizations are increasingly colonizing spheres of life that were once defined as private, communal, or informal—such as child-care (day-care centers) and mate selection (dating services).

---

[1]Adapted from Ashforth, Kreiner et al. (2000).

This has resulted in a multiplicity of roles that many must enact in the course of a week. And this multiplicity has in turn contributed to difficulties in managing or juggling the often conflicting demands of these roles (Tingey, Kiger, & Riley, 1996; K. J. Williams, Suls, Alliger, Learner, & Wan, 1991)—difficulties that are only compounded by the heavy workloads routinely placed on many people (Hochschild, 1997; Schor, 1991).

Moreover, since the industrial revolution, home and work have typically been segmented (Andrews & Bailyn, 1993; Shamir, 1992). Segmentation gave rise to what Kanter (1977) called the *myth of separate worlds*, namely that the two role domains do not and should not overlap. As Andrews and Bailyn (1993) noted, this myth marginalized and privatized work-related family problems, enabling organizations to act almost as if families did not exist and forcing organizational members to seek idiosyncratic solutions to their problems. However, in recent years, the pendulum has begun to swing back such that many organizations have developed policies allowing flextime, child-care services, recreational facilities, telecommuting, and so on (e.g., Glass & Estes, 1997). These policies are greatly abetted by a slew of new technologies including laptop computers, e-mail, pagers, fax machines, and cell phones. Indeed, as electronic connections proliferate, the four walls of the traditional organization are dissolving such that the home and other places are increasingly becoming *work* places. In short, many organizations are fostering greater integration between work and formerly personal spaces. For all its benefits, this integration has fostered significant *role blurring* (e.g., Barrett, Johnson, & Meyer, 1985)—that is, overlap in role boundaries and identities.

These twin forces—role proliferation and role blurring—raise important questions regarding how individuals manage the challenge of frequently transitioning between their multiple roles and, where desired, of segmenting their roles. Although a tremendous amount of research has focused on the nature of interrole conflict (e.g., Kossek & Ozeki, 1998), relatively little attention has focused on the nature of micro role transitions—again, the psychological (and where relevant, physical) movement between simultaneously held roles (Burr, 1972; Richter, 1984). As noted in chapter 1, micro transitions pertain to frequent and usually recurring transitions such as the commute between home and work.

Like macro role transitions, micro transitions include disengagement from one role (role exit) and engagement in another (role entry). For example, how does a new parent change diapers in the morning and run a division in the afternoon? How does a manager enact the role of boss toward her subordinates and then enact the role of subordinate toward her boss? These often abrupt transitions may be difficult to accomplish, and people frequently lament having to "wear different hats" and "shift gears."

Micro transitions are qualitatively different than the macro transitions discussed thus far. First, the role exits and entries tend to be temporary and recurrent. Thus, there is much less need to attain closure via each role exit or to reconstruct identity, meaning, control, and belonging anew with each role entry. Roles are temporarily suspended, not permanently exited, such that the transition processes discussed earlier are experienced in far more muted form. Second, micro transitions necessarily implicate the multiple roles one plays in contemporary society (e.g., spouse, parent, subordinate, coworker, health club member), raising the issue of how and to what extent these roles are differentiated. In short, the creation and maintenance of role boundaries—or *boundary work* (Nippert-Eng, 1996b)—is a critical aspect of micro transitions.

The central question in this chapter is: How do individuals engage in daily role transitions as part of their organizational life? The literatures on boundary creation and boundary crossing provide an overall framework for our argument. We draw on the work of Zerubavel (1991) who described a boundary as a "mental fence" (p. 2), and of Nippert-Eng (1996b) who viewed boundaries as socially constructed "lines" (p. xi) drawn around people, activities, and other entities. Crossing these mental fences or lines has been described metaphorically by Lewin (1951) as unfreezing-movement-freezing (see chap. 1); by Durkheim (1915) as crossing an abyss, by Simmel (1955) as crossing a bridge, and by Zerubavel (1991) as taking a cognitive leap between categories. Similarly, we describe role transitions as a *boundary crossing activity* where one exits and enters roles by surmounting boundaries (Schein, 1971; Van Maanen, 1982).

The model is illustrated with examples from the three major domains of everyday role transitions that involve work: (a) work–home transitions (i.e., commuting and home-based work), (b) work–work or at-work transitions (e.g., between one's roles of subordinate, peer, superordinate, and organization representative or between multiple jobs [moonlighting]), and (c) work–"third place" transitions (i.e., between work and other social domains such as a church, health club, and bar).[2]

Two key assumptions should be noted. First, for purposes of this chapter, we assume that the individual has attained a workable equilibrium

---

[2]Oldenburg (1997) defined *third places* as "the core settings of informal public life" (p. 16). (First and second places refer to home and work.) We focus on third places lodged in organizational settings such as churches and health clubs to simplify the subsequent discussion of role boundary, role identity, and role transitions.

within and across salient roles; that is, that he or she has negotiated more
or less satisfactory definitions of those roles and mechanisms for handling
role demands and conflicts on an ongoing basis. Second, we assume that
individuals generally seek to: (a) minimize the difficulty of desired role
transitions, where *difficulty* is defined as the effort required to become
psychologically and physically disengaged in one role and reengaged in
another role (Burr, 1972),[3] and (b) minimize the difficulty and frequency
of undesired role transitions. Thus, our analysis centers on how individuals minimize the difficulty of role transitions and the frequency of undesired transitions.

The chapter is divided into five sections. First, we revisit the concepts
of role boundary and role identity. Second, we argue that these concepts
contribute to whether roles are relatively segmented or integrated. High
segmentation fosters the transition challenge of crossing role boundaries
via role exit (unfreezing), movement, and role entry (freezing), whereas
high integration fosters the challenge of creating and maintaining role
boundaries. Third, we argue that role transitions become less difficult over
time as individuals develop transition scripts and role schemas. Fourth, the
impact of individual differences are considered. Finally, we speculate on
six areas in which the basic model may be extended.

ROLE BOUNDARIES
AND ROLE IDENTITIES

This section revisits the notion from chapter 1 that a role can be described
in terms of its interface with the environment (boundary) and its nature or
content (identity).

Role Boundaries

It was noted in chapter 1 that individuals erect mental fences as a means
of simplifying and ordering the environment. These mental fences create
more or less discrete domains of activity (e.g., home, work, health club)
and within each domain, more or less discrete bundles of tasks (roles).

---

[3]We recognize that aspects of the transition process may be enjoyable, such as listening to music
during the drive to work. Nonetheless, consistent with the argument that people are "cognitive misers"
(Fiske & Taylor, 1991), it seems likely that people generally prefer a relatively efficient (less difficult)
transition to a relatively inefficient (more difficult) one.

Certain domains, such as home and work, are more or less institutional-ized in the sense that people share a general understanding of the bound-aries of the domains and their associated roles and of the nature of the activities within the domains and roles. At the level of the individual, how-ever, boundaries tend to be constructed somewhat idiosyncratically just as roles tend to be enacted somewhat idiosyncratically (see chap. 7). One person may allow work to cross over into home, whereas another may struggle to keep the two separated (Nippert-Eng, 1996a, 1996b).

Thus, as noted in chapter 1, a role boundary refers to whatever marks the perimeter of a role. Given that work, home, and third place domains tend to be more or less institutionalized, their associated roles tend to be bounded both physically and temporally. Furthermore, as we will see, a variety of symbolic markers, from attire to particular role set members, may supplement these boundaries.

Role Flexibility and Permeability.   Two key concepts affect-ing the process of micro role transitions are the *flexibility* and *permeabil-ity* of a given role boundary. Flexibility is the degree to which the physical and temporal boundaries are pliable (D. T. Hall & Richter, 1988). A role with flexible boundaries can be enacted in various settings and at various times. For example, a man working in the family business may be called on to play the role of son at any point or place during the day. Conversely, inflexible boundaries severely constrain when and where a role may be enacted (e.g., security guard). Permeability is the degree to which a role allows one to be physically located in the role's domain but psychologi-cally and/or behaviorally involved in another role (Pleck, 1977; Richter, 1992). An employee who is able to regularly accept personal calls and vis-its has a permeable work role boundary. Conversely, an employee who has little opportunity (e.g., access, time) to attend to other roles has an imper-meable boundary.

On one hand, the flexibility and permeability of a role boundary may ameliorate interrole conflict by enabling the individual to undertake a role transition when necessary. For example, an employee may be able to leave work early to deal with a problem at his child's school. On the other hand, the very looseness of the boundary may exacerbate conflict by creating confusion among the individual and the members of his or her role sets as to which role is or should be most salient. The man working in the family business may be unsure whether to adopt the role of the supportive son or the critical colleague when appraising his parent's decisions (Kaslow & Kaslow, 1992).

Role Identities

A role identity was defined in chapter 1 as the persona associated with a role, including goals, values, beliefs, norms, interaction styles, and time horizons. As with macro role transitions, a key concept affecting micro transitions is the *contrast* between the identities of the relevant roles, defined in chapter 1 as the number of core and peripheral features that differ between the identities and the extent of the differences where core features are weighted more heavily.

A high contrast can be experienced as undesirable or desirable.[4] On one hand, concepts such as *master identity* (J. D. Brown, 1991), *master status* (Hughes, 1945), and *global identity* (see chap. 2) imply that some individuals experience contrast as fragmentation and seek to minimize contrast by enacting a subjectively important identity in various social domains. Thus, as noted later under "Role Identification," a valued identity may be used as an organizing framework for other role identities.

On the other hand, work, home, and third places may each serve as a foil for the others, providing a valued diversity of experience and thereby complementing one another. According to the compensation model of work–family relationships, home (and presumably third places) may address social-psychological needs and desires not adequately addressed by work (Champoux, 1978; Edwards & Rothbard, 2000). As Nippert-Eng (1996b) described, work and home have become stereotyped in popular culture with symbiotic themes attached to each, including production and consumption, masculine and feminine, instrumental and expressive, achievement and affiliation, and work and play. The richness of these contrasts contributes to the richness of the self.

The Context for Role Transitions

It is important to note that role boundaries and identities, and thus role transitions, are embedded in contexts that are rich in history, culture, structure, and so forth. In particular, our analysis focuses on roles lodged in organizational settings (work and third places) and at home; in other

---

[4]We are referring here to the experience of the contrast per se, not to the experience of the transition between highly contrasting roles (for the latter, see chap. 4, "Low-Magnitude Versus High-Magnitude Transitions"). As noted next, because multiple roles are held simultaneously, the individual may appreciate the diversity in roles for what it contributes to the totality of who he or she is (the global identity).

words, as noted, on roles lodged in social domains that are relatively institutionalized. As such, these domains act as strong situations (see chap. 1), influencing the placement of role boundaries and the nature of role identities within them (Barley, 1989). For example, a bank may require its branch employees to be at their respective branches (spatial boundary) from 9 a.m. to 5 p.m. each day (temporal boundary), it may discourage personal telephone calls and certain non-work-related activities and topics (inflexible and impermeable boundaries), and it may prescribe a certain friendly and service-oriented demeanor (role identity). Thus, in shaping the boundaries and identities of roles, the various social domains shape where a given pair of roles may lie on the role segmentation–role integration continuum, discussed next, and thus the nature of transitions between roles.

THE ROLE SEGMENTATION–ROLE INTEGRATION CONTINUUM

In this section, we argue that combining the concepts of role boundary (flexibility and permeability) and role identity (contrast) suggests that a given pair of roles can be arrayed on a continuum ranging from high segmentation to high integration. This continuum has been invoked by others in describing role boundaries. Based on extensive qualitative work, Nippert-Eng (1996a, 1996b) found that individuals differ in the degree to which they segment or integrate their work and home roles. Similarly, Hartmann (1997) found that individuals vary in the degree to which they have thick (segmented) or thin (integrated) boundaries around roles and other categorizations. Such findings suggest that segmentation and integration can be placed at opposite ends of a continuum. Figure 9.1 illustrates how the concepts of flexibility, permeability, and contrast jointly define a given pair of roles as segmented or integrated. We elaborate below on the rationale for a segmentation–integration continuum. We also argue that high segmentation decreases the blurring of roles but increases the magnitude of change between roles, thus fostering the primary transition challenge of crossing role boundaries. Conversely, high integration decreases the magnitude of change but increases the blurring of roles, thus fostering the challenge of creating and maintaining role boundaries.

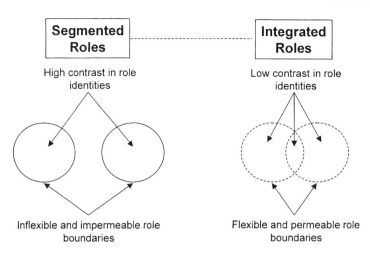

Segmented Roles ---------------- Integrated Roles

Segmented Roles	Integrated Roles
High contrast in role identities	Low contrast in role identities
Inflexible and impermeable role boundaries	Flexible and permeable role boundaries
Primary transition challenge lies in crossing role boundaries (given low blurring of roles and high magnitude of change between roles).	Primary transition challenge lies in creating and maintaining role boundaries (given high blurring of roles and low magnitude of change between roles)

FIG. 9.1. The role segmentation–integration continuum. (Reprinted from B. E. Ashforth, G. E. Kreiner, & M. Fugate, 2000, "All in a day's work: Boundaries and micro role transitions," *Academy of Management Review*, in press. Copyright © 2000 by the Academy of Management. Reprinted by permission of the Academy of Management via the Copyright Clearance Center, Inc.)

Role Segmentation

Inflexible and impermeable role boundaries tend to be associated with relatively large differences in identities between roles. First, the more inflexible and impermeable the boundaries of a given pair of roles, the less likely that their respective identities will "contaminate" one another. Lacking an open interface, there are few channels for the values, beliefs, norms, and so on of one role to infuse those of the other. Second, the more inflexible and impermeable the boundaries of a given pair of roles, the more likely that the respective identities will tend to *diverge* over time (Shamir, 1992). Effectively sequestered, the identities may evolve independently according to pressures from their respective contexts. Third, the greater the contrast between the identities of a given pair of roles, the more likely that relatively inflexible and impermeable boundaries will have become institutionalized over time as a means of *preserving* the essence of each identity. The mental fence is drawn around each identity so that it becomes highly salient within its now-bounded context. Members of a weekly poker game, intent on the game itself, may develop strict norms against discussing work or home life matters.

As shown in Fig. 9.1, roles that are highly differentiated (high contrast), tied to specific settings and times (inflexible), and permit few cross-role interruptions (impermeable) are highly *segmented* (Nippert-Eng, 1996a, 1996b). As Nippert-Eng (1996b) put it, "realm-specific contents not only promote a realm-specific sense of self, but they insulate us from our other-realm selves" (p. 36). Highly segmented roles tend to have little similarity between the contexts that inform each role and between the specific goals, values, beliefs, norms, interaction styles, and time horizons that constitute each role identity, and there tends to be minimal overlap in the physical location or the membership of the role sets. Given low boundary flexibility and low permeability, transitions between highly segmented roles tend to be relatively infrequent—although they may be quite regular (see chap. 4; e.g., a twice a day commute between home and work, a weekly visit to church).

Complete segmentation means that role identities and their associated contexts and role sets are mutually exclusive and perhaps even antithetical. This kind of Jekyll-and-Hyde dualism in roles is relatively rare although examples do exist (C. F. Epstein, 1996). For example, F. E. Katz (1993) described how the chief of the Nazi-run Auschwitz extermination camp routinely supervised mass executions and then walked home to his family where he apparently was a loving spouse and father. Short of complete segmentation, high segmentation is most evident between the domains of work and home (where one commutes rather than telecommutes) and work and third places. High segmentation in the at-work domain is less evident because work roles usually have the organizational context in common together with whatever role identities are implied by that context. Nonetheless, segmentation does occur, particularly among internal and external boundary spanners who must interact with various constituencies with divergent and possibly conflicting goals (J. S. Adams, 1976).

The Primary Transition Challenge for Segmented Roles

We advance the argument in this subsection that segmentation reduces the blurring between roles, thus clarifying the nature of the transition. However, the high contrast associated with segmentation increases the magnitude of the transition. Thus, the primary transition challenge in highly segmented roles lies in *crossing the role boundaries*: To psycholog-ically (and, where relevant, physically) exit one role and enter the other.

Blurring Between Roles.   Segmentation reduces blurring in three ways. First, because each role is associated with specific settings and times, there tend to be clear markers that both cue the appropriate identity and signal that identity to members of the relevant role set. A clerk enter-ing an office building at the start of the workday, a hockey player stepping onto the ice, a factory worker punching a timeclock, and a working parent picking up her daughter from day care are subject to potent cues about the proper role identity to adopt. Indeed, the distinctive settings associated with schools, funeral homes, factories, and so on may have as much to do with signaling distinctive role identities as they do with functional neces-sity (Olins, 1989).

Second, because highly segmented roles tend to be relatively imperme-able, role occupants are less concerned with being distracted by cross-role interruptions. Following Mandler's (1964, 1990) interruption–discrepancy theory, this "peace of mind" enables the incumbent to more thoroughly and exclusively immerse himself or herself in the role.

Third, because of the high contrast between segmented role identities, it is easier to psychologically compartmentalize the identities (Ashforth & Mael, 1989; Nippert-Eng, 1996b). The strong differentiation between the goals, norms, geographical location, role set members, and so on associ-ated with each role identity makes each appear to be a self-contained gestalt.[5] For example, the role-appropriate aggressiveness of a police inter-rogator may have little psychological bearing on the role-appropriate sen-sitivity of that same person as a parent. With compartmentalization, the interrogator–parent is less likely to experience interrole conflict (at least in the long term: In the short term, prior to fully learning and adapting to the role identities, the discontinuity in identities is likely to be quite salient and experienced as jarring; see the later discussion, "Role Schemas"). The upshot is that when either the parent or interrogator role is cued, she is able to more fully immerse herself in the gestalt of the role. In sum, the absence of blurring between the roles—that is, the clarity of the differentiation and associated role boundaries—in turn clarifies the nature of the transition.

---

[5]Thus, compartmentalization enables individuals to internalize a given role identity without hav-ing to resolve or even recognize inconsistencies with other role identities. Compartmentalization thereby helps individuals to cope with the fragmentation and turbulence of modern life discussed in chapter 1—although at the potentially high cost of a fragmented self (Gergen, 1991; Zurcher, 1977).

Magnitude of Transition. However, high segmentation renders the transition more difficult. The contrast in role identities means that there is more of a psychological and possibly physical gulf to bridge. Thus, although the interrogator may well understand that aggressiveness is no longer appropriate once she leaves the police station, it may remain difficult at a visceral level to shed the aggressive identity of the interrogator in favor of the loving identity of the parent. Research on role *spillover* indicates that moods, stress, and thoughts that are generated in one role domain often influence or spill over into other domains (Leiter & Durup, 1996; K. J. Williams & Alliger, 1994). The greater the magnitude of the transition, the more likely that these epiphenomena of role experience will be inappropriate in the next role.[6]

Furthermore, by definition, a transition between highly segmented roles entails multiple boundary crossings including temporal, social, or physical boundaries, or all three. Thus, it may take considerable psychological and perhaps physical effort to move from one role to another. Accordingly, the primary transition challenge in highly segmented roles lies in crossing the role boundaries.

Crossing Role Boundaries

Lewin's (1951) field theory provides a framework for the task of crossing role boundaries. As noted in chapter 1, the theory maintains that social states are quasi-stationary equilibria held in place by counterbalancing forces. For example, a person may stay late at work because the benefits appear to outweigh the costs. However, if the forces were to shift, the relative balance could be upset, resulting in an unfreezing of the equilibrium and movement toward a new equilibrium. Thus, a child's dance recital may upset the positive ratio of benefits to costs and prompt the person to head for home. A freezing of a new equilibrium occurs if the opposing forces again become counterbalanced. Change is thus described as a process of unfreezing-movement-freezing.

In the management literature, field theory is often applied to organizational change and development, that is, to macro transitions involving individuals, subunits, or entire organizations (e.g., Marshak, 1993). However, field theory is also applicable to micro transitions because such

---

[6]Conversely, the smaller the magnitude of the transition, the more likely that these epiphenomena will spill over precisely because of the similarity in role identities and the overlap in role boundaries.

transitions involve movement across boundaries. As the earlier example of the parent suggests, unfreezing corresponds to exiting one role, and freezing corresponds to entering another. The key difference in the application of field theory to micro rather than macro transitions is that the change is temporary rather than permanent, and thus the transition is more a matter of attention or salience than resocialization or unlearning. It should also be noted that for many micro transitions, Lewin's (1951) counterbalancing forces are composed largely of general and domain-specific norms that shape behavior. Thus, the parent may have been ordered to stay late by his boss and may be compelled by company policy to return by 9 a.m.

As also discussed in chapter 1, the unfreezing-movement-freezing framework dovetails nicely with van Gennep's (1960) three rites of passage: Unfreezing is facilitated by rites of separation, movement by rites of transition, and freezing by rites of incorporation (see Fig. 1.1).

Unfreezing: Role Exit and Rites of Separation. Unfreezing involves a disruption of Lewin's (1951) quasi-stationary equilibria such that the individual psychologically disengages from the role. Unfreezing is triggered by external or internal cues, or both. Common external cues include the calendar and clock (particularly given relatively inflexible and impermeable boundaries; Nippert-Eng, 1996a), completion of a project or task, social signals and requests, and interruptions (although segmentation reduces their frequency). Common internal cues include "push" factors such as a sense of closure, exhaustion, hunger and thirst, and the "pull" of the envisaged role to address push concerns or to otherwise provide a desired experience.

J. M. George and Brief (1996) argued that the emotions associated with such cues serve as signals that activate attention and the appropriate role identity. For example, a phone call from one's child is more likely to fully cue the parent identity if the news provokes very negative (e.g., the child had an accident) or very positive feelings (e.g., the child made the football team). However, as argued later under "Role Transitions Over Time," routinized role transitions such as the commute to work may become more or less programmed such that they unfold with little conscious thought or feeling.

Unfreezing may be triggered and facilitated by rites of separation. For example, a commuter may begin to psychologically disengage from her home role and prepare for her work role by following her daily routine of showering, dressing in work attire, reading the business section of the newspaper over breakfast, and listening to traffic reports. The flow of the ritual creates a psychological momentum that effectively overcomes the inertia of the home role and eases her into the work role. Such personalized rites of separation are typically embedded within larger social (e.g., family, friends) and institutionalized rites of separation. For example, disengagement from work at the end of the day may be facilitated by a collective "winding down," where coworkers plan their next day's agenda, turn equipment off, rinse coffee mugs, and so on (Nippert-Eng, 1996b). Once the rites and psychological disengagement have begun, it may be very difficult to fully reengage an individual in workplace issues even if he or she is still physically present in the workplace.

Movement: Rites of Transition.   This stage involves the psychological (and if relevant, physical) movement between roles. The function of rites of transition is not to impart the role identity, as was seen in chapter 6 for macro transitions, but simply to facilitate movement between already learned roles.

Given the external and internal cues that precipitate micro role exit, it is often clear which role is to be entered (e.g., leaving home Monday morning for work). Indeed, particular role exit and entry sequences are frequently routinized (see the later discussion, "Role Transitions Over Time"). If the exit cues are indeterminate ("Do I go to a movie or the club?"), expectancy theory suggests that one would enter the role with the highest anticipated valence (Vroom, 1964). However, unlike some of the momentous decisions researched in expectancy theory (e.g., selecting a job), the ephemeral nature of many micro role transitions likely means that the decision process unfolds in a relatively quick and muted form ("I'm more in the mood for a movie").

Psychological and physical movement is facilitated by rites of transition. Psychological preparation for role entry likely involves a combination of attention and arousal. The individual must adopt not only the appropriate cognitive frame (e.g., husband, employee, soccer coach) but the appropriate degree and nature of affective arousal. For example, some transitions may require heightened arousal (e.g., preparing for a presentation) achieved through a variety of means popularly known as "psyching up" (e.g., visualization, emotional labor, rehearsal; Hochschild, 1983; Murphy & Jowdy, 1992), whereas other transitions may require lowered arousal (e.g., dealing with an irate client) achieved through relaxation techniques (Orlick, 1980). This calibration of role, mind, and body has been described earlier as *flow* (Csikszentmihalyi, 1990; see chap. 2) or as *ideal performance state* (Uneståhl, 1986).

Various rites of transition may help regulate attention and arousal. For example, commuting can be viewed as a rite of transition involving temporal and spatial boundaries. Controlling for the variability in commuting time by car (caused by weather, traffic, etc.), Kluger (1998) found a positive relationship between the length and enjoyment of the commute. Enjoyment was operationalized as time to relax, time to think, valuable private time, conferring energy and waking one up, and reducing stress. Thus, a relatively long but smooth commute appears to provide a valued buffer between role identities (D. T. Hall, 1990).[7]

Freezing: Role Entry and Rites of Incorporation. Freezing involves the establishment of new quasi-stationary equilibria such that the individual is psychologically engaged in the newly entered role. Freezing is facilitated by rites of incorporation. In the macro transitions discussed in chapter 6, rites of incorporation served to test and sanctify one's readiness to assume the role; here, they simply signal one's *re*entry into a role. A police officer provides an example of how the simple act of dressing may serve as a rite of incorporation involving potent boundary markers:

> You put the uniform on and there you go, you have to be serious. You're carrying a defensive baton, which is pretty lethal force if you have to use it; you're carrying pepper spray which could do damage; and you're carrying your .38 [gun], which is deadly force. So, you put on your uniform and it's like putting on a very serious role. (Ashforth & Tomiuk, 1996, p. 5)

In sum, the role segmentation associated with differentiated role identities and relatively inflexible and impermeable role boundaries makes crossing the boundaries problematic. Crossing entails a process of unfreezing-movement-freezing that is often triggered and facilitated by personal and collective rites of separation, transition, and incorporation.

---

[7]Kluger's (1998) findings would appear to contradict the point made in footnote 3 that an efficient commute is preferred to an inefficient one. However, a long commute may be enjoyed precisely because it allows people to clear their mind so that they can arrive home ready to reengage in their family and leisure roles. In this sense, a long commute is actually a relatively efficient way of simultaneously facilitating a physical and psychological shift between roles.

Role Integration

At the opposite end of the continuum from high role segmentation is high role integration. As depicted in Fig. 9.1, integration is denoted by roles that are weakly differentiated (low contrast), are not tied to specific places and times (flexible boundary), and allow cross-role interruptions (permeable boundary). Highly integrated roles tend to have similar identities, be embedded in similar contexts, and overlap in the physical location and the membership of the role sets. Common indicators of work–home integration include working at home, socializing with organizational members, inviting people from work and from one's personal life to the same functions, wearing the same attire at the office and at home, making and receiving personal phone calls at work, displaying family photographs and memorabilia at the workplace, discussing personal issues with colleagues and work issues with family and friends, and reflecting on work issues at home and vice versa (Nippert-Eng, 1996b). Given high boundary flexibility and permeability, transitions between highly integrated roles tend to be relatively frequent and perhaps irregular and unpredictable (e.g., a home-based worker taking time out to attend to a crying child).

Complete integration implies that there are virtually no differences between roles, only "a single, all-purpose mentality, one way of being, one amorphous self" (Nippert-Eng, 1996a, p. 568). The more complete the integration, the more puzzling the notion of a role transition may appear to the individual; indeed, in the absence of role boundaries, there is no awareness of transition (Zerubavel, 1991). However, just as complete segmentation is rare, so too is complete integration. One potential example is members of religious orders living in monasteries and convents (Bruder, 1998). High integration is far more common than complete integration. Examples that lend themselves to high integration are evident in all three transition domains: (a) in the work–home domain where one works at home or in a family business or is a member of a total institution, such as a prison or navy vessel (Goffman, 1961a), (b) in the at-work domain where one's work roles are subsumed under a single organizational context, and (c) in the work–third place domain where one selects third places that reflect a work-based role identity (e.g., an executive joining a golf club) or vice versa or where both work and third place role identities are manifestations of a more global identity (e.g., a religious individual who joins organizations that reflect her religious beliefs).

The Primary Transition Challenge
for Integrated Roles

In this subsection, we argue that whereas the magnitude of the change between integrated roles is far less than between segmented roles, the blurring of the roles is far greater. Role blurring may foster confusion and interruptions such that the primary transition challenge for highly integrated roles is *creating and maintaining boundaries* between the roles.

Magnitude of Transition.   Given the low contrast between role identities and the flexibility and permeability of role boundaries, the transition process for highly integrated roles tends to be less difficult than for highly segmented roles. Thus, the transition process reflected in Fig. 1.1 tends to occur in less elaborate form. For example, Ahrentzen (1990) found that home-based workers tend to engage in relatively simple rituals to get motivated to start work (e.g., have a coffee, read the newspaper). Indeed, the unfreezing-movement-freezing sequence may occur rapidly, with little conscious awareness. A manager may exit one meeting where she was the boss and enter another where she is a peer with little psychological (and physical) effort.

Blurring Between Roles.   However, although the magnitude of the change is far less than for segmented roles, the blurring of the roles is far greater (E. J. Hill, Miller, Weiner, & Colihan, 1998; Shamir, 1992). As noted, highly flexible and permeable boundaries, coupled with overlapping role identities and their respective role sets and contexts, may foster confusion about which role identity is or should be most salient. A prime example is two people who establish what might be termed a *multiplex relationship*—that is, a relationship based on more than one set of roles. Examples include romantic relationships at work (Mainiero, 1986), family businesses where organizational members are both colleagues and family members (Kaslow & Kaslow, 1992), direct sales organizations such as Amway and Tupperware that encourage individuals to commercialize friendships (Butterfield, 1986), and relationship marketing where service agents are encouraged to build personal ties with customers (L. A. Crosby, Evans, & Cowles, 1990). A bank president who became a close friend of one of his customers, an automobile dealer, omitted negative information about the dealer's returned checks and loan payment delinquency when asked for a credit reference. The dealer went bankrupt, and the court ruled that a competing bank had been grossly misled by the president (Anonymous, 1990; see chap. 6, "Going Native," and S. Macdonald, 1995). Thus, role blurring can result in interrole conflict and anxiety for the individual straddling ostensibly separate worlds.

Moreover, high flexibility and permeability render the roles highly accessible such that either role may be interrupted without warning (D. T. Hall, 1990). For example, a meeting between team members (cueing the peer role) may be interrupted by the manager (cueing the subordinate role). Interruptions, as role boundary violations, disrupt the enactment of a role identity and may force an unwanted shift to another role identity. Interruptions thus disturb the ongoing identity maintenance process as role identities compete for attention and primacy (Burke, 1991; Hecht, 1996). However, interruptions do not necessarily involve suspending one role for another; they may require enacting two or more roles *simultaneously*. A team member whose boss pops into a work meeting must simultaneously enact the newly cued subordinate role vis-à-vis the supervisor but continues to be observed by her team members while still in the role of peer. Both roles are being played, but one has interrupted the other's exclusivity and dominance.

Thus, high integration makes it difficult for one to psychologically decouple the roles, fully disengaging from one in favor of another. For example, as noted in chapter 2, Schmid and Jones (1991) found that short-term prison inmates tried to preserve their "true" preprison self by playing the part of the tough but cautious inmate. However, because the prison afforded little privacy, and thus space to be oneself, the inmates were forced to remain in character virtually at all times. As a result, they found it difficult to separate their preprison self from their inmate role identity.

There are two provisos, however, to this argument that role blurring fosters undesired interruptions. First, not all interruptions are experienced negatively (cf. Mandler, 1990). An interruption can serve as a respite, providing a welcome break from a taxing role (Westman & Eden, 1997). For example, as alluded to in chapter 2, ethnographies of work suggest that people often welcome social interaction and horseplay as a distraction from unmotivating tasks (e.g., Balzer, 1976; Roy, 1959–60). Furthermore, an interruption may allow one to deal once and for all with a pressing cross-role problem such that one major interruption effectively forestalls a series of minor interruptions and brings peace of mind.

Second, role integration is likely to *decrease* the affective impact of interruptions. Mandler's (1964, 1990) interruption–discrepancy theory suggests that the degree of discrepancy between role identities determines the level of affect experienced and that the success or failure of accommodation determines whether the affect will be positive or negative. Similarly, according to Burke (1991), negative connections between role identities—that is, spatial or time constraints, meaning contradictions, and dual commitments—exacerbate the impact of interruptions. Consider a child calling his mother during a work meeting, interrupting an otherwise segmented role (Hecht, 1996). To the degree that the mother cannot be in two places at once (spatial or time constraint), cannot merge the meaning of mother and worker into an overriding identity (meaning contradiction), and is committed to enacting both roles (dual commitment), she will experience interrole conflict. The mother must choose between the parent role (and excuse herself from the meeting) or the work role (and call the child later). Thus, K. J. Williams et al. (1991) found that juggling the segmented roles of *mother* and *worker* had immediate and negative effects on task enjoyment and mood.

Given the great potential in highly integrated roles for frequent role confusion and frequent (albeit low impact) interruptions, the primary transition challenge lies in creating and maintaining boundaries between the roles.[8]

Creating and Maintaining Role Boundaries

If the primary transition challenge under high segmentation leads to a process-oriented response, that of crossing role boundaries, then the challenge under high integration leads to a structural response, that of creating and maintaining boundaries. Nippert-Eng (1996b) defined *boundary work* as "the strategies, principles, and practices that we use to create, maintain and modify cultural categories" (p. 7). Boundary work is used to foster either greater segmentation or integration, that is, to construct or modify the temporal, spatial, and other boundaries that demark roles—and in so doing, create "more or less distinct 'territories of the self'" (Nippert-Eng,

---

[8]It should be noted that there are several reasons why integration may be nonetheless desirable. First, integration provides opportunities for *role cross-fertilization,* that is, for attaining synergies in learning and resource utilization by leveraging the opportunities and resources of multiple roles. For example, a salesperson who loves golf may leverage her time by inviting clients to play the game. Second, individuals who strongly identify with a particular role may attain greater personal fulfillment from integrating that role with other roles (see the later discussion of "Role Identification"). Third, newcomers may seek to "throw themselves" into their work as a means of establishing their credibility and confidence, essentially suspending their other roles. For such newcomers, the challenge is not to create and maintain boundaries but to erase them at least until their claims to the work role identity have been validated (e.g., Kunda, 1992).

1996a, p. 569). However, given the great potential for identity confusion and undesired interruptions in highly integrated roles, it seems likely that most individuals will prefer at least some segmentation of their work–home, at-work, and work–third place domains.

Groups, organizations, and society as a whole have developed a number of more or less institutionalized means of partially segmenting or buffering otherwise integrated roles. Examples include taboos against discussing religious, political, or other personally charged issues at work; the demarcation of frontstage and backstage spaces at work; laws that forbid sexual harassment and discrimination based on criteria unrelated to work; norms and company policies that minimize potential conflicts of interests (e.g., friendships with clients); policies that require newly promoted personnel to work for a different department; norms that confine socializing largely to members of one's own rank; rules of etiquette that govern interactions; policies that forbid soliciting for personal causes at work; and the use of organizational time-outs such as office parties and retreats where work role identities are temporarily suspended.

At the individual level, people attain greater segmentation by erecting and defending idiosyncratic boundaries, boundary markers, and means of regulating access. These efforts appear to focus primarily on temporal and spatial boundaries, and there seems to be a limitless variety of boundary work. For example, Ahrentzen (1990) and Mirchandani (1998) discussed how home-based workers carve out work boundaries by creating a physical workspace, marking the territory with equipment and furniture, restricting the access of others, rescheduling domestic tasks, and setting times when people can call or talk to them. Similarly, live-in domestic workers such as maids and nannies often have a difficult time separating their work and nonwork roles. C. L. Macdonald (1996) found that in the absence of the temporal and spatial boundaries implied by off-site living, domestic workers often resort to an assortment of contrived boundaries such as refusing to perform emotionally charged tasks (e.g., cooking one's native cuisine), disparaging and thus distancing themselves from their employers, and routinely spending weekends with friends.

In sum, segmentation is often deliberately fostered through a host of idiosyncratic and collective temporal, spatial, and other boundaries. However, the integration associated with overlapping role identities and their relevant contexts and role set members, and with relatively flexible and permeable role boundaries, often makes it very hard for the individual to create and maintain role boundaries.

ROLE TRANSITIONS OVER TIME: THE DEVELOPMENT OF SCRIPTS AND SCHEMAS

The discussion thus far has not considered the implications of time. In this section, we argue that transition scripts and role schemas tend to emerge over time, easing the difficulty of role transitions and of reentering roles following interruptions.

Transition Scripts

A *script* or *event schema* is a cognitive structure that specifies the typical (descriptive) or appropriate (normative) sequence of behaviors and events in a given goal-oriented situation or process (Fiske & Taylor, 1991; Gioia & Poole, 1984). For example, the transition from work to a health club may involve saying good-bye to one's coworkers, driving to the club, saying hello to the staff, and changing clothes. Thus, *transition scripts* organize transition tasks in a temporal flow, thereby guiding the individual and providing a sense of predictability and control (Lord & Foti, 1986). Scripts vary from strong to weak, depending on how precisely the sequence of events is specified, and often include multiple paths to destinations (Gioia & Poole, 1984).

Like all scripts, a transition script develops as the individual gains direct and vicarious experience with relatively invariant tasks (Goodwin & Ziegler, 1998; P. P. Poole, Gray, & Gioia, 1990)—with "regular transitions" in the language of chapter 4. Tasks become cognitively linked into subroutines (leaving work, driving to the club, and entering the club), subroutines become linked into higher order routines (the work–club transition), and decision rules evolve for handling recurring problems (e.g., if the traffic report indicates jams, leave 30 minutes later). Thus, the greater one's experience, the more elaborate the script and the less difficult the role transition.

Consistent with the discussion of unfreezing-movement-freezing, transition scripts may be cued either externally (e.g., by the alarm clock) or internally (e.g., one feels hungry and so breaks for lunch). Once cued, the enactment of the script may be greatly facilitated by the rites of passage, clear boundary markers, and the actions of others (e.g., family members preparing for their day).

In time, with repeated enactments of a transition script, both the cueing and the enactment of the transition process are likely to become relatively automatic or *mindless* (Ashforth & Fried, 1988; Langer, 1989); that is, performed with little conscious effort or awareness. The specific tasks become cognitively chunked together such that the specifics are effectively forgotten relative to the more abstract overarching subroutines. Thus, the individual may slip easily from one role identity to another. Of course, an otherwise mindless transition may contain unstructured and therefore effortful subroutines such as the flow of conversation during a daily car pool to work.

In sum, the more a role transition is repeated, the more automatic and less difficult the transition tends to become and the more likely that role-specific indicators will trigger a psychological transition automatically.

Role Schemas

A *role schema* is a cognitive structure that organizes one's knowledge about the typical or appropriate behaviors expected of a person occupying a given position (Fiske & Taylor, 1991). For instance, a teacher is expected to discuss curriculum content with students, administer and grade tests, and meet with students' parents. As one gains experience in performing a role, one's role schema becomes more extensive (breadth), more detailed (depth), and more organized (Lord & Foti, 1986; Walsh, 1995).

Like a transition script, the cueing and enactment of a role schema tend to become more automatic over time such that one may enter a role and execute much of it quite reflexively (Ashforth & Fried, 1988; Weiss & Ilgen, 1985). For example, the teacher may launch into a lecture about a familiar topic without consulting his notes. Consequently, the jarring effect of interruptions may be attenuated over time by the development of a role schema. The teacher, interrupted by an emergency telephone call from home, may resume his lecture with little difficulty or loss of continuity. Indeed, individuals may become quite facile at juggling roles and may develop transition scripts for *re*entering roles that are interrupted (Mandler, 1990; Tingey et al., 1996).

In summary, the more a role is enacted, the smaller the affective impact of role boundary violations (interruptions) tends to be.

INDIVIDUAL DIFFERENCES

Nippert-Eng (1996a, 1996b) found wide variation in the degree to which individuals desired to segment or integrate their work and home domains. Similarly, Richter (1984) found distinct individual variations in *transition styles* between work and home: For some, the psychological transition preceded the physical one; for others, the two coincided; and for still others, the physical transition preceded the psychological. Such variations suggest that individual differences may play a major part in transition dynamics. We focus on three differences that are likely to strongly affect both the tendency to segment roles and the difficulty of the psychological transition process: Role identification, personal need for structure, and self-monitoring.

Role Identification

As discussed in chapters 2 and 3, identification occurs when one defines oneself at least partly in terms of the role identity (e.g., "I am a husband, a machinist, a bowler"; Ashforth & Mael, 1989; Pratt, 1998). The role occupant imports the role identity as a (partial) definition of self, essentially *becoming* the role (Ashforth, 1998). The greater the role identification, the more one seeks opportunities to express the role identity as a valued portion of the self-concept (Stryker, 1980). Thus, the greater the identification, the more likely is one to attempt to integrate the role with one's other roles. A strongly identified executive may routinely take work home on weekends and join organizations that will further her career; a strongly identified parent may display family photos in his office and talk about his children; and a strongly identified tennis player may recruit partners at work and talk about her game (e.g., Hochschild, 1997; Nippert-Eng, 1996b). Heinsler, Kleinman, and Stenross (1990) found that strongly identified police detectives had a difficult time *not* seeing crime and criminals on their days off. Indeed, R. H. Turner (1978) noted that a person may be unable or unwilling to "turn off" a valued role in contexts where it is not normatively appropriate (see chap. 2, "Multiple Identities"). However, because most people prefer at least some segmentation between their role domains, there are usually real limits to how much integration is desired.

Paradoxically, role identification also may both decrease and increase the difficulty of the transition process. With regard to *decreasing* the difficulty, it seems likely that the stronger the identification, the more eager one will be to enter the role and the more quickly and thoroughly one will become immersed in the role. Csikszentmihalyi's (1990) analysis of motivational flow indicates that individuals are far more likely to become psychologically and physically immersed in the experience of a role if there is an initial affinity for what the role entails. In terms of Richter's (1984) transition styles, highly identified individuals are more likely to experience the psychological transition in advance of the physical one. With regard to *increasing* the difficulty of the transition, identification may impede role exit (Frone, Russell, & Cooper, 1992; K. J. Williams & Alliger, 1994). Just as individuals may be eager to enter roles with which they identify, they may be reluctant to exit those same roles. Thus, the physical transition may precede the psychological one.

In summary, the greater one's role identification, the more likely one is to at least partly integrate the role with other roles, the less difficult role entry tends to be, and the more difficult role exit tends to be.

Personal Need for Structure

Personal need for structure (PNS) is defined as an aversion to ambiguity and a desire for clarity and certainty (Moskowitz, 1993). As such, PNS is correlated with authoritarianism, cognitive rigidity, dogmatism, and intolerance of ambiguity (Neuberg & Newsom, 1993). The desire for clarity and certainty suggests that high PNS individuals will tend to prefer to segment rather than integrate their role domains. As we have seen, segmentation involves decoupling role identities and their associated role sets and surrounding contexts such that a given role becomes more of a self-contained and internally coherent gestalt. This coherence, supported by relatively rigid and impermeable boundaries, is likely to appeal to the high PNS individual's desire for structure. By the same token, the desire for clarity and certainty may impede the psychological switching of gears required by transitions across segmented role domains. Thus, role transitions may require greater psychological effort.

To summarize, the stronger one's personal need for structure, the more likely one is to segment role domains and the more difficult role transitions tend to be.

Self-Monitoring

As noted in chapter 7, self-monitoring is one's sensitivity to situational cues as guides to behavior, concern for displaying appropriate behavior, and effort to display such behavior (M. Snyder, 1987). The higher one's self-monitoring, the more likely that one will conform to situational cues. Thus, self-monitoring should facilitate role transitions between segmented roles by enabling individuals to better read the role identity cues, boundary markers, preferences of peers and others, and so forth associated with a particular role.

However, self-monitoring may not facilitate transitions between highly integrated roles. The overlap in identity, context, and role sets may obscure situational cues as to which role is most appropriate and exacerbate the sense of confusion and interrole conflict that often accompanies integrated roles. For example, Zahrly and Tosi (1989) found that high self-monitors in a new plant start-up were more aware of the work–family role conflicts caused by work schedules that spilled into family time. Low self-monitors, being less sensitive to social cues, detected less interrole conflict. Indeed, consistent with research by M. Snyder, Gangestad, and Simpson (1983), this analysis suggests that high self-monitors may prefer to segment their roles to reduce the likelihood of such conflicts.

Thus, the stronger one's tendency to engage in self-monitoring, the more likely one is to segment role domains and the easier role transitions between segmented roles tend to be.

EXTENDING
THE BASIC FRAMEWORK

The analysis focused on the psychological dynamics of daily role transitions involving the social domains of work, home, and third places. Combining the concepts of role boundary and identity, we argued that roles can be arrayed on a continuum ranging from high segmentation (i.e., high contrast in role identities and inflexible and impermeable role boundaries) to high integration (i.e., low contrast and flexible and permeable boundaries). High segmentation decreases the blurring of roles but increases the magnitude of change between roles, fostering the primary transition challenge of crossing role boundaries. Exit from one role and entry into another are often facilitated by personal and collective rites of passage that signal to the individual and members of his or her role set(s) the change in roles and attendant identities. In contrast, high integration decreases the magnitude of change but increases role blurring, fostering the challenge of creating and maintaining role boundaries. This challenge is typically addressed by personal and collective boundary work that serves to buffer otherwise integrated roles.

These basic arguments can be extended in at least six promising directions: (a) comparing role domains, (b) comparing work roles, (c) workforce externalization, (d) cross-situational identities, (e) role conflict, ambiguity, overload, and complexity, and (f) other role transitions.

Comparing Role Domains

We argued that transitions in the at-work domain tend to be less difficult because of the common organizational context. In what other ways might the transition process vary across the work–home, at-work, and work –third place domains? For example, Pleck (1977) argued that work and home roles may have "asymmetrically permeable boundaries" (p. 423), as when organizations expect employees to work uninterrupted for certain blocks of time and to juggle their home role to accommodate work demands. This would suggest a greater need to create and maintain boundaries at home to defend against work encroachments than vice versa— particularly with the growing popularity of pagers and other technologies mentioned earlier.

Similarly, we noted that role identities may be loosely coupled (segmentation) or tightly coupled (integration). This begs the issue of why, when, and how individuals select roles that are highly segmented rather than highly integrated. Do individuals tend to seek a certain level of diversity, complementarity, and complexity across their "role system"? Is there an optimal level of segmentation–integration? Are work–third place roles more likely to be segmented than work–home or home–third place roles? Furthermore, there are many types of third places. It seems likely that individuals would be more comfortable with greater integration between work and some third places (e.g., lunchtime restaurant) than others (e.g., gay bar).

Comparing Work Roles

The model of role segmentation–integration (Fig. 9.1) and the role transition process (Fig. 1.1) is intended to generalize to any at-work role, given the assumptions noted earlier (i.e., that one has attained an equilibrium within and across salient roles and that one seeks to minimize the difficulty of transitions). However, because not all work roles are alike, future research might focus on how differences between roles play out in the model. For example, hourly employees tend to have fixed working times and locales, they may be discouraged from handling personal concerns at work, and they may not be expected to do work at home. In short, hourly employees may encounter relatively high segmentation between work and home/third places, suggesting that their primary transition challenge lies in crossing role boundaries. Conversely, salaried employees tend to have more open-ended hours, flexible work locations, and may frequently be expected to do work at home. Thus, they may encounter relatively high integration between roles, suggesting the transition challenge of creating and maintaining role boundaries (Jackall, 1988; Perlow, 1998).

Perhaps the key variables for transition researchers to focus on regarding at-work roles—indeed, all roles—is the nature of normative demands (what others expect) and the degree of autonomy role occupants have to enact or even modify those demands (cf. Karasek, 1979). For example, although a salaried employee may face strong normative demands to work long hours, she may have considerable latitude to determine when and where the work is performed. In general, it seems likely that autonomy over the creation and maintenance of role boundaries (structural control) and the crossing of role boundaries (process control) would reduce the difficulty of micro role transitions. Thus, Duxbury, Higgins, and Lee (1994) found that a general sense of control over one's time, irritations, and so forth was negatively associated with interference of work with family and family with work, and Koslowsky, Kluger, and Reich (1995) argued that perceived control over one's daily commute ameliorates the potential strain of commuting. The pivotal role of autonomy in role transitions suggests that the transition model depicted in Fig. 1.1 might be extended to include constructs such as control, participation, predictability, status, self-efficacy, and negotiation.

Workforce Externalization

Global competition, tight labor markets, and rising customer expectations have caused organizations to seek flexibility by restructuring traditional employment relationships in an effort to minimize costs and respond to rapid fluctuations in demand. In effect, organizations are externalizing their employees, moving them outside of the organization's internal core as signaled by remote location, diminished employment tenure, and indirect reporting relationships (Pfeffer & Baron, 1988). In addition to telecommuting arrangements (i.e., externalization of work location), this trend has led to a surge in contingent employees (i.e., who work on a temporary or part-time basis) and outsourced employees (i.e., who work for an intermediary such as a temporary staffing agency, professional employer organization, or telemarketing service bureau but who provide service for a client organization). The use of externalized employees has more than doubled since the early 1980s (Fierman, 1994; LaPlante, 1995)—and this escalation is likely to continue.

The growth of the externalized workforce presents two related transition challenges for organizations. First, as the discussion of role entry in chapters 6 and 7 suggests, newcomers are typically socialized into an organization's milieu through immersion in a rich and localized context complemented with more or less institutionalized socialization tactics and social support. Externalized employees, particularly outsourced employees, are frequently denied rigorous socialization and ongoing immersion in the organizational context. For instance, it took only 2 hours to train 600 employees of L.L. Bean to answer tourism inquiries for the state of Maine (Moran, 1998). As a result, their understanding of the organizational and role identities and their degree of identification with them may remain weak. In the absence of a visceral conception of and commitment to the organization and role, the transition into the work role may become tentative and incomplete.

Second, because telecommuters and outsourced employees work outside the organization, they lack the typical identity cues that facilitate psychological entry into the organization. Customers phoning Microsoft for assistance frequently make small talk with the service agents about the weather in Seattle or whether the agent has met Bill Gates. The agents respond politely but evasively ("It's overcast" or "No, I've never met him") while keeping secret that they are actually 3,000 miles away in Massachusetts (Auerbach, 1996). The upshot of a remote location is that the transition may, again, become tentative. One implication of these transition challenges for outsourced employees in particular is that the employees are more in danger of going native than are other employees, therefore favoring their direct employer (e.g., the temp agency) or, in the case of service agents, the customers of the client organization that the agent ostensibly works for.

Thus, an intriguing research question is how can organizations effectively socialize and enhance the identification and loyalty of externalized employees such that they more willingly and fully embrace the transition into the organizational role? In other words, how can the organization and its roles be made psychologically real so that the appropriate identities take root and are cued when necessary? As one example, telemarketers at outsourcing provider Matrixx form strong ties with their client organizations through the use of client-provided scripts, client-provided mission statements posted in their work areas, and—in one case—client-provided supervisors (Shermach, 1995).

Cross-Situational Identities

We briefly noted that a global identity may affect one's choice of specific roles across domains. This raises the broader question of how such cross-situational identities as age, gender, ethnicity, and nationality may influence the role transition process. Three examples will suffice. First, some research suggests that given the traditional gendering of work and home roles, men's home role boundaries are more flexible and permeable than their work role boundaries, whereas precisely the opposite is true of women (Pleck, 1977; Richter, 1990). However, these differences may be disappearing from contemporary society (Swanson, Power, & Simpson, 1998; K. J. Williams & Alliger, 1994). Second, we have focused on the role dynamics associated with more or less formal and achieved roles in institutionalized social domains. How might the concepts of role identity, boundary, segmentation–integration, and transition apply to ascribed "roles" such as demographic categories (cf. K. Hall & Bucholtz, 1995; Rosenblum & Travis, 1996)? Questions such as the following provide promising leads for extending the model: What role identities are connoted by, say, *White*, *female*, or *young*? How flexible and permeable are the boundaries of *Whiteness*, *femaleness*, or *youth*? How is *Whiteness*, *femaleness*, or *youth* cued by recurring movement across formal roles? How do individuals reconcile being labeled *young* in one role (e.g., vis-à-vis parents) while being labeled *older* in another (e.g., vis-à-vis subordinates)? Third, research suggests that members of collectivist national cultures such as Japan's are more inclined to integrate their role domains than are members of individualist cultures such as the United States' (Kondo, 1990; Lobel, 1991). How might other cultural differences affect the propensity to segment rather than integrate roles and the dynamics of the transition process itself (cf. Ashforth, Kreiner et al., 2000)?

Role Conflict, Ambiguity, Overload, and Complexity

Our focus on roles raises the question of how such well-known role attributes as conflict, ambiguity, overload, and complexity might apply to the micro transition process. At various points, we noted that interrole conflict is related in complex ways to both segmented roles and integrated roles. Whereas the compartmentalization afforded by segmentation may reduce some conflicts, the high contrast in role identities may create contradictions in values, norms, and so on, and the relatively rigid role boundaries may impair one's ability to deal with pressing issues in one role while in another. Conversely, the role blurring caused by integration may exacerbate some conflicts, whereas the overlap in role identities may reduce contradictions, and the flexible and permeable role boundaries may enable one to manage conflicts when and where needed. Thus, interrole conflict has potentially rich implications for the tendency to segment or integrate roles and for the experience of transition between roles.

Speculative implications can similarly be offered for role ambiguity, overload, and complexity (Burr, 1972). For example, role ambiguity may impair role entry in that it may be difficult to become psychologically immersed in a role that appears unclear. Role overload may induce some individuals to segment their roles as a means of containing the overload and conserving their resources (e.g., an overloaded manager who restricts her accessibility to subordinates); alternatively, following footnote 8, some may integrate roles as a means of leveraging their resources. Role complexity may impair both role entry and exit in that it may be difficult to become fully immersed in the complexities of the role and to later extricate oneself from those same complexities. Furthermore, just as the transition challenge of crossing role boundaries was argued to give rise to rites of passage, the aversiveness of role conflict, ambiguity, and overload may also give rise to such rites. However, as the discussion of "Role Transitions Over Time" suggests, these role attributes may present less of a barrier to transitions as transition scripts and role schemas develop.

Other Role Transitions

Finally, the transition process depicted in Fig. 1.1 could be extended to quasi micro transitions such as vacations, short-term assignments, and infrequent or one-time roles (e.g., defendant, amusement park patron); to recurring ephemeral roles such as bank customer and moviegoer; and to "role extensions" (Johnston & Johnson, 1988) such as where a subordinate must manage the department in his supervisor's absence. For example, a training rotation to a different job and department would be analogous to a transition between somewhat segmented roles, suggesting the potential for difficulty in crossing the boundaries between jobs (cf. Van Maanen, 1982). And a role extension from subordinate to temporary supervisor would be analogous to a transition between somewhat integrated roles (i.e., same department and role set), suggesting the potential for difficulty in creating and maintaining role boundaries (e.g., resisting peers who expect favors).

CONCLUSION

Individuals tend to occupy multiple roles such that a micro role transition involves juggling the salience of a given set of roles. A father does not cease being a father while at work; however, the role identity of father may not be salient, existing as a latent identity to be cued at a later time. Thus, the father may act in quite unfather-like ways if the work role identity calls forth a different persona. Role boundaries and identities help structure and differentiate one's roles, and rites of passage and transition scripts help ease the transition process such that one may slip out of one persona and into another with less psychological effort. These structures and processes also enable one to retain a diverse portfolio of perhaps loosely coupled selves without being incapacitated by potential contradictions between the role identities. In short, what makes micro role transitions intriguing is that to switch roles is to potentially switch worlds; and yet many people do it every day with hardly a second thought.

10

Epilogue: Summary and Major Themes

[Barry] became recognized as one to go to for advice and soon developed a reputation for being a fine teacher. The company decided to take advantage of this talent and put him in a public contact job in the Marketing Department. . . . Since Barry was a showman at heart who loved to be on stage, he thrived on the public relations aspect of this job. . . . his success was rewarded with a promotion. . . . Barry was [later] placed in another marketing supervisor job, this time to develop methods for teaching and implementing functional accounting. . . . This staff position had little appeal to Barry, and he was not doing well. He had begun to abuse travel privileges and to take more sick time. . . . Barry complained that he never received the proper recognition for his speaking ability and public relations value. . . . He said he had grown tired of constantly trying to make a good impression on new bosses, and he was now planning to retire early.

—Howard and Bray (1988, pp. 214–215)

We have covered a lot of ground over the last nine chapters. We have reviewed established ideas such as role learning and life stages, and explored relatively new ones such as transition bridges and role reversals. Along the way, we visited new foremen and retiring coworkers, symphony musicians and condemned prisoners. What has been learned from this winding journey?

In this concluding chapter, I offer a thumbnail summary of the major arguments of the book and close with brief discussions of eight major themes that cross-cut these arguments. Key terms from the book are italicized in the summary and theme discussions.

SUMMARY
OF MAJOR ARGUMENTS

As organizations continue to colonize more and more aspects of everyday life, organizational *roles* or positions continue to proliferate. An individual may be a member of a work organization, a church, and a health club; a patient at a medical clinic; a client of a law firm, a day-care center, and a tax accounting firm; a customer at a grocery store, a bank, and a local theater; and so on. Increasingly, then, the tasks of everyday life are mediated through roles in organizational settings. Moreover, with the globalization of the economy and the explosion of technological developments, the rate of change is escalating. Thus, traditional assumptions about stable roles and predictable work careers are eroding quickly. The upshot is that individuals are constantly in a state of becoming—exploring their roles and their personal resonance with them even as the roles evolve, and moving between various roles over time.

Role transitions are about how one disengages from one role (*role exit*) and engages in another (*role entry*)—whether the roles are held sequentially (the *macro transition* of, say, a promotion) or simultaneously (the *micro transition* of, say, a commute between home and work). What makes the concept of role transition intriguing is that one must shift between different social worlds. Attached to every role is a *role identity*, that is, a set of goals, values, beliefs, norms, interaction styles, and time horizons. Whether a role identity is richly articulated and multifaceted (*strong identity* and wide *scope*; e.g., manager) or is quite limited (e.g., movie patron), it connotes a certain persona or self-in-role schema that channels thought, feeling, and action. To switch roles, then, is to switch personas.

To help preserve the integrity and uniqueness of each role identity, roles are surrounded by a *role boundary*. Given the institutionalized cast of organizations, roles tend to be bounded in space and time and denoted by various *boundary markers* (e.g., building, furniture, attire). By circumscribing domains, boundaries enable one to concentrate more exclusively on whatever domain is currently salient. Thus, role transitions involve crossing boundaries. Various *rites of passage* may be used to facilitate role exit (rites of separation), the journey between roles (rites of transition), and role entry (rites of incorporation). For example, farewell parties may serve as rites of separation, comforting routines and mementos may function as *transition bridges* and thus serve as rites of transition, and newcomer initiation events may serve as rites of incorporation.

Macro Role Transitions

Entering a new role arouses *psychological motives* for *identity* (i.e., self-knowledge, self-expression, self-coherence, self-continuity, self-distinctiveness, and self-enhancement), *meaning* (i.e., meaningfulness and sense-making), *control* (i.e., primary and secondary), and *belonging* (i.e., personalized and depersonalized). These motives are complementary and experienced simultaneously. The more these motives are met, the more likely that one will define oneself at least partly in terms of the role identity; that is, the more likely that one will identify with the role. In turn, the greater the *role identification*, the more faithfully one will enact the role identity: To do otherwise would be to impugn oneself.

The attractiveness or *valence* of a role transition to the transitioner depends on the nature of the role identity and the transition process. A role identity that addresses the four motives is likely to be viewed positively. A role transition process that is of low (vs. high) *magnitude*, is *socially desirable* (vs. undesirable), *voluntary* (vs. involuntary), *predictable* (vs. unpredictable), *collective* (vs. individual), *reversible* (vs. irreversible), and has a long (vs. short) *duration* is also more likely to be viewed positively.

Newcomers often enter roles with unrealistically high expectations or have only an intellectual grasp of the role and therefore experience *entry shock*. Entry shock predisposes newcomers to learn about their role and how they resonate with it (*role learning*), which in turn may predispose them to change the situation (*role innovation*) and to changes in the self (*personal change*). *Socialization* is the process through which newcomers learn about the role identity and wider organizational context. Socialization practices may be relatively unstructured such that newcomers develop more or less idiosyncratic views of their roles and innovative ways of fulfilling them. Conversely, the practices may be relatively structured such that newcomers develop more or less consensual views of their roles and similar ways of fulfilling them (although consensus need not mean conformity). Either way, learning occurs as individuals make sense of myriad formative episodes or *epiphanies* and *turning points*.

The more that newcomers' incoming identities differ from the role and organizational identities and the less that newcomers are willing or able to divest themselves of their incoming identities, the more likely that the organization will attempt to actively strip those identities away via *divestiture*. Newcomers may be temporarily isolated from outsiders and subjected to intense and relentless pressure to adopt the proffered identities.

However, newcomers are not passive vessels; they often engage in a variety of proactive behaviors (*proactivity*) to both learn about their role and context and to shape them more to their preferences. Role innovation is prompted by necessity, autonomy, and unmet expectations. Although work adjustment is often viewed by scholars as a compromise between role innovation and personal change, research suggests that these responses are more or less independent. Indeed, individuals may proactively seek and profit from both role innovation and personal growth.

Role exit is not simply role entry in reverse. Role exit originates from intrarole (*push*) or extrarole (*pull*) forces and may be voluntary or involuntary. The discussion in chapter 5 focused primarily on the most complex intersection of these variables; intrarole and voluntary transitions. A *precipitating event*, such as a disappointment or milestone, may provoke *first doubts* about one's role occupancy. If one is unable or unwilling to alter the situation or reconcile oneself with it, the doubts may escalate. The stronger and more nagging the doubts, the more inclined one becomes to seek confirmation rather than disconfirmation: One becomes motivated to confirm one's misgivings, particularly if validated by valued members of the role set (*social validation*).

If doubts indeed escalate, one may *seek and weigh alternatives*. The degree to which this process is rational and the amount of time devoted to it varies widely across individuals. The alternatives considered are strongly influenced by one's set of hoped-for and feared selves (*possible selves*) and by pragmatic issues. One may begin to identify with favored prospects such that the current role and reference group lose some of their psychological grip. Often, a final precipitating event—a turning point—is required to provoke a complete break with the role. Role exit may lead to *liminality*, where one lacks an identity moor to the relevant domain. Ultimately, however, the psychological impact of role exit depends on the degree to which one is able to construe the exit as a positive and self-affirming act rather than a negative and self-defeating one.

Macro Role Transitions and the Life Span. The experience of a given role can be characterized as a *transition cycle* of preparation→encounter→adjustment→stabilization. Individuals roughly calibrate their transition cycle to correspond to the expected duration of their role tenure. Thus, the cycle may be compressed in short roles (*time compression*), such as camp counselor, and extended in long ones. The *within-role* cycle may be embedded within cycles tied to sequences of similar or integrated roles, and these within- and *between-role* transition cycles are in turn embedded within a larger transition cycle tied to one's *career* and life span. However, given the constant state of becoming that increasingly typifies careers, a major challenge for the individual is to articulate *identity narratives* that weave roles and role transitions into a coherent and meaningful story. Identity narratives may be written prospectively or retrospectively and may both enable and constrain role transitions. Role transitions may also be regulated by the *social clock,* that is, by expectations of what is age-appropriate.

Micro Role Transitions

Unlike macro role transitions, micro transitions tend to be temporary and recurrent and involve the juggling of simultaneous roles rather than movement through sequential roles. Moreover, micro transitions directly implicate roles that are based not only in work organizations but in one's home life and in so-called *third places* (e.g., church, health club).

A given pair of roles can be arrayed on a continuum ranging from *high segmentation* to *high integration.* Highly segmented roles, such as church versus work, have boundaries that are relatively inflexible (i.e., tied to specific settings and times) and impermeable (i.e., permit few cross-role interruptions). Conversely, highly integrated roles, such as in a family business or a navy vessel, have relatively flexible and permeable boundaries. Generally, the greater the segmentation between two roles, the greater the contrast in role identities (*role contrast*). Thus, high segmentation decreases the blurring between role identities and between role boundaries (*role blurring*) but increases the magnitude of the role transition, fostering the transition challenge of *crossing role boundaries.* Boundary crossing is facilitated by personal and collective rites of passage that signal a change in roles and their identities (e.g., dressing for work and car pooling).

In contrast, high integration decreases the magnitude of the role transition but increases role blurring, fostering the transition challenge of *creating and maintaining role boundaries.* This challenge is often surmounted by personal and collective *boundary work* that serves to buffer the roles. For example, a home-based worker may reschedule domestic tasks, create a physical workspace, and restrict the access of others. Transitions tend to become easier over time as individuals develop *transition scripts* for more or less mindlessly transitioning between roles and *role schemas* that enable smooth reentry into interrupted or temporarily exited roles.

MAJOR THEMES

There are at least eight central themes that cross-cut the above arguments: (a) role and self, (b) dynamic interactionism, (c) transitioning, (d) events, (e) normalizing, (f) role exit↔role entry, (g) role identification, and (h) social influence.

Role and Self

In discussing role identities and role transitions, it is easy to lose sight of the individual. The individual is more than a role occupant and more than the sum of his or her internalized role identities. The individual's core sense of self, his or her *global identity*, is comprised of *personal identities* (i.e., idiosyncratic attributes such as dispositions) and *social identities* (i.e., internalized group categories such as gender), the latter of which includes role identities. The global identity is abstracted from countless experiences, particularly positive ones.

There are five key links between the self, as represented by the global identity, and the role, as represented by the role identity. First, the individual's global identity influences his or her selection of roles. Roles are more likely to be entered if they are expected to reinforce, complement, or extend the self in personally and socially desirable ways. Second, once an individual has selected a portfolio of roles (e.g., supervisor, peer, spouse, church member), the *salience* of a particular role to the individual is determined by the role's *subjective importance* and *situational relevance*. Because the global identity shapes what is seen as important and relevant, it therefore also shapes the salience of roles. Third, the global identity informs the individual's enactment of a given role. The individual seeks to express and affirm valued aspects of self through role performance. And the weaker the situation, the more latitude there is for doing exactly that. Fourth, as the global identity becomes more densely articulated over time (and perhaps more tightly integrated, but often not), it tends to become more resistant to information that does not appear to fit. Thus, the global identity filters self-relevant feedback generated by role enactment, preferring that which reinforces, complements, or extends the self in valued ways. Combining these first four tendencies, it is apparent that the global identity tends to function as a positively regarded, self-fulfilling template—although dramatic or repeated disconfirmation of the global identity, as well as normal maturation, significant life events, divestiture processes, and so on may provoke change, whether gradually or abruptly. Fifth, role identities that reflect positively on the self (e.g., through distinctiveness, prestige, high performance, extrinsic and intrinsic rewards) are more likely to be internalized in the global identity as components of the self. Indeed, the global identity can crystallize around certain highly valued role identities.

In sum, the first major theme—that of role and self—suggests that the self (global identity) influences the choice, salience, and enactment of role identities just as surely as the role identities influence the development of the self.

Dynamic Interactionism

The chapters on role exit (chap. 5), role entry (chap. 7), and micro role transitions (chap. 9) raised a host of individual differences that likely moderate transition dynamics. The notion of *dynamic interactionism* suggests that the individual influences the situation just as the situation influences the individual such that the two coevolve over time. In the context of role entry, for example, personal change and role innovation may be mutually reinforcing rather than mutually exclusive, particularly over the long run. Indeed, the potential power of the individual and the situation to shape each other in a dynamic and ongoing manner is so strong that it may be difficult to predict the state of either at some future point from a static set of antecedents. However, the stronger the situation (*strong situation*), the more influence it exerts relative to individual differences.

Given that role identities tend to be differentiated, especially when attached to differentiated social domains (e.g., home vs. work), it is important to underscore the concept of *coherence*. A particular setting is likely to present a more or less unique set of situational attributes, thus rendering particular individual differences more salient. Thus, one's work role may arouse the need for achievement, whereas one's spouse role may arouse the need for affiliation. The dynamic interaction of unique situations and particular individual differences may lead to different adjustment patterns across roles (moderate consistency), and yet the patterns may nonetheless reflect the nature of the person (high coherence). The individual remains true to each sense of self-in-role even if those selves differ markedly across roles. In addition, the more that these various selves are internalized into the global identity, the more that he or she will experience a sense of authenticity in enacting each of these selves. However, if these selves are contradictory, the individual may lack a holistic sense of self (i.e., the global identity may be fragmented and conflicted).

Thus, the theme of dynamic interactionism suggests that not only does the individual influence situations and vice versa, the individual can also enact widely varying role identities and still experience a sense of coherence within each role—although a sense of holism may remain problematic.

Transitioning

As noted, the transition cycle consists of four phases: Preparation, encounter, adjustment, and stabilization. This model is consistent with other models of socialization and work adjustment that argue that individuals gravitate toward a stable state, an equilibrium. However, stabilization is often short-lived or unattainable. As the organizational landscape becomes more turbulent and the frequency of role transitions increases even while the predictability of when, what, and where decreases, individuals are more likely to be perpetually preparing, encountering, and adjusting. In short, many individuals are in a perpetual state of becoming, where change is the norm and stability the exception. Thus, rather than view role transitions as infrequent disruptions of an otherwise stable continuity, it may be more accurate to view them as ongoing processes.

If transitioning is indeed becoming the norm, then the development of *meta-competencies* is likewise becoming important. Meta-competencies refer to a willingness and ability to learn and adapt. Meta-competencies imply certain corollaries: A willingness and ability to experiment and explore, to engage one's environment proactively; a variety of possible selves and identity narratives so that one is willing and able to become immersed in various new role identities; and a variety of experience and knowledge so that one has the requisite variety to engage various new challenges in meaningful ways.

In sum, the third major theme is that role transitions are, fundamentally, ongoing processes.

Events

Organizational life is experienced not as a seamless process but as a series of more or less loosely coupled events. Much of the learning that occurs during role entry and the first doubts that instigate voluntary role exit are associated with particular events. An event may be expected or unexpected, positive or negative, long or short, caused by oneself or some external force, isolated or recurring, and so on through a number of other continua. What makes a specific occurrence "eventful" or noteworthy is the meaning that an individual attributes to it. A client's thank you, the attainment of a work goal, an invitation to join a committee, a peer's resignation, a rebuke from a supervisor, and countless other episodes may be pregnant with meaning for an individual. Thus, individuals routinely decode events to learn about their role identities and contexts and their articulation of the role identities. Indeed, a seemingly innocuous event, such as a chance remark in the hallway, may become an epiphany for an individual.

The notion of events suggests several intriguing implications. First, the timing of events may strongly affect what the individual ultimately concludes about the role and organization. The meaning of a given event depends in part on *when* it occurs in a newcomer's tenure. A newcomer may be more receptive to a message about her behavior when she is 3 weeks into her job rather than 3 months. Second, the sequencing of events may also strongly affect the individual's adjustment. A newcomer who begins with a negative experience (who "gets off on the wrong foot") may never recover his initial enthusiasm and credibility, whereas a newcomer who begins with a string of positive experiences may be buffered from the impact of that same negative experience. Third, the trajectory of an individual's learning and identification may appear somewhat erratic insofar as they are pegged to the occurrence of key events. A newcomer's slow progress may say more about the stimulation afforded by the role than about the newcomer. Fourth, some role exits may be difficult to predict with conventional turnover models. A veteran may more or less mindlessly enact her role until a critical event, such as her 30th birthday or the resignation of a friend, disrupts the status quo and precipitates doubts. Fifth, over one's career, the occurrence of certain events (e.g., becoming pregnant) or the nonoccurrence of normative events (e.g., not being promoted) may affect one's identification with various roles far more strongly than tenure or age per se. Learning and many social labels are tied to what happens over time rather than to the passage of time itself.

Thus, the fourth central theme is that transition dynamics are closely associated with the occurrence and nonoccurrence of meaningful events rather than with the passage of time per se.

Normalizing

Role transitions are partly about rendering the new, the unexpected, the difficult, and the threatening more or less ordinary—about *normalizing* role identities and their enactment. In learning and enacting a role identity, one becomes familiar with the identity such that it may eventually be taken for granted. As suggested by the discussion of the making of a torturer (chap. 6), counternormative or particularly unique identities may be imparted through the intense divestiture process noted earlier. Indeed, history indicates that there are *no* institutionalized roles that cannot be made to appear acceptable to at least a portion of the populace.

Normalizing is also facilitated by a variety of transition bridges, including comforting routines, mementos, and identity narratives (all noted earlier), as well as *transitional roles* (e.g., trainee) and mediatory myths (e.g., "This role will be a developmental experience for you"). Transition bridges provide a sense of continuity between the past, the problematic present, and the desired future, thus helping the individual to settle into the role.

One risk of normalizing is that role occupants may overadapt to the idiosyncrasies of the role such that they find it difficult to exit the role (e.g., a soldier who becomes addicted to the rush of combat; cf. Grossman, 1995) and to unlearn role-specific features that impede entry into subsequent roles (e.g., a newcomer who is constantly saying, "That's not how we did it at IBM").

In sum, the fifth major theme is that individuals and organizations seek to normalize role identities so that individuals can feel comfortable donning and enacting these personas regardless of their content.

Role Exit↔Role Entry

The process of role exit is intimately connected to the process of role entry. The individual's psychological exit from a role often begins long before the physical exit. As noted earlier, an individual mulling over doubts about a role may begin to seek and weigh alternatives. The more attractive a particular alternative, the more likely that the individual will engage in *anticipatory identification* with the hoped-for role and *antici-*

patory deidentification with the current role (although identification with certain features of the current role may generalize to the hoped-for role). The individual's psychological fulcrum shifts from the current role to the anticipated one. Thus, psychological exit from one role may be strongly associated with psychological entry into another.

The individual's psychological exit from the role continues after physical entry into the next role. Deidentification continues, abetted by the compensatory qualities of the current role and by certain transition bridges, notably grieving the exited role, indulging in nostalgic recollections, constructing a salutary *exrole* (e.g., alumni) that enables the individual to attain closure, and by invoking identity narratives that portray the exited role as an important but closed chapter. The individual may even engage in *disidentification* (i.e., actively disavowing features of the old role as self-defining; "That is *not* me") and *selective forgetting* (i.e., unlearning goals, values, beliefs, and norms that are antithetical to the new role) as means of differentiating the old role from the new and distancing himself or herself from the old role.

Thus, the sixth central theme is that role exit continues after subsequent role entry and thus cannot be understood separately from role entry. (Similarly, although it was mentioned more in passing, the nature of role entry influences the likelihood and nature of subsequent role exit.)

Role Identification

Role identification is the sense of oneness with a role, entailing the perception and valuing of that oneness. To identify with a role is to define oneself at least partly in terms of the role identity. Thus, to be true to the role is to be true to oneself. Consequently, role identification helps address the psychological motives for identity, meaning, control, and belonging and facilitates role performance—thereby obviating much of the need for conventional control systems. With regard to micro role transitions, identification also increases one's propensity to integrate roles across social domains (e.g., inviting coworkers home).

Anticipatory identification, as noted earlier, may facilitate role entry. And once immersed in the role, role identification may inhibit role exit: To leave the role is to abandon a portion of oneself. However, the more generalizable the features of the role identity with which one identifies (e.g., *team member* vs. *GE project manager*), the more easily one may transfer one's identification to another role and organization. Moreover, identification may render one less tolerant of deviations from the identity such that one may become *more* likely to exit if the role is altered (e.g., a customer service representative who identifies strongly with service may quit if the company begins stinting on service to save money).

There is a dark side to role identification. Individuals who identify very strongly and more or less exclusively with a role may lose an independent sense of self and overconform to the role identity (e.g., an auditor who becomes a martinet, an actor who becomes a caricature of the parts he has played) and may be devastated if they must exit the role (e.g., an aging athlete who is forced to retire and has no other identity to fall back on). Ultimately, then, it may be healthy for both oneself and one's organization to internalize a diversity of personal and social identities and to maintain a certain *ambivalence* about any one organization-based identity. Ambivalence, where one simultaneously identifies and disidentifies with features of the role identity, enables one to achieve a certain ironic distance from the identity and to inform one's role enactment with other identities. Thus, the enactment may become more personalized and more rounded or enriched.

In sum, the seventh major theme is that defining oneself in terms of a role identity strongly affects one's propensity to enter and exit the role and one's enactment of the identity.

Social Influence

A role is embedded in a *role set* of interdependent positions. Role occupants tend to be concerned with what members of their role set think about their performance because: (a) role occupants recognize that they can learn from their counterparts, (b) role set members have a direct stake in the occupants' performance and may both facilitate and reward effectiveness, and (c) occupants tend to develop personal bonds with role set members and wish to fulfill social expectations. As a result, one's peers, supervisors, subordinates, customers, and so on can strongly shape one's construction and enactment of organizational reality.

Social influence is particularly apparent during role entry as neophytes tend to rely heavily on others for role learning and for instrumental and expressive *social support*. The less experienced the newcomer and the more unique the role or organization, the greater the reliance. Through social interaction and the internalization of social standards and meanings, newcomers come to see themselves somewhat through the eyes of others and construct a more or less stable sense of self-in-role. Social validation by key role set members of one's role behaviors, *identity markers* (e.g., attire, use of jargon), and performance outcomes help one feel like a bona fide exemplar of the role identity.

Social influence is also relevant to role exit. Individuals may turn to trusted role set members for social support and to validate or invalidate their emerging doubts about the role. However, if the doubts escalate, the individuals are more likely to seek confirmation of their doubts than impartial feedback.

Thus, the final central theme is that no man or woman is an island and the views of others in the local context often strongly affect the experience of the role and the propensity to exit it.

CONCLUSION

A career is a series of work roles, a dance between the individual and the personas of the roles that are entered and ultimately exited. Sometimes the dance is fluid and the individual becomes caught up in the flow of the moment; sometimes the dance is awkward and the individual struggles self-consciously. Role transitions are about how and why the individual enters a role and begins the dance anew and how and why the individual subsequently exits the role. The nature of the role transition process strongly affects the nature of the subsequent role enactment and the trajectory of the career.

If the pace of organizational life and change are indeed escalating, then careers will be less about stability punctuated by occasional role transitions than about ongoing transitions—both within and between roles—punctuated by occasional stability. When transitioning is the norm, the processes of role entry and exit become compressed and adaptation becomes a necessary way of life. This is the challenge that awaits tomorrow's men and women.

References

Abrams, D. (1990). How do group members regulate their behaviour? An integration of social identity and self-awareness theories. In D. Abrams & M. A. Hogg (Eds.), *Social identity theory:
Constructive and critical advances* (pp. 89–112). New York: Springer-Verlag.

Abrams, D. (1992). Processes of social identification. In G. M. Breakwell (Ed.), *Social psychology of
identity and the self-concept* (pp. 57–99). San Diego: Academic Press.

Abramson, L. Y., Alloy, L. B., & Metalsky, G. I. (1995). Hopelessness depression. In G. M. Buchanan
& M. E. P. Seligman (Eds.), *Explanatory style* (pp. 113–134). Hillsdale, NJ: Lawrence Erlbaum
Associates.

Abravanel, H. (1983). Mediatory myths in the service of organizational ideology. In L. Pondy, G.
Morgan, & T. Dandridge (Eds.), *Organizational symbolism* (pp. 273–293). Greenwich, CT: JAI.

Adams, G. A., & Beehr, T. A. (1998). Turnover and retirement: A comparison of their similarities and
differences. *Personnel Psychology, 51*, 643–665.

Adams, J. S. (1976). The structure and dynamics of behavior in organizational boundary roles. In M.
D. Dunnette (Ed.), *Handbook of industrial and organizational psychology* (pp. 1175–1199).
Chicago: Rand McNally.

Adkins, C. L. (1995). Previous work experience and organizational socialization: A longitudinal
examination. *Academy of Management Journal, 38*, 839–862.

Adler, P. A., & Adler, P. (1991). *Backboards & blackboards: College athletes and role engulfment.*
New York: Columbia University Press.

Ahrentzen, S. B. (1990). Managing conflict by managing boundaries: How professional homework-
ers cope with multiple roles at home. *Environment and Behavior, 22*, 723–752.

Albert, S., & Whetten, D. A. (1985). Organizational identity. In L. L. Cummings & B. M. Staw (Eds.),
Research in organizational behavior (Vol. 7, pp. 263–295). Greenwich, CT: JAI.

Allen, N. J., & Meyer, J. P. (1990). Organizational socialization tactics: A longitudinal analysis of links to newcomers' commitment and role orientation. *Academy of Management Journal, 33,* 847–858.

Allen, V. L., & van de Vliert, E. (1984). A role theoretical perspective on transitional processes. In V. L. Allen & E. van de Vliert (Eds.), *Role transitions: Explorations and explanations* (pp. 3–18). New York: Plenum.

Allison, A. (1994). *Nightwork: Sexuality, pleasure, and corporate masculinity in a Tokyo hostess club.* Chicago: University of Chicago Press.

Alloy, L. B., Clements, C. M., & Koenig, L. J. (1993). Perceptions of control: Determinants and mechanisms. In G. Weary, F. Gleicher, & K. L. Marsh (Eds.), *Control motivation and social cognition* (pp. 33–73). New York: Springer-Verlag.

Alpert, L., Atkins, B. M., & Ziller, R. C. (1979). Becoming a judge: The transition from advocate to arbiter. *Judicature, 62,* 325–335.

Andrews, A., & Bailyn, L. (1993). Segmentation and synergy: Two models of linking work and family. In J. C. Hood (Ed.), *Men, work, and family* (pp. 262–275). Newbury Park, CA: Sage.

Anonymous. (1990). Credit information exchange: Separating friendships from business. *Journal of Commercial Bank Lending, 72*(7), 57–59.

Archer, J., & Rhodes, V. (1987). Bereavement and reactions to job loss: A comparative review. *British Journal of Social Psychology, 26,* 211–224.

Archer, J., & Rhodes, V. (1995). A longitudinal study of job loss in relation to the grief process. *Journal of Community & Applied Social Psychology, 5,* 183–188.

Argyris, C., & Schön, D. (1978). *Organizational learning: A theory of action perspective.* Reading, MA: Addison-Wesley.

Arluke, A. (1991). Going into the closet with science: Information control among animal experimenters. *Journal of Contemporary Ethnography, 20,* 306–330.

Armstrong, J. S. (1977). Social irresponsibility in management. *Journal of Business Research, 5,* 185–213.

Armstrong-Stassen, M. (1994). Coping with transition: A study of layoff survivors. *Journal of Organizational Behavior, 15,* 597–621.

Arnold, J., & Nicholson, N. (1991). Construing of self and others at work in the early years of corporate careers. *Journal of Organizational Behavior, 12,* 621–639.

Aronson, E., & Mills, J. (1959). The effects of severity of initiation on liking for a group. *Journal of Abnormal and Social Psychology, 59,* 177–181.

Aronson, J., Blanton, H., & Cooper, J. (1995). From dissonance to disidentification: Selectivity in the self-affirmation process. *Journal of Personality and Social Psychology, 68,* 986–996.

Arthur, M. B. (1994). The boundaryless career: A new perspective for organizational inquiry. *Journal of Organizational Behavior, 15,* 295–306.

Arthur, M. B., & Rousseau, D. M. (1996a). Introduction: The boundaryless career as a new employment principle. In M. B. Arthur & D. M. Rousseau (Eds.), *The boundaryless career: A new employment principle for a new organizational era* (pp. 3–20). New York: Oxford University Press.

Arthur, M. B., & Rousseau, D. M. (Eds.). (1996b). *The boundaryless career: A new employment principle for a new organizational era.* New York: Oxford University Press.

Ashby, W. R. (1960). *Design for a brain: The origin of adaptive behavior* (2nd ed.). London: Chapman & Hall.

Ashford, S. J. (1986). Feedback seeking in individual adaptation: A resource perspective. *Academy of Management Journal, 29,* 465–487.

Ashford, S. J., & Black, J. S. (1996). Proactivity during organizational entry: The role of desire for control. *Journal of Applied Psychology, 81,* 199–214.

Ashford, S. J., & Taylor, M. S. (1990). Adaptation to work transitions: An integrative approach. In G. R. Ferris & K. M. Rowland (Eds.), *Research in personnel and human resources management* (Vol. 8, pp. 1–39). Greenwich, CT: JAI.

Ashforth, B. E. (1992). The perceived inequity of systems. *Administration and Society, 24*, 375–408.

Ashforth, B. E. (1998). Becoming: How does the process of identification unfold? In D. A. Whetten & P. C. Godfrey (Eds.), *Identity in organizations: Building theory through conversations* (pp. 213–222). Thousand Oaks, CA: Sage.

Ashforth, B. E., & Fried, Y. (1988). The mindlessness of organizational behaviors. *Human Relations, 41*, 305–329.

Ashforth, B. E., & Gibbs, B. W. (1990). The double-edge of organizational legitimation. *Organization Science, 1*, 177–194.

Ashforth, B. E., & Humphrey, R. H. (1993). Emotional labor in service roles: The influence of identity. *Academy of Management Review, 18*, 88–115.

Ashforth, B. E., & Humphrey, R. H. (1995). Labeling processes in the organization: Constructing the individual. In L. L. Cummings & B. M. Staw (Eds.), *Research in organizational behavior* (Vol. 17, pp. 413–461). Greenwich, CT: JAI.

Ashforth, B. E., & Humphrey, R. H. (1997). The ubiquity and potency of labeling in organizations. *Organization Science, 8*, 43–58.

Ashforth, B. E., & Kreiner, G. E. (1999). "How can you do it?": Dirty work and the challenge of constructing a positive identity. *Academy of Management Review, 24*, 413–434.

Ashforth, B. E., & Kreiner, G. E. (2000). Normalizing emotion in organizations: Making the extraordinary seem ordinary. *Human Resource Management Review*, in press.

Ashforth, B. E., Kreiner, G. E., & Fugate, M. (2000). All in a day's work: Boundaries and micro role transitions. *Academy of Management Review*, in press.

Ashforth, B. E., & Mael, F. (1989). Social identity theory and the organization. *Academy of Management Review, 14*, 20–39.

Ashforth, B. E., & Mael, F. A. (1996). Organizational identity and strategy as a context for the individual. In J. A. C. Baum & J. E. Dutton (Eds.), *Advances in strategic management* (Vol. 13, pp. 19–64). Greenwich, CT: JAI.

Ashforth, B. E., & Mael, F. A. (1998). The power of resistance: Sustaining valued identities. In R. M. Kramer & M. A. Neale (Eds.), *Power and influence in organizations* (pp. 89–119). Thousand Oaks, CA: Sage.

Ashforth, B. E., & Saks, A. M. (1995). Work-role transitions: A longitudinal examination of the Nicholson model. *Journal of Occupational and Organizational Psychology, 68*, 157–175.

Ashforth, B. E., & Saks, A. M. (1996). Socialization tactics: Longitudinal effects on newcomer adjustment. *Academy of Management Journal, 39*, 149–178.

Ashforth, B. E., & Saks, A. M. (2000). Personal control in organizations: A longitudinal investigation with newcomers. *Human Relations, 53*, 311–339.

Ashforth, B. E., Saks, A. M., & Lee, R. T. (1997). On the dimensionality of Jones' (1986) measures of organizational socialization tactics. *International Journal of Selection and Assessment, 5*, 200–214.

Ashforth, B. E., & Tomiuk, M. A. (1996, August). *The experience of emotional labor in service encounters.* Paper presented at the annual meeting of the Academy of Management, Cincinnati, OH.

Ashforth, B. E., & Tomiuk, M. A. (2000). Emotional labour and authenticity: Views from service agents. In S. Fineman (Ed.), *Emotion in organizations* (Vol. 2, pp. 184–203). London: Sage.

Atchley, R. C. (1976). *The sociology of retirement.* Cambridge, MA: Schenkman.

Atchley, R. C. (1991). *Social forces and aging: An introduction to social gerontology* (6th ed.). Belmont, CA: Wadsworth.

Auerbach, J. (1996, March 8). More than a bit player: Stream International catches wave of outsourcing services. *Boston Globe*, p. 77.

Baesler, E. J. (1995). Persuasive effects of an involving disability role play. *Journal of Applied Rehabilitation Counseling, 26*(2), 29–35.

Baker, M. (1986). *Cops: Their lives in their own words.* New York: Pocket Books.

Baker, T., & Aldrich, H. E. (1996). Prometheus stretches: Building identity and cumulative knowledge in multiemployer careers. In M. B. Arthur & D. M. Rousseau (Eds.), *The boundaryless career: A new employment principle for a new organizational era* (pp. 132–149). New York: Oxford University Press.

Balzer, R. (1976). *Clockwork: Life in and outside an American factory.* Garden City, NY: Doubleday.

Banaji, M. R., & Prentice, D. A. (1994). The self in social contexts. In L. W. Porter & M. R. Rosenzweig (Eds.), *Annual review of psychology* (Vol. 45, pp. 297–332). Palo Alto, CA: Annual Reviews.

Bandura, A. (1977). *Social learning theory.* Englewood Cliffs, NJ: Prentice-Hall.

Bandura, A. (1986). *Social foundations of thought and action: A social cognitive theory.* Englewood Cliffs, NJ: Prentice-Hall.

Banks, M., Bates, I., Breakwell, G., Bynner, J., Emler, N., Jamieson, L., & Roberts, K. (1992). *Careers and identities.* Milton Keynes, England: Open University Press.

Bankston, W. B., Forsyth, C. J., & Floyd, H. H., Jr. (1981). Toward a general model of the process of radical conversion: An interactionist perspective on the transformation of self-identity. *Qualitative Sociology, 4,* 279–297.

Barker, J. R. (1993). Tightening the iron cage: Concertive control in self-managing teams. *Administrative Science Quarterly, 38,* 408–437.

Barley, S. R. (1989). Careers, identities, and institutions: The legacy of the Chicago school of sociology. In M. B. Arthur, D. T. Hall, & B. S. Lawrence (Eds.), *Handbook of career theory* (pp. 41–65). Cambridge, England: Cambridge University Press.

Barrett, C. L., Johnson, P. W., & Meyer, R. G. (1985). Expert eyewitness, consultant, advocate: One role is enough. *Social Action and the Law, 11*(2), 56–57.

Barrick, M. R., & Mount, M. K. (1991). The big five personality dimensions and job performance: A meta-analysis. *Personnel Psychology, 44,* 1–26.

Bauer, T. N., & Green, S. G. (1998). Testing the combined effects of newcomer information seeking and manager behavior on socialization. *Journal of Applied Psychology, 83,* 72–83.

Bauer, T. N., Morrison, E. W., & Callister, R. R. (1998). Organizational socialization: A review and directions for future research. In G. R. Ferris (Ed.), *Research in personnel and human resources management* (Vol. 16, pp. 149–214). Greenwich, CT: JAI.

Baumeister, R. F. (1986). *Identity: Cultural change and the struggle for self.* New York: Oxford University Press.

Baumeister, R. F., & Leary, M. R. (1995). The need to belong: Desire for interpersonal attachments as a fundamental human motivation. *Psychological Bulletin, 117,* 497–529.

Becker, H. S. (1960). Notes on the concept of commitment. *American Journal of Sociology, 66,* 32–40.

Becker, H. S. (1964). Personal change in adult life. *Sociometry, 27,* 40–53.

Bedeian, A. G., Ferris, G. R., & Kacmar, K. M. (1992). Age, tenure, and job satisfaction: A tale of two perspectives. *Journal of Vocational Behavior, 40,* 33–48.

Beehr, T. A. (1986). The process of retirement: A review and recommendations for future investigation. *Personnel Psychology, 39,* 31–55.

Beehr, T. A. (1995). *Psychological stress in the workplace.* London: Routledge.

Belk, R. W. (1988). Possessions and the extended self. *Journal of Consumer Research, 15,* 139–168.

Belknap, I. (1969). The mental patient in the hospital ward system. In W. A. Rushing (Ed.), *Deviant behavior and social processes* (pp. 378–387). Chicago: Rand McNally.

Bell, N. E., & Staw, B. M. (1989). People as sculptors versus sculpture: The roles of personality and personal control in organizations. In M. B. Arthur, D. T. Hall, & B. S. Lawrence (Eds.), *Handbook of career theory* (pp. 232–251). Cambridge, England: Cambridge University Press.

Bem, D. J. (1972). Self-perception theory. In L. Berkowitz (Ed.), *Advances in experimental social psychology* (pp. 1–62). New York: Academic Press.

Berman, H. J. (1993). The validity of role reversal: A hermeneutic perspective. *Journal of Gerontological Social Work, 20*(3/4), 101–111.

Berzonsky, M. D. (1990). Self-construction over the life-span: A process perspective on identity formation. In G. J. Neimeyer & R. A. Neimeyer (Eds.), *Advances in personal construct theory* (Vol. 1, pp. 155–186). Greenwich, CT: JAI.

Berzonsky, M. D. (1992). Identity style and coping strategies. *Journal of Personality, 60,* 771–788.

Bettelheim, B. (1960). *The informed heart: Autonomy in a mass age.* New York: The Free Press.

Beyer, J. M., & Hannah, D. R. (1996, August). *Socialization, social identity and the possible self: Who do I want to be?* Paper presented at the annual meeting of the Academy of Management, Cincinnati, OH.

Biddle, B. J. (1979). *Role theory: Expectations, identities, and behaviors.* New York: Academic Press.

Black, J. S. (1988). Work role transitions: A study of American expatriate managers in Japan. *Journal of International Business Studies, 19,* 277–294.

Black, J. S., & Ashford, S. J. (1995). Fitting in or making jobs fit: Factors affecting mode of adjustment for new hires. *Human Relations, 48,* 421–437.

Black, J. S., Gregersen, H. B., & Mendenhall, M. E. (1992). *Global assignments: Successfully expatriating and repatriating international managers.* San Francisco: Jossey-Bass.

Blau, G. (1988). An investigation of the apprenticeship organizational socialization strategy. *Journal of Vocational Behavior, 32,* 176–195.

Blauner, R. (1964). *Alienation and freedom: The factory work and his industry.* Chicago: University of Chicago Press.

Blumer, H. (1969). *Symbolic interactionism: Perspective and method.* Englewood Cliffs, NJ: Prentice-Hall.

Bourassa, L., & Ashforth, B. E. (1998). You are about to party *Defiant* style: Socialization and identity onboard an Alaskan fishing boat. *Journal of Contemporary Ethnography, 27,* 171–196.

Bowlby, J. (1969). *Attachment and loss.* Vol. 1: *Attachment.* New York: Basic Books.

Bowlby, J. (1980). *Attachment and loss.* Vol. 3: *Loss: Sadness and depression.* New York: Basic Books.

Boyanowsky, E. O. (1977). The psychology of identity change: A theoretical framework for review and analysis of the self-role transformation process. *Canadian Psychological Review, 18,* 115–127.

Braithwaite, V. A., Gibson, D. M., & Bosly-Craft, R. (1986). An exploratory study of poor adjustment styles among retirees. *Social Science and Medicine, 23,* 493–499.

Brandtstädter, J., & Rothermund, K. (1994). Self-percepts of control in middle and later adulthood: Buffering losses by rescaling goals. *Psychology and Aging, 9,* 265–273.

Breakwell, G. M. (1986). *Coping with threatened identities.* London: Methuen.

Breese, J. R., & Feltey, K. M. (1996). Role exit from home to homeless. *Free Inquiry in Creative Sociology, 24,* 67–76.

Breese, J. R., & O'Toole, R. (1995). Role exit theory: Applications to adult women college students. *Career Development Quarterly, 44,* 12–25.

Brehm, J. W. (1993). Control, its loss, and psychological reactance. In G. Weary, F. Gleicher, & K. L. Marsh (Eds.), *Control motivation and social cognition* (pp. 3–30). New York: Springer-Verlag.

Brett, J. M. (1980). The effect of job transfers on employees and their families. In C. L. Cooper & R. Payne (Eds.), *Current concerns in occupational stress* (pp. 99–136). Chichester, England: Wiley.

Brett, J. M. (1984). Job transitions and personal and role development. In K. M. Rowland & G. R. Ferris (Eds.), *Research in personnel and human resources management* (Vol. 2, pp. 155–185). Greenwich, CT: JAI.

Brewer, M. B. (1981). Ethnocentrism and its role in interpersonal trust. In M. B. Brewer & B. E. Collins (Eds.), *Scientific inquiry and the social sciences: A volume in honor of Donald T. Campbell* (pp. 345–360). San Francisco: Jossey-Bass.

Brewer, M. B. (1988). A dual process model of impression formation. In T. K. Srull & R. S. Wyer, Jr. (Eds.), *Advances in social cognition* (Vol. 1, pp. 1–36). Hillsdale, NJ: Lawrence Erlbaum Associates.

Brewer, M. B. (1991). The social self: On being the same and different at the same time. *Personality and Social Psychology Bulletin, 17,* 475–482.

Brewer, M. B. (1993). The role of distinctiveness in social identity and group behaviour. In M. A. Hogg & D. Abrams (Eds.), *Group motivation: Social psychological perspectives* (pp. 1–16). New York: Harvester Wheatsheaf.

Brewer, M. B., & Gardner, W. (1996). Who is this "we"? Levels of collective identity and self representations. *Journal of Personality and Social Psychology, 71,* 83–93.

Bridges, W. (1995). *Jobshift: How to prosper in a workplace without jobs.* Reading, MA: Addison-Wesley.

Brief, A. P. (1998). *Attitudes in and around organizations.* Thousand Oaks, CA: Sage.

Brief, A. P., Konovsky, M. A., Goodwin, R., & Link, K. (1995). Inferring the meaning of work from the effects of unemployment. *Journal of Applied Social Psychology, 25,* 693–711.

Brief, A. P., & Nord, W. R. (1990). Work and meaning: Definitions and interpretations. In A. P. Brief & W. R. Nord (Eds.), *Meanings of occupational work: A collection of essays* (pp. 1–19). Toronto, Canada: Lexington.

Brim, O. G., Jr., & Ryff, C. D. (1980). On the properties of life events. In P. B. Baltes & O. G. Brim, Jr. (Eds.), *Life-span development and behavior* (Vol. 3, pp. 367–388). New York: Academic Press.

Briskin, A. (1996). *The stirring of soul in the workplace.* San Francisco: Jossey-Bass.

Brockner, J. (1988). *Self-esteem at work: Research, theory, and practice.* Lexington, MA: Lexington.

Brockner, J., Tyler, T. R., & Cooper-Schneider, R. (1992). The influence of prior commitment to an institution on reactions to perceived unfairness: The higher they are, the harder they fall. *Administrative Science Quarterly, 37,* 241–261.

Brockner, J., & Wiesenfeld, B. (1993). Living on the edge (of social and organizational psychology): The effects of job layoffs on those who remain. In J. K. Murnighan (Ed.), *Social psychology in organizations: Advances in theory and research* (pp. 119–140). Englewood Cliffs, NJ: Prentice-Hall.

Brown, G. W., & Harris, T. O. (Eds.). (1989). *Life events and illness.* New York: Guilford.

Brown, J. D. (1991). Preprofessional socialization and identity transformation: The case of the professional ex-. *Journal of Contemporary Ethnography, 20,* 157–178.

Brown, J. D., Collins, R. L., & Schmidt, G. W. (1988). Self-esteem and direct versus indirect forms of self-enhancement. *Journal of Personality and Social Psychology, 55,* 445–453.

Brown, M. E. (1969). Identification and some conditions of organizational involvement. *Administrative Science Quarterly, 14,* 346–355.

Bruce, R. A., & Scott, S. G. (1994). Varieties and commonalities of career transitions: Louis' typology revisited. *Journal of Vocational Behavior, 45,* 17–40.

Bruder, K. A. (1998). Monastic blessings: Deconstructing and reconstructing the self. *Symbolic Interaction, 21,* 87–116.

Buckley, M. R., Fedor, D. B., Veres, J. G., Wiese, D. S., & Carraher, S. M. (1998). Investigating newcomer expectations and job-related outcomes. *Journal of Applied Psychology, 83,* 452–461.

Bullis, C., & Bach, B. W. (1989). Socialization turning points: An examination of change in organizational identification. *Western Journal of Speech Communication, 53,* 273–293.

Bullis, C. A., & Tompkins, P. K. (1989). The forest ranger revisited: A study of control practices and identification. *Communication Monographs, 56,* 287–306.

Burger, J. M., & Cooper, H. M. (1979). The desirability of control. *Motivation and Emotion, 3,* 381–393.

Burke, P. J. (1991). Identity processes and social stress. *American Sociological Review, 56,* 836–849.

Burke, P. J., & Reitzes, D. C. (1981). The link between identity and role performance. *Social Psychology Quarterly, 44,* 83–92.

Burr, W. R. (1972). Role transitions: A reformulation of theory. *Journal of Marriage and the Family, 34,* 407–416.

Butterfield, S. (1986). *Amway: The cult of free enterprise.* Montreal, Canada: Black Rose Books.

Byrne, D. (1971). *The attraction paradigm.* New York: Academic Press.

Callero, P. L. (1985). Role-identity salience. *Social Psychology Quarterly, 48,* 203–215.

Cappelli, P., Bassi, L., Katz, H., Knoke, D., Osterman, P., & Useem, M. (1997). *Change at work.* New York: Oxford University Press.

Cassell, J. (1991). *Expected miracles: Surgeons at work.* Philadelphia: Temple University Press.

Champoux, J. E. (1978). Perceptions of work and nonwork: A reexamination of the compensatory and spillover models. *Sociology of Work and Occupations, 5,* 402–422.

Chao, G. T., O'Leary-Kelly, A. M., Wolf, S., Klein, H. J., & Gardner, P. D. (1994). Organizational socialization: Its content and consequences. *Journal of Applied Psychology, 79,* 730–743.

Chatman, J. A. (1989). Improving interactional organizational research: A model of person–organization fit. *Academy of Management Review, 14,* 333–349.

Chatman, J. A. (1991). Matching people and organizations: Selection and socialization in public accounting firms. *Administrative Science Quarterly, 36,* 459–484.

Cheney, G. (1983). On the various and changing meanings of organizational membership: A field study of organizational identification. *Communication Monographs, 50,* 342–362.

Cheney, G. (1991). *Rhetoric in an organizational society: Managing multiple identities.* Columbia, SC: University of South Carolina Press.

Church, A. H. (1997). Managerial self-awareness in high-performing individuals in organizations. *Journal of Applied Psychology, 82,* 281–292.

Cialdini, R. B., Borden, R. J., Thorne, A., Walker, M. R., Freeman, S., & Sloan, L. R. (1976). Basking in reflected glory: Three (football) field studies. *Journal of Personality and Social Psychology, 34,* 366–375.

Cleveland, J. N., & Hollmann, G. (1990). The effects of the age-type of tasks and incumbent age composition on job perceptions. *Journal of Vocational Behavior, 36,* 181–194.

Cleveland, J. N., & Shore, L. M. (1992). Self- and supervisory perspectives on age and work attitudes and performance. *Journal of Applied Psychology, 77,* 469–484.

Collinson, D. L. (1992). *Managing the shopfloor: Subjectivity, masculinity and workplace culture.* Berlin: Walter de Gruyter.

Comer, D. R. (1991). Organizational newcomers' acquisition of information from peers. *Management Communication Quarterly, 5,* 64–89.

Cooper, W. H., Graham, W. J., & Dyke, L. S. (1993). Tournament players. In G. R. Ferris (Ed.), *Research in personnel and human resources management* (Vol. 11, pp. 83–132). Greenwich, CT: JAI.

Crocker, J., & Major, B. (1989). Social stigma and self-esteem: The self-protective properties of stigma. *Psychological Review, 96,* 608–630.

Crosby, F. (1984). The denial of personal discrimination. *American Behavioral Scientist, 27,* 371–386.

Crosby, L. A., Evans, K. R., & Cowles, D. (1990). Relationship quality in services selling: An interpersonal influence perspective. *Journal of Marketing, 54*(3), 68–81.

Csikszentmihalyi, M. (1990). *Flow: The psychology of optimal experience.* New York: Harper & Row.

Csikszentmihalyi, M., & Rochberg-Halton, E. (1981). *The meaning of things: Domestic symbols and the self.* Cambridge, England: Cambridge University Press.

Cushman, P. (1986). The self besieged: Recruitment-indoctrination processes in restrictive groups. *Journal for the Theory of Social Behaviour, 16,* 1–32.

Czarniawska, B. (1997). *Narrating the organization: Dramas of institutional identity.* Chicago: University of Chicago Press.

Dalton, G. W., & Thompson, P. H. (1986). *Novations: Strategies for career management.* Glenview, IL: Scott, Foresman.

Danish, S. J., Smyer, M. A., & Nowak, C. A. (1980). Developmental intervention: Enhancing life-event processes. In P. B. Baltes & O. G. Brim, Jr. (Eds.), *Life-span development and behavior* (Vol. 3, pp. 339–366). New York: Academic Press.

Davidson, O. G. (1993). *Under fire: The NRA and the battle for gun control.* New York: Henry Holt.

Davis, F. (1979). *Yearning for yesterday: A sociology of nostalgia.* New York: The Free Press.

Davis, F., & Olesen, V. L. (1963). Initiation into a women's profession: Identity problems in the status transition of coed to student nurse. *Sociometry, 26,* 89–101.

Davis-Blake, A., & Pfeffer, J. (1989). Just a mirage: The search for dispositional effects in organizational research. *Academy of Management Review, 14,* 385–400.

Dawis, R. V., & Lofquist, L. H. (1984). *A psychological theory of work adjustment: An individual-differences model and its applications.* Minneapolis, MN: University of Minnesota Press.

Deaux, K. (1996). Social identification. In E. T. Higgins & A. W. Kruglanski (Eds.), *Social psychology: Handbook of basic principles* (pp. 777–798). New York: Guilford.

DeLong, T. J., & DeLong, C. C. (1992). Managers as fathers: Hope on the homefront. *Human Resource Management, 31*(3), 171–181.

Demo, D. H. (1992). The self-concept over time: Research issues and directions. In J. Blake & J. Hagan (Eds.), *Annual review of sociology* (Vol. 18, pp. 303–326). Palo Alto, CA: Annual Reviews.

Denhardt, R. B. (1987). Images of death and slavery in organizational life. *Journal of Management, 13,* 529–541.

Dentler, R. A., & Erikson, K. T. (1959). The functions of deviance in groups. *Social Problems, 7,* 98–107.

Denzin, N. K. (1989). *Interpretive interactionism.* Newbury Park, CA: Sage.

Derry, R. (1987). Moral reasoning in work-related conflicts. In W. C. Frederick (Ed.), *Research in corporate social performance and policy* (Vol. 9, pp. 25–49). Greenwich, CT: JAI.

Des Pres, T. (1976). *The survivor: An anatomy of life in the death camps.* New York: Oxford University Press.

Dillard, J. P. (1991). The current status of research on sequential-request compliance techniques. *Personality and Social Psychology Bulletin, 17,* 283–288.

Dittmar, H. (1992). *The social psychology of material possessions: To have is to be.* New York: St. Martin's Press.

Donahue, E. M., Robins, R. W., Roberts, B. W., & John, O. P. (1993). The divided self: Concurrent and longitudinal effects of psychological adjustment and social roles on self-concept differentiation. *Journal of Personality and Social Psychology, 64,* 834–846.

Dorsey, D. (1994). *The force.* New York: Random House.

Dubin, R. (1992). *Central life interests: Creative individualism in a complex world.* New Brunswick, NJ: Transaction.

Dukerich, J. M., Golden, B. R., & Jacobson, C. K. (1996). Nested cultures and identities: A comparative study of nation and profession/occupation status effects on resource allocation decisions. In P. A. Bamberger, M. Erez, & S. B. Bacharach (Eds.), *Research in the sociology of organizations* (Vol. 14, pp. 35–89). Greenwich, CT: JAI.

Dukerich, J. M., Kramer, R., & McLean Parks, J. (1998). The dark side of organizational identification. In D. A. Whetten & P. C. Godfrey (Eds.), *Identity in organizations: Building theory through conversations* (pp. 245–256). Thousand Oaks, CA: Sage.

Durkheim, E. (1915). *The elementary forms of the religious life: A study in religious sociology* (J. W. Swain, Trans.). London: Geoge Allen & Unwin.

Dutton, J. E., Dukerich, J. M., & Harquail, C. V. (1994). Organizational images and member identification. *Administrative Science Quarterly, 39,* 239–263.

Duxbury, L., Higgins, C., & Lee, C. (1994). Work–family conflict: A comparison by gender, family type, and perceived control. *Journal of Family Issues, 15,* 449–466.

Ebaugh, H. R. F. (1988). *Becoming an ex: The process of role exit.* Chicago: University of Chicago Press.

Eby, L. T., & Buch, K. (1995). Job loss as career growth: Responses to involuntary career transitions. *Career Development Quarterly, 44,* 26–42.

Eden, D. (1990). *Pygmalion in management: Productivity as a self-fulfilling prophecy.* Lexington, MA: Lexington.

Edwards, J. R., & Rothbard, N. P. (2000). Mechanisms linking work and family: Clarifying the relationship between work and family constructs. *Academy of Management Review, 25,* 178–199.

Eisenberger, R., Huntington, R., Hutchison, S., & Sowa, D. (1986). Perceived organizational support. *Journal of Applied Psychology, 71,* 500–507.

Ekerdt, D. J., & DeViney, S. (1993). Evidence for a preretirement process among older male workers. *Journal of Gerontology, 48*(2), S35–S43.

Elsbach, K. D. (1999). An expanded model of organizational identification. In R. I. Sutton & B. M. Staw (Eds.), *Research in organizational behavior* (Vol. 21, pp. 163–200). Greenwich, CT: JAI.

Elsbach, K. D., & Bhattacharya, C. B. (1996). *Organizational disidentification: A study of social identity and the National Rifle Association.* Unpublished manuscript, University of California–Davis.

Epstein, C. F. (1989). Workplace boundaries: Conceptions and creations. *Social Research, 56,* 571–590.

Epstein, C. F. (1996). The protean woman: Anxiety and opportunity. In C. B. Strozier & M. Flynn (Eds.), *Trauma and self* (pp. 159–173). Lanham, MD: Rowman & Littlefield.

Epstein, S. (1980). The self-concept: A review and the proposal of an integrated theory of personality. In E. Staub (Ed.), *Personality: Basic aspects and current research* (pp. 81–132). Englewood Cliffs, NJ: Prentice-Hall.

Erdner, R. A., & Guy, R. F. (1990). Career identification and women's attitudes toward retirement. *International Journal of Aging and Human Development, 30,* 129–139.

Erez, M., & Earley, P. C. (1993). *Culture, self-identity, and work.* New York: Oxford University Press.

Erikson, E. H. (1963). *Childhood and society* (2nd ed.). New York: Norton.

Erikson, E. H. (1968). *Identity: Youth and crisis.* New York: Norton.

Erikson, K. T. (1976). *Everything in its path: Destruction of community in the Buffalo Creek Flood.* New York: Touchstone.

Falcione, R. L. & Wilson, C. E. (1988). Socialization processes in organizations. In G. M. Goldhaber & G. A. Barnett (Eds.), *Handbook of organizational communication* (pp. 151–169). Norwood, NJ: Ablex.

Farkas, A. J., & Tetrick, L. E. (1989). A three-wave longitudinal analysis of the causal ordering of satisfaction and commitment on turnover decisions. *Journal of Applied Psychology, 74,* 855–868.

Farran, C. J., Herth, K. A., & Popovich, J. M. (1995). *Hope and hopelessness: Critical clinical constructs.* Thousand Oaks, CA: Sage.

Fazio, R. H. (1987). Self-perception theory: A current perspective. In M. P. Zanna, J. M. Olson, & C. P. Herman (Eds.), *Social influence: The Ontario symposium* (Vol. 5, pp. 129–150). Hillsdale, NJ: Lawrence Erlbaum Associates.

Fazio, R. H., & Zanna, M. P. (1981). Direct experience and attitude-behavior consistency. In L. Berkowitz (Ed.), *Advances in experimental social psychology* (Vol. 14, pp. 161–202). New York: Academic Press.

Feather, N. T. (1982). Unemployment and its psychological correlates: A study of depressive symptoms, self-esteem, Protestant ethic values, attributional style, and apathy. *Australian Journal of Psychology, 34,* 309–323.

Feij, J. A., Whitely, W. T., Peiró, J. M., & Taris, T. W. (1995). The development of career-enhancing strategies and content innovation: A longitudinal study of new workers. *Journal of Vocational Behavior, 46,* 231–256.

Fein, M. L. (1990). *Role change: A resocialization perspective.* New York: Praeger.

Feldman, D. C. (1976). A contingency theory of socialization. *Administrative Science Quarterly, 21,* 433–452.

Feldman, D. C. (1994a). The decision to retire early: A review and conceptualization. *Academy of Management Review, 19,* 285–311.

Feldman, D. C. (1994b). Who's socializing whom? The impact of socializing newcomers on insiders, work groups, and organizations. *Human Resource Management Review, 4*, 213–233.

Feldman, D. C., & Brett, J. M. (1983). Coping with new jobs: A comparative study of new hires and job changers. *Academy of Management Journal, 26*, 258–272.

Felson, R. B. (1992). Coming to see ourselves: Social sources of self-appraisals. In E. J. Lawler, B. Markovsky, C. Ridgeway, & H. A. Walker (Eds.), *Advances in group processes* (Vol. 9, pp. 185–205). Greenwich, CT: JAI.

Festinger, L. (1957). *A theory of cognitive dissonance*. Evanston, IL: Row, Peterson.

Festinger, L., Riecken, H. W., & Schachter, S. (1964). *When prophecy fails: A social and psychological study of a modern group that predicted the destruction of the world.* New York: Harper & Row.

Fichman, M., & Levinthal, D. A. (1991). Honeymoons and the liability of adolescence: A new perspective on duration dependence in social and organizational relationships. *Academy of Management Review, 16*, 442–468.

Fierman, J. (1994, January 24). The contingency work force. *Fortune, 129*(2), 30–34, 36.

Figley, C. R., & Leventman, S. (Eds.). (1990). *Strangers at home: Vietnam veterans since the war.* New York: Brunner/Mazel.

Fineman, S. (1983). *White collar unemployment: Impact and stress.* Chichester, England: Wiley.

Fisher, C. D. (1986). Organizational socialization: An integrative review. In K. M. Rowland & G. R. Ferris (Eds.), *Research in personnel and human resources management* (Vol. 4, pp. 101–145). Greenwich, CT: JAI.

Fiske, S. T., & Neuberg, S. L. (1990). A continuum of impression formation, from category-based to individuating processes: Influences of information and motivation on attention and interpretation. In M. P. Zanna (Ed.), *Advances in experimental social psychology* (Vol. 23, pp. 1–74). San Diego: Academic Press.

Fiske, S. T., & Taylor, S. E. (1991). *Social cognition* (2nd ed.). New York: McGraw-Hill.

Fitzgerald, T. H. (1988). The loss of work: Notes from retirement. *Harvard Business Review, 66*(2), 99–103.

Fondas, N., & Stewart, R. (1994). Enactment in managerial jobs: A role analysis. *Journal of Management Studies, 31*, 83–103.

Fournier, V. (1995). Personal change following organizational entry: From a role–person fit model to a PCP framework. In R. A. Neimeyer & G. J. Neimeyer (Eds.), *Advances in personal construct psychology* (Vol. 3, pp. 133–189). Greenwich, CT: JAI.

Frankel, B. (1989). *Transforming identities: Context, power and ideology in a therapeutic community.* New York: Peter Lang.

Frankl, V. E. (1962). *Man's search for meaning: An introduction to logotherapy* (I. Lasch, Trans.). Boston: Beacon.

Freeman, S. F. (1999). Identity maintenance and adaptation: A multilevel analysis of response to loss. In R. I. Sutton & B. M. Staw (Eds.), *Research in organizational behavior* (Vol. 21, pp. 247–294). Greenwich, CT: JAI.

Freilich, M. (Ed.). (1970). *Marginal natives: Anthropologists at work.* New York: Harper & Row.

Friedman, S. A. (1996). *Work matters: Women talk about their jobs and their lives.* New York: Viking.

Frone, M. R., Russell, M., & Cooper, M. L. (1992). Antecedents and outcomes of work–family conflict: Testing a model of the work–family interface. *Journal of Applied Psychology, 77*, 65–78.

Fryer, D. (1985). Stages in the psychological response to unemployment: A (dis)integrative review. *Current Psychological Research & Reviews, 4*, 257–273.

Furnham, A., & Bochner, S. (1986). *Culture shock: Psychological reactions to unfamiliar environments.* London: Methuen.

Ganster, D. C., & Fusilier, M. R. (1989). Control in the workplace. In C. L. Cooper & I. T. Robertson (Eds.), *International review of industrial and organizational psychology 1989* (pp. 235–280). Chichester, England: Wiley.

Garfinkel, H. (1956). Conditions of successful degradation ceremonies. *American Journal of Sociology, 61*, 420–424.

Gecas, V. (1986). The motivational significance of self-concept for socialization theory. In E. J. Lawler (Ed.), *Advances in group processes* (Vol. 3, pp. 131–156). Greenwich, CT: JAI.

George, J. M. (1992). The role of personality in organizational life: Issues and evidence. *Journal of Management, 18*, 185–213.

George, J. M., & Brief, A. P. (1996). Motivational agendas in the workplace: The effects of feelings on focus of attention and work motivation. In B. M. Staw & L. L. Cummings (Eds.), *Research in organizational behavior* (Vol. 18, pp. 75–109). Greenwich, CT: JAI.

George, L. K. (1983). Socialization, roles and identity in later life. In A. C. Kerckhoff (Ed.), *Research in sociology of education and socialization* (Vol. 4, pp. 233–263). Greenwich, CT: JAI.

George, L. K. (1993). Sociological perspectives on life transitions. In J. Blake & J. Hagen (Eds.), *Annual Review of Sociology* (Vol. 19, pp. 353–373). Palo Alto, CA: Annual Reviews.

Gephart, R. P., Jr. (1978). Status degradation and organizational succession: An ethnomethodological approach. *Administrative Science Quarterly, 23*, 553–581.

Gergen, K. J. (1991). *The saturated self: Dilemmas of identity in contemporary life.* New York: Basic Books.

Gergen, K. J., & Gergen, M. M. (1988). Narrative and the self as relationship. In L. Berkowitz (Ed.), *Advances in experimental social psychology* (Vol. 21, pp. 17–56). San Diego: Academic Press.

Gerpott, T. J. (1990). Intracompany job transfers: An exploratory two-sample study of the buffering effects of interpersonal support. *Prevention in Human Services, 8*(1), 113–137.

Gersick, C. J. G. (1988). Time and transition in work teams: Toward a new model of group development. *Academy of Management Journal, 31*, 9–41.

Gersick, C. J. G. (1991). Revolutionary change theories: A multilevel exploration of the punctuated equilibrium paradigm. *Academy of Management Review, 16*, 10–36.

Gibbs, J. J. (1982). The first cut is the deepest: Psychological breakdown and survival in the detention setting. In R. Johnson & H. Toch (Eds.), *The pains of imprisonment* (pp. 97–114). Beverly Hills, CA: Sage.

Gibson, J. T. (1990). Factors contributing to the creation of a torturer. In P. Suedfeld (Ed.), *Psychology and torture* (pp. 77–88). New York: Hemisphere.

Gibson, J. T., & Haritos-Fatouros, M. (1986). The education of a torturer. *Psychology Today, 20*(11), 50–52, 56–58.

Gibson, J. W. (1994). *Warrior dreams: Violence and manhood in post-Vietnam America.* New York: Hill & Wang.

Gioia, D. A., & Poole, P. P. (1984). Scripts in organizational behavior. *Academy of Management Review, 9*, 449–459.

Girodo, M. (1984). Entry and re-entry strain in undercover agents. In V. L. Allen & E. van de Vliert (Eds.), *Role transitions: Explorations and explanations* (pp. 169–179). New York: Plenum.

Glaser, B. G., & Strauss, A. L. (1971). *Status passage.* Chicago: Aldine-Atherton.

Glass, J. L., & Estes, S. B. (1997). The family responsive workplace. In J. Hagan & K. S. Cook (Eds.), *Annual Review of Sociology* (Vol. 23, pp. 289–313). Palo Alto, CA: Annual Reviews.

Glynn, M. A. (1998). Individuals' need for organizational identification (nOID): Speculations on individual differences in the propensity to identify. In D. A. Whetten & P. C. Godfrey (Eds.), *Identity in organizations: Building theory through conversations* (pp. 238–244). Thousand Oaks, CA: Sage.

Goffee, R., & Scase, R. (1992). Organizational change and the corporate career: The restructuring of managers' job aspirations. *Human Relations, 45*, 363–385.

Goffman, E. (1959). *The presentation of self in everyday life.* Garden City, NY: Doubleday.

Goffman, E. (1961a). *Asylums: Essays on the social situation of mental patients and other inmates.* Garden City, NY: Doubleday.

Goffman, E. (1961b). *Encounters: Two studies in the sociology of interaction.* Indianapolis, IN: Bobbs-Merrill.

Goffman, E. (1963). *Stigma: Notes on the management of spoiled identity.* Englewood Cliffs, NJ: Prentice-Hall.

Goodwin, V. L., & Ziegler, L. (1998). A test of relationships in a model of organizational cognitive complexity. *Journal of Organizational Behavior, 19,* 371–386.

Gordon, R. A., & Arvey, R. D. (1986). Perceived and actual ages of workers. *Journal of Vocational Behavior, 28,* 21–28.

Gould, R. L. (1978). *Transformations: Growth and change in adult life.* New York: Simon & Schuster.

Gould, S. (1979). Characteristics of career planners in upwardly mobile occupations. *Academy of Management Journal, 22,* 539–550.

Graafsma, T. L. G., Bosma, H. A., Grotevant, H. D., & de Levita, D. J. (1994). Identity and development: An interdisciplinary view. In H. A. Bosma, T. L. G. Graafsma, H. D. Grotevant, & D. J. de Levita (Eds.), *Identity and development: An interdisciplinary approach* (pp. 159–174). Thousand Oaks, CA: Sage.

Graen, G. (1976). Role-making processes within complex organizations. In M. D. Dunnette (Ed.), *Handbook of industrial and organizational psychology* (pp. 1201–1245). Chicago: Rand McNally.

Graen, G. B., Orris, J. B., & Johnson, T. W. (1973). Role assimilation processes in a complex organization. *Journal of Vocational Behavior, 3,* 395–420.

Granfield, R. (1991). Making it by faking it: Working-class students in an elite academic environment. *Journal of Contemporary Ethnography, 20,* 331–351.

Greenhaus, J. H., & Beutell, N. J. (1985). Sources of conflict between work and family roles. *Academy of Management Review, 10,* 76–88.

Greil, A. L., & Rudy, D. R. (1984). Social cocoons: Encapsulation and identity transformation organizations. *Sociological Inquiry, 54,* 260–278.

Greller, M. M., & Stroh, L. K. (1995). Careers in midlife and beyond: A fallow field in need of sustenance. *Journal of Vocational Behavior, 47,* 232–247.

Grossman, D. (1995). *On killing: The psychological cost of learning to kill in war and society.* Boston: Little, Brown.

Grotevant, H. D. (1987). Toward a process model of identity formation. *Journal of Adolescent Research, 2,* 203–222.

Grove, K. (1992). Career change and identity: Nurse practitioners' accounts of occupational choice. In G. Miller (Ed.), *Current research on occupations and professions* (Vol. 7, pp. 141–155). Greenwich, CT: JAI.

Guimond, S. (1995). Encounter and metamorphosis: The impact of military socialisation on professional values. *Applied Psychology: An International Review, 44,* 251–275.

Gundry, L. K., & Rousseau, D. M. (1994). Critical incidents in communication culture to newcomers: The meaning is the message. *Human Relations, 47,* 1063–1088.

Gupta, N., & Jenkins, G. D., Jr. (1991). Rethinking dysfunctional employee behaviors. *Human Resource Management Review, 1,* 39–59.

Haas, J., & Shaffir, W. (1982). Taking on the role of doctor: A dramaturgical analysis of professionalization. *Symbolic Interaction, 5,* 187–203.

Hackman, J. R., & Oldham, G. R. (1980). *Work redesign.* Reading, MA: Addison-Wesley.

Hafferty, F. W. (1991). *Into the valley: Death and the socialization of medical students.* New Haven, CT: Yale University Press.

Hall, D. T. (1968). Identity changes during the transition from student to professor. *School Review, 76,* 445–469.

Hall, D. T. (1976). *Careers in organizations.* Pacific Palisades, CA: Goodyear.

Hall, D. T. (1986). Breaking career routines: Midcareer choice and identity development. In D. T. Hall & Associates, *Career development in organizations* (pp. 120–159). San Francisco: Jossey-Bass.

Hall, D. T. (1990). Telecommuting and the management of work–home boundaries. In *Paradigms revised: The annual review of communications in society—1989* (pp. 177–208). Nashville, TN: Institute for Information Studies.

Hall, D. T. (1995). Unplanned executive transitions and the dance of the subidentities. *Human Resource Management, 34*, 71–92.

Hall, D. T. (1996). Protean careers of the 21st century. *Academy of Management Executive, 10*(4), 8–16.

Hall, D. T., & Associates. (1996). *The career is dead—long live the career: A relational approach to careers.* San Francisco: Jossey-Bass.

Hall, D. T., & Mirvis, P. H. (1995). The new career contract: Developing the whole person at midlife and beyond. *Journal of Vocational Behavior, 47*, 269–289.

Hall, D. T., & Mirvis, P. H. (1996). The new protean career: Psychological success and the path with a heart. In D. T. Hall & Associates, *The career is dead—long live the career: A relational approach to careers* (pp. 15–45). San Francisco: Jossey-Bass.

Hall, D. T., & Nougaim, K. E. (1968). An examination of Maslow's need hierarchy in an organizational setting. *Organizational Behavior and Human Performance, 3*, 12–35.

Hall, D. T., & Richter, J. (1988). Balancing work life and home life: What can organizations do to help? *Academy of Management Executive, 3*, 213–223.

Hall, K., & Bucholtz, M. (Eds.). (1995). *Gender articulated: Language and the socially constructed self.* New York: Routledge.

Hallsten, L. (1993). Burning out: A framework. In W. B. Schaufeli, C. Maslach, & T. Marek (Eds.), *Professional burnout: Recent developments in theory and research* (pp. 95–113). Washington, DC: Taylor & Francis.

Haney, C., Banks, C., & Zimbardo, P. (1973). Interpersonal dynamics in a simulated prison. *International Journal of Criminology and Penology, 1*, 69–97.

Haney, C., & Zimbardo, P. (1973). Social roles, role-playing, and education: On the high school as prison. *Behavioral & Social Science Teacher, 1*(1), 24–45.

Hardin, C. D., & Higgins, E. T. (1996). Shared reality: How social verification makes the subjective objective. In R. M Sorrentino & E. T. Higgins (Eds.), *Handbook of motivation and cognition* (Vol. 3, pp. 28–84). New York: Guilford.

Haritos-Fatouros, M. (1988). The official torturer: A learning model for obedience to the authority of violence. *Journal of Applied Social Psychology, 18*, 1107–1120.

Harquail, C. V. (1996, August). *When one speaks for many: The influence of social identification on group advocacy in organizations.* Paper presented at the annual meeting of the Academy of Management, Cincinnati, OH.

Harquail, C. V. (1998). Organizational identification and the "whole person": Integrating affect, behavior, and cognition. In D. A. Whetten & P. C. Godfrey (Eds.), *Identity in organizations: Building theory through conversations* (pp. 223–231). Thousand Oaks, CA: Sage.

Harré, R. (1983). Identity projects. In G. M. Breakwell (Ed.), *Threatened identities* (pp. 31–51). Chichester, England: Wiley.

Harrison, D. A., Price, K. H., & Bell, M. P. (1998). Beyond relational demography: Time and the effects of surface- and deep-level diversity on work group cohesion. *Academy of Management Journal, 41*, 96–107.

Hartmann, E. (1997). The concept of boundaries in counselling and psychotherapy. *British Journal of Guidance and Counselling, 25*, 147–162.

Haslam, S. A., Oakes, P. J., Turner, J. C., & McGarty, C. (1996). Social identity, self-categorization, and the perceived homogeneity of ingroups and outgroups: The interaction between social motivation and cognition. In R. M. Sorrentino & E. T. Higgins (Eds.), *Handbook of motivation and cognition* (Vol. 3, pp. 182–222). New York: Guilford.

Hattrup, K., & Jackson, S. E. (1996). Learning about individual differences by taking situations seriously. In K. R. Murphy (Ed.), *Individual differences and behavior in organizations* (pp. 507–547). San Francisco: Jossey-Bass.

Hautaluoma, J. E., Enge, R. S., Mitchell, T. M., & Rittwager, F. J. (1991). Early socialization into a work group: Severity of initiations revisited. *Journal of Social Behavior and Personality, 6*, 725–748.

Hecht, L. M. (1996). *Managing multiple roles: The organization of routine activities, chronic role strains, and psychological well-being.* Unpublished doctoral dissertation, Indiana University, Bloomington.

Heckhausen, J., & Schulz, R. (1995). A life-span theory of control. *Psychological Review, 102,* 284–304.

Hedberg, B. (1981). How organizations learn and unlearn. In P. C. Nystrom & W. H. Starbuck (Eds.), *Handbook of organizational design* (Vol. 1, pp. 3–27). New York: Oxford University Press.

Heider, F. (1958). *The psychology of interpersonal relations.* New York: Wiley.

Heinsler, J. M., Kleinman, S., & Stenross, B. (1990). Making work matter: Satisfied detectives and dissatisfied campus police. *Qualitative Sociology, 13,* 235–250.

Heise, D. R. (1977). Social action as the control of affect. *Behavioral Science, 22,* 163–177.

Helmreich, R. L., Sawin, L. L., & Carsrud, A. L. (1986). The honeymoon effect in job performance: Temporal increases in the predictive power of achievement motivation. *Journal of Applied Psychology, 71,* 185–188.

Henson, K. D. (1996). *Just a temp.* Philadelphia: Temple University Press.

Heppner, M. J., Multon, K. D., & Johnston, J. A. (1994). Assessing psychological resources during career change: Development of the Career Transitions Inventory. *Journal of Vocational Behavior, 44,* 55–74.

Hepworth, S. J. (1980). Moderating factors of the psychological impact of unemployment. *Journal of Occupational Psychology, 53,* 139–145.

Herth, K. (1990). Fostering hope in terminally-ill people. *Journal of Advanced Nursing, 15,* 1250–1259.

Higgins, E. T. (1987). Self-discrepancy: A theory relating self and affect. *Psychological Review, 94,* 319–340.

Higgs, D. C., Canavan, M. M., & Meyer, W. J., III. (1992). Moving from defense to offense: The development of an adolescent female sex offender. *Journal of Sex Research, 29,* 131–139.

Hill, E. J., Miller, B. C., Weiner, S. P., & Colihan, J. (1998). Influences of the virtual office on aspects of work and work/life balance. *Personnel Psychology, 51,* 667–683.

Hill, L. A. (1992). *Becoming a manager: Mastery of a new identity.* Boston: Harvard Business School Press.

Hirschman, A. O. (1970). *Exit, voice, and loyalty: Response to decline in firms, organizations, and states.* Cambridge, MA: Harvard University Press.

Hochschild, A. R. (1983). *The managed heart: Commercialization of human feeling.* Berkeley, CA: University of California.

Hochschild, A. R. (1997). *The time bind: When work becomes home and home becomes work.* New York: Metropolitan.

Hogg, M. A., & Abrams, D. (1988). *Social identifications: A social psychology of intergroup relations and group processes.* London: Routledge.

Hogg, M. A., & Abrams, D. (1990). Social motivation, self-esteem and social identity. In D. Abrams & M. A. Hogg (Eds.), *Social identity theory: Constructive and critical advances* (pp. 28–47). New York: Springer-Verlag.

Hogg, M. A., Terry, D. J., & White, K. M. (1995). A tale of two theories: A critical comparison of identity theory with social identity theory. *Social Psychology Quarterly, 58,* 255–269.

Holland, J. L. (1985). *Making vocational choices: A theory of vocational personalities and work environments* (2nd ed.). Englewood Cliffs, NJ: Prentice-Hall.

Hollander, E. P. (1964). *Leaders, groups, and influence.* New York: Oxford University Press.

Holton, E. F., III, & Russell, C. J. (1997). The relationship of anticipation to newcomer socialization processes and outcomes: A pilot study. *Journal of Occupational and Organizational Psychology, 70,* 163–172.

Hom, P. W., & Griffeth, R. W. (1995). *Employee turnover.* Cincinnati, OH: South-Western.

Hom, P. W., Griffeth, R. W., Palich, L. E., & Bracker, J. S. (1998). An exploratory investigation into theoretical mechanisms underlying realistic job previews. *Personnel Psychology, 51,* 421–451.

Horvath, L., & Glynn, M. A. (1993). *Owning a little piece of the rock: Employee ownership, organizational identification, and self-management in worker cooperatives.* Unpublished manuscript, Yale University, New Haven, CT.

House, R. J., Shane, S. A., & Herold, D. M. (1996). Rumors of the death of dispositional research are vastly exaggerated. *Academy of Management Review, 21,* 203–224.

Howard, A., & Bray, D. W. (1988). *Managerial lives in transition: Advancing age and changing times.* New York: Guilford.

Hughes, E. C. (1945). Dilemmas and contradictions of status. *American Journal of Sociology, 50,* 353–359.

Hughes, E. C. (1958). *Men and their work.* Glencoe, IL: The Free Press.

Hughes, E. C. (1970). The humble and the proud: The comparative study of occupations. *Sociological Quarterly, 11,* 147–156.

Hulin, C. L., Roznowski, M., & Hachiya, D. (1985). Alternative opportunities and withdrawal decisions: Empirical and theoretical discrepancies and an integration. *Psychological Bulletin, 97,* 233–250.

Humphrey, R. H. (1985). How work roles influence perception: Structural-cognitive processes and organizational behavior. *American Sociological Review, 50,* 242–252.

Hunt, S. A., & Benford, R. D. (1994). Identity talk in the peace and justice movement. *Journal of Contemporary Ethnography, 22,* 488–517.

Huntington, M. J. (1957). The development of a professional self-image. In R. K. Merton, G. G. Reader, & P. L. Kendall (Eds.), *The student-physician: Introductory studies in the sociology of medical education* (pp. 179–187). Cambridge, MA: Harvard University Press.

Iannaccone, L. R. (1994). Why strict churches are strong. *American Journal of Sociology, 99,* 1180–1211.

Ibarra, H. (1996, August). *Inauthentic selves: Image, identity and social networks in professional socialization.* Paper presented at the annual meeting of the Academy of Management, Cincinnati, OH.

Ilgen, D. R., & Hollenbeck, J. R. (1990). The structure of work: Job design and roles. In M. D. Dunnette & L. M. Hough (Eds.), *Handbook of industrial and organizational psychology* (2nd ed., Vol. 2, pp. 165–207). Palo Alto, CA: Consulting Psychologists Press.

Jackall, R. (1988). *Moral mazes: The world of corporate managers.* New York: Oxford University Press.

Jackofsky, E. F. (1984). Turnover and job performance: An integrated process model. *Academy of Management Review, 9,* 74–83.

Jackson, S. E., & Dutton, J. E. (1988). Discerning threats and opportunities. *Administrative Science Quarterly, 33,* 370–387.

Jackson, S. E., & Schuler, R. S. (1985). A meta-analysis and conceptual critique of research on role ambiguity and role conflict in work settings. *Organizational Behavior and Human Decision Processes, 36,* 16–78.

Jacobson, D. (1996). Celebrating good-bye: Functional components in farewell parties for retiring employees in Israel. *Journal of Aging Studies, 10,* 223–235.

James, W. (1950). *The principles of psychology* (Vols. 1 and 2). New York: Dover. (Original work published 1890.)

Janis, I. L. (1983). *Groupthink: Psychological studies of policy decisions and fiascoes* (2nd ed.). Boston: Houghton Mifflin.

Janis, I. L., & Mann, L. (1977). *Decision-making: A psychological analysis of conflict, choice, and commitment.* New York: The Free Press.

Jankowski, M. S. (1991). *Islands in the street: Gangs and American urban society.* Berkeley, CA: University of California Press.

Johl, B. M. (1989). *Leadership problems in a bank.* Unpublished undergraduate term paper, Concordia University, Montreal, Canada.

Johnson, R. (1990). *Death work: A study of the modern execution process.* Pacific Grove, CA: Brooks/Cole.

Johnston, D. M., & Johnson, N. R. (1988). Role extension in disaster: Employee behavior at the Beverly Hills Supper Club fire. *Sociological Focus, 22,* 39–51.

Jones, G. R. (1986). Socialization tactics, self-efficacy, and newcomers' adjustments to organizations. *Academy of Management Journal, 29,* 262–279.

Kadushin, C. (1969). The professional self-concept of music students. *American Journal of Sociology, 5,* 389–404.

Kahn, R. L., & Antonucci, T. C. (1980). Convoys over the life course: Attachment, roles, and social support. In P. B. Baltes & O. G. Brim, Jr. (Eds.), *Life-span development and behavior* (Vol. 3, pp. 253–286). New York: Academic Press.

Kahn, W. A. (1990). Psychological conditions of personal engagement and disengagement at work. *Academy of Management Journal, 33,* 692–724.

Kahn, W. A., & Kram, K. E. (1994). Authority at work: Internal models and their organizational consequences. *Academy of Management Review, 19,* 17–50.

Kanter, R. M. (1977). *Work and family in the United States: A critical review and agenda for research and policy.* New York: Russell Sage Foundation.

Kanungo, R. N. (1979). The concepts of alienation and involvement revisited. *Psychological Bulletin, 86,* 119–138.

Karasek, R. A., Jr. (1979). Job demands, job decision latitude, and mental strain: Implications for job redesign. *Administrative Science Quarterly, 24,* 285–308.

Karp, D. A. (1985–86). Academics beyond midlife: Some observations on changing consciousness in the fifty to sixty year decade. *International Journal of Aging and Human Development, 22*(2), 81–103.

Kaslow, F. W., & Kaslow, S. (1992). The family that works together: Special problems of family businesses. In S. Zedeck (Ed.), *Work, families, and organizations* (pp. 312–361). San Francisco: Jossey-Bass.

Katovich, M. A., & Hardesty, M. J. (1986). The temporary. In N. K. Denzin (Ed.), *Studies in symbolic interaction* (Vol. 7, Part B, pp. 333–352). Greenwich, CT: JAI.

Katz, D., & Kahn, R. L. (1978). *The social psychology of organizations* (2nd ed.). New York: Wiley.

Katz, D. R. (1988). *The big store: Inside the crisis and revolution at Sears.* New York: Penguin.

Katz, F. E. (1993). *Ordinary people and extraordinary evil: A report on the beguilings of evil.* Albany, NY: State University of New York Press.

Katz, P. (1990). Emotional metaphors, socialization, and roles of drill sergeants. *Ethos, 18,* 457–480.

Katz, R. (1980). Time and work: Toward an integrative perspective. In B. M. Staw & L. L. Cummings (Eds.), *Research in organizational behavior* (Vol. 2, pp. 81–127). Greenwich, CT: JAI.

Katz, R. (1985). Organizational stress and early socialization experiences. In T. A. Beehr & R. S. Bhagat (Eds.), *Human stress and cognition in organizations* (pp. 117–139). New York: Wiley.

Kaufman, H. G. (1982). *Professionals in search of work: Coping with the stress of job loss and underemployment.* New York: Wiley.

Kegan, R. (1982). *The evolving self: Problem and process in human development.* Cambridge, MA: Harvard University Press.

Kelley, H. H. (1971). *Attribution in social interaction.* Morristown, NJ: General Learning Press.

Kelly, G. A. (1955). *The psychology of personal constructs* (Vols. 1 and 2). New York: Norton.

Kelman, H. C. (1961). Processes of opinion change. *Public Opinion Quarterly, 25,* 57–78.

Kemp, N. J., Wall, T. D., Clegg, C. W., & Cordery, J. L. (1983). Autonomous work groups in a greenfield site: A comparative study. *Journal of Occupational Psychology, 56,* 271–288.

Kenny, D. A., & DePaulo, B. M. (1993). Do people know how others view them? An empirical and theoretical account. *Psychological Bulletin, 114,* 145–161.

Kets de Vries, M. F. R., & Miller, D. (1984). *The neurotic organization: Diagnosing and changing counterproductive styles of management.* San Francisco: Jossey-Bass.

Kilduff, M., Funk, J. L., & Mehra, A. (1997). Engineering identity in a Japanese factory. *Organization Science, 8,* 579–592.

Kinicki, A. J., & Latack, J. C. (1990). Explication of the construct of coping with involuntary job loss. *Journal of Vocational Behavior, 36*, 339–360.

Kluger, A. N. (1998). Commute variability and strain. *Journal of Organizational Behavior, 19*, 147–165.

Kohn, M. L., & Schooler, C. (1983). *Work and personality: An inquiry into the impact of social stratification.* Norwood, NJ: Ablex.

Kondo, D. K. (1990). *Crafting selves: Power, gender, and discourses of identity in a Japanese workplace.* Chicago: University of Chicago Press.

Korman, A. K., Wittig-Berman, U., & Lang, D. (1981). Career success and personal failure: Alienation in professionals and managers. *Academy of Management Journal, 24*, 342–360.

Koslowsky, M., Kluger, A. N., & Reich, M. (1995). *Commuting stress: Causes, effects, and methods of coping.* New York: Plenum.

Kossek, E. E., & Ozeki, C. (1998). Work–family conflict, policies, and the job-life satisfaction relationship: A review and directions for organizational behavior–human resources research. *Journal of Applied Psychology, 83*, 139–149.

Kotter, J. P., & Heskett, J. L. (1992). *Corporate culture and performance.* New York: The Free Press.

Krackhardt, D., & Porter, L. W. (1986). The snowball effect: Turnover embedded in communication networks. *Journal of Applied Psychology, 71*, 50–55.

Kramer, M. (1974). *Reality shock: Why nurses leave nursing.* St. Louis, MO: Mosby.

Kramer, M. W. (1993). Communication and uncertainty reduction during job transfers: Leaving and joining processes. *Communication Monographs, 60*, 178–198.

Kramer, M. W., Callister, R. R., & Turban, D. B. (1995). Information-receiving and information-giving during job transitions. *Western Journal of Communication, 59*, 151–170.

Kramer, R. M. (1991). Intergroup relations and organizational dilemmas: The role of categorization processes. In L. L. Cummings & B. M. Staw (Eds.), *Research in organizational behavior* (Vol. 13, pp. 191–228). Greenwich, CT: JAI.

Krau, E. (1989). The transition in life domain salience and the modification of work values between high school and adult employment. *Journal of Vocational Behavior, 34*, 100–116.

Kroger, J., & Haslett, S. J. (1991). A comparison of ego identity status transition pathways and change rates across five identity domains. *International Journal of Aging and Human Development, 32*, 303–330.

Kübler-Ross, E. (1969). *On death and dying.* New York: Macmillan.

Kunda, G. (1992). *Engineering culture: Control and commitment in a high-tech corporation.* Philadelphia: Temple University Press.

Kurtz, H. (1996). *Hot air: All talk, all the time.* New York: Times Books.

Landfield, A. W. (1988). Personal science and the concept of validation. *International Journal of Personal Construct Psychology, 1*, 237–249.

Langer, E. J. (1989). *Mindfulness.* Reading, MA: Addison-Wesley.

LaPlante, A. (1995, October 9). Telecommuting: Round two—voluntary no more. *Forbes ASAP*, 132–135, 138.

Larrick, R. P., & Boles, T. L. (1995). Avoiding regret in decisions with feedback: A negotiation example. *Organizational Behavior and Human Decision Processes, 63*, 87–97.

Latack, J. C. (1984). Career transitions within organizations: An exploratory study of work, nonwork, and coping strategies. *Organizational Behavior and Human Performance, 34*, 296–322.

Latack, J. C., & Dozier, J. B. (1986). After the ax falls: Job loss as a career transition. *Academy of Management Review, 11*, 375–392.

Latack, J. C., Kinicki, A. J., & Prussia, G. E. (1995). An integrative process model of coping with job loss. *Academy of Management Review, 20*, 311–342.

Laurent, A. (1978). Managerial subordinacy: A neglected aspect of organizational hierarchies. *Academy of Management Review, 3*, 220–230.

Lawrence, B. S. (1980). The myth of the midlife crisis. *Sloan Management Review, 21*(4), 35–49.

Lawrence, B. S. (1987). An organizational theory of age effects. In N. DiTomaso (Ed.), *Research in the sociology of organizations* (Vol. 5, pp. 37–71). Greenwich, CT: JAI.

Lawrence, B. S. (1996a). Interest and indifference: The role of age in the organizational sciences. In G. R. Ferris (Ed.), *Research in personnel and human resources management* (Vol. 14, pp. 1–59). Greenwich, CT: JAI.

Lawrence, B. S. (1996b). Organizational age norms: Why is it so hard to know one when you see one? *The Gerontologist, 36,* 209–220.

Lazarus, R. S. (1984). On the primacy of cognition. *American Psychologist, 39,* 124–129.

Lazarus, R. S., & Folkman, S. (1984). *Stress, appraisal, and coping.* New York: Springer.

Leach, J. (1994). *Survival psychology.* Washington Square, NY: New York University Press.

Leana, C. R., & Feldman, D. C. (1992). *Coping with job loss: How individuals, organizations, and communities respond to layoffs.* New York: Lexington Books.

Lecky, P. (1945). *Self-consistency: A theory of personality.* New York: Anchor.

Lee, R. T., & Ashforth, B. E. (1996). A meta-analytic examination of the correlates of the three dimensions of burnout. *Journal of Applied Psychology, 81,* 123–133.

Lee, T. W., & Mitchell, T. R. (1994). An alternative approach: The unfolding model of voluntary employee turnover. *Academy of Management Review, 19,* 51–89.

Lee, T. W., Mitchell, T. R., Wise, L., & Fireman, S. (1996). An unfolding model of voluntary employee turnover. *Academy of Management Journal, 39,* 5–36.

Leiter, M. P., & Durup, M. J. (1996). Work, home, and in-between: A longitudinal study of spillover. *Journal of Applied Behavioral Science, 32,* 29–47.

Lennox, J. A. (1992). *The appearance of shared meanings: Ambiguity and humour in police communication.* Unpublished doctoral dissertation, Concordia University, Montreal, Canada.

León, F. R. (1981). The role of positive and negative outcomes in the causation of motivational forces. *Journal of Applied Psychology, 66,* 45–53.

Leonard, N. H., Beauvais, L. L., & Scholl, R. W. (1995). A self concept-based model of work motivation. In D. P. Moore (Ed.), *Academy of Management Best Papers Proceedings* (pp. 322–326). Madison, WI: OMNIPRESS.

Levine, J. M., Bogart, L. M., & Zdaniuk, B. (1996). Impact of anticipated group membership on cognition. In R. M. Sorrentino & E. T. Higgins (Eds.), *Handbook of motivation and cognition* (Vol. 3, pp. 531–569). New York: Guilford.

Levinson, D. J. (1986). A conception of adult development. *American Psychologist, 41,* 3–13.

Levinson, D. J., Darrow, C. N., Klein, E. B., Levinson, M. H., & McKee, B. (1978). *The seasons of a man's life.* New York: Knopf.

Lewin, K. (1951). *Field theory in social science: Selected theoretical papers* (D. Cartwright, Ed.). New York: Harper & Brothers.

Lieberman, S. (1956). The effects of changes in roles on the attitudes of role occupants. *Human Relations, 9,* 385–402.

Lifton, R. J. (1961). *Thought reform and the psychology of totalism: A study of "brainwashing" in China.* New York: Norton.

Lifton, R. J. (1993). *The protean self: Human resilience in an age of fragmentation.* New York: Basic Books.

Lobel, S. A. (1991). Allocation of investment in work and family roles: Alternative theories and implications for research. *Academy of Management Review, 16,* 507–521.

Locke, E. A., & Latham, G. P. (1990). *A theory of goal setting and task performance.* Englewood Cliffs, NJ: Prentice Hall.

Lodewijkx, H. F. M., & Syroit, J. E. M. M. (1997). Severity of initiation revisited: Does severity of initiation increase attractiveness in real groups? *European Journal of Social Psychology, 27,* 275–300.

Lofland, J. (1978). Becoming a world saver revisited. In J. Richardson (Ed.), *Conversion careers: In and out of new religion* (pp. 10–23). Beverly Hills, CA: Sage.

Loomes, G., & Sugden, R. (1987). Some implications of a more general form of regret theory. *Journal of Economic Theory, 41*, 270–287.

Lord, R. G., & Foti, R. J. (1986). Schema theories, information processing, and organizational behavior. In H. P. Sims, Jr., D. A. Gioia, & Associates, *The thinking organization: Dynamics of organizational social cognition* (pp. 20–48). San Francisco: Jossey-Bass.

Loseke, D. R., & Cahill, S. E. (1986). Actors in search of a character: Student social workers' quest for professional identity. *Symbolic Interaction, 9*, 245–258.

Louis, M. R. (1980a). Career transitions: Varieties and commonalities. *Academy of Management Review, 5*, 329–340.

Louis, M. R. (1980b). Surprise and sense making: What newcomers experience in entering unfamiliar organizational settings. *Administrative Science Quarterly, 25*, 226–251.

Louis, M. R., Posner, B. Z., & Powell, G. N. (1983). The availability and helpfulness of socialization practices. *Personnel Psychology, 36*, 857–866.

Louis, M. R., & Sutton, R. I. (1991). Switching cognitive gears: From habits of mind to active thinking. *Human Relations, 44*, 55–76.

Lowenthal, M. F., Thurnher, M., Chiriboga, D., & Associates. (1975). *Four stages of life: A comparative study of women and men facing transitions.* San Francisco: Jossey-Bass.

Ludwig, A. M. (1997). *How do we know who we are? A biography of the self.* Oxford, England: Oxford University Press.

Macdonald, C. L. (1996). Shadow mothers: Nannies, *au pairs*, and invisible work. In C. L. Macdonald & C. Sirianni (Eds.), *Working in the service society* (pp. 244–263). Philadelphia: Temple University Press.

Macdonald, S. (1995). Too close for comfort?: The strategic implications of getting close to the customer. *California Management Review, 37*(4), 8–27.

Mael, F. (1988). *Organizational identification: Construct redefinition and a field application with organizational alumni.* Unpublished doctoral dissertation, Wayne State University, Detroit.

Mael, F., & Ashforth, B. E. (1992). Alumni and their alma mater: A partial test of the reformulated model of organizational identification. *Journal of Organizational Behavior, 13*, 103–123.

Mael, F. A., & Ashforth, B. E. (1995). Loyal from day one: Biodata, organizational identification, and turnover among newcomers. *Personnel Psychology, 48*, 309–333.

Magnusson, D., & Endler, N. S. (1977). Interactional psychology: Present status and future prospects. In D. Magnusson & N. S. Endler (Eds.), *Personality at the crossroads: Current issues in interactional psychology* (pp. 3–31). Hillsdale, NJ: Lawrence Erlbaum Associates.

Mainiero, L. A. (1986). A review and analysis of power dynamics in organizational romances. *Academy of Management Review, 11*, 750–762.

Major, D. A., Kozlowski, S. W. J., Chao, G. T., & Gardner, P. D. (1995). A longitudinal investigation of newcomer expectations, early socialization outcomes, and the moderating effects of role development factors. *Journal of Applied Psychology, 80*, 418–431.

Mandler, G. (1964). The interruption of behavior. In D. Levine (Ed.), *Nebraska symposium on motivation* (Vol. 12, pp. 163–219). Lincoln, NE: University of Nebraska Press.

Mandler, G. (1990). Interruption (discrepancy) theory: Review and extensions. In S. Fisher & C. L. Cooper (Eds.), *On the move: The psychology of change and transition* (pp. 13–32). Chichester, England: Wiley.

Mansfield, R. (1972). The initiation of graduates in industry: The resolution of identity–stress as a determinant of job satisfaction in the early months at work. *Human Relations, 25*, 77–86.

Manz, C. C. (1983). *The art of self-leadership: Strategies for personal effectiveness in your life and work.* Englewood Cliffs, NJ: Prentice-Hall.

March, J. G., & Simon, H. A. (1958). *Organizations.* New York: Wiley.

Marcia, J. E. (1966). Development and validation of ego-identity status. *Journal of Personality and Social Psychology, 3*, 551–558.

Marcia, J. E. (1994). The empirical study of ego identity. In H. A. Bosma, T. L. G. Graafsma, H. D. Grotevant, & D. J. de Levita (Eds.), *Identity and development: An interdisciplinary approach* (pp. 67–80). Thousand Oaks, CA: Sage.

Marion, R. (1990). *The intern blues: The private ordeals of three young doctors*. New York: Fawcett Crest.

Markus, H., & Nurius, P. (1986). Possible selves. *American Psychologist, 41*, 954–969.

Marshak, R. J. (1993). Lewin meets Confucius: A re-view of the OD model of change. *Journal of Applied Behavioral Science, 29*, 393–415.

Martinko, M. J. (Ed.). (1995). *Attribution theory: An organizational perspective*. Delray Beach, FL: St. Lucie Press.

Maslach, C. (1982). *Burnout: The cost of caring*. New York: Prentice Hall.

McAdams, D. P. (1987). A life-story model of identity. In R. Hogan & W. Jones (Eds.), *Perspectives in personality* (Vol. 2, pp. 15–50). Greenwich, CT: JAI.

McAdams, D. P. (1992). Unity and purpose in human lives: The emergence of identity as a life story. In R. A. Zucker, A. I. Rabin, J. Aronoff, & S. J. Frank (Eds.), *Personality structure in the life course: Essays on personology in the Murray tradition* (pp. 323–375). New York: Springer.

McAlexander, J. H., & Schouten, J. W. (1989). Hairstyle changes as transition markers. *Sociology and Social Research, 74*, 58–62.

McCall, G. J., & Simmons, J. L. (1978). *Identities and interactions: An examination of human associations in everyday life* (rev. ed.). New York: The Free Press.

McCarl, R. S. (1984). "You've come a long way—and now this is your retirement": An analysis of performance in fire fighting culture. *Journal of American Folklore, 97*, 393–422.

McClelland, D. C. (1985). *Human motivation*. Glenview, IL: Scott, Foresman.

McFadyen, R. G. (1995). Coping with threatened identities: Unemployed people's self-categorizations. *Current Psychology: Developmental•Learning•Personality•Social, 14*, 233–257.

Mead, G. H. (1934). *Mind, self, and society: From the standpoint of a social behaviorist*. Chicago: University of Chicago Press.

Meglino, B. M., DeNisi, A. S., & Ravlin, E. C. (1993). Effects of previous job exposure and subsequent job status on the functioning of a realistic job preview. *Personnel Psychology, 46*, 803–822.

Mellon, J. (Ed.). (1990). *Bullwhip days: The slaves remember: An oral history*. New York: Avon.

Menaghan, E. G. (1989). Role changes and psychological well-being: Variations in effects by gender and role repertoire. *Social Forces, 67*, 693–714.

Menzies, I. E. P. (1960). A case-study in the functioning of social systems as a defence against anxiety. *Human Relations, 13*, 95–121.

Merton, R. K. (1957a). The role-set: Problems in sociological theory. *British Journal of Sociology, 8*, 106–120.

Merton, R. K. (1957b). *Social theory and social structure* (rev. ed.). Glencoe, IL: The Free Press.

Merton, R. K. (1976). *Sociological ambivalence and other essays*. New York: The Free Press.

Meyer, J. P., & Allen, N. J. (1984). Testing the "side-bet theory" of organizational commitment: Some methodological considerations. *Journal of Applied Psychology, 69*, 372–378.

Meyer, J. P., & Allen, N. J. (1997). *Commitment in the workplace: Theory, research, and application*. Thousand Oaks, CA: Sage.

Michaelsen, S., & Johnson, D. E. (Eds.). (1997). *Border theory: The limits of cultural politics*. Minneapolis, MN: University of Minnesota Press.

Miles, R. E., & Snow, C. C. (1996). Twenty-first-century careers. In M. B. Arthur & D. M. Rousseau (Eds.), *The boundaryless career: A new employment principle for a new organizational era* (pp. 97–115). New York: Oxford University Press.

Milgram, S. (1974). *Obedience to authority: An experimental view*. New York: Harper & Row.

Miller, N., Urban, L. M., & Vanman, E. J. (1998). A theoretical analysis of crossed social categorization effects. In C. Sedikides, J. Schopler, & C. A. Insko (Eds.), *Intergroup cognition and intergroup behavior* (pp. 393–420). Mahwah, NJ: Lawrence Erlbaum Associates.

Miller, V. D., & Jablin, F. M. (1991). Information seeking during organizational entry: Influences, tactics, and a model of the process. *Academy of Management Review, 16,* 92–120.

Miller, V. D., Johnson, J. R., Hart, Z., & Peterson, D. L. (1999). A test of antecedents and outcomes of employee role negotiation ability. *Journal of Applied Communication Research, 27,* 24–48.

Mills, C. W. (1940). Situated actions and vocabularies of motive. *American Sociological Review, 5,* 904–913.

Minkler, M., & Biller, R. P. (1979). Role shock: A tool for conceptualizing stresses accompanying disruptive role transitions. *Human Relations, 32,* 125–140.

Mintzberg, H. (1973). *The nature of managerial work.* New York: Harper & Row.

Mintzberg, H. (1979). *The structuring of organizations: A synthesis of the research.* Englewood Cliffs, NJ: Prentice-Hall.

Mintzberg, H. (1983). *Power in and around organizations.* Englewood Cliffs, NJ: Prentice-Hall.

Mirchandani, K. (1998). Protecting the boundary: Teleworker insights on the expansive concept of "work." *Gender & Society, 12,* 168–187.

Mischel, W. (1977). The interaction of person and situation. In D. Magnusson & N. S. Endler (Eds.), *Personality at the crossroads: Current issues in interactional psychology* (pp. 333–352). Hillsdale, NJ: Lawrence Erlbaum Associates.

Mitra, A., Jenkins, G. D., Jr., & Gupta, N. (1992). A meta-analytic review of the relationship between absence and turnover. *Journal of Applied Psychology, 77,* 879–889.

Moran, Y. (1998). Bean answers new calling. *Catalog Age, 15*(6), 81.

More, D. M. (1968). Demotion. In B. G. Glaser (Ed.), *Organizational careers: A sourcebook for theory* (pp. 287–294). Chicago: Aldine.

Moreland, R. L., & Levine, J. M. (1989). Newcomers and oldtimers in small groups. In P. B. Paulus (Ed.), *Psychology of group influence* (2nd ed., pp. 143–186). Hillsdale, NJ: Lawrence Erlbaum Associates.

Morin, E. M. (1995). Organizational effectiveness and the meaning of work. In T. C. Pauchant & Associates, *In search of meaning: Managing for the health of our organizations, our communities, and the natural world* (pp. 29–64). San Francisco: Jossey-Bass.

Morris, J. M. (1997). The job change: A three-part process with variations for men and women. *Sociological Focus, 30,* 263–278.

Morrison, E. W. (1993a). Longitudinal study of the effects of information seeking on newcomer socialization. *Journal of Applied Psychology, 78,* 173–183.

Morrison, E. W. (1993b). Newcomer information seeking: Exploring types, modes, sources, and outcomes. *Academy of Management Journal, 36,* 557–589.

Morrison, E. W. (1995). Information usefulness and acquisition during organizational encounter. *Management Communication Quarterly, 9,* 131–155.

Morrison, R. F., & Holzbach, R. L. (1980). The career manager role. In C. B. Derr (Ed.), *Work, family, and the career: New frontiers in theory and research* (pp. 75–93). New York: Praeger.

Mortimer, J. T., Finch, M. D., & Kumka, D. (1982). Persistence and change in development: The multidimensional self-concept. In P. B. Baltes & O. G. Brim, Jr. (Eds.), *Life-span development and behavior* (Vol. 4, pp. 263–313). New York: Academic Press.

Mortimer, J. T., Lorence, J., & Kumka, D. S. (1986). *Work, family, and personality: Transition to adulthood.* Norwood, NJ: Ablex.

Mortland, C. A. (1987). Transforming refugees in refugee camps. *Urban Anthropology, 16,* 375–404.

Moskowitz, G. B. (1993). Individual differences in social categorization: The influence of personal need for structure on spontaneous trait inferences. *Journal of Personality and Social Psychology, 65,* 132–142.

Munk, N. (1998, March 16). The new organization man. *Fortune, 137*(5), 62–66, 68, 72, 74.

Munton, A. G., & West, M. A. (1995). Innovations and personal change: Patterns of adjustment to relocation. *Journal of Organizational Behavior, 16,* 363–375.

Murphy, S. M., & Jowdy, D. P. (1992). Imagery and mental practice. In T. S. Horn (Ed.), *Advances in sport psychology* (pp. 221–250). Champaign, IL: Human Kinetics.

Mutran, E., & Reitzes, D. C. (1981). Retirement, identity and well-being: Realignment of role relationships. *Journal of Gerontology, 36,* 733–740.

Narváez, P. (1990). "I've gotten soppy": "Send-off parties" as rites of passage in the occupational folklife of CBC reporters. *American Behavioral Scientist, 33,* 339–352.

Near, J. P., & Miceli, M. P. (1987). Whistle-blowers in organizations: Dissidents or reformers? In L. L. Cummings & B. M. Staw (Eds.), *Research in organizational behavior* (Vol. 9, pp. 321–368). Greenwich, CT: JAI.

Neuberg, S. L., & Newsom, J. T. (1993). Personal need for structure: Individual differences in the desire for simple structure. *Journal of Personality and Social Psychology, 65,* 113–131.

Neugarten, B. L. (1977). Adaptation and the life cycle. In N. K. Schlossberg & A. D. Entine (Eds.), *Counseling adults* (pp. 34–46). Monterey, CA: Brooks/Cole.

Neugarten, B. L., Moore, J. W., & Lowe, J. C. (1965). Age norms, age constraints, and adult socialization. *American Journal of Sociology, 70,* 710–717.

Nicholson, N. (1984). A theory of work role transitions. *Administrative Science Quarterly, 29,* 172–191.

Nicholson, N. (1987). The transition cycle: A conceptual framework for the analysis of change and human resources management. In K. M. Rowland & G. R. Ferris (Eds.), *Research in personnel and human resources management* (Vol. 5, pp. 167–222). Greenwich, CT: JAI.

Nicholson, N. (1993). Purgatory or place of safety? The managerial plateau and organizational age-grading. *Human Relations, 46,* 1369–1389.

Nicholson, N., & West, M. A. (1988). *Managerial job change: Men and women in transition.* Cambridge, England: Cambridge University Press.

Nicholson, N., & West, M. (1989). Transitions, work histories, and careers. In M. B. Arthur, D. T. Hall, & B. S. Lawrence (Eds.), *Handbook of career theory* (pp. 181–201). Cambridge, England: Cambridge University Press.

Nicholson, N., West, M., & Cawsey, T. F. (1985). Future uncertain: Expected vs. attained job mobility among managers. *Journal of Occupational Psychology, 58,* 313–320.

Nippert-Eng, C. (1996a). Calendars and keys: The classification of "home" and "work." *Sociological Forum, 11,* 563–582.

Nippert-Eng, C. E. (1996b). *Home and work: Negotiating boundaries through everyday life.* Chicago: University of Chicago Press.

Noble, C. H., & Walker, B. A. (1997). Exploring the relationships among liminal transitions, symbolic consumption, and the extended self. *Psychology & Marketing, 14,* 29–47.

Oakes, P. J. (1987). The salience of social categories. In J. C. Turner, M. A. Hogg, P. J. Oakes, S. D. Reicher, & M. S. Wetherell, *Rediscovering the social group: A self-categorization theory* (pp. 117–141). Oxford, England: Blackwell.

Oakes, P., & Turner, J. C. (1986). Distinctiveness and the salience of social category memberships: Is there an automatic perceptual bias towards novelty? *European Journal of Social Psychology, 16,* 325–344.

Oatley, K. (1990). Role transitions and the emotional structure of everyday life. In S. Fisher & C. L. Cooper (Eds.), *On the move: The psychology of change and transition* (pp. 67–81). Chichester, England: Wiley.

O'Connor, D., & Wolfe, D. M. (1991). From crisis to growth at midlife: Changes in personal paradigm. *Journal of Organizational Behavior, 12,* 323–340.

O'Connor, K., & Chamberlain, K. (1996). Dimensions of life meaning: A qualitative investigation at mid-life. *British Journal of Psychology, 87,* 461–477.

Ogawa, R. T. (1991). Enchantment, disenchantment, and accommodation: How a faculty made sense of the succession of its principal. *Educational Administration Quarterly, 27,* 30–60.

Oldenburg, R. (1997). *The great good place: Cafés, coffee shops, community centers, beauty parlors, general stores, bars, hangouts and how they get you through the day.* New York: Marlowe.

Olins, W. (1989). *Corporate identity: Making business strategy visible through design.* Boston: Harvard Business School Press.

Olver, R. (1990). *The making of champions: Life in Canada's Junior A leagues.* Markham, Canada: Viking.

O'Reilly, C. A., & Chatman, J. A. (1996). Culture as social control: Corporations, cults, and commitment. In B. M. Staw & L. L. Cummings (Eds.), *Research in organizational behavior* (Vol. 18, pp. 157–200). Greenwich, CT: JAI.

Orlick, T. (1980). *In pursuit of excellence.* Champaign, IL: Human Kinetics.

Ornstein, S., Cron, W. L., & Slocum, J. W., Jr. (1989). Life stage versus career stage: A comparative test of the theories of Levinson and Super. *Journal of Organizational Behavior, 10,* 117–133.

Ostroff, C., & Kozlowski, S. W. J. (1992). Organizational socialization as a learning process: The role of information acquisition. *Personnel Psychology, 45,* 849–874.

Ouchi, W. G. (1980). Markets, bureaucracies, and clans. *Administrative Science Quarterly, 25,* 129–141.

Ouellet, L. J. (1994). *Pedal to the metal: The work lives of truckers.* Philadelphia: Temple University Press.

Parkinson, C. N. (1983). *Parkinson: The law, complete.* New York: Ballantine.

Parsons, C. K., Herold, D. M., & Leatherwood, M. L. (1985). Turnover during initial employment: A longitudinal study of the role of causal attributions. *Journal of Applied Psychology, 70,* 337–341.

Parsons, T. (1951). *The social system.* Glencoe, IL: The Free Press.

Pauchant, T. C., & Associates. (1995). *In search of meaning: Managing for the health of our organizations, our communities, and the natural world.* San Francisco: Jossey-Bass.

Perlow, L. A. (1998). Boundary control: The social ordering of work and family time in a high-tech corporation. *Administrative Science Quarterly, 43,* 328–357.

Perry, E. (1997). A cognitive approach to understanding discrimination: A closer look at applicant gender and age. In G. R. Ferris (Ed.), *Research in personnel and human resources management* (Vol. 15, pp. 175–240). Greenwich, CT: JAI.

Petrick, J. A. (1999, June 13). Working at home: For better, for worse. *New York Times,* Section 3, p. 13.

Pfeffer, J. (1981). Management as symbolic action: The creation and maintenance of organizational paradigms. In L. L. Cummings & B. M. Staw (Eds.), *Research in organizational behavior* (Vol. 3, pp. 1–52). Greenwich, CT: JAI.

Pfeffer, J., & Baron, J. N. (1988). Taking the workers back out: Recent trends in the structure of employment. In B. M. Staw & L. L. Cummings (Eds.), *Research in organizational behavior* (Vol. 10, pp. 257–303). Greenwich, CT: JAI.

Pinder, C. C., & Schroeder, K. G. (1987). Time to proficiency following job transfers. *Academy of Management Journal, 30,* 336–353.

Pinder, C. C., & Walter, G. A. (1984). Personnel transfers and employee development. In K. M. Rowland & G. R. Ferris (Eds.), *Research in personnel and human resources management* (Vol. 2, pp. 187–218). Greenwich, CT: JAI.

Pleck, J. H. (1977). The work–family role system. *Social Problems, 24,* 417–427.

Poole, M. E., Langan-Fox, J., & Omodei, M. (1993). Contrasting subjective and objective criteria as determinants of perceived career success: A longitudinal study. *Journal of Occupational and Organizational Psychology, 66,* 39–54.

Poole, P. P., Gray, B., & Gioia, D. A. (1990). Organizational script development through interactive accommodation. *Group & Organization Studies, 15,* 212–232.

Porter, L. W., Lawler, E. E., III, & Hackman, J. R. (1975). *Behavior in organizations.* New York: McGraw-Hill.

Pratt, M. G. (1998). To be or not to be?: Central questions in organizational identification. In D. A. Whetten & P. C. Godfrey (Eds.), *Identity in organizations: Building theory through conversations* (pp. 171–207). Thousand Oaks, CA: Sage.

Pratt, M. G., & Barnett, C. K. (1997). Emotions and unlearning in Amway recruiting techniques: Promoting change through "safe" ambivalence. *Management Learning, 28,* 65–88.

Price, R. H., Friedland, D. S., & Vinokur, A. D. (1998). Job loss: Hard times and eroded identity. In J. H. Harvey (Ed.), *Perspectives on loss: A sourcebook* (pp. 303–316). Philadelphia: Taylor & Francis.

Prussia, G. E., Kinicki, A. J., & Bracker, J. S. (1993). Psychological and behavioral consequences of job loss: A covariance structure analysis using Weiner's (1985) attribution model. *Journal of Applied Psychology, 78*, 382–394.

Quinn, J. B. (1980). *Strategies for change: Logical incrementalism.* Homewood, IL: Irwin.

Rabbie, J. M., & Horwitz, M. (1988). Categories versus groups as explanatory concepts in intergroup relations. *European Journal of Social Psychology, 18*, 117–123.

Rachlin, H. (1991). *The making of a cop.* New York: Pocket Books.

Rachlin, H. (1995). *The making of a detective.* New York: Norton.

Rafaeli, A., & Pratt, M. G. (1993). Tailored meanings: On the meaning and impact of organizational dress. *Academy of Management Review, 18*, 32–55.

Rahim, A. (1996). Stress, strain, and their moderators: An empirical comparison of entrepreneurs and managers. *Journal of Small Business Management, 34*(1), 46–58.

Reed, D. A. (1989). *An orderly world: The social construction of reality within an occupation.* Unpublished doctoral dissertation, Indiana University, Bloomington.

Reichers, A. E. (1987). An interactionist perspective on newcomer socialization rates. *Academy of Management Review, 12*, 278–287.

Reid, D. (1991). *Paris sewers and sewermen: Realities and representations.* Cambridge, MA: Harvard University Press.

Reilly, N. P., & Orsak, C. L. (1991). A career stage analysis of career and organizational commitment in nursing. *Journal of Vocational Behavior, 39*, 311–330.

Richter, J. (1984). *The daily transition between professional and private life.* Unpublished doctoral dissertation, Boston University.

Richter, J. (1990). Crossing boundaries between professional and private life. In H. Y. Grossman & N. L. Chester (Eds.), *The experience and meaning of work in women's lives* (pp. 143–163). Hillsdale, NJ: Lawrence Erlbaum Associates.

Richter, J. (1992). Balancing work and family in Israel. In S. Zedeck (Ed.), *Work, families, and organizations* (pp. 362–394). San Francisco: Jossey-Bass.

Ricks, T. E. (1997). *Making the Corps.* New York: Scribner.

Riemer, J. W. (1979). *Hard hats: The work world of construction workers.* Beverly Hills, CA: Sage.

Ritzer, G. (1996). *The McDonaldization of society: An investigation into the changing character of contemporary social life* (rev. ed). Thousand Oaks, CA: Pine Forge Press.

Riverin-Simard, D. (1988). *Phases of working life.* Montreal, Canada: Meridien Press.

Roberts, B. W., & Donahue, E. M. (1994). One personality, multiple selves: Integrating personality and social roles. *Journal of Personality, 62*, 199–218.

Robinson, S. L. (1996). Trust and breach of the psychological contract. *Administrative Science Quarterly, 41*, 574–599.

Robinson, W. P. (Ed.). (1996). *Social groups and identities: Developing the legacy of Henri Tajfel.* Oxford, England: Butterworth-Heinemann.

Rosen, M. (1985). Breakfast at Spiro's: Dramaturgy and dominance. *Journal of Management, 11*(2), 31–48.

Rosenbaum, E. E. (1988). *The doctor: When the doctor is the patient.* New York: Ivy Books.

Rosenberg, S. (1997). Multiplicity of selves. In R. D. Ashmore & L. Jussim (Eds.), *Self and identity: Fundamental issues* (pp. 23–45). New York: Oxford University Press.

Rosenblum, K. E., & Travis, T.-M. (1996). *The meaning of difference: American constructions of race, sex and gender, social class, and sexual orientation.* New York: McGraw-Hill.

Rosenthal, D. (1990). *At the heart of the bomb: The dangerous allure of weapons work.* Reading, MA: Addison-Wesley.

Rosenthal, R., & Jacobson, L. (1968). *Pygmalion in the classroom: Teacher expectation and pupils' intellectual development.* New York: Holt, Rinehart & Winston.

Ross, L. (1977). The intuitive psychologist and his shortcomings: Distortions in the attribution process. In L. Berkowitz (Ed.), *Advances in experimental social psychology* (Vol. 10, pp. 173–220). New York: Academic Press.

Rossan, S. (1987). Identity and its development in adulthood. In T. Honess & K. Yardley (Eds.), *Self and identity: Perspectives across the lifespan* (pp. 304–319). London: Routledge & Kegan Paul.

Rothbaum, F., Weisz, J. R., & Snyder, S. S. (1982). Changing the world and changing the self: A two-process model of perceived control. *Journal of Personality and Social Psychology, 42,* 5–37.

Rousseau, D. M. (1995). *Psychological contracts in organizations: Understanding written and unwritten agreements.* Thousand Oaks, CA: Sage.

Rousseau, D. M. (1998). Why workers still identify with organizations. *Journal of Organizational Behavior, 19,* 217–233.

Roy, D. F. (1959–60). "Banana time": Job satisfaction and informal interaction. *Human Organization, 18,* 158–168.

Ruble, D. N. (1994). A phase model of transitions: Cognitive and motivational consequences. In M. P. Zanna (Ed.), *Advances in experimental social psychology* (Vol. 26, pp. 163–214). San Diego: Academic Press.

Ruble, D. N., & Seidman, E. (1996). Social transitions: Windows into social psychological processes. In E. T. Higgins & A. W. Kruglanski (Eds.), *Social psychology: Handbook of basic principles* (pp. 830–856). New York: Guilford.

Ryan, J., & Sackrey, C. (1984). *Strangers in paradise: Academics from the working class.* Boston: South End Press.

Saks, A. M., & Ashforth, B. E. (1997). Organizational socialization: Making sense of the past and present as a prologue for the future. *Journal of Vocational Behavior, 51,* 234–279.

Salancik, G. R. (1977). Commitment and the control of organizational behavior and belief. In B. M. Staw & G. R. Salancik (Eds.), *New directions in organizational behavior* (pp. 1–54). Chicago: St. Clair Press.

Salancik, G. R., & Pfeffer, J. (1978). A social information processing approach to job attitudes and task design. *Administrative Science Quarterly, 23,* 224–253.

Salzinger, L. (1991). A maid by any other name: The transformation of "dirty work" by Central American immigrants. In M. Burawoy, A. Burton, A. A. Ferguson, K. J. Fox, J. Gamson, N. Gartrell, L. Hurst, C. Kurzman, L. Salzinger, J. Schiffman, & S. Ur, *Ethnography unbound: Power and resistance in the modern metropolis* (pp. 139–160). Berkeley, CA: University of California Press.

San Giovanni, L. (1978). *Ex-nuns: A study of emergent role passage.* Norwood, NJ: Ablex.

Santee, R. T., & Jackson, S. E. (1979). Commitment to self-identification: A sociopsychological approach to personality. *Human Relations, 32,* 141–158.

Santino, J. (1990). The outlaw emotions: Narrative expressions on the rules and roles of occupational identity. *American Behavioral Scientist, 33,* 318–329.

Savishinsky, J. (1995). The unbearable lightness of retirement: Ritual and support in a modern life passage. *Research on Aging, 17,* 243–259.

Scheff, T. J. (1979). *Catharsis in healing, ritual, and drama.* Berkeley, CA: University of California Press.

Schein, E. H. (1961). *Coercive persuasion.* New York: Norton.

Schein, E. H. (1971). The individual, the organization, and the career: A conceptual scheme. *Journal of Applied Behavioral Science, 7,* 401–426.

Schein, E. H. (1978). *Career dynamics: Matching individual and organizational needs.* Reading, MA: Addison-Wesley.

Schlenker, B. R. (1986). Self-identification: Toward an integration of the private and public self. In R. F. Baumeister (Ed.), *Public self and private self* (pp. 21–62). New York: Springer-Verlag.

Schlenker, B. R., Britt, T. W., & Pennington, J. (1996). Impression regulation and management: Highlights of a theory of self-identification. In R. M. Sorrentino & E. T. Higgins (Eds.), *Handbook of motivation and cognition* (Vol. 3, pp. 118–147). New York: Guilford.

Schlenker, B. R., & Trudeau, J. V. (1990). Impact of self-presentations on private self-beliefs: Effects of prior self-beliefs and misattribution. *Journal of Personality and Social Psychology, 58*, 22–32.

Schlossberg, N. K. (1981). A model for analyzing human adaptation to transition. *Counseling Psychologist, 9*(2), 2–18.

Schmid, T. J., & Jones, R. S. (1991). Suspended identity: Identity transformation in a maximum security prison. *Symbolic Interaction, 14*, 415–432.

Schmid, T. J., & Jones, R. S. (1993). Ambivalent actions: Prison adaptation strategies of first-time, short-term inmates. *Journal of Contemporary Ethnography, 21*, 439–463.

Schmitt-Rodermund, E., & Vondracek, F. W. (1999). Breadth of interests, exploration, and identity development in adolescence. *Journal of Vocational Behavior, 55*, 298–317.

Schneider, B. (1983). Interactional psychology and organizational behavior. In L. L. Cummings & B. M. Staw (Eds.), *Research in organizational behavior* (Vol. 5, pp. 1–31). Greenwich, CT: JAI.

Schneider, B. (1987). The people make the place. *Personnel Psychology, 40*, 437–453.

Schopler, J., & Bateson, N. (1962). A dependence interpretation of the effects of a severe initiation. *Journal of Personality, 30*, 633–649.

Schor, J. B. (1991). *The overworked American: The unexpected decline of leisure.* New York: Basic Books.

Schouten, J. W. (1991). Selves in transition: Symbolic consumption in personal rites of passage and identity reconstruction. *Journal of Consumer Research, 17*, 412–425.

Schrier, D. A., & Mulcahy, F. D. (1988). Middle management and union realities: Coercion and anti-structure in a public corporation. *Human Organization, 47*, 146–151.

Schwartz, H. S. (1987). Anti-social actions of committed organizational participants: An existential psychoanalytic perspective. *Organization Studies, 8*, 327–340.

Schwitzgebel, R. K., & Kolb, D. A. (1974). *Changing human behavior: Principles of planned intervention.* New York: McGraw-Hill.

Scott, C. R. (1997). Identification with multiple targets in a geographically dispersed organization. *Management Communication Quarterly, 10*, 491–522.

Scott, R. A. (1969). *The making of blind men: A study of adult socialization.* New York: Russell Sage Foundation.

Sedikides, C., & Strube, M. J. (1997). Self-evaluation: To thine own self be good, to thine own self be sure, to thine own self be true, and to thine own self be better. In M. P. Zanna (Ed.), *Advances in experimental social psychology* (Vol. 29, pp. 209–269). San Diego: Academic Press.

Semmer, N., & Schallberger, U. (1996). Selection, socialisation, and mutual adaptation: Resolving discrepancies between people and work. *Applied Psychology: An International Review, 45*, 263–288.

Settoon, R. P., & Adkins, C. L. (1997). Newcomer socialization: The role of supervisors, coworkers, friends and family members. *Journal of Business and Psychology, 11*, 507–516.

Shamir, B. (1991). Meaning, self and motivation in organizations. *Organization Studies, 12*, 405–424.

Shamir, B. (1992). Home: The perfect workplace? In S. Zedeck (Ed.), *Work, families, and organizations* (pp. 272–311). San Francisco: Jossey-Bass.

Sheffey, S., & Tindale, R. S. (1992). Perceptions of sexual harassment in the workplace. *Journal of Applied Social Psychology, 22*, 1502–1520.

Sheldon, K. M., Ryan, R. M., Rawsthorne, L. J., & Ilardi, B. (1997). Trait self and true self: Cross-role variation in the big-five personality traits and its relations with psychological authenticity and subjective well-being. *Journal of Personality and Social Psychology, 73*, 1380–1393.

Shermach, K. (1995, June 19). Outsourcing seen as a way to cut costs, retain service. *Marketing News, 29*(13), 5, 8.

Sherman, E. A. (1987). *Meaning in mid-life transitions.* Albany, NY: State University of New York Press.

Shield, R. R. (1988). *Uneasy endings: Daily life in an American nursing home.* Ithaca, NY: Cornell University Press.

Silver, I. (1996). Role transitions, objects, and identity. *Symbolic Interaction, 19,* 1–20.

Simmel, G. (1955). The web of group-affiliations. In K. H. Wolff & R. Bendix (Trans.), *Conflict and the web of group-affiliations* (pp. 125–195). Glencoe, IL: The Free Press. (Original work published 1922.)

Slap shots. (1999, November 14). *Arizona Republic,* p. C8.

Smart, R., & Peterson, C. (1994). Stability versus transition in women's career development: A test of Levinson's theory. *Journal of Vocational Behavior, 45,* 241–260.

Smith, K. K., & Berg, D. N. (1987). *Paradoxes of group life: Understanding conflict, paralysis, and movement in group dynamics.* San Francisco: Jossey-Bass.

Snow, D. A., & Anderson, L. (1993). *Down on their luck: A study of homeless street people.* Berkeley, CA: University of California Press.

Snyder, C. R., & Fromkin, H. L. (1980). *Uniqueness: The human pursuit of difference.* New York: Plenum.

Snyder, C. R., Harris, C., Anderson, J. R., Holleran, S. A., Irving, L. M., Sigmon, S. T., Yoshinobu, L., Gibb, J., Langelle, C., & Harney, P. (1991). The will and the ways: Development and validation of an individual-differences measure of hope. *Journal of Personality and Social Psychology, 60,* 570–585.

Snyder, M. (1987). *Public appearances, private realities: The psychology of self-monitoring.* New York: Freeman.

Snyder, M., Gangestad, S., & Simpson, J. A. (1983). Choosing friends as activity partners: The role of self-monitoring. *Journal of Personality and Social Psychology, 45,* 1061–1072.

Sobel, G. (1989). *Burnout at a summer camp.* Unpublished undergraduate term paper, Concordia University, Montreal, Canada.

Sonnenfeld, J. (1988). *The hero's farewell: What happens when CEOs retire.* New York: Oxford University Press.

Spenner, K. I. (1988). Occupations, work settings and the course of adult development: Tracing the implications of select historical changes. In P. B. Baltes, D. L. Featherman, & R. M. Lerner (Eds.), *Life-span development and behavior* (Vol. 9, pp. 243–285). Hillsdale, NJ: Lawrence Erlbaum Associates.

Staub, E. (1990). The psychology and culture of torture and torturers. In P. Suedfeld (Ed.), *Psychology and torture* (pp. 49–76). New York: Hemisphere.

Staw, B. M. (1980). Rationality and justification in organizational life. In B. M. Staw & L. L. Cummings (Eds.), *Research in organizational behavior* (Vol. 2, pp. 45–80). Greenwich, CT: JAI.

Staw, B. M., & Boettger, R. D. (1990). Task revision: A neglected form of work performance. *Academy of Management Journal, 33,* 534–559.

Staw, B. M., & Ross, J. (1987). Behavior in escalation situations: Antecedents, prototypes, and solutions. In L. L. Cummings & B. M. Staw (Eds.), *Research in organizational behavior* (Vol. 9, pp. 39–78). Greenwich, CT: JAI.

Staw, B. M., Sandelands, L. E., & Dutton, J. E. (1981). Threat-rigidity effects in organizational behavior: A multilevel analysis. *Administrative Science Quarterly, 26,* 501–524.

Steele, C. M. (1988). The psychology of self-affirmation: Sustaining the integrity of the self. In L. Berkowitz (Ed.), *Advances in experimental social psychology* (Vol. 21, pp. 261–302). San Diego: Academic Press.

Steele, C. M., Spencer, S. J., & Lynch, M. (1993). Self-image resilience and dissonance: The role of affirmational resources. *Journal of Personality and Social Psychology, 64,* 885–896.

Steele, P. D., & Zurcher, L. A., Jr. (1973). Leisure sports as "ephemeral roles": An exploratory study. *Pacific Sociological Review, 16,* 345–356.

Steinitz, V. A., & Solomon, E. R. (1986). *Starting out: Class and community in the lives of working-class youth.* Philadelphia: Temple University Press.

Stephens, G. K. (1994). Crossing internal career boundaries: The state of research on subjective career transitions. *Journal of Management, 20,* 479–501.

Sterns, H. L., & Miklos, S. M. (1995). The aging worker in a changing environment: Organizational and individual issues. *Journal of Vocational Behavior, 47*, 248–268.

Stohl, C. (1986). The role of memorable messages in the process of organizational socialization. *Communication Quarterly, 34*, 231–249.

St. Onge, S. (1995). Systematic desensitization. In M. Ballou (Ed.), *Psychological interventions: A guide to strategies* (pp. 95–115). Westport, CT: Praeger.

Stryker, S. (1980). *Symbolic interactionism: A social structural version.* Menlo Park, CA: Benjamin/Cummings.

Stryker, S. (1987). Identity theory: Developments and extensions. In K. Yardley & T. Honess (Eds.), *Self and identity: Psychosocial perspectives* (pp. 89–103). Chichester, England: Wiley.

Stryker, S., & Serpe, R. T. (1982). Commitment, identity salience, and role behavior: Theory and research example. In W. Ickes & E. S. Knowles (Eds.), *Personality, roles, and social behavior* (pp. 199–218). New York: Springer-Verlag.

Stryker, S., & Serpe, R. T. (1994). Identity salience and psychological centrality: Equivalent, overlapping, or complementary concepts? *Social Psychology Quarterly, 57*, 16–35.

Suedfeld, P. (1991). Groups in isolation and confinement: Environments and experiences. In A. A. Harrison, Y. A. Clearwater, & C. P. McKay (Eds.), *From Antarctica to outer space: Life in isolation and confinement* (pp. 135–146). New York: Springer-Verlag.

Super, D. E. (1990). A life-span, life-space approach to career development. In D. Brown (Ed.), *Career choice and development* (2nd ed., pp. 197–261). San Francisco: Jossey-Bass.

Super, D. E., Crites, J. O., Hummel, R. C., Moser, H. P., Overstreet, P. L., & Warnath, C. F. (1957). *Vocational development: A framework for research.* New York: Teachers College, Columbia University.

Sutton, R. I., & Louis, M. R. (1987). How selecting and socializing newcomers influences insiders. *Human Resource Management, 26*, 347–361.

Swann, W. B., Jr. (1990). To be adored or to be known? The interplay of self-enhancement and self-verification. In E. T. Higgins & R. M. Sorrentino (Eds.), *Handbook of motivation and cognition* (Vol. 2, pp. 408–448). New York: Guilford.

Swann, W. B., Jr., & Hill, C. A. (1982). When our identities are mistaken: Reaffirming self-conceptions through social interaction. *Journal of Personality and Social Psychology, 43*, 59–66.

Swanson, V., Power, K. G., & Simpson, R. J. (1998). Occupational stress and family life: A comparison of male and female doctors. *Journal of Occupational and Organizational Psychology, 71*, 237–260.

Sykes, G., & Matza, D. (1957). Techniques of neutralization: A theory of delinquency. *American Sociological Review, 22*, 664–670.

Tajfel, H. (1982). Social psychology of intergroup relations. In M. R. Rosenzweig & L. W. Porter (Eds.), *Annual review of psychology* (Vol. 33, pp. 1–39). Palo Alto, CA: Annual Reviews.

Tajfel, H., & Turner, J. C. (1986). The social identity theory of intergroup behavior. In S. Worchel & W. G. Austin (Eds.), *Psychology of intergroup relations* (2nd ed., pp. 7–24). Chicago: Nelson-Hall.

Taylor, M. S. (1988). Effects of college internships on individual participants. *Journal of Applied Psychology, 73*, 393–401.

Taylor, S. E. (1989). *Positive illusions: Creative self-deception and the healthy mind.* New York: Basic Books.

Taylor Carter, M. A., & Cook, K. (1995). Adaptation to retirement: Role changes and psychological resources. *Career Development Quarterly, 44*, 67–82.

Terkel, S. (1975). *Working.* New York: Avon.

Thoits, P. A. (1989). The sociology of emotions. In W. R. Scott & J. Blake (Eds.), *Annual review of sociology* (Vol. 15, pp. 317–342). Palo Alto, CA: Annual Reviews.

Thoits, P. A. (1991). On merging identity theory and stress research. *Social Psychology Quarterly, 54*, 101–112.

Thoits, P. A., & Virshup, L. K. (1997). Me's and we's: Forms and functions of social identities. In R. D. Ashmore & L. Jussim (Eds.), *Self and identity: Fundamental issues* (pp. 106–133). New York: Oxford University Press.

Thomas, E. J., & Biddle, B. J. (1966). The nature and history of role theory. In B. J. Biddle & E. J. Thomas (Eds.), *Role theory: Concepts and research* (pp. 3–19). New York: Wiley.

Thomas, K. W., & Velthouse, B. A. (1990). Cognitive elements of empowerment: An "interpretive" model of intrinsic task motivation. *Academy of Management Review, 15*, 666–681.

Thompson, K. R., Hochwarter, W. A., & Mathys, N. J. (1997). Stretch targets: What makes them effective? *Academy of Management Executive, 11*(3), 48–60.

Thompson, W. E. (1991). Handling the stigma of handling the dead: Morticians and funeral directors. *Deviant Behavior, 12*, 403–429.

Tingey, H., Kiger, G., & Riley, P. J. (1996). Juggling multiple roles: Perceptions of working mothers. *Social Science Journal, 33*, 183–191.

Tokar, D. M., Fischer, A. R., & Subich, L. M. (1998). Personality and vocational behavior: A selective review of the literature, 1993–1997. *Journal of Vocational Behavior, 53*, 115–153.

Treiman, D. J. (1977). *Occupational prestige in comparative perspective.* New York: Academic Press.

Trice, H. M., & Beyer, J. M. (1984). Studying organizational cultures through rites and ceremonials. *Academy of Management Review, 9*, 653–669.

Trice, H. M., & Morand, D. A. (1989). Rites of passage in work careers. In M. B. Arthur, D. T. Hall, & B. S. Lawrence (Eds.), *Handbook of career theory* (pp. 397–416). Cambridge, England: Cambridge University Press.

Tsuda, T. (1993). The psychosocial functions of liminality: The Japanese university experience. *Journal of Psychohistory, 20*, 305–330.

Turner, J. C. (1984). Social identification and psychological group formation. In H. Tajfel (Ed.), *The social dimension: European developments in social psychology* (Vol. 2, pp. 518–538). Cambridge, England: Cambridge University Press.

Turner, J. C. (1985). Social categorization and the self-concept: A social cognitive theory of group behavior. In E. J. Lawler (Ed.), *Advances in group processes* (Vol. 2, pp. 77–122). Greenwich, CT: JAI.

Turner, J. C., Hogg, M. A., Oakes, P. J., Reicher, S. D., & Wetherell, M. S. (1987). *Rediscovering the social group: A self-categorization theory.* Oxford, England: Basil Blackwell.

Turner, J. C., & Oakes, P. J. (1989). Self-categorization theory and social influence. In P. B. Paulus (Ed.), *Psychology of group influence* (2nd ed., pp. 233–275). Hillsdale, NJ: Lawrence Erlbaum Associates.

Turner, J. C., Oakes, P. J., Haslam, S. A., & McGarty, C. (1994). Self and collective: Cognition and social context. *Personality and Social Psychology Bulletin, 20*, 454–463.

Turner, R. H. (1962). Role taking: Process versus conformity. In A. M. Rose (Ed.), *Human behavior and social processes: An interactionist approach* (pp. 20–40). Boston: Houghton Mifflin.

Turner, R. H. (1978). The role and the person. *American Journal of Sociology, 84*, 1–23.

Turner, V. W. (1967). *The forest of symbols: Aspects of Ndembu ritual.* Ithaca, NY: Cornell University Press.

Turner, V. W. (1969). *The ritual process: Structure and anti-structure.* Chicago: Aldine.

Unestähl, L.-E. (1986). The ideal performance. In L.-E. Unestähl (Ed.), *Sport psychology in theory and practice* (pp. 20–37). Orebro, Sweden: Veje.

Urban, L. M., & Miller, N. (1998). A theoretical analysis of cross categorization effects: A meta-analysis. *Journal of Personality and Social Psychology, 74*, 894–908.

van Gennep, A. (1960). *The rites of passage* (M. B. Vizedom & G. L. Caffee, Trans.). Chicago: University of Chicago Press. (Original work published 1908.)

Van Maanen, J. (1975). Police socialization: A longitudinal examination of job attitudes in an urban police department. *Administrative Science Quarterly, 20*, 207–228.

Van Maanen, J. (1977). Experiencing organizations: Notes on the meaning of careers and socialization. In J. Van Maanen (Ed.), *Organizational careers: Some new perspectives* (pp. 15–45). London: Wiley.

Van Maanen, J. (1982). Boundary crossings: Major strategies of organizational socialization and their consequences. In R. Katz (Ed.), *Career issues in human resource management* (pp. 85–115). Englewood Cliffs, NJ: Prentice-Hall.

Van Maanen, J. (1983). The boss: First-line supervision in an American police agency. In M. Punch (Ed.), *Control in the police organization* (pp. 275–317). Cambridge, MA: MIT Press.

Van Maanen, J., & Kunda, G. (1989). "Real feelings": Emotional expression and organizational culture. In L. L. Cummings & B. M. Staw (Eds.), *Research in organizational behavior* (Vol. 11, pp. 43–103). Greenwich, CT: JAI.

Van Maanen, J., & Schein, E. H. (1979). Toward a theory of organizational socialization. In B. M. Staw (Ed.), *Research in organizational behavior* (Vol. 1, pp. 209–264). Greenwich, CT: JAI.

Vroom, V. H. (1964). *Work and motivation.* New York: Wiley.

Vroom, V. H., & Deci, E. L. (1971). The stability of post-decision dissonance: A follow-up study of the job attitudes of business school graduates. *Organizational Behavior and Human Performance, 6*, 36–49.

Wachtler, S. (1997). *After the madness: A judge's own prison memoir.* New York: Random House.

Walsh, J. P. (1995). Managerial and organizational cognition: Notes from a trip down memory lane. *Organization Science, 6*, 280–321.

Wanberg, C. R. (1997). Antecedents and outcomes of coping behaviors among unemployed and reemployed individuals. *Journal of Applied Psychology, 82*, 731–744.

Wan-Huggins, V. N., Riordan, C. M., & Griffeth, R. W. (1998). The development and longitudinal test of a model of organizational identification. *Journal of Applied Social Psychology, 28*, 724–749.

Wanous, J. P. (1992). *Organizational entry: Recruitment, selection, orientation, and socialization of newcomers* (2nd ed.). Reading, MA: Addison-Wesley.

Wanous, J. P., Poland, T. D., Premack, S. L., & Davis, K. S. (1992). The effects of met expectations on newcomer attitudes and behaviors: A review and meta-analysis. *Journal of Applied Psychology, 77*, 288–297.

Wapner, S., Demick, J., & Redondo, J. P. (1990). Cherished possessions and adaptation of older people to nursing homes. *International Journal of Aging and Human Development, 31*, 219–235.

Warr, P., & Pennington, J. (1994). Occupational age-grading: Jobs for older and younger nonmanagerial employees. *Journal of Vocational Behavior, 45*, 328–346.

Waskul, D. D. (1998). Camp staffing: The construction, maintenance, and dissolution of roles and identities at a summer camp. *Sociological Spectrum, 18*, 25–53.

Waterman, A. S. (1988). Identity status theory and Erikson's theory: Communalities and differences. *Developmental Review, 8*, 185–208.

Waterman, A. S., & Archer, S. L. (1990). A life-span perspective on identity formation: Developments in form, function, and process. In P. B. Baltes, D. L. Featherman, & R. M. Lerner (Eds.), *Life-span development and behavior* (Vol. 10, pp. 29–57). Hillsdale, NJ: Lawrence Erlbaum Associates.

Watkins, K. (1986). When co-workers clash. *Training and Development Journal, 40*(4), 26–27.

Watson, D., & Clark, L. A. (1984). Negative affectivity: The disposition to experience aversive emotional states. *Psychological Bulletin, 96*, 465–490.

Wegner, D. M. (1989). *White bears and other unwanted thoughts: Suppression, obsession, and the psychology of mental control.* New York: Viking.

Weick, K. E. (1979). *The social psychology of organizing* (2nd ed.). Reading, MA: Addison-Wesley.

Weick, K. E. (1995). *Sensemaking in organizations.* Thousand Oaks, CA: Sage.

Weick, K. E. (1996). Enactment and the boundaryless career: Organizing as we work. In M. B. Arthur & D. M. Rousseau (Eds.), *The boundaryless career: A new employment principle for a new organizational era* (pp. 40–57). New York: Oxford University Press.

Weiss, H. M. (1977). Subordinate imitation of supervisor behavior: The role of modeling in organizational socialization. *Organizational Behavior and Human Performance, 19*, 89–105.

Weiss, H. M., & Ilgen, D. R. (1985). Routinized behavior in organizations. *Journal of Behavioral Economics, 14*, 57–67.

Weiss, H. M., Ilgen, D. R., & Sharbaugh, M. E. (1982). Effects of life and job stress on information search behaviors of organizational members. *Journal of Applied Psychology, 67*, 60–66.

Wells, L. E., & Stryker, S. (1988). Stability and change in self over the life course. In D. L. Featherman (Ed.), *Life-span development and behavior* (Vol. 8, pp. 191–229). New York: Academic Press.

Wells, P. A. (1988). The paradox of functional dysfunction in a Girl Scout camp: Implications of cultural diversity for achieving organizational goals. In M. O. Jones, M. D. Moore, & R. C. Snyder (Eds.), *Inside organizations: Understanding the human dimension* (pp. 109–117). Newbury Park, CA: Sage.

Wertsch, M. E. (1992). *Military brats: Legacies of childhood inside the fortress.* New York: Fawcett Columbine.

West, L. J. (1993). A psychiatric overview of cult-related phenomena. *Journal of the American Academy of Psychoanalysis, 21*, 1–19.

West, M. A. (1987). Role innovation in the world of work. *British Journal of Social Psychology, 26*, 305–315.

West, M. A., Nicholson, N., & Rees, A. (1987). Transitions into newly created jobs. *Journal of Occupational Psychology, 60*, 97–113.

West, M., Nicholson, N., & Rees, A. (1990). The outcomes of downward managerial mobility. *Journal of Organizational Behavior, 11*, 119–134.

West, M., & Rushton, R. (1989). Mismatches in the work-role transitions. *Journal of Occupational Psychology, 62*, 271–286.

Westby, D. L. (1960). The career experience of the symphony musician. *Social Forces, 38*, 223–230.

Westman, M., & Eden, D. (1997). Effects of a respite from work on burnout: Vacation relief and fade-out. *Journal of Applied Psychology, 82*, 516–527.

Wicklund, R. A., & Gollwitzer, P. M. (1982). *Symbolic self-completion.* Hillsdale, NJ: Lawrence Erlbaum Associates.

Widdershoven, G. A. M. (1994). Identity and development: A narrative perspective. In H. A. Bosma, T. L. G. Graafsma, H. D. Grotevant, & D. J. de Levita (Eds.), *Identity and development: An interdisciplinary approach* (pp. 103–117). Thousand Oaks, CA: Sage.

Wiener, D. J. (1996). *Burns, falls and crashes: Interviews with movie stunt performers.* Jefferson, NC: McFarland.

Williams, C. P., & Savickas, M. L. (1990). Developmental tasks of career maintenance. *Journal of Vocational Behavior, 36*, 166–175.

Williams, K. J., & Alliger, G. M. (1994). Role stressors, mood spillover, and perceptions of work–family conflict in employed parents. *Academy of Management Journal, 37*, 837–868.

Williams, K. J., Suls, J., Alliger, G. M., Learner, S. M., & Wan, C. K. (1991). Multiple role juggling and daily mood states in working mothers: An experience sampling study. *Journal of Applied Psychology, 76*, 664–674.

Willmott, H. (1993). Strength is ignorance; slavery is freedom: Managing culture in modern organizations. *Journal of Management Studies, 30*, 515–552.

Withey, M. J., & Cooper, W. H. (1989). Predicting exit, voice, loyalty, and neglect. *Administrative Science Quarterly, 34*, 521–539.

Wong, P. T. P., & Weiner, B. (1981). When people ask "why" questions, and the heuristics of attributional search. *Journal of Personality and Social Psychology, 40*, 650–663.

Wood, J. V. (1989). Theory and research concerning social comparisons of personal attributes. *Psychological Bulletin, 106*, 231–248.

Woods, J. D., & Lucas, J. H. (1993). *The corporate closet: The professional lives of gay men in America.* New York: The Free Press.

Wright, L. (1993). *Saints and sinners: Walker Railey, Jimmy Swaggart, Madalyn Murray O'Hair, Anton LaVey, Will Campbell, Matthew Fox.* New York: Knopf.

Wright, T. A., & Bonett, D. G. (1992). The effect of turnover on work satisfaction and mental health: Support for a situational perspective. *Journal of Organizational Behavior, 13*, 603–615.

Yanay, N., & Shahar, G. (1998). Professional feelings as emotional labor. *Journal of Contemporary Ethnography, 27*, 346–373.

Yoder, J. D., & Aniakudo, P. (1996). When pranks become harassment: The case of African American women firefighters. *Sex Roles, 35*, 253–270.

Zahrly, J., & Tosi, H. (1989). The differential effect of organizational induction process on early work role adjustment. *Journal of Organizational Behavior, 10*, 59–74.

Zajonc, R. B. (1984). On the primacy of affect. *American Psychologist, 39*, 117–123.

Zaleznik, A. (1989). *The managerial mystique: Restoring leadership in business.* New York: Harper & Row.

Zamble, E., & Porporino, F. J. (1988). *Coping, behavior, and adaptation in prison inmates.* New York: Springer-Verlag.

Zerubavel, E. (1991). *The fine line: Making distinctions in everyday life.* New York: The Free Press.

Zimbardo, P. G. (1969). The human choice: Individuation, reason, and order versus deindividuation, impulse and chaos. In W. J. Arnold & D. Levine (Eds.), *Nebraska symposium on motivation* (Vol. 17, pp. 237–307). Lincoln, NE: University of Nebraska Press.

Zurcher, L. A., Jr. (1970). The "friendly" poker game: A study of an ephemeral role. *Social Forces, 49*, 173–186.

Zurcher, L. A., Jr. (1977). *The mutable self: A self-concept for social change.* Beverly Hills, CA: Sage.

Zurcher, L. A. (1978). Ephemeral roles, voluntary action, and voluntary associations. *Journal of Voluntary Action Research, 7*(3/4), 65–74.

Zurcher, L. A. (1979). Role selection: The influence of internalized vocabularies of motive. *Symbolic Interaction, 2*(2), 45–62.

Author Index

206, 207, 215, 220, 225, 226, 227, 228,
230, 231, 235, 236, 239, 245, 246, 248,
252, 254
Nippert-Eng, C. E., 5, 13, 261, 263, 264, 265,
267, 268, 270, 271, 273, 276, 279, 280
Noble, C. H., 176
Nord, W. R., 64
Nougaim, K. E., 228, 248
Nowak, C. A., 256
Nurius, P., 36, 47, 56, 62, 88, 121

O

Oakes, P. J., 24, 25, 30, 32, 60
Oatley, K., 2
O'Connor, D., 251
O'Connor, K., 64
Ogawa, R. T., 145
Oldenburg, R., 261
Oldham, G. R., 19, 64, 72, 73, 206
O'Leary-Kelly, A. M., 92, 187, 203, 204
Olesen, V. L., 135, 174
Olins, W., 268
Olver, R., 185
Omodei, M., 85
O'Reilly, C. A., 153, 155, 156, 168
Orlick, T., 271
Ornstein, S., 249
Orris, J. B., 200
Orsak, C. L., 226
Osterman, P., 2, 8, 9
Ostroff, C., 187, 188
O'Toole, R., 120, 228
Ouchi, W. G., 153
Ouellet, L. J., 216
Overstreet, P. L., 245, 246, 248, 250
Ozeki, C., 260

P

Palich, L. E., 124, 159
Parkinson, C. N., 230
Parsons, C. K., 114
Parsons, T., 4, 213
Pauchant, T. C., 64
Peiró, J. M., 197
Pennington, J., 50, 253
Perlow, L. A., 284
Perry, E., 27
Peterson, C., 249

Peterson, D. L., 92, 189
Petrick, J. A., 259
Pfeffer, J., 18, 64, 94, 116, 154, 284
Pinder, C. C., 92, 202
Pleck, J. H., 263, 283, 286
Poland, T. D., 159
Poole, M. E., 85
Poole, P. P., 278
Popovich, J. M., 221
Porporino, F. J., 98, 222
Porter, L. W., 146, 157
Posner, B. Z., 189, 190
Powell, G. N., 189, 190
Power, K. G., 286
Pratt, M. G., 31, 56, 62, 64, 70, 82, 84, 154,
155, 156, 169, 217, 280
Premack, S. L., 159
Prentice, D. A., 41, 56, 57, 62
Price, K. H., 255
Price, R. H., 138
Prussia, G. E., 109, 135, 139, 140

Q

Quinn, J. B., 198

R

Rabbie, J. M., 24
Rachlin, H., 63, 101, 164
Rafaeli, A., 217
Rahim, A., 189
Ravlin, E. C., 124
Rawsthorne, L. J., 19, 41
Redonodo, J. P., 176
Reed, D. A., 76, 161
Rees, A., 92, 95, 207
Reich, M., 284
Reicher, S. D., 24, 32
Reichers, A. E., 229
Reid, D., 80
Reilly, N. P., 226
Reitzes, D. C., 82, 140
Rhodes, V., 128, 129
Richter, J., 3, 13, 260, 263, 279, 280, 286
Ricks, T. E., 46, 101, 149, 166, 168, 174
Riecken, H. W., 69
Riemer, J. W., 166, 173, 217
Riley, P. J., 260, 279
Riordan, C. M., 154

Subject Index